Washington County Tennessee

Death Record

Abstracts

1908-1916

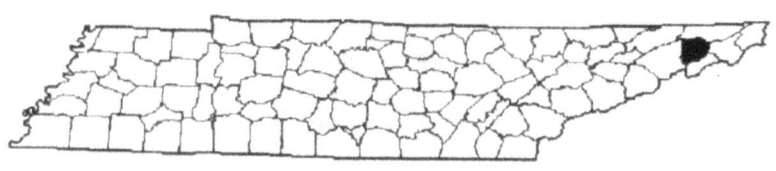

Eddie M. Nikazy

HERITAGE BOOKS
2007

HERITAGE BOOKS
AN IMPRINT OF HERITAGE BOOKS, INC.

Books, CDs, and more—Worldwide

For our listing of thousands of titles see our website at
www.HeritageBooks.com

Published 2007 by
HERITAGE BOOKS, INC.
Publishing Division
65 East Main Street
Westminster, Maryland 21157-5026

Copyright © 1994 Eddie M. Nikazy

Other books by the author:
Abstracts of Death Records for Johnson County, Tennessee, 1908 to 1941
Carter County, Tennessee Deaths, 1926-1934
Carter County, Tennessee Record Abstracts, Death Records, 1908-1925
Carter County, Tennessee Record Abstracts, Marriages, 1871-1920
Forgotten Soldiers: History of the 2nd Tennessee Volunteer Infantry Regiment (USA), 1861-1865
Forgotten Soldiers: History of the 4th Tennessee Volunteer Infantry Regiment (USA), 1863-1865
Greene County, Tennessee Death Record Abstracts, 1908-1918
Sullivan County, Tennessee Death Records, 1908-1918, Volume 1
Sullivan County, Tennessee Death Records, 1919-1925, Volume 2
Unicoi County, Tennessee Death Record Abstracts, 1908-1936

All rights reserved. No part of this book may be reproduced or transmitted in any form or by any means, electronic or mechanical, including photocopying, recording or by any information storage and retrieval system without written permission from the author, except for the inclusion of brief quotations in a review.

International Standard Book Number: 978-0-7884-0100-9

TABLE OF CONTENTS

Preface v

Death Record Abstracts 1

Index 267

Foreword

This volume contains abstracts of death records for Washington County, Tennessee for the years 1908 through 1916. In addition to the local residents who died in Washington County during this period, the deaths of many patients at the National Soldiers Home at Johnson City are also recorded.

Washington County was established in 1777 as a part of the Territory South of the River Ohio. The original county comprised almost the entire Eastern half of the current State of Tennessee. The county seat, Jonesborough (established 1779), is the oldest town in Tennessee. Earlier, in 1769, Captain William Bean moved his family to the "new country" and built a cabin at a point between the Watauga River and Boones Creek, in what is now Washington County. The Beans' are credited with being the first permanent settlers in Tennessee. Washington County certainly is one of the most important early East Tennessee counties.

Many entries contained in this volume are descendants of the original pioneer families who settled this county. In this compilation of Washington County death records:

1.) Where the reported place of birth is different from the local county, the place of birth is stated.
2.) Name spelling variations have been preserved. When looking for a particular surname, it is may be necessary to check other possible spelling variations.
3.) Where possible, the cause of death is quoted as it appears in the record.
4.) Parenthetical entries following parents names indicate the reported place of the parents birth.
5.) Parenthetical entries following the informants name indicate place of residence.
6.) Record numbers, correspond with the official death record numbers on file in the Tennessee State Archives.

W.H. TAPP, age: 81 years, born in Unicoi County, married, death cause: dropsy, died in the 4th District on 11 Jun 1912, record (1908-12): 92050.

James JOHNSON, age: 75 years, born in Carter County, single, death cause: "pneumonia", died in the 4th District on 7 Mar 1912, record (1908-12): 92051.

Martha TAYLOR, colored, age: 65 years, married, death cause: "consumption", died in the 4th District on 7 Dec 1911, record (1908-12): 92052.

Martha DUFFIELD, colored, age: 8 months, death cause: "consumption", died: 4th District on 5 Feb 1912, record: 92053.

Nora DUFFIELD, colored, age not recorded, married, death cause: "consumption", died: 4th District, 6 Mar 1912, record: 92054.

M.E. BOOTH, female, age: 59 years and 7 months, married, death cause: "asthma", died in the 4th District on 22 Dec 1911, record (1908-12): 92055.

Myrtle KYKER, age: 18 years, single, death cause: "typhoid fever", died in the 4th District on 6 Jul 1911, record: 92056.

James R. PRICE, age: 83 years and 7 months, born in Carter County, death cause: "Brights disease", died: 4th District, 22 Sep 1911, record (1908-12): 92057.

Eva Bell BOOTH, age: 1 year and 5 months, death cause: "burned to death", died: 4th District, 24 Apr 1912, record: 92058.

Carry CONSTABLE, age: 7 weeks, death cause: "bold hives", died in the 4th District on 7 Mar 1912, record (1908-12): 92059.

Frank HICKS, age: 36 years, born in Johnson County, married, death cause: "neuralgia of stomach", died: 1st District on 9 May 1912, record (1908-12): 92060.

Allen RHEA, colored, age: 22 years, single, death cause: "consumption", died in the 3rd District on 9 Mar 1912, record: 92061.

Ed MATHES, colored, age: 3 years, born at Limestone, death cause: "measles", died at Limestone on 15 Jan 1912, record: 92062.

D.S. GREENWAY, age: 34 years, married, death cause: "consumption", died at Washington College on 21 May 1912, record: 92063.

D.F. LAFALETT, age: 46 years, born in Greene County, married, death cause: "kicked by mule", died at Washington College, 3 Jun 1912, record: 92064.

G.W. BROYLES, age: 81 years, married, death cause: "lock bowels", died at Washington College, 3 Dec 1911, record: 92065.

Charty WASSOM, age: 50 years, born in Jefferson County, married, death cause: "heart trouble", died at Telford on 8 Dec 1911, record (1908-12): 92066.

Mary C. CAMPBELL, age: 51 years, born in Virginia, married, death cause: "heart trouble", died at Washington College on 17 Oct 1911, record: 92067.

Guy SAULTS, age: 2 years, death cause: "measles", died at Washington College on 2 Jan 1912, record (1908-12): 92068.

R.D. BEARD, age: 78 years, married, death cause: not recorded, died at Limestone on 20 Aug 1911, record (1908-12): 92069.

Infant BAILEY, female, age: 4 months, death cause: not stated, died in the 2nd District on 5 Jun 1912, record (1908-12): 92070.

Mary BAILEY, age: 4 years, death cause: "pneumonia", died in the 2nd District on 15 Feb 1912, record (1908-12): 92071.

Sarah PHILLIPS, age: 78 years, married, death cause: "age", died in the 2nd District on 7 Jun 1912, record (1908-12): 92072.

Maggie HINLEY, age: 54 years, married, death cause: "rheumatism", died: 2nd District on 17 Feb 1912, record (1908-12): 92073.

Henry HUMPHREYS, age: 13 years, death cause: "typhoid", died in the 2nd District on 15 Aug 1911, record (1908-12): 92074.

Edith CHASE, age: 68 years, married, death cause: "cancer", died in the 2nd District on 26 Jan 1912, record (1908-12): 92075.

Infant AUSTIN, male, death cause: "unknown", died in the 2nd District on 6 Mar 1911, record (1908-12): 92076.

Florence HYLTON, age: 41 years, married, death cause: "diarrhoea", died: 2nd District on 1 Aug 1911, record (1908-12): 92077.

Mamie SMITH, age: 18 years, single, death cause: "typhoid fever", died: 1st District on 15 Oct 1911, record (1908-12): 92078.
Hobart MATHES, death cause: "stillborn", died: 1st District on 17 May 1912, record (1908-12): 92079.
Hubert MATHES, death cause: not stated, died: 1st District on 17 May 1912, record (1908-12): 92080.
G.W. WALTERS, age: 67 years, married, death cause: "pneumonia", died in the 1st District on 23 Feb 1912, record (1908-12): 92081.
Mary E. MARTIN, age: 7 months, death cause: "brain fever", died in the 1st District on 27 Oct 1911, record (1908-12): 92082.
Simeon BROYLES, age: 73 years, married, death cause: "heart failure", died in the 1st District on 16 Jun 1912, record: 92083.
Henrietta ROBERTS, age: 5 months, death cause: "diphtheria", died at Johnson City on 8 Jan 1912, record (1908-12): 92084.
Waieta CULVERSON, colored, age: 3 years, death cause: "whooping cough", died at Johnson City on 6 Nov 1911, record: 92085.
Grant LAWSON, Jr., age: 21 months, death cause: "spinal trouble", died: Johnson City on __ Sep 1911, record (1908-12): 92086.
Isaac DICKENS, age: 19 years, single, electrician, death cause: "electrocuted", died at Johnson City on 25 Jan 1912, record (1908-12): 92087.
Bessie FOX, age: 5 weeks, death cause: "bold hives", died: Chuckey, 5 Nov 1911, record (1908-12): 92088.
William SNODGRASS, age: 92 years, born in Virginia, married, death cause: "old age", died at Johnson City on 25 Ap 1912, record (1908-12): 92089.
Elizabeth (illegible), age: 65 years, born in Washington County, VA., married, death cause: "consumption", died at Johnson City on 23 Jan 1912, record (1908-12): 92090.
Ada SCOTT, age: 32 years, born at Watauga, married, death cause: "consumption", died at Johnson City on 7 Mar 1912, record: 92091.

Donald PHILLIPS, age: 5 years, death cause: "whooping cough", died in Johnson City on 8 Apr 1912, record (1908-12): 92092.
Lois REEVES, age: 24 years, born at Jonesboro, single, death cause: not recorded, died at Abingdon, VA., on 16 Oct 1911, record (1908-12): 92093.
David ROSS, age: 72 years, born in Greene County, married, death cause: "consumption", died at Johnson City on 12 Apr 1912, record (1908-12): 92094.
A.H. TATE, age: 68 years, born in Chilhowie, VA., married, death cause: "heart disease", died at Johnson City on 8 Jan 1912, record (1908-12): 92095.
Margaret JONES, age: 7 months, death cause: "pneumonia", died at Johnson City on 25 Apr 1912, record (1908-12): 92096.
Brownie CLARK, age: 22 years, single, death cause: "consumption", died at Johnson City on 26 Apr 1912, record (1908-12): 92097.
Nancy CLARK, age: 56 years, born in Unicoi County, married, death cause: "consumption", died in Carter County on 26 May 1912, record (1908-12): 92098.
H.M. W-- (illegible), age: 63 years, born in Ohio, married, death cause: "heart disease", died: Johnson City on 12 Dec 1911, record (1908-12): 92099.
Cecil WISE, age: 2 days, death cause: "unknown", died: Johnson City on __ Dec 1911, record: 92100.
Marion LOVELL, colored, age: 24 years, born at Sandis, GA., married, death cause: "consumption", died: Johnson City on 27 Jan 1912, record: 92101.
G.R. WEBSTER, age: 53 years, born in Hawkins County, married, death cause: "stomach trouble", died: Johnson City, 23 Mar 1912, record (1908-12): 92102.
Silas HYPSHIRE, colored, age: 12 years, born a Morristown, death cause: "consumption", died at Johnson City, 21 May 1912, record (1908-12): 92103.
J. Mat MARTIN, age: 64 years, married, death cause: "heart trouble", died at Johnson City on 13 Nov 1911, record (1908-12): 92104.
Loyd C. BREEDING, age: 36 years, born at Morristown, married, death cause: "pneumonia", died at Johnson City on 4 Apr 1912, record (1908-12): 92105.

Mollie TINKER, age: 12 days, death cause: not stated, died in the 1st District on 26 Oct 1909, record (1908-12): 92106.
Lara SHIELDS, age: 56 years, single, death cause: "tumor of liver", died near Boonesboro on 10 May 1910, record: 92107.
Bella BUCHANAN, black, age: 17 years, single, death cause: "lagrippe", died at Pilot Hill on 20 May 1910, record: 92108.
Hazel MARTIN, age: 1 year, death cause: "flux", died at Pilot Hill , 1st District on 9 Aug 1909, record (1908-12): 92109.
Trula May PAINTER, age: 16 months, death cause: "pneumonia", died at Liberty Church, 1st District on 23 Jan 1910, record (1908-12): 92110.
Johnie GRAHAM, age: not stated, twin, died in 1st District on 1 Jun 1910, record (1908-12): 92111.
Willie GRAHAM, twin, death cause: "stillborn", died: 1st District on 1 Jun 1910, record (1908-12): 92112.
Melvina GREENWAY, death cause: "stillborn", died at Clarks Creek, 1st District on 20 Mar 1910, record (1908-12): 92113.
Mary Ann BAINES, age: 80 years, widow, death cause: "paralysis", died: 17th District on 24 May 1911, record (1908-12): 92114.
Mary CONLEY, age: 76 years, widow, death cause: "tuberculosis", died: 17th District on 16 Feb 1911, record (1908-12): 92116.
Martha KINLEY, age: 30 years, married, death cause: "heart disease", died: 17th District on 5 May 1911, record (1908-12): 92117.
Levicy A. BRODRICK, age: 74 years, widow, death cause: "heart disease, d17 on 19 Jul 1910, record (1908-12): 92118.
Efie BASKETT, age: 2 years, death cause: "pneumonia fever", died: 17th District on 16 Dec 1910, record (1908-12): 92119.
J.H. MOORE, age: 58 years, married, death cause: "consumption of bowels", died: 17th District, 8 Feb 1911, record: 92120.

Birnie D. WINTON, age: 11 months, death cause: "meningitis", died: 17th District on 5 Jul 1910, record (1908-12): 92121.

Martha DICKERSON, age: 67 years, born in Greene County, widow, death cause: "consumption", died: 17th District on 1 Oct 1910, record (1908-12): 92122.

Rhoda E. DUNN, age: 77 years, born in Carter County, death cause: "pneumonia fever", died: 17th District on 12 Jan 1911, record (1908-12): 92123.

I.F. MOORE, age: 62 years, married, death cause: "consumption", died: 17th District on 3 Feb 1911, record (1908-12): 92124.

Marietta EAMES, age: 88 years, widow, death cause: "grippe and pneumonia", died: 17th District on 8 Mar 1911, record: 92125.

Conie M. STFFORD, age: 25 years, married, death cause: "consumption", died: 17th District on 28 May 1911, record (1908-12): 92126.

Bessie M. KEYS, age: 29 years, single, death cause: illegible, died: 17th District on 1 Sep 1910, record (1908-12): 92127.

Mahala COLLIER, age: 84 years, born in Greene County, widow, death cause: "old age", died: 17th District on 10 May 1911, record (1908-12): 92128.

Hollie ARMNTRANT, age: 11 years, death cause: "shot accidentally", died: 17th District on 2 Feb 1911, record: 92129.

Ellen JENKINS, age: 26 years, married, death cause: "dropsy of heart", died: 15th District on 20 Nov 1910, record: 92130.

Claud M. STOUT, age: 18 months, death cause: "croup", died: 15th District on 7 Apr 1911, record (1908-12): 92131.

John BAILEY, age: 82 years, born in Unicoi County, married, death cause: "paralysis", died: 15th District on 29 Jun 1911, record (1908-12): 92132.

Mary RHUDY, age: 35 years, born in Washington County, VA., married, died: 15th District on 25 Aug 1910, record: 92133.

Sallie SHAW, age: 23 years, married, death cause: "tuberculosis", died: 15th District on 30 Apr 1911, record (1908-12): 92134.

Mary E. SHAW, age: 5 months, death cause: not stated, died: 15th District on 10 Jun 1911, record (1908-12): 92135.

Lara PHILLIPS, age: 12, death cause: "epilepsy", died: 15th District on 13 Sep 1910, record (1908-12): 92136.

Francis LANDINGHAM, age: 44 years, married, death cause: "spinal meningitis", died: 15th District on 8 Jan 1911, record: 92137.

John TOMPKINS, age: 78 years, married, death cause: "old age", died: 15th District on 25 Jan 1911, record (1908-12): 92138.

Ira BOOTH, female, age: 22 years, married, death cause: "spinal meningitis", died: 15th District on 12 Mar 1911, record: 92139.

Ely SIMPSON, colored, age: 22 years, born in Hamblin County, single, death cause: "tuberculosis", died: 15th District on 28 Mar 1911, record (1908-12): 92140.

Barte CLAYDE, age: 77 years, married, death cause: "heart failure", died: 15th District on 12 Apr 1911, record (1908-12): 92141.

Luke SMITH, age: 22 years, single, death cause: "epilepsy", died: 15th District on 7 Jun 1911, record (1908-12): 92142.

Unnamed Infant, female, age: 10 months, death cause: "tuberculosis", died: 15th District on 14 Nov 1910, record: 92143.

Dan OSBORNE, colored, age: 36 years, born in Virginia, married, death cause: "typhoid fever", died: 15th District on 4 Apr 1911, record (1908-12): 92144.

Blanch CLOYD, age: 10 years, death cause: "typhoid fever", died: 15th District on 1 Feb 1911, record (1908-12): 92145.

Richard BAILEY, age: 2 months, death cause: "pneumonia", died: 15th District on 4 Dec 1910, record (1908-12): 92146.

Dalton, MCGUIRE, age: 3 years, born in Sullivan County, death cause: "burned", died: 15th District on 11 Feb 1910, record (1908-12): 92147.

Infant KEYS, age: 6 weeks, death cause: "pneumonia", died: 15th District on 8 Dec 1910, record (1908-12): 92148.

Henry STUART, colored, age: 23 years, single, death cause: "tuberculosis", died: 15th District on 10 Aug 1910, record (1908-12): 92149.

Elizabeth CUNNINGHAM, colored, age: 64 years, married, death cause: "paralysis", died: 15th District on 18 May 1911, record (1908-12): 92150.

Charles CRAYLE, age: 3 days, death cause: "hives", died: 15th District on 15 Jul 1910, record (1908-12): 92151.

Nannie BYRD, age: 37 years, married, death cause: not stated, died: 15th District on 22 Dec 1910, record (1908-12): 92152.

Mollie C. BOWMAN, age: 37 years, born in Carter County, married, death cause: "tumor", died: 15th District on 8 Dec 1910, record (1908-12): 92153.

Martha BAILEY, colored, age: 61 years, born in Sullivan County, married, death cause: "pneumonia fever", died: 15th District on 31 Jan 1911, record (1908-12): 92154.

Anna P. GREENLEE, colored, age: 5 years, death cause: "appendicitis", died: 15th District on 21 Jun 1911, record: 92155.

Mary V. PURSELL, age: 53 years, born in Sullivan County, married, death cause: "tuberculosis", died: 15th District on 25 Jul 1910, record (1908-12): 92156.

H. Howard WARLICK, age: 22 years, single, death cause: "tuberculosis", died: 15th District on 21 Apr 1911, record: 92157.

Elizabeth CHESTER, age: 83 years, married, death cause: "old age", died: 15th District on 7 May 1911, record (1908-12): 92158.

Charley MCPHERSON, age: 55 years, single, death cause: not stated, died: 15th District on 25 Aug 1910, record (1908-12): 92159.

Melvina BARKLEY, age: 74 years, born in Wythe County, VA., married, death cause: "paralysis of heart", died: 15th District on 27 Sep 1910, record (1908-12): 92160.

Mariah Sneyd FEBRUARY, age: 87 years, born in Staffordshire, England, married, death cause: "general debility", died: 15th District on 5 Apr 1911, record: 92161.

Samuel Jacob KIRKPATRICK, age: 69 years, born in Hamblen County, married, death cause: "general debility", died at Jonesboro on 5 Nov 1910, record (1908-12): 92162.

Amelia KEEN, age: 90 (?), years and 6 months, born at Woodstock, VA., married, death cause: "indigestion", died: 15th District on 27 Apr 1911, record: 92163.

William Gentry MAY, age: 13 days, death cause: not stated, died: 15th District on 31 Oct 1910, record (1908-12): 92164.

J.W. HOSS, age: 51 years, married, death cause: "heart failure", died: 15th District on 7 Jul 1910, record (1908-12): 92165.

Elizabeth RUSSELL, age: 76 years, married, death cause: "ennema", died: 15th District on 5 Jan 1911, record (1908-12): 92166.

Sarah SAULTS, age: 85 years, single, death cause: "general debility", died at Jonesboro on 8 Mar 1911, record (1908-12): 92167.

Sarah CARMACK, age: 71 years, born in Bedford County, PA., married, death cause: "old age", died: 16th District on 29 Nov 1910, record (1908-12): 92168.

Clarence BALL, age: 15 days, death cause: not stated, died: 16th District on 7 Jun 1911, record (1908-12): 92169.

Susie MCLIN, age: 76 years, married, death cause: "old age", died: 3 Nov 1910, record (1908-12): 92170.

Anna MORRELL, age: 5 years, death cause: "meningitis", died: 14th District on 3 Apr 1911, record (1908-12): 92171.

William PRICE, age: 3 months, death cause: "spinal meningitis", died: 14th District on 14 Jun 1911, record (1908-12): 92172.

Stuart F. MORRELL, age: 1 year, death cause: "croup", died: 14th District on 5 Jan 1911, record (1908-12): 92173.

Ellen ALLISON, colored, age: 35 years, born in Hamblen County, married, died: 14th District on 20 Jan 1911, record: 92174.

Rosco H. JENKINS, age: 7 years, death cause: "blood poison", died: 14th District on 28 Apr 1911, record (1908-12): 92175.

Jessie P. MURRAY, age: 20 years, single, death cause: "hurt by horse", died: 14th District on 25 Feb 1911, record: 92176.

James BACON, age: 52 years, married, death cause: "tubeculosis", died: 14th District on 16 Mar 1911, record (1908-12): 92177.

Elbert DOUGLAS, age: 82 years, married, death cause: "cancer", died: 14th District on 17 Dec 1910, record (1908-12): 92178.

John SIFFORD, age: 78 years, born in North Carolina, married, death cause: "lagrippe", died: 14th District on 15 Jan 1911, record (1908-12): 92179.

Luck B. BALES, age: 45 years, married, death cause: "tuberculosis", died: 14th District on 16 Apr 1911, record (1908-12): 92180.

Louise ARCHER, age: 3 days, death cause: not stated, died: 14th District on 20 Sep 1910, record (1908-12): 92181.

Johnnie PRICE, age: 2 years, death cause: "croup", died: 14th District on 9 Dec 1910, record (1908-12): 92182.

Dora MITCHELL, age: 7 weeks, death cause: "stomach trouble", died: 13th District on 22 May 1911, record (1908-12): 92183.

Robert BACON, age: 17 years, 11 months and 10 days, single, death cause: "blood poison", died: 13th District on 10 Aug 1910, record (1908-12): 92184.

Adam SHIPLEY, age: 71 years, married, death cause: "ira siplars", died: 13th District on 11 Nov 1910, record (1908-12): 92185.

Nila May CHASE, age: 5 months and 24 days, death cause: "enlargement of head", died: 13th District on 12 Nov 1910.

Mattie COX, age: 48 years, born in Sullivan County, married, death cause: "consumption", died: 13th District on 24 Oct 1910, record (1908-12): 92187.

William M. FULKERSON, age: 76 years and 3 months, married, death cause: "blood poison", died: 13th District on 2 Jan 1911, record (1908-12): 92188.

Hattie Marie MARTIN, age: 6 years and 9 months, death cause: "pneumonia", died at Boones Creek on 12 Nov 1910, record: 92202.

Julia M. HAWS, age: 56 years, born in Greene County, married, death cause: "pneumonia", died at Limestone on 30 Apr 1911, record (1908-12): 92189.

Myrtle Blanch MCCRACKEN, age: 7 years, death cause: "brain fever", died at Limestone on 15 Jul 1911, record (1908-12): 92190.

Troy FOWLER, colored, age: 22 years, born: Chuckey, single, death cause: "consumption", died at Limestone on 8 Oct 1910, record (1908-12): 92191.

R.C. BROWN, age: 75 years, born at Bedford County, VA., married, death cause: "heart trouble", died at Limestone on 12 Jun 1911, record (1908-12): 92192.

Burnie Franklin GRAY, age: 3 years, born at Horse Creek, death cause: "typhoid fever, died at Limestone on 28 Jun 1911, record (1908-12): 92193.

Catherine Murrell WILLIAMS, age: 2 years, death cause: "indigestion", died: Limestone on 5 Jun 1911, record: 92194.

O.P. HENDERSON, age: 73 years, born in South Carolina, married, death cause: "pneumonia", died at Limestone on 22 Apr 1911, record (1908-12): 92195.

Mary Ann KLEPPER, age: 84 years and 2 months, married, death cause: "old age", died at Limestone on 25 Feb 1911, record (1908-12): 92196.

William Henry ANDERSON, age: 5 months, death cause: "pneumonia", died at Limestone on 28 Dec 1911, record (1908-12): 92197.

Riley Hasson KEEBLER, age: 21 months, death cause: "dysentery", died at Limestone on 11 Jun 1911, record (1908-12): 92198.

J.O. MCCOURY, age: 64 years, born in North Carolina, marrid, death cause: "heart, kidney and consumption", died at Boones Creek on 19 Apr 1911, record: 92199.

Hiram JOHNSON, age: 74 years, born in Virginia, married, death cause: "Brights disease", died at Boones Creek on 18 Apr 1911, record (1908-12): 92200.

Martha SELLARS, age: 52 years and 25 days, widow, death cause: "general break down", died at Boones Creek on 21 Jun 1911, record (1908-12): 92201.

Mary MOODY, age: 20 years, married, death cause: "consumption", died at Boones Creek on 19 Feb 1911, record (1908-12): 92203.

Brown REEDY, age: 4 years and 8 months, death cause: "dyptheria", died at Boones Creek on 16 Sep 1910, record: 92204.

James Lee KEEFAUVER, age: 6 weeks, death cause: "pneumonia", died at Boones Creek on 4 Feb 1911, record (1908-12): 92205.

Grant RIFFEY, age: 3 years, death cause: "dyptheria", died at Boones Creek on 19 Feb 1911, record (1908-12): 92206.

D.G. BASHOR, age: 2 years, death cause: "dyptheria", died at Boones Creek on 13 Feb 1911, record (1908-12): 92207.

Cecil JOHNSON, age: 7 years, death cause: "dyptheria", died at Boones Creek on 10 Nov 1910, record (1908-12): 92208.

Denver HODGES, age: 8 years, death cause: "blood poison", died at Boones Creek on 17 May 1911, record (1908-12): 92209.

James MAUPIN, age: 2 months and 8 days, death cause: "brain fever", died at Boones Creek on 14 Mar 1911, record: 92210.

Louisa HARWOOD, age: 63 years, born in Sullivan County, widow, death cause: "indigestion", died at Boones Creek on 13 Sep 1910, record (1908-12): 92211.

Ben H. CROSS, age: 71 years, single, death cause: "typhoid fever", died at Boones Creek on 12 Sep 1910, record (1908-12): 92212.

W.B. BOWMAN, age: 72 years, married, death cause: "indigestion", died at Boones Creek on 3 Sep 1910, record (1908-12): 92213.

John MITCHELL, age: 72 years, married, death cause: "cancer", died at Boones Creek on 7 Oct 1910, record (1908-12): 92214.

Stella ISENBURG, age: 5 years, death cause: "dyptheria", died at Boones Creek on 17 Dec 1910, record (1908-12): 92215.

John WILBORN, age: 54 years, born in Virginia, married, death cause: "indigestion", died at Boones Creek on 15 Jun 1911, record (1908-12): 92216.

Samuel HILBERT, age: 66 years, born in Virginia, married, death cause: "heart trouble", died at Boones Creek on 26 Jun 1911, record (1908-12): 92217.

Mamey SEATON, age: 12 years, death cause: "flux", died: 1st District on 14 Jun 1911, record (1908-12): 92218.

Francis BROYLES, age: 76 years, widow, death cause: "asma", died: 1st District on 16 Apr 1911, record (1908-12): 92219.

Glades PAMTER, age: 7 months, death cause: "hives", died: 1st District on 2 Jun 1911, record (1908-12): 92220.

Bet LANDERS, female, age: 85 years, born at Shelton Laurel, NC., single, death cause: "dropsy", died: 1st District on 1 Nov 1910, record (1908-12): 92221.

Isaac N. DUNBAR, death cause: "still born", died: 1st District on 26 Mar 1911, record (1908-12): 92222.

Bevie LANDERS, male, age: 72 years, born at Shelton Laurel, NC., married, death cause: "Brights disease", died: 1st District on 15 Jun 1911, record (1908-12): 92223.

Fred BROYLES, age: 18 years, single, death cause: "fever", died: 1st District on 26 Dec 1910, record (1908-12): 92224.

D.M. FELLERS, age: not stated, married, death cause: "diabetes", died: 1st District on 7 Mar 1911, record (1908-12): 92225.

William SALTS, age: 11 months, death cause: "cholera infantum", died: 1st District on 11 Aug 1910, record (1908-12): 92226.

Luther MATHES, age: 1 year and 11 days, death cause: "cholera infantum", died: 1st District on 11 Aug 1910, record: 92227.

Clyde COLE, age: 13 days, death cause: "bowel trouble", died: 1st District on 16 Jun 1911, record (1908-12): 92228.

W.M. BROYLES, age: 65 years, married, death cause: "heart trouble", died: 1st District on 31 Oct 1910, record (1908-12): 92229.

Viola LANDERS, age: 14 months, death cause: "flux", died: 1st District on 3 Jun 1911, record (1908-12): 92230.

William W. MASTERS, age: 76 years, born in Wilkesboro, NC., married, death cause: "old age and break down", died: 1st District on 28 Nov 1910, record (1908-12): 92231.

R.A. MOORE, age: 64 years, married, death cause: "consumption", died: 1st District on 24 Feb 1911, record (1908-12): 92232.

Jennie MITCHELL, age: 50 years, born in Yancey County, NC., married, death cause: "paralysis", died: 1st District on 1 Jun 1911, record (1908-12): 92233.

Lena MAY, age: 20 years, married, death cause: "child birth", died at Limestone on 28 Jul 1910, record (1908-12): 92235.

Lena MAY, age: 14 days, death cause: "convulsions", died: Limestone on 10 Aug 1910, record (1908-12): 92236.

Dan BUCHANAN, black, age: 22 years, single, death cause: "consumption", died: 1st District on 15 Dec 1911, record: 92234.

George W. PARKER, age: 50 years, born in Greene County, married, death cause: "heart failure", died: 10 Mar 1911, record: 92237.

Mary A. KIMERLY (or Simerly ?), age: 76 years, married, death cause: "dropsy", died: 2nd District on 27 Aug 1910, record (1908-12): 92238.

Mary J. THOMAS, age: 61 years, single, death cause: "paralysis", died: 2nd District on 18 Jun 1911, record (1908-12): 92239.

Mary Elizabeth BASS, age: 2 months, death cause: illegible, died: 2nd District on 6 Dec 1910, record (1908-12): 92240.

Bertha BOYD, age: 6 years, born in North Carolina, death cause: "diptheria", died: 2nd District on 16 Dec 1910, record: 92241.

Amantha STEPP, age: 76 years, born in Virginia, death cause: not stated, died: 2nd District on 16 Oct 1910, record: 92242.

M.L. BROWN, female, age: 77 years, married, death cause: "pneumonia", died: 2nd District, 15 Feb 1911, record: 92243.

John E. HUMPHREYS, age: 4 years, born in Illinois, death cause: "typhoid", died: 2nd District on 8 Oct 1910, record: 92244.

Daniel WAGNER, age: 79 years, born in Johnson County, married, death cause: "kidney trouble", died: 3rd District on 22 Apr 1910, record (1908-12): 92245.

Frank F. MILLER, age: 56 years, married, death cause: "suciocidi (?)" died: 3rd District on 10 Nov 1909, record: 92246.

J.A. MAUK, age: 54 years, married, death cause: "heart trouble", died: 3rd District on 20 Jun 1910, record (1908-12): 92247.

Walter A. HUNT, age: 21 years, single, death cause: "drowned", died at Limestone on 11 Jul 1909, record (1908-12): 92248.

M.J. WEST, age: 71 years, married, death cause: "Brights disease", died at Washington College on 13 Jul 1910, record: 92249.

Amanda C. BRIGHT, age: 43 years, born in Greene County, single, death cause: "heart trouble", died: 3rd District on 4 Mary 1910, record (1908-12): 92250.

Emma J. BROYLES, age: 73 years, married, death cause: "pneumonia", died: 3rd District on 4 Mar 1910, record (1908-12): 92251

Lizzie BROBECK, age: 61 years, single, death cause: "liver trouble, died: 2nd District on 14 Nov 1909, record (1908-12): 92252.

Emanuel ESTEP, age: 19 years, born in North Carolina, single, death cause: "serofula", died in North Carolina on 6 May 1910, record (1908-12): 92253.

Herald LOYD, age: 3 months, death cause: "cholera infantum", died: 2nd District on 10 May 1909, record (1908-12): 92254.

William D. SANDERSON, age: 35 years, married, death cause: "consumption", died: 2nd District on 12 Mar 1910, record: 92255.

Mag ODELL, age: 50 years, married, death cause: "stomach trouble", died: 2nd District on 12 Sep 1909, record (1908-12): 92256.

Jessie BAYLESS, age: 5 years, born in Illinois, death cause: "croup", died: 2nd District on 29 Oct 1909, record: 92257.

Mary E. KIMERY, age: 76 years, married, death cause: "bowel trouble", died: 2nd District on 21 May 1910, record: 92258.

Robert GILLESPIE, Jr., age: 37 years, single, death cause: "kidney trouble", died: 2nd District on 6 Apr 1910, record: 92259.

Charlie MCKEE, age: 18 years, single, death cause: "typhoid fever", died: 2nd District on 18 Sep 1909, record (1908-12): 92260.

Louise RUBLE, age: 8 years, death cause: "diptheria", died: 2nd District on 1 Oct 1909, record (1908-12): 92261.

Infant RUBLE, male, age: 1 day, son of E.E. RUBLE, death cause: not stated, died: 2nd District on 19 Sep 1909, record: 92262.

J.R. PAYNE, age: 70 years, married, death cause: "hemorrhage", died: 3rd District on 10 Dec 1910, record (1908-12): 92263.

Hester PAYNE, age: 66 years, married, death cause: "pneumonia", died: 3rd District on 5 Jan 1911, record (1908-12): 92264.

Jacob BAXTER, age: 94 years, born at Lacy Springs, VA., married, death cause: "old age", died: 3rd District on 11 Jan 1911, record (1908-12): 92265.

S.W. TONEY, age: 66 years, born in Carter County, married, death cause: "rhumatism", died at Telford on 27 Nov 1910, record (1908-12): 92266.

James McChesney WAGNER, age: 1 day, death cause: "unknown", died at Washington College on 27 Jun 1911, record (1908-12): 92267.

Isaac BARKLEY, colored, age: 95 years, married, death cause: "old age", died at Washington College on 10 Jul 1910, record (1908-12): 92267, record (1908-12): 92268.

Tessie BARKLEY, colored, age: 90 years, married, death cause: "rhumatism", died at Washington College on 28 Dec 1910, record (1908-12): 92269.

Alice MILLER, age: 39 years, 2 months and 4 days, married, death cause: "poisoned", died 4th District on 3 Apr 1911, record: 92270.

B.F. SWINGLE, age: 95 years, married, death cause: "heart failure", died: 4th District on 10 May 1911, record (1908-12): 92271.

E.E. WILSON, age: age 76 years, married, death cause: "paralysis", died: 4th District on 30 Oct 1910, record (1908-12): 92272.

Jane (ILLEGIBLE), death cause: "stillborn", died 4th District on 5 Jun 1911, record (1908-12): 92273.

James PRESNELL, age: 38 years, born in Mitchell County, NC., married, death cause: "typhoid fever", died 4th District on 20 Oct 1910, record (1908-12): 92274.

Jane RUSSELL, age: 73 years, married, death cause: "consumption", died: 4d on 29 Jan 1911, record (1908-12): 92275.

Nancy J. HOSS, age: 62 years, married, death cause: "consumption", died: 4d on 21 Oct 1910, record (1908-12): 92276.

Margaret BAYLESS, age: 76 years and 11 months, single, death cause: "paralysis", died: 29 Jun 1911, record (1908-12): 92277.

Henry Jackson BUCHANAN, age: 9 months, death cause: "lung trouble", died: 4d on 7 Feb 1911, record (1908-12): 92278.
Ana BOOTH, age: 27 years, married, death cause: "consumption", died: 4d on 19 Mar __ (1911 ?), record (1908-12): 92279.
Rachel YOUNG, age: 45 years, married, death cause: "heart disease", died: 4d on 15 Apr 1911, record (1908-12): 92280.
Mary C. MAY, age: 78 years, married, death cause: "old age", died: 5th District on 5 Dec 1910, record (1908-12): 92281.
D.D. MARKWOOD, age: 74 years, married, death cause: "heart disease", died: 5th District on 28 Dec 1910, record (1908-12): 92282.
Raymon CANE, age: 3 years, death cause: "croup", died: 5th District on 13 May 1911, record (1908-12): 92283.
Martin FORD, black, age: 65 years, married, death cause: "accident", died: 5th District on 29 Jan 1911, record (1908-12): 92284.
Unnamed Infant, male, death cause: "stillborn", died: 5th District on 1 Aug 1910, record (1908-12): 92285.
Unnamed Infant, male, age: 2 weeks, death cause: "heart trouble", died: 5th District on 25 Mar 1911, record (1908-12): 92286.
S.D. HELBERT, age: 52 years, married, death cause: "meningitis", died at Knoxville on 28 Dec 1910, record (1908-12): 92287.
Lizzie CLARK, age: 42 years, married, death cause: "consumption", died: 5th District on 12 Mar 1911, record (1908-12): 92288.
Unnamed Infant, male, death cause: "stillborn", died: 5th District on 12 Mar 1911, record (1908-12): 92289.
Edith FREEMAN, age: 1 year and 1 month, death cause: "consumption", died at Embreeville on 9 Jun 1911, record: 92290.
Unnamed Infant, male, age: 3 weeks, death cause: "bold hives", died at Embreeville on 13 Mar 1911, record (1908-12): 92291.

Albert YATES, age: 18 years, single, death cause: "typhoid fever", died at Embreeville on 23 Jun 1911, record (1908-12): 92292.

Georgia Hazel LIGHT, age: 5 days, death cause: "pneumonia", died at Fall Branch on 20 Oct 1910, record (1908-12): 92293.

Erma MOULTON, age: 18 years, 5 months and 17 days, born in Sullivan County, single, death cause: "tuberculosis", died at Fall Branch on 1 Jul 1910, record (1908-12): 92294.

Joseph C. BOYER, age: 18 years, death cause: "typhoid", died at Fall Branch on 2 Sep 1910, record (1908-12): 92295.

Eli P. WARREN, age: 44 years, born at Piney Flats, married, death cause: "abscess of liver", died at Fall Branch on 7 Jun 1911, record (1908-12): 92296.

Onie Lee GOOD, age: 3 years and 5 months, death cause: "scroffula", died at Fall Branch on 23 Jun 1911, record: 92297.

N.L. BEARD, age: 58 years, born in Sullivan County, married, death cause: "cancer", died in Dallas, Texas on 6 Jun 1911, record (1908-12): 92298.

Jake W. SMITH, age: 44 years, born in Virginia, married, death cause: "tuber-culosis", died at Fall Branch on 31 Oct 1910, record (1908-12): 92299.

Rena BAYLESS, age: 79 years, born in Franklin County, VA., married, death cause: "nervous breakdown", died: 8th District on 5 Apr 1911, record (1908-12): 92300.

Elice W. DAVENPORT, male, age: 9 months, death cause: "diptheria", died: 8th District on 9 Oct 1910, record (1908-12): 92301.

Allie MCINTURFF, age: 2 years, death cause: "cholera", died: 8th District on 19 Jan 1911, record (1908-12): 92302.

Orpha DULANEY, age: 91 years, married, death cause: "cancer", died: 8th District on 10 Apr 1911, record (1908-12): 92303.

Harry Olen MULLEN, age: 1 year, born in Johnson County, death cause: "cholera infantum", died: 8th District on 3 Feb 1911, record (1908-12): 92304.

Infant VANCE, male, son of J.M. VANCE, death cause: "stillborn", died: 8th District on 21 Mar 1911, record (1908-12): 92305.

Adam GREER, age: 75 years, born in Ashe County, NC., married, death cause: "rhumatism", died: 8th District on 9 Jun 1911, record (1908-12): 92306.

Rena Pearl HUGHS, age: 5 years, born in Mitchell County, NC., death cause: "lock jaw", died: 8th District on 23 Ju 1911, record (1908-12): 92307.

Edith GROSS, age: 2 years and 7 months, death cause: "croup", died at Boones Creek on __ Nov 1910, record (1908-12): 92308.

Cumi PHILLIPS, age: 35 years, married, death cause: "fever", died: 8th District on 5 Jan 1911, record (1908-12): 92309.

Cary B. PATRICK, age: 21 years, married, death cause: "consumption", died: 5 Jul 1910, record (1908-12): 92310.

A.G. RIDDLE, Jr., age: 4 years, death cause: "pneumonia", died: Johnson City on 3 Jan 1911, record (1908-12): 92311.

Infant FEATHERS, black, female, born at Watauga, TN., death cause: not stated, died at Watauga on 5 Dec 1910, record: 92312.

James H. MCINTYRE, age: 16 years and 9 months, death cause: "heart failure", died: Johnson City on 25 Feb 1911, record: 92313.

R.W. MCFALL, age: 66 years, born at Watauga, TN., married, death cause: "rhumatism", died: Watauga on 17 Feb 1911, record: 92314.

Lottie A. MCINTYRE, age: 2 years and 6 months, death cause: "whooping cough", died: Johnson City on 20 Apr 1911, record: 92315.

Infant FULKERSON, male, age: 2 days, death cause: not stated, died: Johnson City on 3 Dec 1910, record (1908-12): 92316.

Infant MORRELL, female, lived 1 hour, death cause: not stated, died: Johnson City on 11 Mar 1911, record (1908-12): 92317.

Eugene PRICE, age: 6 weeks, born at Morristown, death cause: not stated, died: Johnson City on 28 Jul 1910, record: 92318.

Jenie RHEA, age: 8 days, death cause: "hives", died: Johnson City on 23 Nov 1910, record: 92319.

John SMITH, age: 15 years, death cause: illegible, died: Johnson City on 6 Apr 1911, record: 92320.

Mattie TAYLOR, age: 66 years, born at Hendersonville, NC., married, death cause: "erysipelas", died: Johnson City on 19 Mar 1911, record (1908-12): 92321.

Malcome COLLETTE, age: 1 year, death cause: "whooping cough", died: Johnson City on 30 Nov 1911, record (1908-12): 92322.

Mildred DAVIDSON, age: 1 month and 19 days, death cause: "pneumonia", died: Johnson City on 19 Feb 1911, record (1908-12): 92323.

Infant CARROLL, male, lived 4 hours, child of Dr. CAROLL, death cause: "unknown", died: Johnson City on 17 Jan 1911, record: 92324.

Hester EMMERT, age: 69 years, born in Carter County, death cause: "kidney trouble", married, died: Johnson City on 12 Jun 1910, record: 92325.

Edgar LAWSON, lived 2 hours, death cause: not stated, died: Johnson City on 7 Oct 1909, record (1908-12): 92326.

Francis CLAY, age: 4 months, death cause: "stomach trouble", died: Johnson City on 11 Jun 1910, record (1908-12): 92327.

J.F. LANDIS, age: 21 years, born in Birmingham, married, death cause: "tuberculosis", died at Bristol on 20 Nov 1908, record (1908-12): 92328.

Irene ORR, age: 16 months (or years ?), death cause: "consumption, died at Johnson City on 5 Feb 1910, record (1908-12): 92329.

Alice RHEA, black, age: 39 years, married, death cause: "heart failure", died at Johnson City on 3 Jul 1909, record (1908-12): 92330.

Elizabeth HAYES, age: 79 years, born in Carter County, widow, death cause: "lagrippe", died at Johnson City on 30 Apr 1910, record: 92331.

Sallie ARON, age: 75 years, born in Stokes County, NC., single, death cause: "dropsy", died at Johnson City on 4 Oct 1909, record (1908-12): 92332.

James Milton AYERS, age: 70 years, born in Butler County, Ohio, married, death cause: "penumonia", died at Johnson City on 26 Feb 1910, record (1908-12): 92333.
E.H. CAMPBELL, age: 48 years, married, death cause: "suicide", died at Johnson City on 9 Mar 1910, record (1908-12): 92334.
Charlie VAUGHT, age: 1 year and 9 months, death cause: "stomach trouble", died at Johnson City on 23 Jul 1909, record (1908-12): 92335.
Stuart HENDERSON, age: 4 years, death cause: "pneumonia", died: 9d on 23 Mar 1910, record (1908-12): 92336.
Ella PARSONS, age: 38 years, born in Knox County, married, death cause: "cancer of liver", died: Morganton, NC., on 3 Dec 1909, record: 92337.
Ina D..., age: 22 years, born at Stonaker, VA., death cause: "typhoid fever", married, death cause: 23 Dec 1909, record (1908-12): 92338.
Gertrude RANGE, age: 24 years, married, death cause: "tuberculosis", died at Johnson City on 20 Feb 1910, record (1908-12): 92339.
John ARWOOD, age: 83 years, born at Big Rock Creek, NC., preacher, widower, death cause: "dropsy", died in Carter County on 14 Jul 1909, record: 92340.
Thomas EVANS, age: 63 years, born in Greene County, married, death cause: "bowel trouble", died at Johnson City on 24 Dec 1909, record: 92341.
Will GREAR, age: 25 years, born at Elk Park, NC., married, death cause: "stomach trouble", died at Johnson City on 27 Jul 1909, record: 92342.
T.D. ROWE, age: 33 years, born at Little Rock Creek, NC., married, death cause: "measles", died at Knoxville on 15 Feb 1910, record (1908-12): 92343.
Isaac CLARKE, age: 23 years, born in Carter County, single, death cause: "tuberculosis", died at Johnson City on 29 Mar 1910, record (1908-12): 92344.
Jesse REEDY, age: 87 years, born in Grayson County, VA., married, death cause: "old age", died at Johnson City on 25 Jun 1910, record: 92345.

Martha HOBSON, age: 7 months, death cause: "summer complaint", died in Johnson City on 12 Jul 1909, record (1908-12): 92346.
Minnie LEONARD, age: 30 years, married, death cause: "tuberculosis", died at Johnson City on 9 May 1910, record (1908-12): 92347.
Alfred D. TAYLOR, age: 72 years, born in Carter County, married, death cause: "stomach trouble", died in Johnson City on 1 May 1910, record: 92348.
James LOW, age: 8 months, death cause: "summer complaint", died in Johnson City on 30 Aug 1910, record (1908-12): 92349.
Hester EMMERT, age: 69 years, born in Elizabethton, widow, death cause: "unknown", died at Johnson City on 12 Jun 1910, record (1908-12): 92350.
Anna GEAGLEY, age: 42 years, born in Greene County, married, death cause: "diabetes", died at Afton on 5 Nov 1909, record (1908-12): 92351.
Hewey ROSENBALM, age: 16 months, death cause: "sarafula", died 1 Jul 1910, record: 92352.
Infant STOUT, female, child of J.B. STOUT, death cause: "stillborn", died at Johnson City on 20 May 1910, record (1908-12): 92353.
H. RUSSELL, age: 57 years, born in Michigan, married, death cause: "heart failure", died in Johnson City on 8 Dec 1909, record (1908-12): 92354.
Georgia GIVENS, age: 10 weeks, death cause: "bronchitis", died at Johnson City on 17 Nov 1909, record (1908-12): 92355.
Edward ROGAN, age: 67 years, born in Kingsport, married, death cause: "grippe", died: Johnson City on 6 Apr 1910, record (1908-12): 92356.
Walter MCPEAK, age: 27 years, married, city officer, death cause: "killed, stabbed", died: Johnson City on 23 Jun 1910, record (1908-12): 92357.
R.B. BLACK, age: 53 years, born in Ashe County, NC., married, death cause: "blood poison", died: Johnson City on 25 Aug 1909, record (1908-12): 92358.
Infant OVERSTREET, female, child of Will OVERSTREET, death cause: "stillborn", died: Johnson City on 1 Feb 1910, record (1908-12): 92359.

Archie R. CHANDLER, age: 1 year and 11 months, death cause: "flux", died: Johnson City on 30 May 1901, record (1908-12): 92360.

Eva Grace MOODY, age: 11 weeks, death cause: "cholera infantum", died: Johnson City on 10 Jun 1910, record (1908-12): 92361.

Fred BELTON, age: 2 years, death cause: "bronchial penumonia", died: Johnson City on 8 May 1910, record (1908-12): 92362.

Infant WILSON, female, child of Walter WILSON, death cause: "stillborn", died at Johnson City on 7 Nov 1910, record (1908-12): 92363.

Samuel Taft PHILIPS, lived 2 hours, death cause: "weakness", died at Clarke Creek on 23 May 1909, record (1908-12): 92364.

Eveline GREENWAY, age: 63 years, married, death cause: "dropsy", died at Clarke Creek on 19 Jun 1909, record (1908-12): 92365.

Rena R. FOX, age: 15 months, death cause: "cholera infantum", died at Pilot Hill on 20 Jun 1909, record (1908-12): 92366.

Swiney SNODEN, age: 8 years, death cause: "pneumonia fever", died at Pilot Hill on 27 Jan 1909, record (1908-12): 92367.

Elen FOSTER, age: 23 years and 6 months, married, death cause: "consumption", died: 1st District on 4 Sep 1908, record (1908-12): 92368.

Arvel FOSTER, age: 1 month and 18 days, death cause: "stomach trouble", died: 1st District on 30 May 1909, record (1908-12): 92369.

Sarah ROUSE, age: 27 years and 15 days, born at White Rock, NC., married, death cause: "rhumatism", died: 30 Jun 1909, record (1908-12): 92370.

Cora E. FANNING, age: 30 years, born at Herman, Greene County, single, death cause: "consumption", died at Chuckey on 27 Feb 1909, record: 92371.

Burson STANTON, age: 1 year and 24 days, death cause: not stated, died at Chuckey on 29 Jun 1909, record (1908-12): 92372.

Birdie STANTON, age: 1 month and 18 days, death cause: not stated, died at Chuckey on 25 Jun 1909, record (1908-12): 92373.

Jessie PAINTER, age: 93 years, married, death cause: "pneumonia", died at Chuckey on 7 May 1909, record (1908-12): 92374.

Anie PAINTER, lived 1 hour, death cause: not stated, died at Painter, TN., on 5 May 1909, record: 92375.

T.S. LINCOLNFELLOW, age: 59 years, born in Pennsylvania, widower, death cause: "heart trouble", died: Johnson City on 17 Mar 1909, record: 92376.

Noah YATES, lived one hour, died in Johnson City on 24 May 1909, record (1908-12): 92377.

Unnamed Infant, female, death cause: "born dead", died: Johnson City on 22 Apr 1909, record: 92378.

Haney (?) CULBERSON, age: 19 months, death cause: "fever", died: Johnson City on 31 Oct 1908, record (1908-12): 92379.

Ethel R. FELTS, age: 5 years, born in Knoxville, death cause: "burned", died: Johnson City on 9 Nov 1908, record (1908-12): 92380.

H.H. ELLIS, colored, age: 38 years, married, death cause: "consumption", died: 23 Feb 1909, record (1908-12): 92381.

Edgar SEVADLEY, age: 11 months, death cause: "fever", died: Johnson City on 30 Jun 1909, record (1908-12): 92382.

Lucian MOORE, age: 6 years, born in Hawkins County, death cause: "flux", died: Johnson City on 25 Jun 1909, record (1908-12): 92383.

Goldie MOORE, age: unknown, death cause: "child birth", died: Johnson City on 10 Jun 1909, record (1908-12): 92384.

James ALFRED, age: 10 months, death cause: "bronchitis", died at Hampton, TN., on 20 Sep 1908, record (1908-12): 92385.

Charlie David DYER, age: 2 years and 5 months, death cause: "whooping cough", died: Johnson City on 7 Feb 1909, record (1908-12): 92386.

Miltie REDWINE, female, age: 60 years, born in Abingdon, VA., married, death cause: "cancer", died: Johnson City on 13 Sep 1908, record: 92387.

Unnamed Infant, female, death cause: "stillborn", died: Johnson City on 25 Jan 1909, record: 92388.

G... WILLIAMS, female, age 4 Weeks, death cause: "unknown", died: Johnson City on 8 Oct 1908, record (1908-12): 92389.

Unnamed Infant, male, lived 4 days, death cause: "unknown", died: Johnson City on 19 Jun 1909, record (1908-12): 92390.

Clara May SPENSE, age: 16 years, born in Virginia, death cause: "consumption", died: Johnson City on 28 Aug 1908, record (1908-12): 92391.

Robert RANGE, age: 21 years, single, death cause: "consumption", died: Johnson City on 1 Jun 1909, record (1908-12): 92392.

Mary Hester WOODS, colored, age: 10 weeks, born at Bristol, VA., death cause: "bold hives", died at Bristol on 7 Apr 1909, record (1908-12): 92393.

Mary JONES, age: 28 years, married, death cause: "stomach trouble", died at Johnson City on __ Jun 1909, record (1908-12): 92394.

Bessie MILHORN, age: 7 years, born at Boones Creek, death cause: "scarlet fever", died: Johnson City on 5 Mar 1909, record (1908-12): 92395.

James CHINOTH, age: 3 years, death cause: "brain fever", died: Johnson City on 1 Sep 1908, record (1908-12): 92396.

_____ COLDWELL, colored, age: 46 years, born in Bert County, NC., married, death cause: "heart dropsy", died at Knoxville on 9 Dec 1908, record: 92397.

Howard BRANCH, age: 6 months, born in Elizabethton, death cause: "heart trouble", died: Johnson City on 22 Oct 1908, record (1908-12): 92398.

Loman JOHNSON, age: 68 years, born in New York, married, death cause: "tumor of stomach", died at Soldier's Home on 26 Mar 1909, record: 92399.

Jessie WILLARD, female, age: 30 years, born in Lawrence, Kansas, widow, death cause: "tuberculosis of lungs", died: Johnson City on 8 May 1909, record (1908-12): 92400.

Unnamed Infant, female, lived 2 hours, death cause: "small pox", died: Johnson City on 28 Jun 1909, record (1908-12): 92401.

Allie MOODY, age: 3 years, death cause: "fever", died: Johnson City on 13 Oct 1908, record: 92402.

Thomas MARTIN, age: 29 years, born in Wilkes County, NC., married, death cause: "killed by shaft in mill", died at Elkins, NC., on 23 Dec 1908, record (1908-12): 92403.

James CAMPBELL, age: 24 years, born in Virginia, death cause: "killed by train", died in Oklahoma on __ May 1909, record (1908-12): 92404.

Fannie B. COLLINS, age: 26 years, born at Chuckey, married, death cause: "dropsy", died: Johnson City on 30 Oct 1908, record (1908-12): 92405.

Coy Jerome COLLINS, age: 7 months, death cause: "unknown", died: Johnson City on __ Oct 1908, record (1908-12): 92406.

James ERVIN, colored, age: 9 months, death cause: "bornchitis", died: Johnson City on __ Oct 1908, record (1908-12): 92407.

Howard HOSS, age: 4 months, death cause: "unknown", died: Johnson City on __ Sep 1908, record: 92408.

Ollie YOUNG, colored, age: 20 years, born in Jonesboro, death cause: "fever", died: Johnson City on 28 Mar 1909, record (1908-12): 92409.

George SMITH, colored, age: 18 years, single, death cause: "killed by shooting", died: Johnson City on 16 May 1909, record (1908-12): 92410.

Lena JACKSON, colored, age: 21 years, born at Jonesboro, death cause: "measles", died: Johnson City on 9 apr 1909, record (1908-12): 92411.

Annie MCCALLISTER, colored, age: 25 years, born at Jonesboro, widow, death cause: "consumption", died: Johnson City on __ Jun 1909, record: 92412.

Maggie HALE, colored, age: 24 years, born in Maryville, TN., married, death cause: "pneumonia", died at Johnson City on 20 Mar 1909, record: 92413.

Milton CARRIGER, colored, age: 25 years, married, death cause: "consumption", died at Johnson City on 21 Feb 1909, record (1908-12): 92414.

Unnamed Infant, female, lived 3 days, death cause: "unknown", died at Johnson City on 22 Aur 1908, record (1908-12): 92415.

S.L. HAMPTON, age: 38 years, born in North Carolina, married, death cause: "tonsillitis", died at Johnson City on 1 Jul 1908, record (1908-12): 92416.

Robert Eugene GRAY, age: 4 months, death cause: "stomach trouble", died at Johnson City on 27 Jun 1909, record (1908-12): 92417.

Bertha BAKER, age: 21 years, born at Jonesboro, married, death cause: "flux", died at Johnson City on 26 Jun 1909, record (1908-12): 92418.

Iris PICKERING, age: 16 months, death cause: "summer complaint", died at Johnson City on 19 Jun 1909, record (1908-12): 92419.

James M. BROYLES, age: 49 years, born at Embreeville, married, death cause: "killed", died at Johnson City on 4 Oct 1908, record (1908-12): 92420.

Emma E. RICHARDSON, age: 54 years, born in North Carolina, married, death cause: "nervous prostration", died at Johnson City on 9 Oct 1908, record (1908-12): 92421.

Samuel HILTON, age: 66 years, married, death cause: "general debility", died at Johnson City on 24 Mar 1909, record (1908-12): 92422.

Annie LANGHREN, age: 53 years, married, death cause: "cancer of stomach", died at Johnson City on 5 Jul 1909. record (1908-12): 92423.

Nova CURTIS, death cause: "born dead", died at Johnson City on 3 Dec 1909, record (1908-12): 92424.

Walter RHEA, colored, age: 38 years, born in Sullivan County, single, death cause: "heart dropsy", died at Johnson City on 8 May 1909, record (1908-12): 92425.

Eugene JONES, colored, age: 5 years, death cause: "killed by train", died at Johnson City on 10 jan 1909, record (1908-12): 92426.

Unnamed Infant, female, lived 1 day, death cause: "bleeding death", died at Johnson City on 15 Dec 1908, record (1908-12): 92427.

Unnamed Infant, male, lived 1 day, death cause: "bold hives, died at Johnson City on 21 May 1908, record (1908-12): 92428.

Jacob LITTLE, age: 74 years, born at Embreeville, widower, death cause: "old age", died at Johnson City on 31 Dec 1908, record (1908-12): 92429.

Glenine PICKERING, age: 3 months, death cause: "summer complaint", died at Johnson City on 30 Jun 1909, record (1908-12): 92430.

Mary HOBSON, age: 5 months, death cause: "summer complaint", died at Johnson City on 8 Jun 1909, record (1908-12): 92431.

Mrs. T.J. CLOYD, age: 74 years, born in Carter County, widow, death cause: "heart failure", died at Johnson City on 19 Feb 1909, record: 92432.

Frederick FISHER, age: 42 years, born in Dayton, Ohio, married, death cause: "tuberculosis of bowels", died at Johnson City on 11 Jun 1909, record (1908-12): 92433.

J.B. WHITE, age: 16 years, born at Whitesburg, TN., death cause: "drowned in Watauga River", died at Johnson City on 8 Jun 1909, record (1908-12): 92434.

George ALLEN, age: 50 years, born at Richmond, VA., married, death cause: "stomach trouble", died at Johnson City on 14 Apr 1909, record: 92435.

Robert MOODY, age: 9 months, death cause: "whooping cough", died at Johnson City on 22 May 1909, record (1908-12): 92436.

Mrs. Alice Robinson REEVES, age: 57 years, born in Sullivan County, married, death cause: "gall stones", died at Johnson City on 17 Mar 1909, record (1908-12): 92437.

Nellie May BRUMMITT, age: 14 months, death cause: "fever and measles", died at Johnson City on 12 Oct 1908, record (1908-12): 92438.

Robert Clyde OVERSTREET, age: 13 months, death cause: "measles and fever", died at Johnson City on __ Aug 1908, record (1908-12): 92439.

Joe RAINWATER, age: 1 month and 5 days, death cause: "measles", died at Johnson City on 26 Jan 1909, record (1908-12): 92440.

Mrs. Elizabeth LENEN (?), age: 61 years, born in London England, married, death cause: "stomach trouble, died at Johnson City on 29 Oct 1908, record (1908-12): 92441.

Mrs. Jane TAYLOR, age: 67 years, born in Carter County, widow, death cause: "paralysis", died at Johnson City on 15 Jun 1909, record: 92442.

Elsie MAUPIN, age: 18 months, death cause: "summer disease", died: 11th District on __ Aug 1908, record (1908-12): 92443.

_____ WHITE, age: 10 years, death cause: "spinal trouble", died: 11th District on __ Mar 1909, record (1908-12): 92444.

_____ TAYLOR, female, age: 2 years, death cause: not stated, died: 11th District on __ Sep 1908, record (1908-12): 92445.

Archey BAILEY, age: 13 years, born in Sullivan County, death cause: "drowned", died: 11th District on 27 Jun 1909, record (1908-12): 92446.

J.R. BOWMAN, age: 39 years, married, death cause: "typhoid fever", died: 11th District on 25 Jan 1909, record (1908-12): 92447.

Decator CROUCH, age: 51 years, married, merchant, death cause: "liver trouble", died: 11th District on 24 Jan 1909, record (1908-12): 92448.

Jane Galoway CROUCH, age: 87 years, born in Sullivan County, married, death cause: "old age", died: 11th District on 23 Jan 1909, record (1908-12): 92449.

Ruben TYRE, age: 80 years, born in Virginia, married, farmer, death cause: "enlargement of heart", died: 11th District on 22 Jun 1909, record (1908-12): 92450.

Ollie SAYLOR, age: 8 days, death cause: "weakness", died: 11th District on 13 Jul 1909, record: 92451.

Clay CREESY, age: 10 weeks, death cause: "bold hives", died: 11th District on __ __ 1909, record (1908-12): 92452.

Infant HALE, female, age: 29 days, death cause: "starvation", died: 11th District on 7 Feb 1909 (08?), record (1908-12): 92453.

Cora E. HALE, age: 26 years, married, farmer's wife, death cause: "consumption", died: 11th District on 4 Sep 1908, record (1908-12): 92454.

Infant HENSON, male, child of John HENSON, death cause: "died at birth", died: 10th District on 27 Mar 1909, record (1908-12): 92455.

Delilah SMITHPETERS, age: 60 years, married, death cause: "tuberculosis", died: 10th District on 22 Aug 1908, record (1908-12): 92456.

Virgie B. MILLER, age: 19 months, death cause: "whooping cough", died: 10th District on 19 Sep 1908, record (1908-12): 92457.

Henry HODGE, age: 34 years, married, machinist, death cause: "caught in machinery (sawmill), died at Stone Gap, VA., on 29 May 1909, record: 92458.

Jessie E. HALE, age: 3 months and some days, death cause: "bold hives", died: 10th District on 21 Nov 1908, record (1908-12): 92459.

James COLLINS, age: 48 years, married, farmer, death cause: "diabetes", died: 10th District on 14 Aug 1908, record (1908-12): 92460.

Bertha BAKER, age: 20 years, married, death cause: "cattarh of stomach", died: 10th District on 10 Jun 1909, record (1908-12): 92461.

Bessie BAKER, age: 1 year and 1 months, death cause: "flux", died: 10th District on 20 Apr 1909, record (1908-12): 92462.

Nellie E. BOWMAN, age: 37 years, married, death cause: "stomach trouble", died: 10th District on 25 Sep 1908, record (1908-12): 92463.

Cordie KELLESY, age: 11 years, death cause: "meningitis", died: 10th District on 15 Oct 1908, record (1908-12): 92464.

Lucy BAKER, age: 2 years, death cause: "whooping cough", died: 10th District on 22 Jul 1908, record (1908-12): 92465.

Jasper N. CHRISTY, age: 78 years, widower, blacksmith, death cause: "paralysis", died: 10th District on 7 May 1909, record (1908-12): 92466.

Billy SMITH, age: 5 days, death cause: "bold hives", died: 9th District on 2 Jan 1909, record: 92467.

Mildred MILHORN, age: 4 weeks, death cause: "cholera infantum", died at Johnson City on 15 Jul 1909, record (1908-12): 92468.

Robert BLEVINS, age: 7 weeks, death cause: "heart failure", died at Johnson City on 15 Apr 1910, record (1908-12): 92469.

J. CRUMLEY, age: 75 years, born in Sullivan County, widower, lumberman, died at Johnson City on 20 Jan 1901, record (1908-12): 92470.

Ada M. HARR, age: 38 years, born in Arkansas, married, death cause: "tuberculosis", died in Johnson City on 18 Apr 1910, record: 92471.

Dr. J.A. KIRKPATRICK, age: 65 years, born in Hawkins County, married, physician, death cause: "Brights disease", died in Johnson City on 16 Feb 1910, record (1908-12): 92472.

R.W. WINSTON, black, age: 42 years, born in Richmond, VA., married, minister, death cause: "tuberculosis", died in Johnson City on 9 Oct 1909, record (1908-12): 92473.

Alex TURNER, age: 36 years, born in Knoxville, married, stone mason, death cause: "epileptic fit", died at Bristol on 26 Jul 1909, record: 92474.

Araline BORING, female, age: 14 months, death cause: "cutting teeth", died at Johnson City on 18 Dec 1909, record (1908-12): 92475.

James HOSS, age: 15 years, death cause: "typhoid fever", died at Johnson City on 3 Aug 1909, record (1908-12): 92476.

Infant JOHNSON, female, age: 6 months, death cause: "tonsilitis", died at Johnson City on 17 Jun 1910, record (1908-12): 92477.

Elsie JOHNSON, age: 3 years, death cause: "tonsilitis", died at Johnson City on 15 Feb 1910, record (1908-12): 92478.

James BOOHER, age: not stated, born in Ohio, married, laborer, death cause: "killed by wagon", died in Ohio on __ Aug 1909, record (1908-12): 92479.

Mary JONES, age: 5 years, death cause: "fever", died: Johnson City on 20 May 1910, record (1908-12): 92480.

Jake JONES, age: 23 years, born in North Carolina, married, laborer, death cause: "tuberculosis", died at Johnson City on 9 May 1910, record: 92481.

Infant BUSHAGE, female, death cause: "stillborn", died at Johnson City on 27 Dec 1909, record (1908-12): 92482.

J.J. JOHNSON, black, age: 64 years, born at Chuckey River, married, death cause: "dropsy", died at Johnson City on 7 Apr 1910, record (1908-12): 92483.

Gertrude PEARCE, age: 22 years, born in Elizabethton, single, death cause: "over worked", died at Johnson City on 19 Jan 1910, record: 92484.

John COPNEY, black, age: 1 years, death cause: "weakling", died at Johnson City on __ Apr 1910, record (1908-12): 92485.

Mina E. WALLACE, age: 19 years, married, death cause: "child birth", died at Green Mountain on 8 Jun 1910, record (1908-12): 92486.

Caroline GRUMP, age: 75 years, born in Germany, married, death cause: "pneumonia", died at Johnson City on 22 Dec 1909, record (1908-12): 92487.

Susie WAGNER, age: 84 years, widow, death cause: "rhumatism", died at Johnson City on 20 Jun 1910, record (1908-12): 92482.

Tennessee LUSK, age: 82 years, born in Carter County, widower, teacher, death cause: "old age and broken leg", died at Johnson City on 1 Feb 1910, record (1908-12): 92483.

Jessie GREENLEE, black, age: 21 years, born in Jonesboro, married, death cause: "killed by explosion", died at Johnson City on __ Apr 1910, record (1908-12): 92484.

Harriett SCOTT, age: 77 years, born in Carter County, widow, death cause: "broken arm", died at Johnson City on 10 Apr 1910, record: 92485.

John K..., age: 3 months, born at Keebler Cross Roads, death cause: "stomach trouble", died at Johnson City on 28 Jun 1910, record: 92486.

Jacob R. RANGE, age: 74 years, married, miller, death cause: "jaundice", died at Johnson City on __ Apr 1910, record: 92487.

Hassie CAMPBELL, age: 54 years, married, death cause: "dropsy", died at Johnson City on 4 Jun 1910, record (1908-12): 92488.

Elsie (illegible), age: 11 months, death cause: "summer complaint", died at Johnson City on 30 Jun 1910, record (1908-12): 92495.

Nancy GEISLER, age: 89 years, born in Sullivan County, widow, death cause: "cancer", died at Johnson City on 2 May 1910, record (1908-12): 92496.

Mrs. M.W. DICKEY, age: 34 years, born in Watauga, TN., married, death cause: "ptomaine poison", died at Johnson City on 5 Mar 1901, record: 92497.

Charles (illegible), black, age: 39 years, born at Mountain City, married, soldier, died in Nebraska on __ Jan 1910, record (1908-12): 92498.

Tom DAVIS, age: 26 years, born at Telford, married, clerk, death cause: "killed by lightening", died at Johnson City on 29 Aug 1909, record: 92499.

John JACKSON, black, death cause: "stillborn", died at Johnson City on 9 Nov 1909, record: 92500.

R.M. JACKSON, age: 51 years, married, painter, death cause: "consumption", died at Johnson City on __ Apr 1910, record (1908-12): 92501.

Alex KELLEY, age: 74 years, born in Ireland, married, stone mason, death cause: "kidney trouble", died at Johnson City on 5 Jun 1910, record: 92502.

Jim GLEAN, age: 50 years, born in Russell County, Va., married, death cause: "pneumonia fever", died: 8th District on 7 Nov 1909, record (1908-12): 92503.

Mary E. PRICE, age: 52 years, single, death cause: "consumption", died: Johnson City on 19 Apr 1910, record (1908-12): 92504.

Worley TOPPER, age: 19 years, single, farmer, death cause: "consumption", died: Johnson City on 27 Apr 1910, record (1908-12): 92505.

Mariah TREADWAY, age: 62 years, born at Embreeville, widow, death cause: "broken down", died at Johnson City on 7 Dec 1910, record (1908-12): 92506.

J.L. HUNTER, age: 34 years, born at Limestone, married, furnace keeper, death cause: "shot, killed", died at Johnson City on 9 Jun 1910, record (1908-12): 92507

Bettie WHITE, age: 5 years, death cause: "pneumonia", died at Johnson City on 2 Jan 1910, record (1908-12): 92508.

Pearl BLEVINS, age: 16 years, death cause: "typhoid", died at Johnson City on 1 Aug 1909, record (1908-12): 92509.

Andrew SHIPLEY, age: 57 years, married, laborer, tanning, death cause: "suicide", died at Johnson City on 7 Jan 1910, record (1908-12): 92510.

Mary MATHEWS, age: 56 years, born in North Carolina, married, death cause: "bronchitis", died at Johnson City on 31 Mar 1910, record (1908-12): 92511.

Edward KENT, age: 18 years, born at Olney, Illinois, single, death cause: "consumption", died at Johnson City on 23 Dec 1909, record (1908-12): 92512.

Lula YATES, age: 28 years, born in Embreeville, married, death cause: "stomach trouble", died at Johnson City on 2 May 1910, record (1908-12): 92513.

Thomas WILLIAMS, age: 46 years, born in Abingdon, VA., married, laborer, death cause: "stomach trouble", died at Johnson City on 14 Feb 1910, record (1908-12): 92514.

Infant CORSON, black, female, death cause: "stillborn", daughter on Lewis CORSON, died at Johnson City on 20 Jun 1910, record: 92515.

Mary J. WOODBY, age: 54 years, born in Yancey County, NC., married, knitter, death cause: "penumonia fever", died at Johnson City on 14 Jun 1910, record (1908-12): 92516.

David CARATHERS, age: 72 years, widower, farmer, death cause: "heart failure", died: 10th District on 8 Feb 1910, record (1908-12): 92517.

Newton A. PATTERSON, age: 81 years, born in Hamblen County, married, truck farmer, death cause: "general breakdown", died: 10th District on 28 Apr 1910, record (1908-12): 92518.

William LEE, age: 78 years, widower, farm labor, death cause: "bladder and kidney trouble", died: 10th District on 11 May 1910, record: 92519.

James W. CARMICHEL, age: 26 years, single, teamster, death cause: "wreck on trolley line", died: 10th District on 3 Jul 1909, record (1908-12): 92520.

Joseph BOWMAN, age: 77 years, widower, farmer, death cause: "rhumatism", died: 10th District on 13 May 1910, record (1908-12): 92521.

John A. FORD, age: 87 years, married, farmer, death cause: "dropsy", died: 10th District on 27 Feb 1910, record (1908-12): 92522.

Hubert TRENT, age: 4 years, death cause: "scarletina", died: 10th District on 1 Sep 1909, record (1908-12): 92523.

William C. HALE, age: 71 years, married, miller, death cause: "asthma and heart failure", died: 10th District on 31 Aug 1909, record (1908-12): 92524.

Wildon W. DEVAULT, age: 47 years, married, farmer, death cause: "abscess and consumption of bowels", died: 10th District on 29 Mar 1910, record: 92525.

George W. FULMER, age: 89 years, widower, farmer, death cause: "paralysis", died: 10th District on 28 Jul 1909, record (1908-12): 92526.

Daniel GLASS, age: 101 years, born in North Carolina, widower, farmer, death cause: "cancer and old age", died: 10th District on 12 Jan 1910, record (1908-12): 92527.

John BOWMAN, age: 74 years, single, farmer, death cause: "disordered liver", died: 10th District on 24 Jan 1910, record (1908-12): 92528.

Sarah A. BASKET, age: 66 years, farmer's wife, death cause: "dropsy", died: 11th District on 10 Jan 1910, record (1908-12): 92529.

Nancy WRIGHT, age: 72 years, single, death cause: "pneumonia (?)", died: 7 Jan 1910, record: 92530.

E.B. HALL, age; 67 years, married, farmer, death cause: "heart trouble", died: 11th District on 11 Oct 1909, record (1908-12): 92531.

Thomas HALE, age: 74 years, married, farmer, death cause: "cancer", died: 11th District on 18 Dec 1909, record (1908-12): 92532.

D. MATHERLY, male, age: 8 years, death cause: "unknown", died: 11th District on 3 Dec 1910, record (1908-12): 92533.

Elva WHITE, age: 3 years, death cause: "unknown", died: 11th District on 29 Mar 1910, record: 92534.

Infant WATKINS, black, age: 1 year, death cause: not stated, died: 11th District on __ Feb 1910, record (1908-12): 92535

Elizabeth HAMMIT, age: 38 years, farmer widow, death cause: "typhoid fever", died: 11th District on 21 Aug 1909, record (1908-12): 92536.

Virgie CHATMAN, age: 3 weeks, death cause: not stated, died: 11th District on 21 Oct 1909, record (1908-12): 92537.

Robert W. GALLOWAY, age: 19 days, death cause: "bold hives", died: 11th District on 26 Jan 1910, record (1908-12): 92538.
Luceil CROUCH, age: 7 months, death cause: not stated, died: 11th District on 27 Jun 1910, record (1908-12): 92539.
Wiley HAMBY, age: 16 days, death cause: "croup", died: 11th District on 10 Feb 1910, record: 92540.
Thomas TYREE, age: 17 years, single, death cause: "typhoid fever", died: 11th District on __ Nov 1909, record (1908-12): 92541.
Sarah GARST, age: 70 years, farmer's wife, death cause: "consumption", died: 11th District on 21 Nov 1909, record (1908-12): 92542.
Bertie CREESY, age: 22 years, framer's wife, death cause: "consumption", died: 11th District on 28 May 1910, record (1908-12): 92543.
Dessie HARWOOD, age: 4 years, death cause: "lock jaw", died: 11th District on 29 May 1910, record (1908-12): 92544.
Mary A. FOX, age: 68 years, doctor's wife, death cause: "dropsy", died: 28 Mar 1910, record: 92545.
Infant HALE, female, death cause: "still born", died: 11th District on 10 Feb 1910, record: 92546.
Clarence HEDGEPATH, black, age: 6 years, born in North Carolina, died: 9th District date not stated, record recorded on 16 Jul 1910, record: 92547.
Florence YOUNG, black, age: 1 year and 7 months, death cause: "indigestion", died: 9th District on 10 Apr 1910, record (1908-12): 92548.
Sallie YOUNG, black, age: 60 years, married, death cause: "consumption", died: 9th District on 13 May 1910, record (1908-12): 92549.
Maggie CARROLL, age: 3 weeks, death cause: "bold hives", died: 9th District on 2 Aug 1909, record (1908-12): 92550.
William YOUNG, black, age: 41 years, born in Yancey County, NC., married, blacksmith, death cause: "accidentally", died in Dante, VA., 18 Dec 1909. record (1908-12): 92551.

Florence DALLI.., age: 15 years, born in North Carolina, death cause: "typhoid fever", died: 9th District on 23 Oct 1909, record (1908-12): 92552.

Joe CLARK, age: 54 years, single, farmer, death cause: "paralysis", died: 9th District on 27 Nov 1909, record (1908-12): 92553.

Abbie HOWARD, age: 2 years, born in Fayetteville, Arkansas, death cause: "bowl hives", died: 9th District on 28 Jan 1910, record (1908-12): 92554.

Callie BRASWELL, age: 9 months, death cause: "spinal trouble", died: 9th District on 23 Jun 1910, record (1908-12): 92555.

Nancy SMITH, age: 79 years, born in Hawkins County, widow, death cause: "stomach trouble", died: 9th District on 7 Mar 1910, record (1908-12): 92556.

Wallie FEATHERS, age: 3 years, death cause: "diptheria", died: 9th District on 17 Oct 1908, record (1908-12): 92557.

William GIBSON, age: 65 years, married, farmer, death cause: "rhumatism and Brights disease", died: 9th District on 10 Jan 1909, record: 92558.

Earnest SUTFIN, death cause: "stillborn", died: 9th District on 31 Aug 1908, record (1908-12): 92559.

Dicie ERVIN, colored, born: 22 Oct 1799 (age: 110 years), death cause: "rhumatism and old age", died: 9th District on 16 Mar 1909, record: 92560.

Matilda DELOACH, age: 55 years, born in Hampton, Carter County, married, death cause: "tuberculosis", died: 9th District on 20 Dec 1908, record: 92561.

Ina Bell KNIPE, age: 7 years, born in Hamblin County, death cause: "whooping cough", died: 9th District on 2 Nov 1908, record (1908-12): 92562.

Abbie HARRELL, age: 34 years, born in Mitchell County, NC., married, death cause: "tuberculosis", died: 23 Dec 1908, record (1908-12): 92563.

H.G. SPROUL, age: 72 years, born in Virginia, carpenter and farmer, single, died: 9th District on 1 Feb 1909, record (1908-12): 92564.

J.M. HOUSTON, age: 71 years, married, death cause: "heart trouble", died: 9th District on 25 Dec 1908, record (1908-12): 92565.

Cora V. DEAKINS, age: 23 years, married, death cause: "tuberculosis", died: 9th District on 8 Sep 1908, record (1908-12): 92566.
Mary A. LEACH, age: 2 years, death cause: "croup", died: 8th District on 21 Jan 1909, record: 92567.
Arthor DENTON, age; 3 years, death cause: "croup",died: 8th District on 20 Jan 1909, record (1908-12): 92568.
Jennings LOW, age: 1 year, death cause: "cholera", died: 8th District on 27 Jun 1909, record: 92569.
Viner LEACH, age: 29 years, single, death cause: "abscess", died: 8th District on 13 Apr 1909, record (1908-12): 92570.
Lola TIPTON, age: 5 years, death cause: "liver trouble", died: 8th District on 17 Jan 1909, record (1908-12): 92571.
Lucille LEACH, age: 2 years, death cause: "croup", died: 8th District on 11 Feb 1909, record: 92572.
Charley SHELL, age: 23 years, single, death cause: "appendicitis", died: 8th District on 9 Aug 1909, record (1908-12): 92573.
Sarah A. LILLY, age: 7 years, death cause: "diptheria", died: 8th District on 23 Oct 1909, record (1908-12): 92574.
Maeria HARVEY, age: 38 years, married, death cause: "blood poison", died; 8th District on 26 Apr 1909, record (1908-12): 92575.
Vestle FREEMAN, age: 2 years and 3 months, death cause: "summer complaint", died at Chuckey Valley on 27 Jul 1909, record (1908-12): 92576.
Era Glee BACON, lived 3 hours, death cause: not stated, died at Fall Branch on 20 Apr 1909, record (1908-12): 92577.
Clifford SHERFEY, age: 4 months, death cause: "penumonia", died at Fall Branch on 17 Oct 1909, record (1908-12): 92578.
Telete MOORE, female, age: 78 years, 1 month and 18 days, born in Jefferson County, married, death cause: not stated, died: 7th District on 28 Jun 1909, record (1908-12): 92579.

Dicy HENSLEY, age: 62 years, married, death cause: "stomach trouble", died: 7th District on 6 Sep 1908, record (1908-12): 92580.
Nettie Blanch FULKERSON, age: 3 years, 5 months and 6 days, death cause: "typhoid", died: 7th District on 10 Oct 1909, record (1908-12): 92581.
Nellie Pauline   , age: 1 year and 8 months, death cause: "whooping cough", died: 7th District on 4 Dec 1908, record (1908-12): 92582.
Annie Myrtle COPASS, age: 1 month and 8 days, death cause: "whooping cough", died: 7th District on 6 Nov 1908, record (1908-12): 92583.
Nancy C. STEVENS, age: 57 years and 6 months, widow, death cause: "heart trouble", died at Roan Mountain on 10 Oct 1908, record (1908-12): 92584.
Ruby Lucile RIGGS, age: 1 month and 15 days, death cause: "penumonia", died: 7th District on 5 Feb 1909, record (1908-12): 92585.
William RODGERS, age: 14 months, death cause: "summer complaint", died: 6th District on 15 Jul 1909, record (1908-12): 92586.
Willie SMITH, age: 5 weeks, death cause: "summer complaint", died at Chuckey Valley on 26 Apr 1909, record (1908-12): 92587.
Miss L.L. BUTLER, age: 63 years, single, death cause: "heart trouble", died: 5th District on 8 Feb 1909, record (1908-12): 92588.
Eleanor MARKWOOD, age: 1 year, born in Lenoir City, death cause: "disentery", died: 5th District on 9 Nov 1908, record (1908-12): 92589.
R.L. ARMATROUT, age: 35 years, single, farmer, death cause: "apoplexy", died: 5th District on 12 Nov 1908, record (1908-12): 92590.
Nina PACK, age: 5 days, death cause: illegible, died: 5th District on 28 Oct 1909, record: 92591.
Claude HUNTER, black, age: 3 years, death cause: "bronchitis", died: 5th District on 8 Dec 1908, record (1908-12): 92592.
Infant MURRAY, black, death cause: not stated, son of John MURRAY, died: 5th District on 17 Mar 1909, record (1908-12): 92593.

E.G. MCCLURE, age: 69 years, married, farmer, death cause: "kidney trouble", died: 5th District on 7 Nov 1908, record (1908-12): 92594.
Infant SMITH, male, age: 5 days, son of W.H. SMITH, death cause: "spasms", died: 5th District on 4 Sep 1908, record (1908-12): 92595.
Fred HENSLEY, age: 7 weeks, death cause: "hives", died: 18 Mar 1909, record (1908-12): 92596.
Clara STORY, age: 3 months, death cause: not stated, died: 4th District on 2 Mar 1909, record: 92597.
Maniard LAUSN, age: 9 months, death cause: not stated, died: 4th District on 11 Jun 1909, record (1908-12): 92598.
J.K. AUSTIN, age: 53 years, married, farmer, death cause: "consumption", died: 4th District on 8 May 1909, record (1908-12): 92599.
Sallie PHILLIPS, age: 25 years, born in North Carolina, married, death cause: "consumption", died: 4th District on 10 Feb 1909, record: 92600.
Nola SHIELDS, age: 1 month, death cause: not stated, died: 4th District on 14 May 1909, record: 92601.
Charley MCGEE, lived 2 days, death cause: not stated, died: 4th District on 16 Apr 1909, record (1908-12): 92602.
Jackson KYKER, age: 67 years, married, death cause: "hemorrhage of lungs", died: 4th District on __ May 1909, record (1908-12): 92603.
Alfred TAYLOR, black, age: 27 years, single, soldier, death cause: "consumption", died: 7 Mar 1909, record (1908-12): 92604.
Lottie Belle MILLER, age: 1 year and 8 days, death cause: "meningitis", died: 4th District on 14 Jul 1909, record (1908-12): 92605.
Ray Millard MABERY, age: 2 years, 10 months and 3 days, cod not stated, died at Limestone on 10 Sep 1908, record (1908-12): 92606.
Mae PIERSON, age: 7 years, cod "flux", died at Washington College on 9 Aug 1908, record: 92607.
Mrs. Sarah PIERSON, age: 47 years, married, cod "flux", died at Washington College on 10 Aug 1908, record (1908-12): 92608.

Gabe PAYNE, age: 65 years, married, farmer, cod "phenumonia", died at Washington College on 12 Mar 1909, record (1908-12): 92609.

Samuel MCCRACKEN, age: 56 years, married, farmer, cod "consumption", died at Washington College on 16 May 1909, record (1908-12): 92610.

Lebert BROYLES, age: 4 years and 6 months, cod "croup", died at Pilot Hill on 18 Jan 1911, record (1908-12): 92611.

Watesil FOSTER, age: 2 months and 7 days, death cause: "hives", died at Cassey Creek on 27 Jun 1912, record (1908-12): 92612.

Walter MATHIS, age: 8 months, death cause: "cholera infantum", died: 1st District on 27 Jul 1911, record (1908-12): 92613.

Benjamin BOWMAN, age: 51 years, married, death cause: "penumonia fever", died: near Liberty Church on 31 Mar 1912, record (1908-12): 92614.

Robert M. S.. (illegible), age: 47 years, widower, death cause: "softening of brain", died: 15th District on 21 Nov 1911, record (1908-12): 92615.

Emma HALE, colored, age: 50 years, single, death cause: "tuberculosis", died: 15th District on __ Jun 1912, record (1908-12): 92616.

Mary KEYS, age: 18 months, death cause: "measles", died: 15th District on __ Mar 1912, record: 92617.

Hary LEINS (?), colored, age: 20 years, single, death cause: "heart failure", died: 15th District on 30 Jan 1912, record (1908-12): 92618.

S.M. MCKAMEY, age: 73 years, born in Sullivan County, married, school teacher, death cause: "dropsy", died: 9d on 26 Jul 1909, record: 92619.

Delia GREENFIELD, age: 38 years, born in Knox County, married, death cause: "abscess", died at Knoxville on 7 May 1910, record (1908-12): 92620.

R.P. GREENFIELD, age: 60 years, born in Coldwell County, NC., married, death cause: "heart trouble", died in Johnson City on 2 Sep 1909, record: 92621.

Mrs. T.A.R. NELSON, age: 42 years, born in Sullivan County, married, death cause: "dropsy", died in Johnson City on 28 Jun 1910, record: 92622.

John TARNY, black, age: 32 years, born at Norfolk, VA., single, died at Johnson City on 14 Apr 1910, record (1908-12): 92623.

Ed. TAYLOR, black, age: not stated, born in Carter County, married, death cause: "dropsy", died in Johnson City on 21 Apr 1910, record: 92624.

Maurine RUTLEDGE, age: 13 years, death cause: "fever", died at Johnson City on 27 Aug 1909, record (1908-12): 92625.

Ralph MOORE, age: 3 years, born in Greenville, death cause: "penumonia fever", died at Johnson City on 9 Apr 1910, record (1908-12): 92626.

Jessie CAMPBELL, age: 22 years, married, death cause: "not known", died at Johnson City on 18 May 1910, record (1908-12): 92627.

Nellie STONECIPHER, age: 6 weeks, death cause: "pneumonia", died at Johnson City on 10 Dec 1909, record (1908-12): 92628.

Jack STONECIPHER, age: 7 months, death cause: "pneumonia", died at Johnson City on 24 May 1910, record (1908-12): 92629.

Millie ESTEP, age: 3 years, death cause: "diabetes", died at Johnson City on 19 Jul 1909, record: 92620.

C.W. GUTHRIE, age: 51 years, born in Augusta County, VA., married, bookkeeper, death cause: "typhoid fever", died at Johnson City on 17 Aug 1909, record (1908-12): 92631.

Charley ONKS, age: 3 years, born in Carter County, death cause: "diabetes", died at Johnson City on 14 Feb 1910, record (1908-12): 92632.

Infant CARROLL, male, age: 2 days, death cause: "yellow jaundice", child of J.W. CARROLL, died at Johnson City on 26 Apr 1910, record: 92633.

Emily BARLOW, age; 73 years, born in Smith County, VA., married, death cause: "dropsy", died at Johnson City on 18 Nov 1909, record (1908-12): 92634.

Infant MORRISON, male, child of H.G. MORRISON, death cause: "stillborn", died at Johnson City on 18 Aug 1909, record (1908-12): 92635.

Isaac FORD, age: 60 years, born in Kentucky, married, death cause: "tuberlosis", died: 14th District on 9 Mar 1910, record (1908-12): 92636.

Mary E. LEADFORD, age: 28 years, married, death cause: "tuberculosis", died: 14th District on 2 May 1910, record (1908-12): 92637.

Nannie E. MILHORN, age: 13 years, death cause: "typhoid", died: 14th District on 5 Nov 1909, record (1908-12): 92638.

Martha MILHORN, age: 80 years, widow, death cause: "tuberculosis", died: 14th District on 24 Aug 1909, record (1908-12): 92639.

Martha CROW, age: 65, married, death cause: "tuberculosis", died: 14th District on 25 Oct 1909, record (1908-12): 92640.

Joseph WILCOX, age: 82 years, born in North Carolina, married mechanic, death cause: "dropsy", died: 14th District on 20 Jul 1909, record: 92641.

Infant LEAB, female, lived 1 day, child of Oscar LEAB, death cause: not stated, died: 14th District on 29 Jan 1910, record (1908-12): 92642.

Jacob E. BROWN, age: 60, born in Virginia, married, death cause: "tuberculosis", died: 14th District on 10 May 1910, record (1908-12): 92643.

Marry A. COMBS, age: 68 years, single, death cause: "fire, burns", died: 13th District on 19 Mar 1910, record (1908-12): 92644.

Nettie Francis WHITLOCK, age: 2 years, 4 months and 3 days, death cause: "throat trouble", died: 13th District on 7 Nov 1909, record (1908-12): 92645.

Josie GRAY, colored, age: 68 years, born in Virginia, married, death cause: "consumption", died: 18 Oct 1909, record (1908-12): 92646.

W.M. DEAKINS, age: 50 years, single, "throat and lung trouble", died: 13th District on 29 May 1910, record (1908-12): 92647.

Haskel, Lee MITCHELL, age: 13 days, "premature birth", died: 13th District on 13 Feb 1910, record (1908-12): 92648.

William E. SHERFEY, age: 36 years, married, "dropsy and lung trouble", died: 13th District on 27 Dec 1910, record (1908-12): 92649.

Nora JACKSON, age: 16 years, "consumption", died: 13th District on 5 Dec 1909, record: 92650.

Ellen H. OLIVER, age: 61 years, born in Yancey County, NC., married, "cancer", died: 15th District on 17 Sep 1909, record (1908-12): 92651.
Clarence A. HEAD, lived 9 hours, "premature birth", died: 15th District on 18 Aur 1909, record (1908-12): 92652.
Mary HOWARD, colored, age: 71 years, born in Missouri, married, "paralysis", died: 15th District on 2 Feb 1910, record (1908-12): 92653.
Allen F. BROWN, age: 62 years, born in Virginia, married, "heart failure", died: 15th District on 11 May 1910, record (1908-12): 92654.
E.T. WILKERSON, age: 32 years, born in Cataba County, NC., married, engineer, "penumonia fever", died: 15th District on 18 Aug 1909, record: 92655.
Walter R. MCPEAK, age: 27 years, married, policeman, "homicide", died: 15th District on 28 Jun 1910, record (1908-12): 92656.
Mellie PHILLIPS, age: 25 years, born in North Carolina, married, "tuberculosis", died: 15th District on 27 Nov 1909, record (1908-12): 92657.
Andrew J. SLAGLE, age: 44 years, born in Carter County, married, school teacher, "homicide", died: Coke (Cocke ?) County on 24 Aug 1909, record: 92658.
Rettie HILBERT, age: 43 years, married, "not known", died: 15th District on 31 Jul 1909, record (1908-12): 92659.
Elizabeth FOX, age: 71 years, married, death cause: "penumonia fever", died: 15th District on 22 Feb 1910, record (1908-12): 92660.
Tula F. BOYD, age: 38 years, married, death cause: "cattarrh", died: 15th District on 27 Jun 1912, record (1908-12): 92661.
John K. WHITE, age: 69 years, married, farmer, death cause: "softening of brain", died: 15th District on 27 May 1912, record (1908-12): 92662.
Richard CRAWFORD, colored, age: 97 years, married, death cause: "heart failure", died: 15th District on 14 Jun 1912, record (1908-12): 92663.
Lizzie ANDERSON, colored, age: 70 years, born in Sullivan County, married, death cause: "paralysis", died: 15th District on 4 Jun 1912, record: 92664.

Molly RYAN, colored, age: 28 years, married, death cause: "tuberculosis", died: 15th District on 4 Jun 1912, record (1908-12): 92665.

Ellen MCQUEEN, age: 2 years, death cause: "measles", died: 15th District on 7 Mar 1912, record: 92666.

Virginia SIMS, age: 7 weeks, death cause: "cholera infantum", died: 15th District on 11 Aug 1911, record (1908-12): 19667.

Paul BROOKS, age: 2 years, death cause: "tuberculosis", died: 15th District on 13 May 1912, record (1908-12): 92668.

Charles B. THOMAS, age: 52 years, married, death cause: "heart failure", died: 15th District on 11 Jun 1912, record (1908-12): 92669.

Walace M. WALKER, age: 11 years, death cause: "typhoid fever", died: 15th District on 9 Apr 1912, record (1908-12): 92670.

Andrew FRANCIS, age: 72 years, married, farmer, death cause: "Brights disease", died: 15th District on 26 Sep 1911, record (1908-12): 92671.

John S. KEYS, age: 65 years, married, farmer, death cause: "dropsy", died: 15th District on 17 Jul 1911, record (1908-12): 92672.

William MALONE, age: 94 years, born in Wake County, NC., married, death cause: "debility", died: 15th District on 2 Jul 1912, record (1908-12): 92673.

Salley FAGANS, age: 60 years, married, death cause: "dropsy", died: 15th District on 28 May 1912, record (1908-12): 92674.

Jennie REEDY, age: 71 years, married, death cause: "fits", died: 15th District on 12 Mar 1912, record (1908-12): 92675.

Metchel MCLEAN, colored, age: not recorded, single, death cause: "fits", died: 15th District on 26 Mar 1912, record (1908-12): 92676.

Isaac WATKINS, age: 91 years, born in New Jersey, married, death cause: "paralysis", died: 15th District on 14 Mar 1912, record (1908-12): 92677.

Robert PRITCHARD, age: 45 years, born in Johnson County, married, death cause: "dropsy", died: 15th District on 24 Feb 1912, record (1908-12): 92678.

Ellen JACKSON, age: 27 years, married, death cause: "siphels", died: 15th District on 25 Jan 1912, record (1908-12): 92679.

Harry SELF, age: 46 years, married, fireman, death cause: "dropsy", died: 15th District on 27 Apr 1912, record (1908-12): 92680.

Martha E. VAUGHN, age: 75 years, born in Sullivan County, married, death cause: "neuralgia of heart", died: 15th District on 23 May 1912, record: 92681.

George T. ADAMS, age: 35 years, married, death cause: "typhoid fever", died: 15th District on 16 Jul 1911, record (1908-12): 92682.

Nellie Loucile CONSTABLE, age: not stated, single, death cause: not stated, died: 4th District on 30 Aug 1909, record (1908-12): 92683.

John SEYMORE, black, lived 2 hours, death cause: not stated, died: 4th District on 4 Apr 1910, record (1908-12): 92684.

Ida SEYMORE, black, age: 25 years, married, death cause: "asthma", died: 4th District on 8 Apr 1910, record (1908-12): 92685.

John M. TAYLOR, black, age: 69 years, born in Carter County, married, death cause: "Brights disease", died: 4th District on 27 Sep 1909, record: 92686.

John STORY, age: not stated, death cause: not stated, died: 4th District on 15 Nov 1909, record (1908-12): 92687.

Florence RENFRO, death cause: "born dead", died: 4th District on 20 Apr 1910, record (1908-12): 92688.

Henry Leone HICKS, age: 1 year, death cause: "croup", died: 4th District on 6 Dec 1909, record (1908-12): 92689.

Margaret STORY, age: 70 years, married, death cause: "bronchitis", died: 4th District on 12 Feb 1910, record (1908-12): 92690.

Maniard LOWERY, age: 10 months, death cause: not stated, died: 4th District on 14 Aug 1909, record (1908-12): 92691.

Robert R. LOYD, age: 63 years, married, death cause: "heart disease", died: 4th District on 17 Feb 1910, record (1908-12): 92692.

George STORY, age: 72 years, born in Wilkes County, NC., married, death cause: "cattarah", died: 4th District on 24 Feb 1910, record (1908-12): 92693.

John Hardin JONES, age: 1 year, death cause: not stated, died: 4th District on 13 Jan 1910, record (1908-12): 92694.

Georg ELLIOT, age: 20 years, born in Unicoi County, single, death cause: "consumption", died: 4th District on 18 Nov 1909, record (1908-12): 92695.

C.G. LILLY, age: 75 years, born in Sullivan County, married, death cause: "kidney and bladder disease", died: 4th District on 29 Dec 1909, record: 92696.

Mary Francis BRADLEY, age: 2 days, death cause: "not known", died: 4th District on 8 Apr 1910, record (1908-12): 92697.

Florence RAY, age: 23 years, single, death cause: "liver trouble", died: 4th District on 13 Jul 1909, record (1908-12): 92698.

Mamie SAMS, age: 23 years, born in Unicoi County, married, death cause: "consumption",died: 26 Nov 1909, record (1908-12): 92699.

Ida SALTS, age: 19 years, born in Carter County, single, death cause: "typhoid fever", died at Chuckey Valley on 7 Oct 1909, record: 92400.

James BOGART, age 3 months and 11 days, death cause: "bold hives", died at Embreeville on 1 Feb 1910, record (1908-12): 92701.

John Clifton WHITE, age: 19 years, single, death cause: "by gun shot", died at Embreeville on 10 Oct 1909, record (1908-12): 92702.

Paulien ORTON, lived 1 day, death cause: "unknown", died at Embreeville on 15 Jun 1910, record: 92703.

Johnie ORTON, age: 7 months, death cause: "flux", died at Embreeville on 20 Dec 1909, record: 92704.

Mary GOOD, age: 2 years, death cause: "measles", died at Johnson City on 15 Aug 1911, record: 92705.

Infant FEATHERS, male, death cause: not stated, child of Carl FEATHERS, died at Johnson City on 3 Nov 1911, record: 92706.

Ethel Lee SPAIN, age: 4 years, death cause: "penumonia", died at Johnson City on 27 Mar 1912, record (1908-12): 92707.

Maria WHITE, age: 79 years, married, death cause: "consumption and dropsy", died at Johnson City on 25 Apr 1911, record (1908-12): 92708.

George WATSON, age: 22 years, single, death cause: "killed by train", died at Johnson City on 8 Jun 1912, record (1908-12): 92709.

G.L. MOORE, age: 40 years, married, tannery foreman, death cause: "typhoid fever", died at Johnson City on 9 Jul 1911, record (1908-12): 92710.

John CRUSENBERRY, age: 2 years, death cause: "pneumonia", died at Johnson City on 30 Mar 1912, record (1908-12): 92711.

Paul EARP, age: 2 years, death cause: "pneumonia" died at Johnson City on 6 Mar 1912, record: 92712.

McDowell SWALTS, age: 4 years, death cause: "measles and whooping cough", died at Johnson City on 23 Jun 1912, record (1908-12): 92713.

C.J. KEGLEY, age: 53 years, born in Wythe County, VA., married, death cause: "pellagra", died at Johnson City on 9 Jun 1912, record (1908-12): 92714.

Willie H. ROBINSON, age: 3 years, born at Allentown, TN., death cause: "dropsy", died at Johnson City on 16 Dec 1911, record (1908-12): 92715.

Infant ROBINSON, female, death cause: "stillborn", child of D.V. ROBINSON, died at Johnson City on 15 Apr 1912, record (1908-12): 92716.

Infant NORRIS, male, lived 30 minutes, death cause: "coughing by mother", child of Frank NORRIS, died at Johnson City on 27 Feb 1912, record: 92717.

Kennith CHRISTIE, age: 67 years, married, blacksmith, death cause: "consumption of bowels", died at Johnson City on __ Jan 1912, record: 92718.

Idella WALKER, colored, age not stated, death cause: "teething", died at Johnson City on __ Feb 1912, record (1908-12): 92719.

Robert HENSON, age: 86 years, born in South Carolina, married, death cause: not recorded, died at Johnson City on 14 Oct 1911, record: 92720.

Charles FAW, colored, age: 23 years, married, death cause: "pneumonia", died at Johnson City on 29 Jan 1912, record (1908-12): 92721.

Andrew TAYLOR, colored, age: 68 years, born in Jonesboro, married, death cause: "dropsy", died at Johnson City on 6 Jan 1912, record (1908-12): 92722.

Robert Lee RAY, age: 9 months, death cause: "measles and whooping cough", died at Johnson City on 8 Apr 1912, record (1908-12): 92723.

Minnie L. BRUMITT, age: 30 years, born in Carter County, married, death cause: "consumption of bowels", died at Johnson City on 9 Oct 1911, record (1908-12): 92724.

Marcella DRAI... (?), age: 42 years, born in Greene County, married, death cause: "consumption", died at Johnson City on 12 Jan 1912, record: 92725.

Infant WATKINS, female, death cause: "stillborn", died at Johnson City on 1 Jan 1912, record: 92726.

Redgley JONES, colored, age: about 50 years, born in Oklahoma, married, death cause: "knife stab", died at Johnson City on 20 Feb 1912, record: 92727.

J.K. KETRON, age: 65 years, born in Sullivan County, married, death cause: "kidney and stomach trouble", died at Boones Creek on 8 Nov 1911, record: 92728.

Blanche WISHONG, age: 26 years, born in Sullivan County, married, death cause: "consumption", died in Johnson City on 9 Jan 1912, record (1908-12): 92729.

Ralph FELTS, age: 3 years, death cause: "diarrhoea", died at Johnson City on 6 Aug 1911, record: 92730.

Edd CRUMBLEY, age: 32 years, single, death cause: "consumption", died at Telford on 7 May 1909, record (1908-12): 92731.

G.A. ROGERS, age: 39 years, married, death cause: "heart trouble", died at Telford on 5 Dec 1908, record (1908-12): 92732.

W.D. PATTON, age: 59 years, married, death cause: "consumption", died at Washington College on 22 Nov 1908, record (1908-12): 92733.

Matilda GRESHAM, age: 95 years, born in Virginia, widow, death cause: "pneumonia and heart trouble", died: 12th District on 31 May 1910, record: 92734.

Willie FORD, age: 7 years, death cause: "croup", died: 12th District on 30 Nov 1909, record (1908-12): 92735.

William T. FORD, age: 65 years, married, death cause: "pneumonia and heart trouble", died: 12th District on 6 May 1910, record (1908-12): 92736.

G.W. HODGE, age: 85 years, married, death cause: "rhumatism and heart trouble", died: 12th District on 15 Nov 1909, record (1908-12): 92737.

Isaac WISE, age: 90 years, born in Shenandoah County, VA., sigle, death cause: "heart failure", died: 12th District on 4 Jan 1910, record: 92738.

Infant MARTIN, male, death cause: "stillborn", child of Sid MARTIN, died: 12th District on 3 Aug 1909, record (1908-12): 92739.

George CARROLL, age: 19 years, born in Sullivan County, single, death cause: "killed by train", died: 12th District on 15 Dec 1909, record: 92740.

Thomas TYREE, age: 17 years, single, death cause: "fever", died: 12th District on 6 Nov 1908, record (1908-12): 92741.

Mary A. FOX, age: 69 years, married, death cause: "rhumatism and tuberculosis", died: 12th District on 28 Mar 1910, record (1908-12): 92742.

Frank HUNTER, black, age: 5 years, death cause: "tuberculosis", died: 5th District on 22 Sep 1909, record (1908-12): 92743.

Mabel HUMPHREY, age: 2 years, death cause: "meningitis", died: 5th District on 3 Jun 1910, record (1908-12): 92744.

Frank FURGUSON, age: 67 years, born in Washington County, VA., married, death cause: "tuberculosis", died in Greene County on 23 Jan 1910, record: 92745.

David MURR, age: 65 years, married, death cause: "general break down", died: 5th District on 10 Mar 1910, record (1908-12): 92746.

Nina BRIGMAN, age: 23 years, born in Greene County, married, died: 5th District on 26 Jan 1910. record (1908-12): 92747.

Mary DILINGHAM, age: 73 years, single, death cause: "heart trouble", died: 5th District on 26 Dec 1908, record (1908-12): 92748.

M.W. BARNES, age: 46 years, married, death cause: "pneumonia", died: 5th District on 3 Jan 1910, record (1908-12): 92749.

Guy WALKER, age: 2 months, death cause: "dysentery", died: 5th District on 10 Aug 1909, record: 92750.

F.M. BUNTON, female, age: 39 years, born in North Carolina, married, death cause: "fever", died: 5th District on 2 Oct 1909, record (1908-12): 92751.

Anderson MARKLAND, age: 5 years, death cause: "indigestion", died: 5th District on 25 Nov 1909, record (1908-12): 92752.

T.C. PATTON, age: 65 years, single, death cause: "stomach trouble", died: 5th District on 25 Apr 1910, record (1908-12): 92753.

Kate BOYD, age: 55 years, born in Knox County, KY., married, death cause: "eresipelas, blood poison", died: 5th District on 26 Dec 1909, record: 92754.

Thomas J. ARNOLD, age; 52 years, born in Hawkins County, married, death cause: "blood poison", died: 16th District on 11 Mar 1912, record: 92755.

Louize CAMPBELL, age: 86 years, widow, death cause: "penumonia", died: 16th District on 12 Apr 1912, record (1908-12): 92756.

Anna HASTINGS, age: 39 years, born at Flagpond, TN., married, death cause: "heart trouble", died: 16th District on 26 Feb 1912, record (1908-12): 92757.

Martha E. BACON, age: 44 years, married, death cause: "growth bowels", died: Memorial Hospital, Knoxville, on 20 Jan 1912, record (1908-12): 92758.

Julia A. LANGHREIN, age: 62 years, born in Yancey County, NC., married, death cause: "measles", died: 16th District on 12 Feb 1912, record: 92759.

Farrell Clay TAYLOR, age: 3 weeks and 5 days, death cause: "measles", died: 16th District on 22 Jan 1912, record (1908-12): 92760.

Wiley HENLEY, age: 38 years, single, death cause: "consumption", died: 18th District on 23 Jan 1912, record (1908-12): 92761.

Elia GRAYHAM, male, age: 4 years, born at Bumpers Cove, death cause: "measles", died: Clarks Creek on 14 Feb 1912, record (1908-12): 92762.

J.M. SEATON, Esq., age: 79 years, married, death cause: "old age", died: 1st District on 7 May 1912, record (1908-12): 92763.

Viola THOMAS, age: 45 years, born in Washington County, VA., married, death cause: "Brights disease", died at Limestone on 23 Jun 1912, record (1908-12): 92764.
Maud GARRSION, age: 31 years, married, death cause: "tuberculosis", died at Limestone on 13 Jul 1911, record (1908-12): 92765.
E.D. GRAY, age: 74 years, born in Sullivan County, married, death cause: "old age", died at Limestone on 17 May 1912, record (1908-12): 92766.
Luta WILLIAMS, age: 36 years, born in Ashville, NC., married, death cause: "tuberculosis", died at Limestone on 12 Sep 1911, record (1908-12): 92767.
Mary Alice SHIELDS, age: 57 years, married, death cause: "stomach, liver and bowel trouble", died at Cherokee on 30 Jul 1911, record (1908-12): 92768.
Ned WALKER, age: 1 day, death cause: "birth", died at Limestone on 3 Feb 1912, record (1908-12): 92769.
Paul DAVIS, age: 1 day, death cause: "incident to birth", died at Limestone on 23 Oct 1911, record (1908-12): 92770.
William Harrison HAWS, age: 71 years, married, death cause: "old age", died at Limestone on 2 Jun 1912, record (1908-12): 92771.
Walter KINLEY, age: 3 months, death cause: "cholera infantum", died: 17th District on 2 Jul 1911, record (1908-12): 92772.
Anna Mary ODELL, age: 2 years and 2 months, death cause: "croup", died: 17th District on 6 Nov 1911, record (1908-12): 92773.
William JONES, age: 64 years, born in Sullivan County, married, death cause: "heart failure", died: 17th District on 27 Oct 1911, record: 92774.
Billie KEYS, age: 12 years, death cause: "appendicitis", died: 17th District on 13 Nov 1911, record (1908-12): 92775.
Bettie TENSTER, age: 3 years and 11 months, death cause: "measles", died: 17th District on 7 Feb 1912, record (1908-12): 92776.
William MERCER, age: 33 years, born in Casey, Illinois, married, death cause: "consumption", died: 9d on 14 Sep 1909, record (1908-12): 92777.

T.A. BRABSON, age: 64 years, married, death cause: "stomach trouble", died: 17th District on 29 Aug 1911, record (1908-12): 92778.

William PACK, age: 1 year, death cause: "spinal trouble", died: 5th District on 25 Jul 1911, record (1908-12): 92779.

Frank LING, age: 66 years, born in Pennsylvania, married, moulder, died: 5th District on 15 Jan 1912, record (1908-12): 92780.

M.L. MOTTERN, age: 51 years, married, death cause: "pneumonia", died: 5th District on 15 Jan 1912, record (1908-12): 92781.

Lockey WALLACE, female, age: 6 years, death cause: "croup", died: 5th District on 20 Nov 1911, record (1908-12): 92782.

M.J. BROWN, female, age: 70 years, married, death cause: "heart failure", died: 5th District on 1 Apr 1912, record (1908-12): 92783.

Lee BAILEY, black, age: 84 years, married, death cause: "old age", died: 5th District on 10 Oct 1912, record (1908-12): 92784.

Rachel BRIGMAN, black, age: 22 years, born in Sullivan County, married, death cause: "family way", died: 5th District on 17 Feb 1912, record: 92785.

Infant TEAGUE, female, death cause: "stillborn", child of Will TEAGUE, died: 5th District on 18 Jun 1912, record (1908-12): 92786.

Sarafine SIMPSON, age: 73 years, single (once married), death cause: "old age", died: 5th District on 15 Mar 1912, record (1908-12): 92787.

Matilda MURRAY, black, age: 92 years, single, death cause: "old age", died: 5th District on 10 Jul 1911, record (1908-12): 92788.

John FOSTER, age: 72 years, born in North Carolina, married, death cause: "heart failure", died: 5th District on 8 Apr 1912, record (1908-12): 92789.

Ida Bell STORY, age: 18 years, married, death cause: "consumption", died: 4th District on 11 Jun 1912, record (1908-12): 92790.

Joseph HILTON, age: 26 years, born in Mitchell County, NC., married, death cause: "consumption", died: 4th District on 12 Jan 1912, record: 92791.

George B. COX, death cause: "born dead", died: 4th District on 23 Jul 1912, record (1908-12): 92792.
John HOSS, age: 37 years, single, death cause: "epilepsy", died in Knox County on 21 Feb 1912, record (1908-12): 92793.
Tessie Ona STORY, age: 14 years, death cause: "consumption", died: 4th District on 3 Mar 1912, record (1908-12): 92794.
Mrs. G.V. MCCOWN, age: 19 years, born in Jefferson City, death cause: "ruptured blood vessel", died at Greeneville on 20 Jan 1911, record (1908-12): 92795.
Catherine BEASLEY, age: 65 years, born in Canoy County, W.VA., married, death cause: "heart failure", died at Johnson City on 15 Nov 1910, record (1908-12): 92796.
Infant OVERSTREET, male, lived 3 hours, death cause: "unknown", child of Will OVERSTREET, died at Johnson City on 29 Mar 1911, record (1908-12): 92797.
John CHESSER, age: 27 years, born in Gilmore County, GA., married, death cause: "tuberculosis", died at Chicamauga, GA., 25 Jan 1911, record: 92798.
Flora BRITT, age: 2 years, death cause: "whooping cough", died at Johnson City on 1 Apr 1911, record (1908-12): 92799.
Thersa DENNY, colored, age: 8 months, death cause: "tuberculosis", died at Johnson City on 28 Feb 1911, record (1908-12): 92800.
Euna RICHARD, age: 34 years, married, death cause: "tuberculosis", died at Johnson City date not stated, recorded: 6 Jul 1911, record: 92801.
Nauia GODSEY, colored, age: 11 days, death cause: "unknown", died at Johnson City on 18 Feb 1911, record (1908-12): 92802.
Ruth GODSEY, colored, age: 11 days, death cause: "unknown", died at Johnson City on 18 Feb 1911, record (1908-12): 92803.
Bessie WINSTON, colored, age: 21 years, born at Big Stone Gap, VA., married, death cause: "tuberculosis", died at Johnson City on __ Jan 1911, record (1908-12): 92804.

Robert WINSTON, colored, age: 3 years, born at Meadow View, VA., death cause: "tuberculosis", died at Johnson City on __ Jan 1911, record: 92805.
Mrs. Ressa LYLE, age: 74 years, born in Staunton, VA., married, death cause: "pneumonia", died at Johnson City on 31 May 1911, record: 92806.
J.W. CROWELL, age: 42 years, born in Washington County, VA., married, supt. of furniture factory, death cause: "asthma", died at Lexington, NC. on 1 May 1911, record (1908-12): 92807.
Thomas BURNETT, age: 1 month, death cause: "unknown", died at Johnson City on 17 Jun 1911, record (1908-12): 92808.
Willie BOWMAN, age: 9 days, death cause: "unknown", died at Johnson City on 25 Jun 1911, record: 92809.
Earl ARCHER, age: 12 years, death cause: not stated, died at Johnson City on 3 Oct 1911, record: 92810.
Lena POSTER, age: 25 years, born in Sullivan County, married, death cause: "tuberculosis", died at Johnson City on 12 Jun 1911, record: 92811.
Kate SOUTH, age: 69 years, born in Abingdon, VA., death cause: "penumonia fever", died at Johnson City on 11 Dec 1910, record (1908-12): 92812.
Will JACKSON, colored, age: 42 years, married, death cause: "tuberculosis", died at Johnson City on 27 Jun 1911, record (1908-12): 92813.
Lora PICKERING, age: 24 years, born at Chuckey, married, died at Johnson City on 5 Sep 1910, record (1908-12): 92814.
Hattie WINSTON, colored, age: 17 years, born in Corbin, VA., death cause: "tuberculosis", died at Johnson City on __ May 1911, record: 92815.
Thomas WINSTON, colored, age: 11 years, born at Meadow View, VA., death cause: "tuberculosis", died at Johnson City on __ Jun 1911, record: 92816.
Martha KINKADE, colored, age: 50 years, married, death cause: "fever", died at Johnson City on __ May 1911, record (1908-12): 92817.
Troop SMITH, colored, age: 1 year, death cause: "croup", died at Johnson City on 7 Oct 1910, record (1908-12): 92818.

George BUCHANAN, colored, age: 50 years, born in Sullivan County, single, death cause: "locked bowels", died at Johnson City on 12 Sep 1910, record (1908-12): 92819.

Willie Mae MALONE, age: 4 months, born at Bristol, death cause: "cholera infantum", died at Bristol on 30 Aug 1910, record (1908-12): 92820.

Robert E. BODENHEIMER, age: 7 months, death cause: "intestinal toxemia", died Johnson City on 10 Jun 1911, record (1908-12): 92821.

Grace SEAVERS, age: 17 years, death cause: "diptheria", died at Johnson City on 12 Oct 1911, record (1908-12): 92822.

Bird WATSON, age: 43 years, born in Virginia, single, railroader, death cause: "heart failure", died at Johnson City on 21 May 1911, record: 92823.

Nathaniel SNOW, age: 3 months, death cause: "unknown", died at Johnson City on 10 Aug 1910, record (1908-12): 92824.

Everett LACY, age: 3 years, born in Bluefield, W.VA., death cause: "dyptheria", died at Johnson City on 18 Oct 1910, record (1908-12): 92825.

Maggie GOBBLE, age: 42 years, married, death cause: "paralysis", died at Johnson City on 31 Mar 1911, record (1908-12): 92826.

Ruth LYLE, age: 18 years, single, death cause: "typhois", died at Johnson City on 17 Aug 1910, record (1908-12): 92827.

Mary HOUSTON, colored, age: 68 years, born in Sullivan County, widow, death cause: "dropsy", died at Johnson City on 15 Dec 1910, record: 92828.

Lula GARDNER, colored, age: 3 years, death cause: "bronchitis", died at Johnson City on __ Oct 1910, record (1908-12): 92829.

Martha BASS, age; 70 years, born in South Carolina, married, death cause: "dropsy", died: Johnson City on 22 Feb 1911, record (1908-12): 92830.

Mrs. Rhoda WEAVER, age: 24 years, married, death cause: "childbirth", died at Johnson City on 8 Nov 1910, record (1908-12): 92831.

Margaret WEAVER, lived 4 hours, death cause: "stillborn", died at Johnson City on 8 Nov 1910, record (1908-12): 92832.

Roy WEAVER, age: 6 years, death cause: "unknown", died at Johnson City on 14 Aug 1910, record: 92833.

Lillie GILLESPIE, age: 22 years, born in Alabama, married, death cause: "tuberculosis", died at Johnson City on 26 Dec 1910, record: 92834.

Infant SONDY, male, death cause: "stillborn", died at Johnson City on __ Nov 1910, record: 92835.

Susie FIELDS, age: 18 years, born at Piney Flats, single, death cause: "tuberculosis", died at Johnson City on 11 Jun 1911, record (1908-12): 92836.

Glennie DICKSON, age: 3 years, death cause: "pneumonia fever", died at Johnson City on 16 Mar 1911, record (1908-12): 92837.

Bonnie DICKSON, age: 14 months, death cause: "bronchitis", died at Johnson City on 10 Jun 1911, record (1908-12): 92838.

John FLETCHER, age: 26 years, married, death cause: "pneumonia fever", died at Johnson City on 18 Sep 1910, record (1908-12): 92839.

Tempie FESS, age: 7 years, death cause: "measles", died at Johnson City on 18 Apr 1911, record: 92840.

Nellie K. SMITH, age: 6 weeks, death cause: "unknown", died at Johnson City on 23 Mar 1911, record (1908-12): 92841.

Lizzie GLENN, age: 17 years, born in Carter County, single, death cause: "tuberculosis", died at Johnson City on 3 Nov 1910, record (1908-12): 92842.

Ethel CANNY, age: 29 years, born in Virginia, married, death cause: "consumption of bowels", died in Johnson City on 28 Apr 1911, record: 92843.

Willie JENKINS, age: 13 years, born in Carter County, death cause: "brain fever", died: 19 Mar 1910, record (1908-12): 92844.

Stella PRITCHARD, age: 3 years, death cause: "summer complaint", died in Johnson City on 29 Jul 1910, record (1908-12): 92845.

Clarence WRIGHT, age: 16 months, death cause: "penumonia", died in Johnson City on 4 Nov 1910, record (1908-12): 92846.

Tate L. EARNEST, age: 49 years, widower, death cause: "accident by gun shot", died near Johnson City on 11 Nov 1910, record (1908-12): 92847.
Henry ROSENBAUM, age: 15 months, death cause: "tuberculosis", died at Johnson City on 2 Jul 1910, record (1908-12): 92848.
Lula Pauline Bushage MILHORN, age: 6 months and 6 days, death cause: "cholera infantum", died: Johnson City on 3 Jun 1911, record (1908-12): 92849.
Jamie LOVE, colored, age: 34 years, born in North Carolina, married, death cause: "stabbed", died at Johnson City on 18 Feb 1911, record: 92850.
Mrs. Venie CARTER, age: 19 years, born at Chuckey, married, death cause: "tuberculosis", died at Johnson City on 25 Jul 1910, record: 92851.
Mary HENSON, age: 30 years, married, death cause: "consumption of bowels", died at Johnson City on 9 Jul 1911, record (1908-12): 92852.
Hazel HENSON, age: 1 week, death cause: "bowel trouble", died at Johnson City on 12 Jun 1911, record (1908-12): 92853.
Irwin GREEN, age: 12 years, death cause: "tuberculosis", died at Johnson City on 11 Jan 1911, record (1908-12): 92854.
Francis LANDINGHAM, age: 48 years, born in Greene County, married, death cause: illegible, died at Jonesboro on 7 Jan 1911, record (1908-12): 92855.
Henry Jackson LEWIS, age: 7 months, death cause: "pneumonia", died at Johnson City on 22 Oct 1910, record (1908-12): 92856.
Lois LOVE, colored, age: 15 months, death cause: "fever", died at Johnson City on 25 Jan 1911, record (1908-12): 92857.
Marlin ELLIS, colored, age: 25 years, born in Sullivan County, single, soldier, death cause: "hanged", died at Etarn, Vermont, died: 15 May 1911, record (1908-12): 92858.
Mollie SNOW, colored, age: 22 years, born at Dry Creek, married, death cause: "unknown", died at Johnson City on 11 Jul 1910, record: 92859.

James LAMKINS, age: 73 years, born at Kingsport, married, death cause: "consumption", died at Johnson City on 1 Nov 1910, record (1908-12): 92860.

Alice CHRISTENBURG, age: 39 years, born at Cherokee, married, death cause: "typhoid fever", died at Johnson City on 14 Oct 1910, record: 92861.

Elkana TOLLIE, age; 24 years, born in Unicoi County, married, miner, death cause: "killed in mine", died at Cranberry, NC., on 17 Jun 1911, record: 92862.

Louise SMALLING, age: 3 years, born at Jonesboro, death cause: "croup", died at Johnson City on 2 Oct 1911, record (1908-12): 92863.

Mary G. GOODMAN, age: 24 years, single, death cause: "tuberculosis", died: 10th District on 10 May 1911, record (1908-12): 92864.

Ralph R. SANDERS, age: 6 months and 13 days, death cause: "disease of spine", died: 10th District on 13 Jun 1911, record (1908-12): 92865.

Montgomery STANT, age: 83 years, widower, death cause: "paralysis", died: 10th District on 15 Jul 1910, record (1908-12): 92866.

Mary E. CRUMLEY, age: 69 years, born in Sullivan County, single, death cause: "tuberculosis", died: 10th District on 12 Apr 1911, record: 92867.

Anna SHIPLEY, age: 19 years, born in Carter County, single, death cause: "Brights disease", died: 10th District on 23 Mar 1911, record (1908-12): 92868.

Ida SWADLEY, age: 30 years, single, death cause: "nervous prostration", died: 10th District on 7 May 1911, record (1908-12): 92869.

Jessie J. KIRTH, age: 16 days, death cause: "eryesipelas", died: 10th District on 22 Jun 1911, record (1908-12): 92870.

(illegible) WHITAKER, female, age: 15 years, death cause: "paralysis", died: 10th District on 8 Apr 1911, record (1908-12): 92871.

Wilber PRICE, age: 7 years, death cause: "diptheria", died: 10th District on 24 Dec 1910, record (1908-12): 92872.

Mary R. MOODY, age: 21 years, married, death cause: "tuberculosis", died: 12th District on 19 Feb 1911, record (1908-12): 92873.

Anderson J. GRAY, age: 83 years, widower, death cause: "general break down", died: 12th District on 4 Aug 1910, record (1908-12): 92874.

Jessie M. COX, Sr., age: 51 years, married, death cause: "tuberculosis", died: 12th District on 6 Sep 1910, record (1908-12): 92875.

Delia REPASS, age: 26 years, married, death cause: "tuberculosis", died: 12th District on 6 Nov 1910, record (1908-12): 92876.

Henry A. DILLOW, age: about 80 years, born in Sullivan County, married, death cause: "heart trouble", died: 12th District on 7 Mar 1911, record (1908-12): 92877.

S.B. ELLIS, age: 82 years, single, death cause: "rheumatism and heart failure", died: 12th District on 13 Mar 1911, record (1908-12): 92878.

Rebecca A. BARNES, age: 58 years, married, death cause: "organic heart trouble", died: 12th District on 17 Mar 1911, record (1908-12): 92879.

Robert Burl SELLS, age: 2 months and 22 days, death cause: "bold hives", died: 12th District on 13 Nov 1910, record (1908-12): 92880.

Lela May FORD, age: 1 month and 10 days, death cause: "bold hives", died: 12th District on 21 Nov 1910, record (1908-12): 92881.

Sarah RIGSBY, age: 73 years, born in Sullivan County, married, death cause: "burned to death", died: 12th District on 3 May 1911, record: 92882.

Alice May BUCKINGHAM, age: 2 months and 23 days, death cause: "bold hives", died: 12th District on 13 Oct 1910, record (1908-12): 92883.

Hassie CONNER, age: 1 month, death cause: "bold hives", died: 12th District on 25 Oct 1910, record (1908-12): 92884.

Smith FORD, age: 60 years, married, death cause: "kidney trouble", died: 12th District on 20 Mar 1911, record (1908-12): 92885.

Elvira FORD, age: 61 years, widow, death cause: not stated, died: 12th District on 20 Apr 1911, record (1908-12): 92886.

Robert ADAMS, age: 42 years, married, death cause: not stated, died: 12th District on 13 Dec 1910, record (1908-12): 92887.

Leotis CLEVINGER, male, age: 2 years and 6 months, death cause: "summer complaint", died at Johnson City on 10 Jun 1911, record (1908-12): 92888.

Infant VANCE, age: 2 months, male, child of James VANCE, death cause: not stated, died: 8th District on 14 May 1912, record (1908-12): 92889.

Hobart GREEN, age: 13 years, death cause: "measles", died: 8th District on 13 Feb 1912, record: 92890.

Francis MILLER, age: 97 years, born in North Carolina, married, death cause: "old age", died: 8th District on 29 Sep 1911, record (1908-12): 92891.

G.W. OLIVER, age: 71 years, married, death cause: "heart trouble", died: 8th District on 22 Sep 1911, record (1908-12): 92892.

Henry DEAKINS, age: 69 years, single, death cause: "tuberculosis", died: 14th District on 13 Aug 1911, record (1908-12): 92893.

Infant BARLOW, male, age: 9 months, child of James BARLOW, death cause: "unknown", died: 8th District on 29 Nov 1911, record (1908-12): 92094.

Infant SAYLOR, male, age: 10 days, child of James SAYLOR, death cause: "heart trouble", died: 8th District on 23 May 1912, record (1908-12): 92895.

Mary MADEN, age: 77 years, born at Knob Creek, widow, death cause: "old age", died at Buffalo Ridge on 10 Jun 1909, record (1908-12): 92896.

Unnamed INFANT, female, death cause: "stillborn", died at Buffalo Ridge on 12 Apr 1909, record: 92897.

Fannie MILLER, lived 6 hours, death cause: not stated, died: 15th District on 24 Mar 1909, record (1908-12): 92898.

Robert HILBERT, lived 36 hours, death cause: "not known", died: 15th District on 10 Jan 1909, record (1908-12): 92899.

Piny HETTON, female, age: 2 years, 1 month and 20 days, death cause: "indigestion", died: 15th District on 26 Sep 1908, record (1908-12): 92900.

Nancy BROOKS, lived 22 days, death cause: "croup", died: 15th District on 5 Nov 1908, record: 92901.

Mary RILEY, age: 67 years, born in Hamblen County, single, death cause: "cancer", died: 8 Dec 1908 (?), record (1908-12): 92902.

Norma LEONARD, age: 83 years, born in Yancey County, NC., single, death cause: "apoplexy", died: 15th District on 23 Jun 1909, record (1908-12): 92903.

Lavina Ellen MOHLER, age: 27 years, single, death cause: "tuberculosis", died: 15th District on 19 Jan 1909, record (1908-12): 92904.

Alexander HOMES, age: 78 years, married, death cause: "bronchitis", died: 15th District on 2 Jun 1909, record (1908-12): 92905.

Jane JOHNSON, age: about 55 years, married, death cause: "cancer", died: 15th District on 8 Apr 1909, record (1908-12): 92906.

Susan FURGUSON, age: about 80 years, born in Virginia, single, death cause: "nervous diability", died: 15th District on 4 Jun 1908, record: 92907.

Henry MCNEIL, age: 69 years, born in Massachusetts, married, death cause: "paralysis", died: 15th District on 13 Aug 1908, record (1908-12): 92908.

James A. MCPHERSON, age: 57 years, married, death cause: "partisis", died: 15th District on 20 Jul 1908, record (1908-12): 92909.

Unnamed INFANT, female, lived 19 hours, death cause: "not known", died: 15th District on 26 Feb 1909, record (1908-12): 92910.

Francis RICE, age: 64 years, married, death cause: "apoplexy", died: 15th District on 24 May 1909, record (1908-12): 92911.

Martha E. NELMS, age: 71 years, single, death cause: "pneumonia", died: 15th District on 26 Mar 1909, record (1908-12): 92912.

Hannah MELEAR, age: 48 years, born in Sullivan County, single, death cause: "cancer", died: 15th District on 30 Jun 1909, record (1908-12): 92913.

Grover C. HOUSTON, age: 23 years, born in Carter County, married, death cause: "typhoid fever", died: 15th District on 16 Dec 1908, record: 92914.

Maggie E. CARWOOD, age: 17 years, born in Sullivan County, death cause: "locked bowels", died: 25 Apr 1909, record (1908-12): 92915.

Preston HUFF, age: 56 years, married, death cause: "paralysis", died: 15th District on 10 Aug 1908, record (1908-12): 92916.

Walter HILL, colored, age: 19 years, single, death cause: "tuberculosis", died in Sullivan County on 20 Dec 1908, record (1908-12): 92917.

Jerry EDWARDS, colored, age: 73 years, single, death cause: "paralysis", died: 15th District on 3 Dec 1908, record (1908-12): 92818.

Clara GREENLEE, colored, age: 3 months and 11 days, death cause: "whooping cough", died: 15th District on 10 May 1909, record (1908-12): 92919.

Fannie TUCKER, age: 38 years, married, death cause: "tuberculosis", died: 15th District on 7 Sep 1908, record (1908-12): 92920.

Unnamed INFANT, female, age: 1 month and 7 days, death cause: "whooping cough", died: 15th District on 12 Feb 1909, record (1908-12): 92921.

Samuel A. ARMSTRONG, age: 38 years, single, death cause: "locomotor atuxia", died: 15th District on 30 Dec 1908, record (1908-12): 92922.

Lucindy B. ROLLER, colored, age: 9 months, death cause: "fever", died: 15th District on 4 Mar 1909, record (1908-12): 92923.

Thomas SCOT, colored, age: 38 years, born in Unicoi County, married, death cause: "tuberculosis", died: 15th District on 6 Mar 1909, record: 92924.

Elbert A. SHIPLEY, age: 59 years, married, death cause: "liver and stomach", died: 15th District on 15 Apr 1908, record (1908-12): 92925.

Josephine CAMPBELL, age: 7 months and 8 days, death cause: "dropsy", died: 15th District on 27 Sep 1908, record (1908-12): 92926.

Mary A. WILLIAMSON, age: 74 years, born in Bedford County, VA., married, death cause: "stomach trouble", died: 15th District on 20 Jun 1908, record (1908-12): 92927.

Mary SHIPLEY, age: 80 years, married, death cause: "old age", died: 15th District on 28 Jul 1909, record (1908-12): 92928.

Walter J. BROWN, age: 17 years, born in Ashe County, NC., death cause: "shock from railroad accident", died in Pulaski, VA. on 22 Feb 1909, record: 92929.

William Newton STEPHENS, age: 30 years, married, death cause: "tuberculosis", died: 16th District on 24 Apr 1909, record (1908-12): 92930.

Amantha J. BALL, age: 51 years, married, death cause: "paralysis", died near Leesburg on 8 Apr 1909, record (1908-12): 92931.

Bertie CAMPBELL, age: 40 years, married, death cause: "Brights disease", died near Leesburg on 16 Dec 1908, record (1908-12): 92932.

Calelia SMITH, age: 9 years, death cause: "meningitis", died near Leesburg on 22 Dec 1908, record (1908-12): 92933.

James A. CROOKSHANK, age: 55 years, married, death cause: "Brights disease", died near Leesburg on 12 Jun 1909, record (1908-12): 92934.

S.H. GARBER, age: 56 years, married, minister, death cause: "cancer of stomach", died near Leesburg on 27 Aug 1908, record (1908-12): 92935.

Bertie L. BAINES, age: 38 years, married, merchant's wife, death cause: "childbirth", died at Knoxville on 8 Aug 1908, record (1908-12): 92936.

Sally BAINES, age: 28 years, married, farmer's wife, death cause: "liver complaint", died: 17th District on 24 Apr 1909, record (1908-12): 92936.

John Wesley LUSTER, age: 49 years, married, death cause: "pneumonia", died: 17th District on 4 Mar 1909, record (1908-12): 92938.

Bertha V. MITCHELL, age: 27 years, married, death cause: "lung trouble", died: 17th District on 3 May 1909, record (1908-12): 92939.

Ruth MORELOCK, age: 1 year and 10 months, death cause: "gastro enteritis", died: 17th District on 9 Jun 1909, record (1908-12): 92940.

Infant BAILEY, female, lived 1 day, death cause: "not known", child of Wesley BAILEY, died: 17th District on 7 Nov 1908, record (1908-12): 92941.

I.G. SQUIBB, age: 71 years, single, death cause: "consumption of bowels", died: 15 Aug 1908, record (1908-12): 92942.

Addie TESNEER, age: 37 years, married, death cause: "consumption", died: 17th District on 20 Dec 1909, record (1908-12): 92943.

William KELLEY, age: 76 years, married, death cause: "rheumitism", died: 18th District on 30 Jun 1908, record (1908-12): 92944.

Unnamed INFANT, male, death cause: "cord disarranged", died: 18th District on 21 Jun 1909, record (1908-12): 92945.

George BAILEY, black, age: 23 years, single, death cause: "fever", died at Limestone on 14 Apr 1909, record (1908-12): 92946.

Mary ANDERSON, age: 4 years, death cause: "worms", died: 18th District on __ Mar 1909, record: 92947.

Nancy Adaline BAILEY, age: 50 years, born in Greene County, married, death cause: "tuberculosis", died at Limestone on 20 Jul 1908, record: 92948.

Samuel T. PLEASANT, age: 56 years, born in Johnson County, married, death cause: "tuberculosis", died: 18th District on 6 May 1909, record: 92949.

Martha MCCRACKEN, age: 71 years, born in Caldwell County, NC., married, death cause: "paralysis", died: 18th District on 11 Jun 1909, record: 92950.

Alice MCCRACKEN, age: 4 years, death cause: "pneumonia and bronchitis", died: 18th District on 21 Jun 1909, record (1908-12): 92951.

William Calvin KEEZEL, age: not stated, born in Rockingham County, VA., married, death cause: "consumption", died at Limestone on 5 Nov 1907, record (1908-12): 92952.

Lula Bell BARKLEY, black, age: 11 years, death cause: "spinal affection", died at Limestone on 7 Aug 1907, record (1908-12): 92953.

Mary FORD, black, age: 39 years, married, death cause: "cancer", died: 18th District on 6 Jan 1908, record (1908-12): 92954.

John W. PYLES, age: not stated, born in Sullivan County, married, death cause: "heart disease", died near Limestone on 9 Sep 1908, record: 92955.

Clyde ROWLS, age: 4 years, death cause: "dysentery", died at Limestone on 2 Jul 1908, record: 92956.

Delilah BROWN, age: 76 years, born near Telford, married, death cause: "paralysis", died at Limestone on 9 Feb 1909, record (1908-12): 92957.
Sue HALE, age: 70 years, widow, death cause: "tuberculosis", died: 12th District on 28 Jun 1909, record (1908-12): 92958.
Infant SELLS, female, lived 4 days, death cause: "unknown", died: 12th District on 26 Feb 1909, record (1908-12): 92959.
Lillie ARCHER, age: 7 years, 5 months and 3 days, death cause: "diptheria", died: 12th District on 5 Dec 1908, record (1908-12): 92960.
Allen CREASEY, age: about 3 months, death cause: "unknown", died: 12th District on 15 Feb 1909, record (1908-12): 92961.
Finnie D. ANDERSON, age: 69 years, married, death cause: "malaria", died at Umatila, Florida on 11 Feb 1909, record (1908-12): 92962.
Infant HALE, female, death cause: "born dead", died: 12th District on 1 Nov 1909, record: 92963.
Infant HAWK, female, death cause: "stillborn", died: 12th District on 21 Jun 1909, record: 92964.
John DEAKINS, age: 72 years, born at Morning Star, TN., married, death cause: "cancer", died: Harmony, 13th District, 28 Mar 1909, record (1908-12): 92965.
Chrissie HOPPER, age: 35 years, married, death cause: "liver disease", died at Fall Branch on 20 Dec 1908, record (1908-12): 92966.
Willie COX, age: 6 years, death cause: "throat disease", died at Fall Branch on 27 May 1909, record (1908-12): 92967.
Jasper N. LEWIS, age: 70 years, born at Spartainburg, SC., married, death cause: "heart failure", died at Jonesboro on 3 Mar 1909, record (1908-12): 92968.
Melvina GRAY, age: 63 years, married, death cause: "cancer of stomach", died at Jonesboro on 16 Jan 1909, record (1908-12): 92969.
William BUCK, age: 33 years, born in Carter County, married, death cause: "consumption", died at Fall Branch on 9 Feb 1909, record (1908-12): 92970.

Julia BACON, age: 63 years, married, death cause: "consumption", died at Jonesboro on 5 Jun 1909, record (1908-12): 92971.

Merlin WHEELOCK, age: 13 months, death cause: "catarrh of bowels", died at Jonesboro on 25 May 1909, record (1908-12): 92972.

Elijah CAREY, age: 76 years, married, death cause: "cancer of stomach", died at Jonesboro on 6 Sep 1908, record (1908-12): 92973.

Mary HALSE, age: 18 years, single, death cause: "tuberculosis of leg", died: 13th District on 7 Apr 1909, record (1908-12): 92974.

Mary Ellen HYDER, age: 3 years, death cause: "bronchitis", died at Nolachucky on 28 Jul 1908, record (1908-12): 92975.

Infant AUSTIN, male, age: 3 months, death cause: "fever", died: 2nd District on 18 Mar 1909, record (1908-12): 92976.

Everitt SNAPP, age: 4 months, death cause: "flux", died at Boonesboro on 8 Jun 1909, record: 92977.

Joseph DUNCAN, age: 19 years, single, death cause: "consumption", died at Boonesboro on 22 Oct 1908, record (1908-12): 92978.

Sarah Edna HUMPHREYS, age: 5 months, death cause: "hives", died: 2nd District on 14 Dec 1908, record (1908-12): 92979.

Doyle MCCRACKEN, age: 8 months, death cause: "bowel trouble", died: 2nd District on 13 Nov 1908, record (1908-12): 92980.

Will CLICK, age: 55 years, married, death cause: "bowel trouble", died: 2nd District on 14 Jan 1909, record (1908-12): 92981.

Infant KYKER, male, death cause: not stated, died: 2nd District on 26 Mar 1909, record: 92982.

Sallie BRICKER, age: 35 years, married, death cause: "consumption", died: 2nd District on 15 Mar 1909, record (1908-12): 92983.

Abe FOSTER, age: 54 years, married, death cause: "dropsy", died: 2nd District on 25 Apr 1909, record (1908-12): 92984.

F.K. WADDELL, age: 74 years, married, death cause: "pneumonia", died: 2nd District on 15 Feb 1909, record (1908-12): 92985.

H.F. BAILEY, age: 78 years, married, death cause: "heart failure", died: 2nd District on 20 Jan 1909, record (1908-12): 92986.

Mrs. John SLEMONS, age: 48 years, married, death cause: "fever", died: 2nd District on 12 Mar 1909, record (1908-12): 92987.

John DEMPSEY, age: 24 years, married, death cause: "diabetes", died: 15th District on 20 Nov 1909, record (1908-12): 92988.

Grace HARRIS, colored, age: 21 years, death cause: "not known", died: 15th District on 15 Sep 1909, record (1908-12): 92989.

Kate MORGAN, colored, age: 33 years, born in Virginia, single, death cause: "not known", died: 15th District on 25 Mar 1910, record: 92990.

William DAVIS, age: 35 years, single, death cause: "epilepsy", died: 15th District on 1 Mar 1910, record (1908-12): 92991.

Eliga PHIPPS, age: 86 years, born in North Carolina, married, death cause: "old age", died: 15th District on 28 May 1910, record (1908-12): 92992.

Margaret HELTON, age: 69 years, married, death cause: "dropsy", died: 15th District on 24 May 1910, record (1908-12): 92993.

Carrie LAWS, age: 4 years, death cause: "scarlet fever", died: 15th District on 18 Nov 1909, record (1908-12): 92994.

Luke HANKLE, age: 2 (?), death cause: "scarlet fever", died: 15th District on 5 Dec 1909, record (1908-12): 92995.

Cora CARTER, age: 81 years, married, death cause: "tumor", died in Sullivan County on 19 Aug 1909, record (1908-12): 92996.

James TAYLOR, age: 48 years, born in North Carolina, married, death cause: "heart failure", died: 7 Oct 1909, record (1908-12): 92997.

William CARDER, age: 66 years, married, death cause: "rheumatism", died: 15th District on 20 Jul 1909, record (1908-12): 92998.

Hattie MARSHALL, age: 31 years, single, death cause: "consumption", died: 15th District on 25 Nov 1909, record (1908-12): 92999.

Lee STUART, colored, age: 23 years, married, death cause: "tuberculosis", died in Ohio on 22 Aug 1909, record (1908-12): 93000.

Barney CUNNINGHAM, colored, age: 99 years, married, death cause: "dropsy", died: 15th District on 27 Apr 1910, record (1908-12): 93001.

June BURTON, age: 79 years, married, death cause: "tuberculosis", died: 15th District on 6 Mar 1910, record (1908-12): 93002.

William ENSOR, age: 78 years, married, shoe maker, death cause: "tuberculosis", died: 15th District on 30 May 1910, record (1908-12): 93003.

Mary LYTTE, age: 65 years, married, death cause: "abscess", died: 15th District on 15 Oct 1909, record (1908-12): 93004.

Carl WHITE, age: 3 months, death cause: "pneumonia fever", died: 15th District on 12 Sep 1909, record (1908-12): 93005.

Zell MARSHALL, colored, age: 2 months, death cause: "spasm", died: 15th District on 13 Apr 1910, record (1908-12): 93006.

William PILL (?), age: 23 years, single, death cause: "burned" died in Virginia on 28 Jan 1910, record (1908-12): 93007.

Lucy FINK, age: 85 years, born in Virginia, married, death cause: "paralysis", died: 15th District on 13 Oct 1909, record (1908-12): 93008.

Angela E. MASON, age: 80 years, widow, death cause: not stated, died: 15th District on 17 Oct 1909, record (1908-12): 93009.

D.J. CRUMLEY, age: 63 years, born in Washington County, VA., married, death cause: "bladder trouble and prostate gland", died: 16th District on 20 Jan 1910, record (1908-12): 93010.

A.T. HILBERT, age: 38 years, married, farmer, death cause: "typhoid fever", died: 16th District on 30 Aug 1909, record (1908-12): 93011.

Catherine MATHES, age: 75 years, born in McDowell County, NC., married, death cause: "pneumonia", died near Leesburg on 4 Nov 1910, record: 93012.
John T. MATHES, age: 96 years, born near Charleston, SC., married, basket maker, death cause: "old age", died in Johnson City on 3 Jan 1910, record: 93013.
John Cordell GRAYBEAL, age: 4 years, born in Watauga County, NC., death cause: "meningitis", died near Leesburg on 5 May 1910, record (1908-12): 93014.
Preston ARMENTROUT, age: 79 years, born in Rockingham County, VA., widower, shoe maker, death cause: "consumption", died: 17th District on 15 Sep 1909, record (1908-12): 93015.
Samantha HUFFMAN, age: 76 years, born in Rockingham County, VA., married, death cause: "paralysis", died: 17th District on 24 May 1910, record: 93016.
Cora E. ARMENTROUT, age: 40 years, single, death cause: "consumption", died: 17th District on 16 May 1910, record (1908-12): 93017.
Sarah SLAGLE, age: 76 years, widow, death cause: "internal abscess", died: 17th District on 20 Dec 1909, record (1908-12): 93018.
Nile HARRIS, age: 6 months, death cause: "tuberculosis", died: 17th District on 14 Jan 1910, record (1908-12): 93019.
N.W. MITCHELL, age: 55 years, widower, death cause: "pneumonia fever", died: 17th District on 5 Dec 1909, record (1908-12): 93020.
Nancy Ann HOUNT, age: 79 years, widow, death cause: "heart failure", died: 17th District on 25 May 1910, record (1908-12): 93021.
Cintha A. MOORE, age: 76 years, single, weaver, death cause: "cancer and bronchitis", died: 17th District on 13 Sep 1909, record (1908-12): 93022.
Jesse MOORE, age: 66 years, married, death cause: "asthma and Brights disease", died: 17th District on 24 Nov 1909, record (1908-12): 93023.
Alice HORNE, age: 58 years, born in Sullivan County, widow, death cause: "cancer", died: 17th District on 24 Nov 1909, record (1908-12): 93024.

Sarah A. MARTIN, age: 64 years, married, death cause: "typhoid fever", died: 17th District on 9 Dec 1909, record (1908-12): 93025.

Martha A. BAILEY, age: 60 years, married, death cause: "consumption", died: 12th District on 10 Jul 1909, record (1908-12): 93026.

Unnamed INFANT, female, death cause: "stillborn", died: 18th District on 13 Oct 1909, record: 93027.

Dexey IVANS, age: 3 months, death cause: "hives", died: Limestone, 13 Apr 1910, record: 93028.

Sarah F. BURGNER, age: about 47 years, born in Greene County, married, death cause: "lagrippe", died: 27 Jun 1910, record (1908-12): 93029.

Clara May RIPPEY, death cause: "sillborn", died at Limestone on 12 Aug 1909, record (1908-12): 93030.

Mary D. HULSE, age: 18 years, single, death cause: "tuberculosis", died: 14th District on 7 Apr 1909, record (1908-12): 93031.

Sarah A. FORD, age: 84 years, widow, death cause: "old age", died: 14th District on 11 Jun 1909, record (1908-12): 93032.

L.A. KEYS, female, age: 78 years, widow, death cause: "tuberculosis", died near Sulphur Springs on 22 Oct 1908, record (1908-12): 93033.

Sallie ALISON, colored, age: 40 years, born in Kingsport, married, death cause: "tuberculosis, died at Locust Mount on 13 Mar 1909, record: 93034.

Ortie ALISON, colored, age: 2 years, death cause: "tuberculosis", died: Locust Mount on 13 Feb 1909, record (1908-12): 93035.

Mary J. SHIPLEY, age: 44 years, married, death cause: "childbirth", died at Morning Star on 18 May 1909, record (1908-12): 93036.

Mary JORDAN, age: 1 year, death cause: "tuberculosis", died at Pleasant Valley on 25 Jun 1909, record (1908-12): 93037.

Daniel BARFIELD, age: 24 years, single, death cause: "tuberculosis", died near Morning Star on 28 Apr 1909, record (1908-12): 93038.

Eli STORY, age: 72 years, born in Mitchell County, NC., married, death cause: "heart trouble", died: 8th District on 16 May 1912, record: 93039.

Paul C. GREEN, age: 3 months, death cause: "croup", died: 8th District on 11 Apr 1912, record: 93040.

Rosa LUNDY, age: 39 years, born in Wytheville, VA., married, death cause: "cancer of womb, died on operating table", died: 8th District on 18 Nov 1912, record (1908-12): 93041.

James NORRIS, age: 61 years, born in Unicoi County, married, death cause: "consumption", died: 8th District on 11 Apr 1912, record (1908-12): 93042.

William F. WEBB, age: 24 years, single, death cause: "consumption", died: 8th District on 30 Jan 1912, record (1908-12): 93043.

Edna OVERSTREET, age: 23 years, born in Unicoi County, married, death cause: "consumption", died: 8th District on 2 Jun 1912, record (1908-12): 93044.

Moses R. ESTEPP, age: 37 years, born in Carter County, married, died: 8th District on 31 May 1912, record (1908-12): 93045.

Sarah L. DENTON, age: 52 years, married, death cause: "heart trouble", died: 8th District on 24 Mar 1912, record (1908-12): 93046.

Thomas LILLY, age: 71 years, born: Sullivan County, married, cooper, death cause: "paralysis", died: 8th District, 24 Jun 1912, record: 93047.

Mary Anna HAWS, infant (age not stated), death cause: "unknown", died at Fall Branch on 12 Apr 1912, record (1908-12): 93048.

Henry SHELTON, age: 9 years, death cause: "catarrh on head", died at Cassey Creek on 21 Mar 1912, record (1908-12): 93049.

Charles GARDNER, age: 29 years, born in North Carolina, single, death cause: "typhoid fever", died at Johnson City on 25 Apr 1911, record: 93050.

Elizabeth SELLARS, age: 53 years, born in Greene County, married, death cause: "tuberculosis", died: 5 May 1911, record (1908-12): 93051.

Walter GIBSON, age: 3 years, death cause: "diptheria", died at Watauga on 5 Nov 1910, record (1908-12): 93052.

Ethel COOK, colored, age: 12 years, born in Abingdon, VA., death cause: "tuberculosis", died at Abingdon, VA., 17 Jan 1911, record: 93053.

74

Eddie COOK, colored, age: 17 years, born at Abingdon, VA., death cause: "tuberculosis", died at Abingdon on 18 Jul 1910, record (1908-12): 93054.

Cherry May COOK, age: 17 years, born at Abingdon, VA., death cause: "tubeculosis", died at Abingdon on 4 Dec 1910, record (1908-12): 93055.

Jenie COOK, age: 36 years, born at Abingdon, VA., married, death cause: "tuberculosis", died at Abingdon on 12 Jan 1910, record (1908-12): 93056.

Anderson COOK, colored, age: 72 years, born at Pulaski, VA., married, death cause: "tuberculosis", died: Abingdon, VA., 31 Jan 1910, record: 93057.

Luke SMITH, age: 21 years, born in Hawkins County, single, death cause: "convulsions", died at Jonesboro on 7 Jan 1911, record (1908-12): 93058.

Maggie STUART, colored, age: 32 years, married, death cause: "child bed fever", died: 20 Nov 1909, record (1908-12): 93059.

Mary BERKHART, age: 64 years, born in Bavaria, Germany, married, death cause: "heart failure", died at Johnson City on 7 Nov 1910, record: 93060.

Josephine STREET, age: 22 years, born at Bakersville, NC., married, death cause: "cancer", died at Johnson City on 12 Aug 1910, record: 53061.

Frank GIBBS, colored, age: 54 years, born in Hawkins County, married, death cause: "asthma", died in Johnson City on 2 Oct 1910, record (1908-12): 93062.

Caroline P. MOSS, age: 11 months, death cause: "teething", died a Johnson City on 31 Mar 1911, record (1908-12): 93063.

Blan WHITE, colored, age: 23 years, born in Knoxville, married, death cause: "appolexy", died at Bristol on 9 Sep 1910, record (1908-12): 93064.

John HARDY, age: 49 years, born in North Carolina, married, death cause: "killed in mine", died at Cranes, W.VA., on 20 Apr 1911, record: 93065.

Samuel DAVIDSON, age: 5 years, born in Rutherford County, NC., death cause: "tuberculosis", died in Johnson City on 18 May 1911, record: 93066.

Lizzie Jones YOUNG, colored, age: 45 years, born in Virginia, married, death cause: "unknown", died: Johnson City, __ Aug 1910, record: 93067.

Henry SPURGEON, colored, age: 77 years, born at Jonesboro, married, death cause: "old age", died at Johnson City on 7 Jul 1910, record (1908-12): 93068.

Infant RYANS, colored, age: 1 month, child of Horace RYANS, death cause: "unknown", died at Johnson City on 25 May 1911, record (1908-12): 93069.

William RYANS, colored, age: 46 years, married, brick mason, death cause: "shot (murdered)", died at Johnson City on 10 Nov 1910, record: 93070.

Ossie RYANS, colored, age: 46 years, born at Blountville, married, death cause: "shot (murdered)", died at Johnson City on 10 Nov 1910, record (1908-12): 93071.

Joseph RYANS, colored, age: 7 years, death cause: "unknown", died at Johnson City on 23 May 1911, record (1908-12): 93072.

Earl SMITH, colored, age: 13 years, death cause: "fever", died at Johnson City on 30 Jun 1911, record (1908-12): 93073.

Carl GOINS, colored, age: 7 months, death cause: "flux", died at Johnson City on 29 Jun 1911, record (1908-12): 93074.

Frank ROBERTS, age: 1 year, death cause: "croup", died at Johnson City on 12 Sep 1910, record: 93075.

Addie O. MILLER, age: 63 years, born in Blountville, married, death cause: "female trouble", died at Johnson City on 21 Mar 1911, record: 93076.

Dr. E.S. MILLER, age: 68 years and 1 day, married, physician, death cause: "gall poisoning", died at Johnson City on 12 Apr 1911, record: 93077.

Frank GILMAN, age: 18 years, death cause: "consumption", died at Johnson City on 13 Sep 1910, record (1908-12): 93078.

Riley H. KELLEY, female, age: 14 months, death cause: "cholera infantum", died at Johnson City on 11 Jun 1911, record (1908-12): 93079.

Bertha SHOWMAN, age: 28 years, born in Sullivan County, married, death cause: "tuberculosis", died at Johnson City on 22 Jan 1911, record: 93080.

George H. SHOWMAN, age: 2 years, death cause: "pneumonia", died at Johnson City on 17 Jun 1911, record (1908-12): 93081.

Jeniva MILLER, colored, age: 8 months, death cause: "pneumonia", died at Johnson City on 21 Dec 1910, record (1908-12): 93082.

Clarence MCNEIL, colored, age: 6 years, born at Roan Mountain, death cause: "burned", died at Johnson City on 20 Feb 1911, record (1908-12): 93083.

Ann BURGINS, colored, age: 65 years, born in Carter County, widow, death cause: "heart failure", died at Johnson City on 21 May 1911, record: 93084.

H. Stanley MILLER, age: 27 years, married, death cause: "artero sclerosis", died at Johnson City on 25 Apr 1911, record (1908-12): 93085.

Charlie H-- (illegible), age: 30 years, born at Buffalo Ridge, married, engineer, death cause: "heart failure", died at Okalona on 6 Apr 1911, record (1908-12): 93086.

Walter RHEA, colored, age: 27 years, married, brakeman, death cause: "accident", died at Johnson City on 17 Mar 1911, record (1908-12): 93087.

Thomas P. SUMMERS, age: 82 years, born in North Carolina, widower, school teacher and minister, death cause: "dropsy", died at Johnson City on 25 Dec 1910, record (1908-12): 93088.

Infant BAILEY, male, lived 1 day, death cause: "unknown", child of David BAILEY, died at Johnson City on 20 May 1911, record (1908-12): 93098.

Infant DAVIS, colored, lived 3 hours, child of Sam DAVIS, death cause: "unknown", died at Johnson City on 7 Jun 1912, record (1908-12): 93090.

Nelon MOORE, colored, age: 75 years, born in North Carolina, married, death cause: "asthma", died at Johnson City on 21 Jan 1912, record: 93091.

Hannah MCNUTT, age: 21 months, born at Bristol, death cause: "teething", died at Bristol on 3 Dec 1911, record (1908-12): 93092.

Sallie ANDERSON, colored, age: about 60 years, single, death cause: "pneumonia", died at Johnson City on __ Mar 1912, record (1908-12): 93093.

Marsh DOWELL, colored, age: 2 years, death cause: "bowel trouble", died at Johnson City on __ Nov 1912, record (1908-12): 93094.

Lucy M. HELSOM, colored, age: 45 years, born in Lynchburg, VA., married, death cause: "jaundice", died in Virginia on 22 Dec 1911, record: 93095.

George MILLER (?), colored, age: 39 years, married, death cause: "dropsy", died at Johnson City on 12 May 1912, record (1908-12): 93096.

Bertha R. BROWN, age: 72 years, born in Germany, married, death cause: "Brights disease", died in Johnson City on 18 Jul 1911, record: 93097.

William SMITH, age: 1 year, death cause: "cholera infantum", died in Johnson City on 25 Jun 1912, record (1908-12): 93098.

Elizabeth G-- (illegible), age: 48 years, born in Hamblen County, married, death cause: "cancer", died in Johnson City on 15 Apr 1912, record: 93099.

Fred WOODWARD, age: 3 years, death cause: "croup", died in Johnson City on 15 Feb 1912, record: 93100.

Infant DAVIS, colored, lived 15 minutes, child of James DAVIS, death cause: "unknown", died at Johnson City on __ Jul 1911, record (1908-12): 93101.

Leona WILLIAMS, age: 18 months, death cause: not stated, died at Johnson City on 20 Apr 1912, record (1908-12): 93102.

Elizabeth WILLIAMS, age: 74 years, born in Virginia, widow, death cause: "old age", died at Johnson City on 29 Jun 1912, record (1908-12): 93103.

Infant FULKERSON, male, child of Martin FULKERSON, death cause: "stillborn", died at Johnson City on 29 Jun 1912, record (1908-12): 93104.

Mary Nell CAMPBELL, lived 6 days, death cause: "unknown", died at Johnson City on 16 Jul 1911, record (1908-12): 93105.

Kate STOUT, age: 4 years, death cause: "diptheria", died in Johnson City on __ Oct 1911, record: 93106.

Dan REEVES, colroed, age: 70 years, married, death cause: "dropsy", died at Johnson City on __ Sep 1911, record (1908-12): 93107.

Sam SMITH, colored, age: 6 years, death cause: "whooping cough", died at Johnson City on 10 Nov 1911, record (1908-12): 93108.

Dewitt BEARD, age: 22 years, single, death cause: "cancer", died: 10th District on 6 May 1912, record (1908-12): 93109.

Gladys LEONARD, age: 3 months and 3 days, death cause: "spinal disease", died: 5 Nov 1909, record (1908-12): 93110.

Margaret THORNBURG, age: 59 years, married, death cause: "consumption", died: 8th District on 19 Apr 1910, record (1908-12): 93111.

Sarah P. HUFFINE, age: 63 years, married, death cause: "liver trouble", died: 8th District on 24 May 1910, record (1908-12): 93112.

Mary E. LEACH, age: 52 years, married, death cause: "general break down", died: 8th District on 24 Mar 1910, record (1908-12): 93113.

William D. SLAGLE, age: 3 years, death cause: "poisoned", died: 8th District on 15 Feb 1910, record (1908-12): 93114.

Lucy VANCE, age: 25 years, married, death cause: "confinement", died: 8th District on 27 Apr 1910, record (1908-12): 93115.

Dennis HICKS, age: 19 years, single, death cause: "tree falling on him", died: 9 Apr 1910, record (1908-12): 93116.

Pernesy WOLFE, age: 81 years, born in Watauga, married, death cause: "old age", died at Watauga on 28 Jun 1910, record (1908-12): 93117.

J.H. PAINTER, age: 87 years, born in New Jersey, widower, death cause: "old age", died at Bristol on 23 Mar 1910, record (1908-12): 93118.

Thomas EVANS, age: 62 years, married, soldier, death cause: "dysentery", died at Johnson City on 24 Dec 1909, record (1908-12): 93119.

Stoward EVANS, age: 2 years, born in Arkansas, death cause: "hives", died: Johnson City on 25 Jun 1910, record (1908-12): 93120.

Myra Clark REEVES, age: 54 years, born in Sullivan County, married, death cause: "cancer", died in Johnson City on 22 Jun 1910, record: 93121.

Earnest JOHNSON, age: 2 years, born in Nashville, death cause: "cholera infantum", died in Johnson City on 5 Aug 1909, record (1908-12): 93122.

J.M. CHILDRESS, age: 58 years, 5 months and 14 days, born in Sullivan County, married, death cause: "Brights disease", died: 7th District on 13 Nov 1909, record (1908-12): 93123.

Ethel RIGGS, age: 28 years, born in Sullivan County, married, death cause: "consumption", died at Fall Branch on 7 Mar 1910, record (1908-12): 93124.

Virgie WHITLOCK, age: 26 years and 2 months, single, death cause: "consumption", died at Fall Branch on 21 Mar 1910, record (1908-12): 93125.

T.M. WELLS, age: 54 years and 8 months, married, lawyer, death cause: "tuberculosis", died at Fall Branch on 21 Oct 1909, record (1908-12): 93126.

James BOYER, age: 21 years, 3 months and 15 days, single, death cause: "caught on saw mill", died at Fall Branch on 6 Apr 1910, record (1908-12): 93127.

Anna HAWS, death cause: "stillborn", born at Biggsville, Illinois, died: 12 Oct 1909, record (1908-12): 93128.

Harvey HALL, age; 4 years, death cause: "stroke of lightning", died in Greene County on 23 Oct 1909, record (1908-12): 93129.

Patsy HALL, age: 69 years and 9 months, born in Hawkins County, widow, death cause: "Brights disease", died at Fall Branch on 23 Jul 1909, record (1908-12): 93130.

Bernica BARRETT, age: 84 years, born in Hawkins County, widow, death cause: "paralysis", died: 7th District on 11 Dec 1909, record (1908-12): 93131.

Berrencia BARRETT: identical to above record, record (1908-12): 93132.

Infant BURCHFIELD, male, death cause: "stillborn", child of C.E. BURCHFIELD, died at Johnson City on 13 Jun 1911, record (1908-12): 93133.

James VALLEY, age: 17 years, born in Clintwood, VA., death cause: "pneumonia", died at Johnson City on 3 Apr 1911, record (1908-12): 93134.

Fred KETCHAM, age: 5 months, death cause: "bowel trouble", died in Johnson City on 20 Sep 1910, record (1908-12): 93135.

Ida MARTIN, age: 18 years, born in Carter County, married, death cause: "dysentery", died at Johnson City on 16 Jun 1911, record (1908-12): 93136.

Lucinda MARTIN, age: 85 years, born in Carter County, married, death cause: "old age", died in Johnson City on 4 Feb 1911, record (1908-12): 93137.

Hazel LOOPER, age: 2 years, born in Yancey County, NC., death cause: "stomach trouble", died in Johnson City on __ Nov 1910, record (1908-12): 93138.

Mary E. LOVE, age: 2 months, death cause: "cholera infantum", died in Johnson City on 20 Jun 1911, record (1908-12): 93139.

Clara May BERKHATZ, age: 11 months, death cause: "unknown", died at Johnson City on 22 Nov 1910, record (1908-12): 93140.

William D. GOOD, age: 51 years, born in Greeneville, married, death cause: "paralysis", died in Johnson City on 1 Apr 1911, record (1908-12): 93141.

John LONG, colored, death cause: "stillborn", died at Fall Branch on 18 Jun 1912, record: 93142.

Keith REED, age: 1 year, born at Okalona, death cause: "croup and pneumonia", died: 11th District on 10 Oct 1911, record (1908-12): 93143.

Cecil DEPEW, age: 9 years and 2 months, death cause: "diabetes", died at Fall Branch on 26 Mar 1912, record (1908-12): 93144.

Richard M. HOPPER, age: 84 years and 9 months, born in North Carolina, married, death cause: "general break down", died at Fall Branch on 2 Oct 1911, record (1908-12): 93145.

Fannie MCCLAIN, colored, age: 30 years, single death cause: "tuberculosis", died at Johnson City on __ Dec 1910, record (1908-12): 93146.

Amos R. MOULTON, age: 81 years, born in Sullivan County, married, blacksmith, married, death cause: "pleurisy", died at Fall Branch on 23 Apr 1912, record (1908-12): 93147.

Berl LANE, death cause: "stillborn", died: 7th District on 17 Dec 1911, record (1908-12): 93148.

Walter HICKMAN, age: 28 years, single, death cause: "apendicitis", died in Dante, VA., on 21 Apr 1912, record (1908-12): 93149.

Katie MORRISON, age: 47 years, married, death cause: "scarofula", died at Fall Branch on 16 Apr 1912, record (1908-12): 93150.

Franklin HICKS, age: 11 months and 12 days, death cause: "unknown", died at Embreville on 22 Dec 1911, record (1908-12): 93151.

Infant LAFLIN, black, male, death cause: "stillborn", died in 5th District, 15 Apr 1912, record (1908-12): 93152.

Mary MOORE, age: 65 years, single, death cause: "pneumonia", died in 5th District, 3 Feb 1912, record (1908-12): 93153.

Bell BARRON, age: 33 years, married, death cause: "consumption", died in 5th District, 17 Nov 1911, record (1908-12): 93154.

Vessie HARRELL, age: 3 years, born in Unicoi County, death cause: "pneumonia", died in 5th District, 3 Feb 1912, record (1908-12): 93155.

Cynthia MAHONEY, age: 30 years, single, death cause: "consumption", died in 5th District on 22 May 1912, record (1908-12): 93156.

Ray LOYD, age: 5 months, death cause: "croup", died in 5th District on 5 Oct 1911, record: 93157.

Lucy SHIPLEY, age: 34 years, married, death cause: "consumption", died in 5th District on 1 Sep 1911, record (1908-12): 93158.

Z. WALKER, age: 73 years, married, death cause: "paralysis", died 14th District, 17 Oct 1911, record (1908-12): 93159.

Ralph ROGERS, lived 2 days, death cause: "not known", died in 14th District, 4 Jun 1912, record (1908-12): 93160.

Fred MOYERS, age: 23 years, single, death cause: "typhoid fever", died in 14th District, 24 Apr 1912, record (1908-12): 93161.

May Sue ARCHER, age: 41 years, married, death cause: "cancer", died in 14th District, 17 Oct 1911, record (1908-12): 93162.

Phoebe M. CROW, age: 33 years, married, death cause: "tuberculosis", died in 14th District, 23 May 1912, record (1908-12): 93163.

Sallie KEEN, age: 32 years, born in Johnson County, married, death cause: "fever", died in 14th District on 29 Sep 1911, record (1908-12): 93164.

Mollie R. KEEN, age: 8 months, death cause: "whooping cough", died in 14th District on 24 Jan 1912, record (1908-12): 93165.

A.J. SHERFEY, age: 62 years, married, death cause: "tuberculosis", died in 14th District on 27 Nov 1911, record (1908-12): 93166.

Amanda BACON, age: 87 years, married, death cause: "old age", died in 14th District on 16 May 1912, record (1908-12): 93167.

Atta ARCHER, male, age: 17 years, death cause: "heart failure", died in 14th District on 25 Aug 1911, record (1908-12): 93168.

Hubert SHERFEY, age: 15 years, death cause: "caused by fall", died in 14th District, 24 Jan 1912, record (1908-12): 93169.

Ramon HAMITT, age: 17 months, death cause: "unknown", died in 11th District, __ Sep 1911, record (1908-12): 93170.

Infant CHATMAN, female, lived 2 hours, death cause: "unknown", died in 11th District, 14 Feb 1912, record (1908-12): 93171.

Offie WILBUN, age: 2 weeks, death cause: "consumption of kidneys", died in 11th District, 3 Mar 1912, record (1908-12): 93172.

Virnen TYREE, male, age: 3 days, death cause: "hives", died in 11th District, 22 Mar 1912, record (1908-12): 93173.

Maud WILLIS, age: 27 years, born in Sullivan County, married, death cause: "serofula", died in 11th District, 9 Mar 1912, record (1908-12): 93174.

Zullie NORRIS, age: 3 months, death cause: "spinal trouble", died in 11th District, 2 Apr 1912, record (1908-12): 93175.

Susan MCFALL, age: 60 years, married, death cause: "heart disease", died in 11th District, 20 Mar 1912, record (1908-12): 93176.

W.R. BRUMMITT, age: 47 years, married, death cause: "consumption", died: 11th District, 26 Jun 1912, record (1908-12): 93177.

Syman HOSTON, black, age: 2 months, death cause: "croup", died in Carter County, __ May 1912, record (1908-12): 93178.

Fred MATHERLY, age: 2 years and 8 months, death cause: "consumption of bowels", died in 11th District, 16 Dec 1911, record (1908-12): 93179.

E.D. HALL, age: 64 years, married, death cause: "paralysis", died in 11th District, 28 Apr 1912, record (1908-12): 93180.

Sudie CROUCH, age: about 60 years, death cause: "tumor on bowels", died in 11th District, 14 Nov 1911, record (1908-12): 93181.

J.E. HARLAN, age: 61 years, born in Virginia, married, death cause: "heart trouble", died in 11th District, 10 Jun 1912, record (1908-12): 93182.

Mary FOX, age: 80 years, born in Sullivan County, single, death cause: "fractured hip", died in 11th District, 19 Dec 1911, record (1908-12): 93183.

Daniel SNIDER, age: 92 years, married, death cause: "old age", died in 11th District, 21 Oct 1911, record (1908-12): 93184.

Thomas GALLOWAY, age: 86 years, married, miller, death cause: "old age", died in 11th District, 21 Oct 1911, record (1908-12): 93185.

Elizabeth RIFFY, age: 59 years, married, death cause: "measles", died in 11th District, 4 Apr 1912, record (1908-12): 93186.

Enoch Houston MOODY, lived 9 hours, death cause: not stated, died at Fall Branch, 16 Apr 1910, record (1908-12): 93187.

J.H. FORD, age: 73 years, widower, death cause: "consumption", died in 12th District, 21 May 1912, record (1908-12): 93188.

William SELLS, lived 9 days, death cause: "not known", died in 12th District, 1 Oct 1912, record (1908-12): 93189.

Rose SELLS, lived 9 days, death cause: "unknown", died in 12th District, 1 Oct 1912, record: 93190.

John R. MOHLER, age: 1 month and 27 days, death cause: "measles", died in 12th District, 3 May 1912, record (1908-12): 93191.

Mattie HARRISON, age: 39 years, married, death cause: "gall stone", died in 12th District, 10 Nov 1912, record (1908-12): 93192.

L.H. BACHMAN, age: 89 years, born in Sullivan County, widower, death cause: "general break down", died in 12th District, 5 Aug 1912, record: 93193.

Elizabeth JENKINS, age: 75 years, born in Sullivan County, widow, death cause: "dropsy and heart trouble", died in 12th District, 24 Sep 1911, record (1908-12): 93194.

Sarah PRICE, age: 93 years, widow, death cause: "old age and heart trouble", died in 12th District, 17 Feb 1912, record (1908-12): 93195.

Infant HARRISON, female, lived 9 days, daughter of Daniel HARRISON, death cause: "unknown", died in 12th District, 15 Nov 1911, record (1908-12): 93196.

Margie WATKINS, lived 9 days, death cause: "weakly when born", died in 13th District, 28 Jan 1912, record (1908-12): 93197.

Samuel LUSTES, age: 7 years, born in Greene County, death cause: "pneumonia", died near Leesburg, 30 Dec 1909, record (1908-12): 93198.

Pauline ORRAN, age: 22 months, death cause: "diarrhoea", died in Johnson City, 11 Jun 1912, record (1908-12): 93199.

Porter LACY, age: 16 years, born at Watauga, death cause: "penumonia", died in Johnson City, 6 Feb 1912, record (1908-12): 93200.

Anna M. HUNT, age: 70 years, born at New Bethlehem, PA., married, death cause: "paralysis", died at Johnson City, 27 Jun 1912, record (1908-12): 93201.

Thomas WHITE, colored, age: 82 years, single, death cause: "old age", buried at Abingdon, VA., died: __ May 1912, record (1908-12): 93202.

Phebey CROW, age: 32 years, married, death cause: "dropsy", died in 13th District (record also in 14th District), 22 May 1912, record (1908-12): 93203.

Illegible INFANT, lived 2 days, female, death cause: "unknown", died in 13th District, 12 Jun 1912, record (1908-12): 93204.

Francis E. HARTMAN, age: 6 years, death cause: "tuberculosis", died in 13th District, 26 Feb 1912, record (1908-12): 93205.

G.K. BROWN, age: 80 years, 3 months and 26 days, married, death cause: "cancer of bladder", died in 13th District, 26 Dec 1911, record (1908-12): 93206.

Ollie SISENBERRY, lived 2 days, death cause: "murdered", died in 13th District, 30 Mar 1912, record (1908-12): 93207.

Lula Velma KEYS, age: 6 weeks, death cause: "whooping cough", died in 13th District, 9 Apr 1912, record (1908-12): 93208.

Infant HAWS, male, lived 1 day, son of Frank and Ollie HAWS, death cause: "unknown", died in 13th District, 27 Apr 1912, record (1908-12): 93209.

Johnie M. MCNEIL, age: 3 months, death cause: "unknown", died in 14d, 8 Apr 1912, record: 93210.

Maud M. HALE, age: 24 years, married, death cause: "diarrhoea", died in 10th District, 15 Oct 1911, record (1908-12): 93211.

Elizabeth SWADLEY, age: 62 years, married, cdeath cause: "nervous prostration", died in 10th District, 7 Jul 1911, record (1908-12): 93212.

Clema DAWSON, age: 52 years, born in Carter County, married, death cause: "tuberculosis", died in 10th District, 10 Nov 1911, record (1908-12): 93213.

Niles KEYS, age: 3 months, death cause: "unknown", died in 11d, 27 Mar 1912, record (1908-12): 93214.

Eddie HAMITT, age: 8 years, death cause: "scarlet fever", died in 11d, __ Sep 1911, record: 93215.

A.P. LITTLE, age: 74 years, married, minister, death cause: "heart disease", died in 10th District, 17 Apr 1912, record (1908-12): 93216.

Roscoe MASTERS, age: 8 years, death cause: "pneumonia fever", died in 10th District, 28 Nov 1911, record (1908-12): 93217.

Amos HALE, age: 2 years and 9 monts, death cause: "paralysis", died in 10th District, 6 Mar 1912, record (1908-12): 93218.

Ollie BOUTON, male, age: 19 years, death cause: "brain fever", died in Johnson City, 18 Sep 1912, record (1908-12): 93219.

J.M. CARR, age: 75 years, widower, lumberman, death cause: "bowel and kidney trouble", died in Johnson City, 3 Ju 1912, record (1908-12): 93220.

John MAHONEY, age: not stated, born in Greene County, married, minister, death cause: "dropsy", died at Watauga, 27 Aug 1911, record: 93221.

Mattie B. ST JOHN, age: 69 years, born at Loudin, TN., married, death cause: "heart failure", died at Loudin, 2 May 1912, record (1908-12): 93222.

(illegible) May BLEVINS, age: 11 months, born at Piney Flats, death cause: "indigestion", died at Watauga, 6 Apr 1912, record (1908-12): 93223.

Toy Henry HILTON, age: 14 months, death cause: "measles and whooping cough", died at Johnson City, 23 Apr 1912, record (1908-12): 93224.

Sinde E. MARTIN, age: 23 years, single, death cause: "tuberculosis", died at Johnson City, 12 May 1912, record (1908-12): 93225.

Albert JOHNSON, age: 23 months, death cause: "cholera infantum", died at Johnson City, 14 Jul 1911, record (1908-12): 93226.

Fred COX, age: 7 months, death cause: "heart failure", died in Johnson City, 3 Sep 1911, record (1908-12): 93227.

O.S. BISHOP, age: 23 years, born in Elizabethton, single, death cause: "tuberculosis", died at Johnson City, 15 May 1912, record (1908-12): 93228.

Onida ROBINS, age: 11 years, death cause: "measles", died at Johnson City, 7 Mar 1912, record: 93229.

Martha KINKAID, colored, age: 66 years, married, death cause: "fever", died at Johnson City, 12 Dec 1911, record (1908-12): 93220.

George MILLER, colored, age: 45 years, born at Limestone, married, death cause: "dropsy", died at Johnson City, 7 Jun 1912, record (1908-12): 93231.

Bessie WINSTON, colored, age: 20 years, born in Kentucky, married, death cause: "consumption", died in Johnson City, __ Dec 1911, record: 93232.

Robert WINSTON, colored, age: 3 years, death cause: "consumption", died at Johnson City, __ Dec 1911, record (1908-12): 93233.

Thomas WINSTON, colored, age: 10 years, death cause: "consumption", died at Johnson City, 10 Jul 1911, record (1908-12): 93234.

Alice CHRISTIANBERRY, age: 40 years, married, death cause: "typhoid fever", died at Johnson City, 14 Oct 1911, record (1908-12): 93235.

Ada CHRISTIANBERRY, age: 10 years, death cause: "accidental burn", died at Johnson City, 6 Feb 1912, record (1908-12): 93236.

Clarence ARNETT, age: 2 months, death cause: "unknown", died at Johnson City, 7 Jul 1911, record (1908-12): 93337.

George TUNNELL, age: 50 years, born in Hawkins County, married, death cause: "pleurisy", died in Johnson City, __ Oct 1911, record (1908-12): 93338.

T.O. ALLEN, age: 75 years, born in South Carolina, married, death cause: "heart trouble", died in Johnson City, 3 Feb 1912, record (1908-12): 93339.

Anna MORRIS, colored, age: 20 years, born in Jonesboro, single, death cause: "rheumatism", died in Johnson City, __ Mar 1912, record: 93340.

Bell JOHNSTON, age: 36 years, married, death cause: "rheumatism", died at Johnson City on 6 Jul 1911, record (1908-12): 93241.

Elizabeth WEBSTER, age: 67 years, born in North Carolina, widow, death cause: "consumption", died in Johnson City on 28 Jun 1912, record: 93242.

Mary ELLIS, colored, age: 43 years, born in Virginia, married, death cause: "bronchitis", died in Johnson City on 15 May 1912, record: 93243.

May BAXTER, age: 8 years, death cause: "consumption", died in Johnson City on 5 Mar 1912, record (1908-12): 93244.

Gladys ELLIS, age: 4 years, death cause: "scaofula", died in Johnson City on 19 Feb 1912, record: 93245.

Lucy MORELAND, colored, age: 76 years, born in Carter County, single, died in Johnson City on 7 Nov 1911, record (1908-12): 93246.

Sallie CARRIER, age: 1 years and 6 months, born at Milligan, death cause: "measles", died at Johnson City on 10 Oct 1911, record (1908-12): 93247.

Nellie BURKET, age: 4 months, death cause: "whooping cough", died at Johnson City on 12 May 1912, record (1908-12): 93248.

Pearl JENKINS, age: 30 years, born in North Carolina, married, death cause: "tuberculosis", died at Johnson City on 22 Apr 1912, record: 93249.

Joe MALONEE, age: 1 week, death cause: "jaundice", died in Johnson City on 3 Jun 1912, record: 93250.

Infant MALONEE, male, death cause: "stillborn", died in Johnson City on 23 May 1912, record: 93251.

Ruth HOSS, age: 2 years and 3 months, death cause: "bowel trouble", died in Johnson City on 10 Aug 1911, record (1908-12): 93252.

John ALMANY, age: 58 years, born in Bulff City, married, death cause: "consumption of bowels", died in Johnson City on 4 Apr 1912, record: 93253.

James MARTIN, age: 3 years, death cause: "consumption", died in Johnson City on 29 Feb 1912, record (1908-12): 93254.

Carrie DESANTES, age: 19 years, married, death cause: "killed by train", died in Johnson City on 1 Jun 1912, record (1908-12): 93255.

John A. DYER, age: 22 years, born in Maryland, single, death cause: "heart failure", died in Johnson City on 26 Apr 1912, record: 93256.

Infant ARWOOD, female, death cause: "stillborn", child of Frank ARWOOD, died in Johnson City on 24 Jan 1912, record (1908-12): 93257.

John H. LONG, age: 6 months, death cause: "stomach trouble", died in Johnson City on 7 Jul 1911, record (1908-12): 93258.

Walter MURRAY, colored, age: 40 years, born in Morristown, married, death cause: "consumption", died in Johnson City on 4 Apr 1912, record: 93259.

Cilbert ALFRED, age: 11 days, death cause: "heart disease", died in Johnson City on 13 Jun 1912, record (1908-12): 93260.

Marcella Lee HINCHMAN, born: 25 Sep 1913 in Kentucky, parents: Walton Lee HINCHMAN (W.VA) and Kate MILLER, death cause: "dyspensia", informant: Walter HINCHMAN (Johnson City), buried: Miller Cemetery, died: 24 Jan 1914, record (1914): 44.

Isaac N. TYREE, born: 4 Feb 1914, parents: Nick TYREE (VA) and Belle PENIX, death cause: "yellow jaundice", informant: father (Johnson City), died: 5 Feb 1914, record (1914): 43.

Johnathan CLEEK, age: 77 years, widower, parents: not stated, death cause: not stated, died: 6th District on 9 Jan 1914, record (1914): 42.

Adam C. FOX, born: __ Aug 1837, widower, retired physician, parents: Daniel FOX (VA) and Anna PORTER, death cause: "lagrippe and old age", died: 12d on 13 Jan 1914, record (1914): 41.

William OWENS, born: 10 Jan 1830, single, parents: not stated, death cause: "senile debility", informant: W.H. JONES (Jonesboro), buried: Bethesda Cemetery, died: 14 Jan 1914, record (1914): 40.

Alfred M. CROUCH, born: 28 Feb 1826, widower, parents: James CROUCH and Susanna BOWMAN, death cause: "heart failure, uremia", informant: Dr. J.L. CLARK (Jonesboro), buried: Boones Creek, died: 18 Jan 1914, record (1914): 39.

Infant DURHAM, female, born: 4 Jan 1914, parents: Thomas DURHAM (NC) and Adah (illegible), death cause: "lagrippe", informant: Dr. F.T. MASSINGILL (Jonesboro), buried: Boones Creek, died: 5 Jan 1914, record (1914): 38.

S. GREENLEE, black, age: 56 years, single, parents: not stated, death cause: "parlaysis", informant: Eli STANTON (Jonesboro), buried: County Farm, died: 30 Jan 1914, record (1914): 37.

Mrs. Annie HODGE, born: __ Jan 1888 in Carter County, married, parents: Milburn LEWIS (Carter Co.) and Nancy GARLAND (Carter Co.), death cause: "tuberculosis", informant: J.S. HODGE (Jonesboro), died: 12th District, buried: Carter County, died: 26 Jan 1914, record (1914): 36.

George IRWIN, black, age: 70 years, born in North Carolina, widower, parents: not stated, death cause: "heart disease", informant: Eli STANTON (Jonesboro), buried: County Farm, died: 18 Jan 1914, record: 35.

Monroe NEATHERLAND, black, age: about 22 years, single, parents: not stated, death cause: "heart disease, rheumatism", buried: County Farm, died: 15 Jan 1914, record (1914): 34.

Elsie May BEACH, born: 28 Aug 1906 in Iowa, parents: John BEACH and Daisy FURCHES (Watauga County, NC), death cause: "clothing caught fire, burns", informant: M.S. FURCHES, Columbus, Iowa, died: 14 Jan 1914, record (1914): 33.

Martin Mathias LOCKNER, age: 93 years, born in Germany, married, minor, parents: not stated, death cause: "old age", died: 6th District on 9 Jan 1914, record (1914): 32.

Lulie SHOWMAN, born: 24 Dec 1893, single, parents: John M. SHOWMAN (Greene County) and Elizabeth SALTS, death cause: "pulmonary tuberculosis", informant: father (Limestone), died: 31 Jan 1914, record: 31.

Sarah Matilda KEYS, born: 10 Nov 1843, married, parents: William WALKER and Mary BROWN, death cause: "pulmonary tuberculosis", informant: W.H. KEYS (Jonesboro), buried: Pleasant Grove, died: 17 Jan 1914, record (1914): 30.

Mary M. CARMACK, age; 78 years, born at Paperville, married, parents: W.L. RUDER and mother not stated, death cause: "broncho pneumonia", informant: Thomas FERGUSON (Jonesboro), buried: Leesburg, died: 27 Jan 1914, record (1914): 29.

Infant WALKER, male, parents: Henry H. WALKER and Addie HUNT, death cause: "stillborn", informant: father (Jonesboro), buried: Sulphur Springs, died: 30 Jan 1914, record (1914): 28.

Joseph BACON, age: 68 years, married, parents: Johnathon BACON and mother not stated, death cause: "apoplexy, cerebral hemorrhage", informant: John C. BACON, Jr.(Fall Branch), died: 21 Jan 1914, record (1914): 27.

Ethel BLEDSOW, colored, born: 27 Jan 1894, married, parents: Mose MORRIS (GA) and Mary GREEN, death cause: "(illegible) following childbirth", informant: Ella MORRIS (Johnson City), buried: Fariview Cemetery, died: 9 Jan 1914, record: 26.

Joseph SMITH alias James H. CARR, age: 68 years, born in Canada, old veteran, parents: not stated, death cause: "intestinal nephritis", died at

Soldier's Home, buried: Pineville, KY., died: 18 Jan 1914, record (1914): 25.

Infant DAVIDSON, colored, female, parents: James DAVIDSON (NC) and Lizzie HARDIN (NC), death cause: "stillborn", buried: West Lawn Cemetery, died: 19 Jan 1914, record (1914): 23.

Infant GARDNER, colored, female, parents: Isaac GARDNER and mother's name illegible, death cause: "premature birth", died in Johnson City on 8 Jan 1914, record (1914): 22.

Selma HORTON, colored, born: 6 May 1892 in North Carolina, parents: John HORTON (NC) and Idline SLUDER (NC), death cause: "influenza", buried: West Lawn Cemetery, died in Johnson City on 23 Jan 1914, record (1914): 20.

J.S. JENNINGS, age: 77 years, married, retired minister, parents: not stated, death cause: "heart failure", died at Indian Springs on 14 Jan 1914, record (1914): 19.

Carl WHITLOCK, age: 29 years, 1 month and 14 days, born in Jefferson City, married, parents: Pleasant Franklin WHITLOCK (Granger County) and Octavia S. HULL (Granger County), death cause: "asphixia", informant: W.F. KIPPLING (Johnson City), buried: Oak Hill, died: 23 Jan 1914, record (1914): 18.

Infant LOVELACE, male, parents: Pat LOVELACE (NC) and (illegible) MORRIS, death cause: "premature birth", informant: father (Jonesboro), buried: Buena Vista, died: 25 Jan 1914, record (1914): 17.

Tennessee BOWLING, female, born: 11 Apr 1866, married, parents: J.B. BOWLING and Jane MILLER, death cause: "operation for cancer", informant: J.W. BOWLING (Roan Mountain), buried: Roan Mountain, died: 29 Jan 1914, record (1914): 16.

Sarah Elizabeth BARNES, born: 5 Jun 1841, widow, parents: Henry SAYLOR and mother not stated, death cause: "tuberculosis", informant: Charles BARNES (Johnson City), buried: Barnes Cemetery, died: 29 Jan 1914, record (1914): 15.

William H. ABEL, age: 70 years, born in Pennsylvania, widower, parents: not stated, death cause: "general peritonitis", buried: Soldier's

Home, died: Soldier's Home on 1 Jan 1914, record (1914): 13.

Mark E. SWENEY, age: 50 years, born in Missouri, married, parents: not stated, death cause: "pulmonary tuberculosis", died: Soldier's Home, 4 Jan 1914, record (1914): 12.

John C. RAYMOND, age: 76 years, born in Wisconsin, single, death cause: "lobar pneumonia", died: Soldier's Home, 4 Jan 1914, record (1914): 11.

Joseph S. PARKER, age; 75 years, born in Massachusetts, single, parents: not stated, death cause: "nephritis", died: Soldier's Home, 23 Jan 1914, record (1914): 10.

Thomas M. ALLEN, age: 77 years, born in New York, married, parents: not stated, died: Soldier's Home on 24 Jan 1914, record (1914): 9.

William FLECK, age: 81 years, born in New York, single, parents: not stated, death cause: "pulmonary tuberculosis", died: Soldier's Home on 28 Jan 1914, record (1914): 8.

Annie HOLDEN, born: 11 Apr 1886, married, parents: Finley MCQUEEN (Carter County) and Elizabeth WAGNER (Carter County), death cause: "tuberculosis", buried: Butler, TN., died: 14 Jan 1914, record (1914): 7.

Lucinda SCOTT, born: 6 Aug 1866 in North Carolina, married, parents: Hugh HARMAN (NC) and mother not stated, death cause: "pellagra", informant: Will SCOTT (Johnson City), buried: Milligan, died: 14 Jan 1914, record (1914): 6.

Sallie E. ONKS, age: 45 years, married, parents: Frank HENSON and mother not stated, death cause: "nephritis", buried: Onks Cemetery, died: 13 Jan 1913, record (1914): 5.

John STOUT, born: 22 Sep 1912, parents: J.B. STOUT (NC) and Nettie CARLTON (NC), death cause: "burns", informant: father (Johnson City), buried: Slagle Cemetery, died: 12 Jan 1914, record (1914): 4.

Eliza MILLER, born: 6 May 1821, widow, parents: Jacob RANGE and Susan RANGE, death cause: "anemia of brain and old age", buried: Oak Hill Cemetery, died: 7 Jan 1914, record (1914): 3.

Alexander HOWELL, age: 69 years, born in Kentucky, single, parents: not stated, death cause: "gangrene", died: Soldier's Home, buried: Philadelphia, PA., died: 4 Jan 1914, record: 2.

Lizzie DAVENPORT, colored, born: 28 Dec 1911, parents: Judge DAVENPORT and Emma KINDLE (NC), death cause: "convulsions", informant: father (Johnson City), buried: Hyder Cemetery, died: 5 Jan 1914, record (1914): 1.

Frederick STEINLEIN, age: 77 years, born in Germany, widower, parents: not stated, death cause: "influenza", died: Soldier's Home, 2 Feb 1914, record (1914): 42.

John BELL, age: 71 years, widower, parents: not stated, death cause: "carcinoma of groin", died: Soldier's Home, 1 Feb 1914, record (1914): 43.

Hiram STEVENS, age: not stated, born: New York, widower, parents: not stated, death cause: "cardiac dilitation", died: Soldier's Home, 31 Jan 1914, record (1914): 44.

Henry MILLER, age: 74 years, born in Germany,, old veteran, widower, parents: not stated, death cause: "lobar pneumonia", died: Soldier's Home, 22 Feb 1914, buried: Brooklyn, NY., record (1914): 45.

Josiah A. RUDDERSON, age: 71 years, single, old veteran, parents: not stated, death cause: "cerabral hemorrhage", died: Soldier's Home, 22 Feb 1914, buried: Morristown, record (1914): 46.

Robert Aubria PURCELL, born: 30 Jan 1914, parents: J.C. PURCELL and Nora D. ARCHER, death cause: "pneumonia", buried: Pleasant Valley, died: 21 Feb 1914, record (1914): 47.

Craig GARRON, born: 5 Feb 1914, parents: Curtis GARRON (Ashville) and Fannie BACON, death cause: illegible, buried: Oak Hill Cemetery, died: Johnson City, 20 Feb 1914, record (1914): 48.

Warren P. BECKELHIMER, born: 10 Aug 1895, single, parents: W.D. BECKELHIMER (Jiles County, VA) and Henrietta Vance BECKELHIMER (Washington County, VA), death cause: "Brights disease", buried: Buna Vista, Johnson City, died: 20 Feb 1914, record (1914): 49.

Infant VINES, female, parents: D.A. VINES and Mable JACKSON, death cause: "six months", informant: father (Johnson City), born/died: 17 Feb 1914, record (1914): 50.

Lizzie DAVIDSON, colored, age: 36 years, 6 months and 1 day, born in South Carolina, married, parents: (illegible) HARDEN (SC) and mother not stated, death cause: "confinement and syptic infection", informant: J.A. DAVIDSON (Johnson City), buried: West Lawn, died: 16 Feb 1914, record (1914): 51.

Dick CARSON, colored, age: 3 years, 1 month and 24 days, born in North Carolina, parents: James CARSON (NC) and Janie PARTRUM (NC), death cause: "nephritis", informant: father (Johnson City), buried: West Lawn, died: 12 Feb 1914, record: 52.

Mrs. Sarah MCPEAK, age: 58 years, born: __ Jul 1858, married, parents: John PRICHARD and Mary PRICHARD, death cause: "pneumonia", died: Johnson City, 5 Feb 1914, buried: Boones Creek, record (1914): 53.

Charles GODSEY, colored, age: 47 years, born in Russell County, VA, married, parents: Andrew GODSEY and mother not stated, death cause: "pulmonary tuberculosis", informant: Daisey GODSEY (Johnson City), buried: West Lawn, died: 9 Feb 1914, record (1914): 54.

John GODSEY, colored, born: 10 Feb 1912, parents: Charles GODSEY (VA) and Daisey LOUDERBOCK, death cause: "meningitis, pneumonia", informant: Alex AYERS (Johnson City), buried: West Lawn, died: 2 Feb 1914, record (1914): 55.

George Baline RIDDLE, born: 9 Jan 1913, parents: John RIDDLE and Rebecca HARRIS, death cause: "measles", informant: Foster WILSON (Johnson City), buried: McKinly Cemetery, died: 2 Feb 1914, record (1914): 56.

Worley Howard SMITH, born: 8 Jan 1014, parents: Creed SMITH (Hawkins County) and Nellie LADY (Sullivan County), death cause: "probably congenital syphilis", informant: father (Johnson City), buried: Oak Hill, died: 2 Feb 1914, record (1914): 57.

Vernilie WHITE, age: 78 years, single, parents: J. STOSMER and mother not stated, death cause:

"pneumonia", informant: G.W. WHITE (Jonesboro), buried: White Cemetery, died: 21 Feb 1914, record (1914): 58.

Jackson L. CROSS, age: 84 years, born in Sullivan County, parents: Abraham __ and __ GITT, death cause: "influenza, general debility", informant: J.H. CROSS (Jonesboro), died: 17 Feb 1914, record (1914): 59.

Vollie LEONARD, male, born: 16 Jul 1893, single, parents: Isaac LEONARD and Florence MILLION, death cause: "blood poison", informant: Louiza LEONARD (Jonesboro), buried: Boones Creek, died: 23 Feb 1914, record (1914): 60.

William E. COMBS, born: 22 Feb 1859, married, parents: Elijah COMBS and mother not stated, death cause: "lagrippe and pneumonia", informant: E.J. COMBS (Jonesboro), buried: Bethany Cemetery, died: 28 Feb 1914, record (1914): 61.

Elbert Marion CANNON, born: 12 Dec 1854, married, parents: Patrick CANNON (Afton) and Catherine CLICK (Afton), death cause: "heart disease", died: 1st District on 9 Feb 1914, buried: Liberty Cemetery, record (1914): 62.

Margaret Lanise SHIELDS, born: 11 Jun 1841, single, parents: John C. SHIELDS and Nancy SHIELDS, death cause: "carcinoma of stomach", informant: Sam W. SHIELDS (Jonesboro), buried: Philadelphia, died: 15 Feb 1914, record (1914): 63.

Harvy BROYLES, born: 11 Jun 1845, married, parents: Jackson BROYLES and mother not stated, death cause: "heart disease", informant: Amanda WALTER (Chucky), buried: Philadelphia, died: 17 Feb 1914, record (1914): 64.

Hubert VAUGHN, born: 28 Nov 1899, invalid, parents: David VAUGHN and Mary LANE, death cause: "chronic spinal trouble", informant: Jake FERGUSON (Jonesboro), buried: Cherokee Cemetery, died: 8 Feb 1914, record (1914): 65.

Anna HILBERT, born: 15 Nov 1900, parents: Jake HILBERT and Minnie BACON, death cause: "heart trouble all her life", informant: father

(Jonesboro), buried: Boones Creek, died: 25 Feb 1911, record (1914): 66.

Henry C. HUFFMAN, born: 12 Jun 1859 in Virginia, married, parents: H. (illegible) HUFFMAN (VA) and Josephine WILKINS (VA), death cause: "lobar pneumonia", informant: J.D. HUFFMAN (Telford), buried: Washington College, died: 27 Jan 1914, record (1914): 67.

Ester L. NICHOLS, born: __ Aug 1828, in New York, widow, parents: not stated, death cause: "paralysis", informant: Alice HULBERT (Johnson City), died: 24 Feb 1914, record (1914): 68.

Edward GILLIGAN, age: 48 years, born in Canada, single, parents: not stated, death cause: "pulmonary tuberculosis", died: Soldier's Home on 22 Feb 1914, record (1914): 69.

Edgar H. COOPER, age: 76 years, born in Vermont, married, parents: not stated, death cause: "mitral insufficiency", died: Soldier's Home on 14 Feb 1914, record (1914): 70.

Ira A. NICHOLS, age: 71 years, born in New York, parents: not stated, death cause: "pulmonary tuberculosis", died: Soldier's Home on 21 Feb 1914, record (1914): 71.

Walker THOMASON, black, age: 85 years, born in Kentucky, single, parents: not stated, death cause: "cardiac dilitation", died: Soldier's Home on 28 Feb 1914, record (1914): 72.

John MCEVOY, age: 55 years, born in Ireland, widower, parents: not stated, death cause: "nephritis", died: Soldier's Home on 15 Feb 1914, record (1914): 73.

Hugh B. MERWIN, age: 68 years, born in Pennsylvania, single, parents: not stated, death cause: "pulmonary tuberculosis", died at Soldier's Home on 12 Feb 1914, record: 74.

Thomas MULLINS, age: 77 years, born in Ireland, single, parents: not stated, death cause: "angina pectoris", died: Soldier's Home on 9 Feb 1914, record (1914): 75.

Vincent VALENTINE, age: 68 years, born in Maryland, single, parents: not stated, death cause: "acute alcoholism", died: Soldier's Home on 2 Feb 1914, record (1914): 76.

Infant ANDERSON, male, parents: Joseph M. ANDERSON and Sarah SEATON, death cause: "stillborn", informant: father (Telford), born/died: 19 Mar 1914, record (1914): 77.

Infant BASHOR, female, parents: Orsa BASHOR and Louise SPEARS (Greene County), death cause: "stillborn", informant: father (Washington College), died: 3 Mar 1914, record (1914): 78.

Henry E. BOWMAN, born: 18 Sep 1875 in Greene County, single, parents: Sparling BOWMAN (Green Co) and Caroline MORELOCK (Green Co), death cause: "influenza and paralysis", informant: father (Rt 4, Johnson City), buried: Greene County, died: 8 Apr 1914, record (1914): 79.

Fannie Whitlock TUCKER, born: 30 Jul 1895, single, parents: S.S. TUCKER and Lina MILLER, death cause: "pulmonary tuberculosis", informant: mother (Telford), died: 9 Mar 1914, record (1914): 80.

Shelton KEEFAUVER, born: 18 Oct 1840, married, parents: Nicholas KEEFAUVER and Dice BACON, death cause: "paralysis", informant: John KEEFAUVER (Jonesboro), buried: Pleasant Valley, died: 3 Mar 1914, record (1914): 81.

Roland G. ZIMMERMAN, born: 24 Mar 1852 in Sullivan County, married, parents: Samuel ZIMMERMAN (Germany) and Sallie HAMILTON, death cause: "lobar pneumonia", informant: Sarah W. ZIMMERMAN (Jonesboro), buried: Greenwood Cemetery, died: 4 Mar 1914, record: 82.

Henry C. JACKSON, born: 2 Feb 1847, single, parents: A.E. JACKSON (Philadelphia, PA) and Sarafine TAYLOR (Carter County), death cause: "hemiplegia", informant: Phil S. TAYLOR (Jonesboro), died: 30 Mar 1914, record (1914): 83.

Charles F. DECKER, born: 4 Apr 1832 in Baden Germany, widower, potter, parents: not stated, death cause: "bronchial pneumonia", informmant: R.H. DECKER (Jonesboro), died: 11 Mar 1914, record: 84.

Edith Garture LEE, colored, born: 13 Oct 1899, parents: Benton LEE (VA) and Katie GRIMES (NC), death cause: "diabetes", died: 6th District on 20 Mar 1914, record (1914): 85.

Robert P. SPENCER, age: 78 years, born in Virginia, widower, parents: Walker SPENCER (VA) and Eliza BIBB (VA), death cause: "grippe, asthma, heart trouble", died at Johnson City on 21 Mar 1914, record: 86.

C.F. WILSON, male, age: not stated, born: Cranberry, NC., parents: not stated, death cause: "extensive burns", buried: Cranberry, NC., died: 19 Mar 1914, record (1914): 87.

Michael MCMANCES, age: 70 years, widower, old veteran, death cause: "acute alcoholism", died: Soldier's Home on 17 Mar 1914, buried: Wilmington, Deleware, record (1914): 88.

Infant KILGORE, male, parents: Thomas KILGORE and Virgie MUSE, death cause: "premature birth", informant: father (Johnson City), born/died: 18 Mar 1914, buried: Whitesburg, TN., record (1914): 89.

George HALE, colored, born: 12 Sep 1864, married, parents: not stated, death cause: "dropsy", died Johnson City, buried: West Lawn Cemetery, died: 14 Mar 1914, record (1914): 90.

Nancy ROLLIN, colored, age: 67 years, born in North Carolina, widow, death cause: "peritonitis", informant: Mary CARSON, daughter (Johnson City), buried: West Lawn, died: 12 Mar 1914, record: 91.

Mrs. Emma KINDLE, born: 31 Dec 1861 in Gaston County, NC., married, parents: Adam WEBBER (NC) and Betsy ROBERTSON (NC), death cause: "dropsy", died in Johnson City on 8 Mar 1914, record (1914): 92.

James William CARRELL, born: 2 Nov 1913, parents: Charles CARRELL and Lizzie EDWARDS (Erwin), death cause: "convulsions", informant: father (Johnson City), buried: Onks Cemetery, died: 8 Mar 1914, record (1914): 93.

Mary Lee JONES, born: 4 Mar 1914, parents: J.P. JONES (Unicoi) and Marthy M. JONES (Unicoi), death cause: "hemorrhage from stomach", buried: Greeneville, died: 6 Mar 1914, record (1914): 94.

Galdis J. PHILLIPS, born: 8 Jan 1914, parents: W.L. PHILLIPS (Yancey County, NC) and Florence CHRISTIE, death cause: "broncho pneumonia", buried: Austin Springs, died: 6 Mar 1914, record (1914): 95.

George EVANS, age: 40 years, born in Virginia, married, parents: Perry EVANS (VA) and Nancy FIELDS (Russell County, VA), death cause: "leukemia", buried: Buena Vista Cemetery, died: 4 Mar 1914, record (1914): 96.

Infant RAY, female, colored, parents: Burnas GRINDSTAFF and Edith RAY, death cause: "premature", informant: Edith RAY (Johnson City), buried: West Lawn Cemetery, born/died: 4 Mar 1914, record: 97.

William Albert THOMPSON, colored, age: 3 months, born in North Carolina, parents: John THOMPSON (NC) and Cora HALL (NC), death cause: "neglect and pneumonia", informant: H.N. HALE (Johnson City), buried: West Lawn, died: 4 Mar 1914, record: 98.

Benjamin MILLER, age: 72 years, born in Ohio, single, coal miner, parents: not stated, death cause: "pulmonary tuberculosis", died: Soldier's Home on 4 Mar 1914, record (1914): 99.

Charles FRANK, age: 74 years, born in Germany, widower, shoe maker, parents: not stated, death cause: "nephritis", died: Soldier's Home on 4 Mar 1914, record (1914): 100.

Albert H. BISBING, age: 72 years, born in Pennsylvania, widower, parents: not stated, death cause: "hemiplegia", died: Soldier's Home on 3 Mar 1914, record (1914): 101.

Edward LAPMAN, age: 72 years, born in Connecticut, single, parents: not stated, death cause: "pneumonia", died: Soldier's Home on 4 Mar 1914, record (1914): 102.

William SWANER, born: 15 Mar 1865, married, parents: Amos SWANER and Katherine BANKS, death cause: "heart disease", informant: Dilet SWANER (Johnson City), buried: Buena Vista Cemetery, died: 26 Mar 1914, record (1914): 103.

William H. HYDER, born: 1 Apr 1859, married, parents: John HYDER and Martha HAYNES, death cause: "pulmonary tuberculosis", informant: Mrs. William HYDER (Johnson City), buried: Happy Valley, died: 24 Mar 1914, record (1914): 104.

Henry H. CARR, born: 29 Nov 1839, lawyer, married, parents: Alford CARR and Elizabeth KING, death cause: "carcinoma . (illegible)", informant: Paul B. CARR (Johnson City), buried: Oak Hill Cemetery, died: 24 Mar 1914, record (1914): 105.

Mattie E. CURTIS, born: 28 Mar 1860, married, parents: Smith HALE and Caroline TOPPIN, death cause: "heart disease", informant: James CURTIS (Johnson City), buried: Oak Hill, died: 22 Mar 1914, record (1914): 106.

Richman CARBLEY, age: 74 years, born in Ohio, widower, parents: Newton CARBLEY (Ohio) and Hulda CROSLEY (Ohio), death cause: "nephritis", died: 9th District, buried: Chattanooga, died: 19 Mar 1914, record (1914): 107.

Jiles ELSWICK, age: 73 years, born in Virginia, widower, parents: father not stated, and Martha ELIOTT (VA), death cause: "pellagra", died: Johnson City, buried: Shipley Cemetery, died: 29 Mar 1914, record (1914): 108.

William Jackson LACY, parents: James A. LACY and Nannie FEATHERS (Carter County), death cause: "premature birth", died: 9th District, buried: Watauga, died: 28 Mar 1914, record (1914): 109.

Nathaniel A. THOMPKINS, age: 75 years, widower, parents: not stated, death cause: "traumatism from railroad accident", died: Soldier's Home on 26 Mar 1914, record (1914): 110.

George W. DIPPLE, age: 71 years, born in New York, single, parents: not stated, death cause: "cystitis", died: Soldier's Home, 24 Mar 1914, record (1914): 111.

George W. BINNIX, age: 70 years, born in Maryland, married, parents: not stated, death cause: "mitral insufficiency", died: Soldier's Home, 20 Mar 1914, record (1914): 113.

George H. HOLMES, age: 46 years, married, single, death cause: "pulmonary tuberculosis", died: Soldier's Home, 20 Mar 1914, record (1914): 112.

Thomas WILSON, age: 70 years, born in Kentucky, single, parents: not stated, death cause:

"hemiplegia", died: Soldier's Home, 15 Mar 1914, record (1914): 114.

Robert W. JACK, age: 44 years, born in Virginia, single, coal miner, parents: not stated, death cause: "pulmonary tuberculosis", died: Soldier's Home, 10 Mar 1914, record (1914): 115.

John EICKHORN, age: 79 years, born in Germany, widower, butcher, death cause: "mitral insufficiency", died: Soldier's Home, 7 Mar 1914, record (1914): 116.

Matthew, DONOHUE, age: 72 years, born in Pennsylvania, widower, death cause: "mitral insufficiency", died: Soldier's Home, 5 Mar 1914, record (1914): 117.

A.W. BROOKS, born: 19 Dec 1851 in Unicoi, married, parents: David BROOKS (Unicoi) and Nancy MILLER, death cause: "paralysis", informant: Mose BROOKS (Jonesboro), buried: Simpson Cemetery, died: 25 Mar 1914, record (1914): 118.

Infant CLOYD, male, born: 28 Feb 1914, parents: Joe CLOYD and Annie POORE, death cause: not stated, informant: Lizzie CAMPBELL, died: 1st District, 19 Mar 1914, record (1914): 119.

Ira BROYLES, born: 20 Sep 1852, married, parents: Jackson BROYLES and mother not stated, death cause: "paralysis", informant: Walter GOURLEY (Chuckey), buried: Philadelphia, died: 14 Mar 1914, record (1914): 120.

Philip Parks TINKER, born: 23 Nov 1831, married, parents: James TINKER and Nancy PARKS, death cause: "nephritis", informant: Jake TINKER (Jonesboro), died: 10 Mar 1914, record (1914): 121.

Annie PAINTER, age: 68 years, 7 months and 10 days, married, parents: Wilson MOORE and Mary GANN, death cause: "hepatic cirrhosis", informant: Jake DUNCAN (Jonesboro), buried: Liberty Cemetery, died: 12 Mar 1914, record (1914): 122.

Nathan Elijah CRAWFORD, born: 25 Jan 1841 in Greene County, married, parents: Jake CRAWFORD (Greene Co) and Elizabeth ENGLISH (Greene Co), death cause: "heart trouble", buried: Pleasant Vale, died: Limestone on 21 Mar 1914, record (1914): 123.

Infant GOOD, male, born: 8 Mar 1914, parents: Charley GOOD and __ HAMMET, death cause: not stated, informant: John CHATMAN (Jonesboro), buried: Boones Creek, died: 12 Mar 1914, record (1914): 124.
Fannie CURTIS, age: 70 years, married, parents: Chinouth HALE and Nancy CHASE, death cause: "gastritis", informant: A.C. CURTIS (Jonesboro), buried: Hales Chapel, died: 12 Mar 1914, record (1914): 125.
Infant MILBURN, male, parents: George MILBURN and Annie (illegible), death cause: "stillborn", informant: father (Jonesboro), buried: Buffalo Ridge, born/died: 30 Mar 1914, record (1914): 126.
James PAINTER, born: 12 Oct 1895, single, parents: John W. PAINTER (Sullivan County) and Jennie E. MCCRARY, death cause: "abdominal tuberculosis", informant: J.W. PAINTER (Fall Branch), died: 1 Apr 1914, record (1914): 127.
Infant MILLER, colored, male, lived 8 hours, parents: Fleming MILLER and Clara JOHNSON, death cause: "premature birth", informant: father (Johnson City), buried: West Lawn Cemetery, died: 28 Apr 1914, record (1914): 128.
William H. CARRIER, born: 26 Jan 1838, widower, cooper, parents: Thomas CARRIER (VA) and Malinda HATCHER (VA), death cause: "cerebral hemorrhage", informant: R.R. CARRIER (Johnson City), buried: Hughes Cemetery, died: 29 Apr 1914, record: 129.
Patel Eugene JACKSON, born: 2 Nov 1913, parents: Arbel JACKSON (NC) and Eugenie CANTER, death cause: "meningitis", informant: father (Johnson City), buried: Oak Hill, died: 30 Apr 1914, record: 130.
William SANFORD, age: 53 years, born in Washington, D.C., single, parents: not stated, death cause: "mitral insufficiency", died: Soldier's Home, 1 Apr 1914, record (1914): 131.
Henry HANDROP, age: 71 years, born in Iowa, widower, parents: not stated, death cause: "mitral insufficiency", died: Soldier's Home, 9 Apr 1914, record (1914): 132.
Charles BURNSIDES, age: 78 years, born in Pennsylvania, single, parents: not stated, death

cause: "choleithiosis", died: Soldier's Home, 14 Apr 1914, record (1914): 133.

Prescott, MCMINDES, age: 72 years, born in New York, married, parents: not stated, death cause: "mitral insufficiency", died: Soldier's Home, 22 Apr 1914, record (1914): 134.

Levi J. SMITH, age: 71 years, widower, parents: not stated, death cause: "mitral insufficiency", died: Soldier's Home, 28 Mar 1914, record (1914): 135.

Albert KERNICK, age: 58 years, born in Austria, widower, parents: not stated, death cause: "nephritis", died: Soldier's Home, died: 29 Mar 1914, record (1914): 136.

Henry DUNHAM, age: 72 years, born: New York, single, parents: not stated, death cause: "nephritis", died: Soldier's Home, 30 Apr 1914, record (1914): 137.

Infant DEARMOND, male, parents: J.G. DEARMOND (LA) and Nannie LOVELL, death cause: "born dead", informant: father (Johnson City), buried: Oak Hill, died: 10 Apr 1914, record: 138.

George D. HOUSTON, born: 30 Aur 1865 in Sullivan County, married, parents: John W. HOUSTON (Sullivan Co) and Ruth WEBB (Sullivan Co), death cause: "both legs crushed by train", informant: E.S. WOLFE (Johnson City), buried: Bluff City, died: 11 Apr 1914, record (1914): 139.

Rush WILLIAMS, colored, age: 18 years, single, parents: not stated, death cause: illegible, buried: West Lawn Cemetery, died: 9th District on 12 Apr 1914, record: 140.

Kathryn RILEY, born: 19 Oct 1888, single, parents: Peter RILEY (Ireland) and Nannie DARDY (VA), death cause: "pulmonary tuberculosis", died: Johnson City, 15 Apr 1914, record (1914): 141.

Hesikiah LITTLE, born: 12 May 1845, married, parents: John LITTLE and Ruth BOREING, death cause: "heart disease, dropsy", informant: Mrs. LITTLE (Johnson City), buried: Loves Cemetery, died: 13 Apr 1914, record (1914): 142.

Infant SILVERS, female, parents: William SILVERS (Romania) and Annie STRAUSS (Rusha), death cause: "stillborn", informant: father (Johnson City), buried: Jewish Cemetery, died: 17 Apr 1914, record (1914): 143.

Aluby Herman BROYLES, born: 17 Dec 1883, married, lumberman, parents: William BROYLES and Mollie SEATON, death cause: "pneumonia", informant: Herman HARRISON (Johnson City), buried: Chuckey, died: 17 Apr 1914, record (1914): 144.

Robert Owen MAUPIN, born: 22 May 1913, parents: Willis MAUPIN and Bessie BLEVINS, death cause: "pneumonia", informant: father (Rt. 5, Johnson City), buried: Blevins Cemetery, died: 17 Apr 1914, record (1914): 145.

Henry L. DAVENPORT, Negro, age: 42 years, born in North Carolina, married, parents: Richard DAVENPORT (NC) and L. STEELE (NC), death cause: "bronchitis, pneumonia", informant: Bradis HORTON (Johnson City), buried: West Lawn, died: 18 Apr 1914, record: 146.

Daniel H. BAILEY, born: 28 Jul 1900, parents: George B. BAILEY and Cora L. TIPTON (VA), death cause: "heart disease", died: Johnson City, 20 Apr 1914, buried: Buna Vista, record (1914): 147.

Albert MILLER, born: 20 Apr 1911, parents: A.S. MILLER (Sullivan County) and Lucy FURGERSON (VA), death cause: "toxemia, gastro intestinal", informant: W.H. MILLER (Johnson City), buried: Oak Hill Cemetery, died: 21 Apr 1914, record: 148.

Matilda E. HICKS, born: 20 Feb 1846 in Virginia, widow, parents: John J. WHITKER (VA) and Elizabeth HURST (VA), death cause: "lagrippe", informant: E.W. WHITKER (Bristol, VA), buried: Oak Hill, died: 22 Apr 1914, record (1914): 149.

Emaline OVERSTREET, born: 12 Mar 1820 in Tennessee, married, parents: __ OVERSTREET and Pollie GLOVER, death cause: "asthma and age", informant: Parley SOUTH (Johnson City), buried: Slagel Cemetery, , died: 20 Apr 1914, record (1914): 150.

Sallie GARDNER, colored, age: 48 years, born in North Carolina, widow, parents: Thomas RAY (NC) and Harriet RAY (NC), death cause: "pulmonary tuberculosis", informant: Charles GARDNER (Johnson City), buried: West Lawn, died: 27 Apr 1914, record (1914): 151.

Mrs. Belle HALE, born: 3 Oct 1873, married, parents: Thomas SAYLOR and Ellen BORING, death cause: "nephritis", informant: John HALE (Johnson City), died: Oak Hill, 27 Apr 1914, record (1914): 152.

Myrtle Selma STUMP, born: 20 Jul 1896 in Virginia, single, parents: J.H. STUMP (VA) and Mary EPPERLY (VA), death cause: "tuberculosis", died: Johnson City, buried: Onks Cemetery, died: 7 Apr 1914, record (1914): 153.

Lucy E. SWINEY, born: 11 Jul 1840 in Virginia, married, parents: __ REED and mother not stated, death cause: "cancer of stomach", died: Limestone, 13 Apr 1914, record (1914): 154.

James MORRIS, born: 1 Mar 1862 in Carter County, married, parents: Verge MORRIS and mother not stated, death cause: "consumption of bowels", informant: Charles H. GOFF (Jonesboro), died: 27 Apr 1914, record (1914): 155.

Mary J. MCCORKLE, born: 17 Nov (18__) (illegible), married, parents: James HOLLY and Mary BARRY, death cause: "cerebral hemorrhage", informant: J.J. MCCORKLE, buried: Elizabethton, died: 1 Apr 1914, record (1914): 156.

Eilza J. THOMPSON, colored, born: 21 Jan 1873 in Virginia, married, parents: Cornelius MARTIN (VA) and Nancy GILMAN (VA), death cause: "paretic dementia", buried: West Lawn, died: 1 Apr 1914, record (1914): 157.

Arthur Augustus GIBSON, born: 11 Oct 1891, single, parents: Thomas Jefferson GIBSON and Jennie HARVEY (Piney Flats), death cause: "meningitis", buried: Gibson Cemetery, died: Watauga, 4 Apr 1914, record (1914): 158.

William C. LEE, born: 27 Nov 1829 in Texas, married, hotel proprietor, parents: not stated, death cause: "heart disease", informant: Isaac RAY (Johnson City), buried: Oak Hill, died: 6 Apr 1914, record (1914): 159.

Mrs. W.M. LUTRETT, born: 30 Jan 1882, married, parents: John HULSE and Angie KEENE, death cause: "ruptured tubal pregnancy", informant: Angie HULSE (Jonesboro), died: 6 Apr 1914, record (1914): 160.

Myrtle Selma STUMP, born: 20 Jul 1896 in Virginia, single, parents: J.H. STUMP (VA) and Nancy EPPERLY (VA), death cause: "tuberculosis", informant: father (Johnson City), buried: Onks Cemetery, died: 7 Apr 1914, record (1914): 161.

Thomas E. KANE, age: 38 years, born in Massachusetts, soldier, parents: not stated, death cause: "pulmonary tuberculosis", died: Soldier's Home, buried: Connecticut, died: 6 Apr 1914, record (1914): 162.

G.W. WADDELL, age: 51 years, born: Cleveland, TN., married, mechanic, parents: not stated, death cause: "self inflicted gun shot wound, suicide", buried: Oak Hill, died: 3 Apr 1914, record (1914): 163.

Samuel C. BLAIR, age: 74 years, married, parents: Robert L. BLAIR and Martha CUNNINGHAM, death cause: "heart disease", informant: Robert W. BLAIR (Johnson City), buried: Oak Hill, died: 11 Apr 1914, record (1914): 164.

Porter C. BURNS, age: 77 years, born: Pennsylvania, widower, parents: not stated, death cause: "mitral insufficiency", died: Soldier's Home, 9 Apr 1914, buried: Pennsylvania, record (1914):: 165.

Bessie Sue LEAB, born: 3 Apr 1884, married, parents: John NELSON and Julia KEYS, death cause: "pulmonary tuberculosis", informant: Oscar LEAB (Jonesboro), buried: Sulphur Springs, died: 15 Apr 1914, record (1914): 166.

Marvis MILLER, colored, female, born: 23 Jan 1914, parents: Robert MILLER and Mag Nell MILLER, death cause: "found dead in bed", died: Limestone, 10 Apr 1914, record (1914): 167.

Infant JAYNES, male, born: 8 Jan 1914, parents: Clarence JAYNES and Daisy BRADLEY, death cause: "premature birth", died: Limestone, 9 Jan 1914, record (1914): 168.

Infant TAYLOR, male, parents: James TAYLOR and Ethel LOVEGROVE (?), death cause: "stillborn", buried: Sulphur Springs, died: 18th District on 15 Apr 1914, record (1914): 169.

Nora Bell CHATMAN, born: 14 Jan 1914, parents: John CHATMAN and Rebecca BISHOP, death cause:

"(illegible) of brain", informant: Mrs. J.F. COFFMAN (Jonesboro), buried: Boones Creek, died: 19 Apr 1914, record (1914): 170.

James GARDNER, born: 15 Aug 1881 in Ireland, married, parents: John GARDNER (Ireland) and Maggie GARRIETY (Ireland), death cause: "tuberculosis of lungs", informant: J.A. HAMILTON (Jonesboro), buried: Boones Creek, died: 20 Apr 1914, record (1914): 171.

Infant ELLIS, male, parents: Vollie ELLIS (Greene County) and Martha SCOTT (Greene County), death cause: "stillborn", informant: J.E. SHIPLEY (Jonesboro), born/died: 7 Mar 1914, record: 172.

Ray LOVEGROVE, born: 5 Apr 1914, parents: Albert LOVEGROVE and Callie Irene (illegible), death cause: "premature", informant: father (Jonesboro), died: 5 Apr 1914, record (1914): 173.

Robert LOVEGROVE, born: 5 Apr 1914, parents: Albert LOVEGROVE and Callie Irene (illegible), death cause: "premature", informant: father (Jonesboro), died: 5 Apr 1914, record (1914): 174.

Ethel MURRAY, colored, born: 27 Jun 1878, married, parents: M.D. LOVE (NC) and Pechia MEVERIC, death cause: "tuberculosis", informant: Lizzie RUSSELL (Telford), buried: Union Grove, died: 19 Apr 1914, record (1914): 175.

Annia MURRAY, colored, born: 30 Jun 1903, parents: John C. MURRY and Ethel LOVE, death cause: "pulmonary tuberculosis", informant: Jude LOFLIN (Telford), buried: New Victory, died: 17 Apr 1914, record (1914): 175.

Robert Franklin MCCULLEY, born: 11 Dec 1857 in Sullivan County, married, parents: John MCCULLEY (Sullivan Co) and Margaret COX (Sullivan Co), death cause: "tuberculosis", informant: Mary E. HALE (Jonesboro), died: 27 Apr 1914, record (1914): 176.

David H. MILLER, born: 15 Sep 1872, married, parents: Isaac MILLER and Nancy J. HEWET (VA), death cause: "broncho pneumonia", informant: C.E. WALTERS (Johnson City), buried: Onks Cemetery, died: 15 Apr 1914, record (1914): 177.

Walter Homer MILLER, born: 14 Dec 1913, parents: John R. MILLER and Nannie M. JONES (Unicoi County), death cause: "whooping cough and bronchitis", informant: father (Jonesboro), died: 25 Apr 1914, record (1914): 178.

Onnie HOWERN, female, born: 15 Jan 1914, parents: Charles J. TIPTON and Ella HOWERN, death cause: "diptheria", died: 6th District, 4 Apr 1911, record (1914): 179.

Lynn Doak BAILEY, born: 10 Apr 1914, parents: Joseph BAILEY and Stella MCCOURLEY, death cause: "lack of neutrition, hairlip and cleft palate", informant: S.B. MORELOCK (Limestone), died: 26 Apr 1914, record (1914): 180.

Bennie A. SEATON, born: 22 Dec 1900, parents: M.L. SEATON and A.H. TINKER, death cause: "fracture of radius ... septicemia, internal injuries", informant: Jake TINKER (Jonesboro), died: 3 Apr 1914, record (1914): 181.

Sarah Elizabeth COFF, age: 71 years, 4 months and 2 days, married, parents: David ROGERS and ___ LETTERAL, death cause: "softening of brain", informant: Emily GILTON (Chuckey), buried: Liberty, died: 10 Apr 1914, record (1914): 182.

Sophronia MCNEIL, age: 60 years, 4 months and 23 days, born in Wilkes County, NC., married, parents: Peter ELLER and mother not stated, death cause: "papillary . (illegible) of laba", informant: L.F. GREENE (Jonesboro), buried: Sulphur Springs, died: 28 Apr 1914, record (1914): 183.

Uriah H. HUNT, born: 7 Oct 1828, widower, parents: Jesse HUNT and Martha RYAN (Greene County), death cause: "Brights disease", informant: Jesse HUNT (Union Mill, NC.), buried: Hunt Cemetery, died: 27 Apr 1914, record (1914): 184.

J.C. BACON, born: 26 Apr 1851, married, parents: Jessie BACON and Patsy ELLIS, death cause: "acute indigestion", informant: R.H. BACON (Jonesboro), buried: Sulphur Spring, died: 26 Apr 1914, record (1914): 185.

Elmynar Ellen INGLE, born: 9 Sep 1882, married, parents: G.W. PRICE (GA) and Adie PRICE (NC), death

cause: "diabetes", informant: Burton INGLE (Jonesboro), buried: Sulphur Springs, died: 1 Apr 1914, record (1914): 186.
Infant GARST, male, parents: John H. GARST and Mae GARBER, death cause: "stillborn", informant: father (Jonesboro), buried: Pleasant Valley, died: 1 Apr 1914, record (1914): 187.
John WHITE, born: 7 Dec 1861, married, parents: William E. WHITE and Elizabeth DEAKINS, death cause: "nephritis, hypertrophy of heart", informant: Mrs. Celia WHITE (Telford), buried: Mt. Wesley, died: 3 May 1914, record (1914): 188.
Infant BOWMAN, male, born: 11 May 1914, parents: John B. BOWMAN and Cleo CAMPBELL, death cause: "premature", informant: S.B. MORELOCK (Limestone), died: 16 May 1914, record (1914): 189.
Infant WALKER, female, parents: William Melvin WALKER and Fanny Mary MARTIN, death cause: "stillborn", buried: Sulphur Springs, died: 20 Mar 1914, record (1914): 190.
Celil Eugene BARNES, born: 31 Dec 1899, parents: A.M. BARNES and Sarah J. MADEN, death cause: "heart trouble", informant: father (Jonesboro), buried: Maden Cemetery, died: 29 May 1914, record: 191.
Jessie James NORRIS, born: 31 May 1858, married, parents: James NORRIS and Susan MILLER, death cause: "carcinoma of (illegible)", informant: H.W. NORRIS (Fordtown), died: 24 May 1914, record (1914): 192.
Henry ROGERS, parents: David ROGERS and Vestie TAITTAN, death cause: "premature", informant: Rev. John ADAMS (Chuckey), buried: Liberty Cemetery, born/died: 29 May 1914, record (1914): 193.
Tebartha JONES, born: 20 May 1839 in North Carolina, married, parents: James RANDOLPH (NC) and Sarah SAMS (NC), death cause: "tuberculosis", informant: O.S. JONES (Chuckey), buried: Githseminie, died: 20 May 1914, record (1914): 194.
Ruby L. MILLER, born: 23 Dec 1913 in Virginia, parents: Bud MILLER and __ JONES (VA), death cause: "congestion of lungs", informant: James LAWS (Chuckey), buried: Philadelphia, died: 11 May 1914, record (1914): 195.

James SNOTGRASS, black, age: "unknown", married, parents: not stated, death cause: "heart failure", informant: Tom RUTLEDGE (Jonesboro), died: 20 May 1914, record (1914): 196.

J.K.P. BOWMAN, born: 23 Dec 1844, married, parents: Sam BOWMAN and Catherine GOODMAN, death cause: "dropsy", informant: Homer BOWMAN (Jonesboro), buried: Boones Creek, died: 21 May 1914, record (1914): 197.

Calidona HALE, age: about 100 years, born in Yancey County, NC., widow, parents: T. BAILEY (NC) and Elizabeth FILIPS (NC), death cause: "heart failure and age", informant: J.A. HAMILTON (Jonesboro), buried: Boones Creek, died: 15 May 1914, record (1914): 198.

Mrs. Bettie MOTTERN, born: 23 May 1861, widow, parents: John BEALS and Marthy E. BAILES, death cause: "chronic direah", informant: Eugene MOTTERN (Jonesboro), buried: 16th District, died: 9 May 1914, record (1914): 199.

Chester Homer BELL, born: 27 Mar 1890, single, parents: Thomas BELL and Retta VINES, death cause: "epilepsy attack", informant: Niles N. WARLICK (Jonesboro), buried: Vines Cemetery, died: 27 Mary 1914, record (1914): 200.

Lois Coretta CONSTABLE, born: 20 May 1913, parents: James CONSTABLE and Bessie CLOYD, death cause: "whooping cough", informant: T.J. TURNER (Jonesboro), buried: New Victory Cemetery, died: 25 May 1914, record (1914): 201.

Henry HOSS, age: 68 years and 11 months, married, parents: Calvin HOSS and Ashia DEAKINS, death cause: "alcoholism, rheumatism affected brain", buried: Cherokee Church, died: 28 May 1914, record: 202.

Frank STORY, born: 3 May 1914, parents: Thomas A. STORY and Lizzie VANCE, death cause: not stated, informant: Doss BUCHANAN (Jonesboro), buried: Dry Creek, died: 5 May 1914, record (1914): 203.

Brook STORY, born: 3 May 1914, parents: Thomas A. STORY and Lizzie VANCE, death cause: not stated, informant: Doss BUCHANAN (Jonesboro), buried: Dry Creek, died: 5 May 1914, record (1914): 204.

Infant BROYLES, male, born: 18 Feb 1914, parents: Arthur BROYLES and Lizzie (illegible), death cause: illegible, informant: Ray HARTSELL (Jonesboro), buried: Cherokee, died: 6 Jun 1914, record: 205.

Andrew Jackson CONKLEN, born: 1 Apr 1847, married, parents: Hagen CONKLEN and Barbara MOULTON, death cause: "intestinal obstruction", informant: J.H. VINCENT (Fall Branch), died: 14 May 1914, record (1914): 206.

Paul TIPTON, age: 9 years, parents: Walter TIPTON (NC) and mother not stated, death cause: "rheumatism involving heart", died: Embreeville on 11 May 1914, record (1914): 207.

Addie BAILEY, born: 17 Oct 1904, parents: Neely BAILEY and Tempa PAINTER, death cause: "pulmonary tuberculosis", informant: father (Limestone), buried: Liberty, died: 11 May 1914, record: 208.

Selma May FAIR, born: 1 Jan 1914, parents: William M. FAIR and Cassie TROXELL, death cause: "asphyxiation", informant: father (Johnson City), buried: Watauga, died: 16 May 1914, record: 211.

Franklin TRAMMEL, colored, born: 29 Nov 1913, parents: Henry TRAMMEL (GA) and Carry TAYLOR, death cause: "bronchitis", informant: Cary TAYLOR (Johnson City), buried: Roan Hill Cemetery, died: 13 May 1914, record (1914): 212.

Mrs. F.B. LAWSON, age: 45 years, married, parents: L. GIFFORD (Blountville) and Mary T. HAINES (Carter County), death cause: "paralysis", buried: Simmerly Cemetery, died: 12 May 1914, record (1914): 213.

W.G. STOCKTON, age: 23 years, single, parents: Peter STOCKTON and mother not stated, death cause: "electric shock, fractured skull", informant: W.M. BOAZ (Johnson City), buried: Wyndale, VA., died: 12 May 1914, record (1914): 214.

Infant SCALF, female, parents: John SCALF (Watauga) and Lula NUCKOLDS, death cause: "stillborn", informant: father (Johnson City) buried: Buena Vista, died: 11 May 1914, record (1914): 215.

Soloman Spencer VEST, born: 29 Apr 1914, parents: John J. VEST and Donnie LARIMER, death cause: "organic heart disease", informant: father (Johnson

City), buried: Watauga, died: 5 May 1914, record (1914): 216.

John T. GLOVER, age: 84 years, born in New York, widower, parents: not stated, death cause: "cerebral hemorrhage", died: Soldier's Home, 2 May 1914, record (1914): 217.

John BIRCHFIELD, Jr., parents: John BIRCHFIELD and Josie BIRCHFIELD, death cause: "stillborn", buried: Milligan, died: 1 May 1914, record (1914): 218.

Arthur Dewitt STALLORDS, born: 17 Apr 1892 in Virginia, married, railroad brakeman, parents: A.J. STALLARDS and mother not stated, death cause: "run over by train", buried: Virginia, died: 1 May 1914, record (1914): 219.

Eliza HUFF, born: 27 Aug 1872, single, parents: Harrison HUFF and Mary CARTER, death cause: "paralysis", informant: Leon H. COLLEY (Jonesboro), buried: Pleasant Valley, died: 24 May 1914, record (1914): 220.

William H. BEAR, age: 70 years, born in Pennsylvania, single, parinter, death cause: "right hemiplegia", died: Soldier's Home, 28 May 1914, record (1914): 224.

George A. WARREN, age: 70 years, born in Tennessee, widower, parents: not stated, death cause: "arterio sclerosis", died: Soldier's Home, 22 May 1914, record (1914): 222.

James H. STULL, age: 83 years, born in New York, single, death cause: "interstitial nephritis", died: Soldier's Home, 20 May 1914, record (1914): 223.

George PAYNE, age: 67 years, born in Ohio, single, parents: not stated, death cause: "pneumonia", died: Soldier's Home, 15 May 1914, record (1914): 224.

Zachariah T. GUY, age: 68 years, born in Mississippi, single, parents: not stated, death cause: "nephritis", died: Soldier's Home, 15 May 1914, record (1914): 225.

Margie Novella PICKERING, born: 1 Jan 1914, parents: Sam H. PICKERING and Lucy SHEETS, death cause: "bronchitis", informant: father (Johnson City), buried: Buena Vista, died: 30 May 1914, record (1914): 226.

Infant TAYLOR, male, parents: S.J. TAYLOR (NC) and Cora WILSON (NC), death cause: "malformation", informant: father (Johnson City), buried: Marion, NC., died: 26 May 1914, record (1914): 227.

Infant EDWARDS, male, parents: B.L. EDWARDS (NC) and Elizabeth HOWUTHRON (NC), death cause: "stillborn", informant: R.L. EDWARDS (Johnson City), buried: Buena Vista, died: 24 May 1914, record (1914): 228.

Andrew OLESON, age: 75 years, born: Sweden, widower, parents: not stated, death cause: "cystitis", buried: Lacrosse, Wisconsin, died: Soldier's Home, 25 May 1914, record (1914): 229.

Mary Evans MILLER, born: 29 Feb 1836, widow, parents: David EVANS and Judith EVANS, death cause: "diearrhoea", buried: Shelbyville, TN., died: Johnson City, 22 May 1914, record (1914): 230.

Coy Elmore VANCE, born: 12 Mar 1914, parents: James A. VANCE and Lena HAMMITT, death cause: "gastro enteritis", informant: father (Johnson City), buried: Cherokee Cemetery, died: 23 May 1914, record (1914): 231.

John T. STEPHENS, age: 67 years, born: Kentucky, married, parents: not stated, death cause: "cerebral hemorrhage", buried: Indianapolis, Indiana, died: Soldier's Home, 17 May 1914, record (1914): 232.

Mary A. SMITH, born: 23 Aug 1823, widow, parents: Samuel M. MAUK and Mary BROYLES, death cause: "cancer of neck and face", informant: Ross SMITH (Jonesboro), died: 29 Jun 1914, record (1914): 233.

Mrs. Dora O'BRIEN, born: 2 Dec 1874, married, parents: I.U. BABB and Ruth Jane TUCKER (Roan, TN), death cause: "heart trouble and (illegible)", informant: Mrs. J.W. REDWINE (Jonesboro), died: 21 Jun 1914, record (1914): 234.

Rebecca SULLANBARGER, born: 7 Apr 1842, widow, parents: __ LAMORE (VA) and Sussie CROUSE, death cause: "heart trouble", informant: James LYEMORE (Jonesboro), buried: Boones Creek, died: 12 Jun 1914, record (1914): 235.

Adolphus ALLISON, black, age: not stated, born: North Carolina, widower, parents: not stated, death cause: "pneumonia", died: 14th District, 22 Jun 1914, record (1914): 236.

Viola Mellion ROGERS, born: 6 May 1913, parents: Calvin Rutledge ROGERS and Ida May JAMES, death cause: "whooping cough", informant: father (Telford), buried: Pleasant Grove, died: 28 Apr 1914, record (1914): 237.

Daniel MILLER, born: 3 Dec 1836 in Virginia, widower, parents: Samuel MILLER (VA) and Elizabeth WINE (VA), death cause: "typhoid fever, uremia", informant: Isaac MILLER (Jonesboro), buried: Pleasant Valley, died: 6 Jul 1914, record: 238.

John W. PAINTER, born: 10 Jan 1856 in Sullivan County, married, parents: William PAINTER (VA) and Mary TAYLOR (VA), death cause: "cancer of tongue", informant: Martin PAINTER (Jonesboro), died: 11 Jul 1914, record (1914): 239.

Mrs. F.A. PARKER, age: 67 years, born in Emery, Virginia, widow, parents: E.E. WILEY (Mass) and Elizabeth HAMMOND (Conn), death cause: "nephritis, uremia", buried: Emery, VA., died: Johnson City, 10 Jun 1914, record (1914): 240.

Millie Edith SNEED, born: 21 Feb 1901, parents: John SNEED (VA) and Tenie ABLE (VA), death cause: "arterial hardening and (illegible) of heart", informant: father (Johnson City), buried: Oak Hill, died: 9 Jun 1914, record (1914): 241.

Dimple PEREGORY, born: 29 Mar 1913, parents: D.M. PEREGORY and Callie GLOVER, death cause: "gastro enteritis", informant: father (Johnson City), buried: Peregory Cemetery, died: 9 Jun 1914, record (1914): 242.

Mrs. Sarah GODSEY, age: 78 years, born in Virginia, widow, parents: not stated, death cause: "Brights disease", informant: Ed SMITH (Johnson City), buried: Oak Hill, died: 8 Jun 1914, record: 243.

Infant BROWN, colored, male, parents: father not stated and Gertrude BROWN, death cause: "stillborn", buried: West Lawn, died: 8 Jun 1914, record: 244.

Walter Boyd PICKERING, born: 21 May 1914, parents: J.H. PICKERING and Bertie JESSIE, death cause: "lung and heart condition", informant: father (Johnson

City), buried: Oak Hill, died: 8 Jun 1914, record (1914): 245.

Gustavia ELLIS, colored, female, born: 17 Feb 1896, single, nurse, parents: John ELLIS and Nancy GAINS (VA), death cause: "fell from elevator shaft at Soldier's Home", informant: H. ELLIS (Johnson City), buried: Hyder Cemetety, died: 3 Jun 1914, record (1914): 246.

Isaac GABY, age: 78 years and 7 months, married, parents: Isaac GABY (VA) and Martha HIBARGER (VA), death cause: "paralysis", informant: Mrs. J.E. BLACK (Limestone), died: 13 May 1914, record (1914): 247.

Luscinda Elizabeth MOON, born: 22 Sep 1874 in Unicoi County, married, parents: Howell EDWARDS and Louisa HULSEY (Unicoi Co.), death cause: "typhoid fever", informant: J.B. MOON (Limestone), buried: Bethel, died: 2 Jun 1914, record (1914): 248.

David V. FINE, born: 3 May 1895, widower, parents: Ross FINE and Maranda SCOTT, death cause: "consumption", informant: R.A. FINE (Jonesboro), buried: Dulaney Cemetery, died: 30 Jun 1914, record (1914): 249.

Robert KEEN, age: 37 years, single, parents: J.H. KEEN and Mary E. SLAGLE, death cause: "killed by locomotive", informant: father (Johnson City), buried: Jones Keen Farm, died: 17 Jun 1914, record (1914): 250.

W.C. ELROD, age: 77 years, 5 months and 4 days, born in Virginia, married, parents: David ELROD (VA) and Sarah BINKLEY (NC), death cause: "cerebral hemorrhage", informant: J.A. HUFFINE (Johnson City), buried: Pleasant View, died: 13 Jun 1914, record (1914): 251.

Christly NAVE, born: 25 Dec 1861, married, parents: William NAVE and Vicie PETERS, death cause: "typhoid fever", informant: Ross M. NAVE (Johnson City), buried: Longmire Cemetery, died: 25 Jun 1914. record (1914): 252.

Margaret BOWMAN, born: 16 Nov 1827 in North Carolina, widow, parents: Johnathon MILLER (NC) and Margaret CARTER (NC), death cause: "dropsy", informant: C.H. BOND (Johnson City), buried: Knob Creek, died: 20 Jun 1914, record (1914): 253.

Nathan L. HODGE, born: 1 Sep 1853, married, physician, parents: James HODGE and Mary (illegible), death cause: "cancer of liver", buried: Hodge Cemetery, died: Johnson City, 21 Apr 1914, record (1914): 254.

Mollie LAMOUS, born: __ Jul 1901, parents: William LAMOUS and Sarah SLIGER, death cause: "cerebral tumor, meningitis", informant: Ernest KYKER (Jonesboro), buried: New Victory Cemetery, died: 5 Jul 1914, record (1914): 255.

Alexander FLEUNSTEIN, age: 74 years, born in Germany, widower, parents: not stated, death cause: "paralysis", buried: Oak Hill, died: Johnson City, 25 Jun 1915, record (1914): 256.

Violet PRICE, black, parents: John PRICE (NC) and Flora PRICE (NC), death cause: "diarrhoea", died: Johnson City, 25 Jun 1914, record (1914): 257.

John MILLER, age: 70 years and 19 days, born in Sullivan County, married, brick mason, parents: Isaac MILLER and Lizzie MILLER, death cause: "cancer of neck", informant: Frank MILLER (Johnson City), buried: Weaver Cemetery, died: 21 Jun 1914, record (1914): 258.

A.L. HARMON, Jr., age: 1 year and 5 months, parents: A.L. HARMON (GA) and Mary SWATZEL (Greeneville), death cause: "ileo colitis", buried: Greeneville, died: 21 Jun 1914, record (1914): 259.

David B. ALDRICH, age: 75 years, born in Canada, married, parents: not stated, death cause: "nephritis", buried: Phillips, NC., died: Soldier's Home, 20 Jun 1914, record (1914): 260.

Lillie J. MALLICOT, born: 21 May 1870, married, parents: Jacob MCNEESE and mother not stated, death cause: "pneumonia", informant: C.A. MALLICOT (Johnson City), buried: Oak Hill, died: 20 Jun 1914, record (1914): 261.

Robert KEEN, age: 37 years, single, parents: J.H. KEEN and Mary E. SLAGLE, death cause: "killed by train", died: Johnson City, 17 Jun 1914, record (1914): 262.

William J. SMALLING, born: 22 Feb __, age: 69 years, married, parents: Duke SMALLING and Nancie BAKER (VA), death cause: "heart disease", informant: R.W. SMALLING (Johnson City), buried: Peoples Cemetery, died: 15 Jun 1914, record (1914): 263.

W.C. ELROD, age: 77 years, born in Virginia, married, parents: not stated, death cause: "heart trouble", buried: Pleasant View Cemetery, died: 15 Jun 1914, record (1914): 264.

Infant STOUT, male, parents: Clint STOUT and Bessie SAYLOR, death cause: "premature birth", informant: Charles SNODGRASS (Johnson City), buried: Barns Cemetery, died: 1 Jun 1914, record (1914): 265.

Infant TAYLOR, female, parents: Bruce B. TAYLOR and mother not stated, death cause: "stillborn", buried: Oak Hill, died: Johnson City, 12 Jun 1914, record (1914): 266.

Mary Elizabeth THOMPSON, age: 63 years, married, parents: father not stated and __ RENFRO, death cause: "pneumonia", died: Johnson City, 12 Jun 1914, record (1914): 267.

Lizzie E. CAMPBELL, age: 47 years, married, parents: John CURTIS and Anna SHIPLEY, death cause: "acute indigestion", buried: Boones Creek, died: Johnson City, 11 Jun 1914, record (1914): 268.

Joe Anna VINES, age: 1 year and 3 months, parents: James A. VINES and Lillie ROSENBLATT, death cause: illegible, informant: D.A. VINES (Johnson City), buried: Oak Hill, died: 11 Jun 1914, record: 269.

Winston COLBERTSON, colored, age: 1 month and 21 days, parents: Winston COLBERTSON (NC) and Francis MATTERSON, death cause: illegible, buried: Hyder Cemetery, died: Johnson City, 30 Jun 1914, record (1914): 270.

Thomas R. MATHIS, age: 73 years, born: Tennessee, widower, parents: not stated, death cause: "diarrhoea", died: Soldier's Home, 27 Jun 1914, record (1914): 271.

George H. COOK, age: 67 years, born: Tennessee, married, parents: not stated, death cause: "pulmonary tuberculosis", died: Soldier's Home, 27 Jun 1914, record (1914): 272.

Charles H. OSGOOD, age: 73 years, born: Massachusetts, parents: not stated, death cause: "cardiac dilatation", died: Soldier's Home, 23 Jun 1914, record (1914): 273.

Simon KEHOE, age: 74 years, born: Ireland, single, parents: not stated, death cause: "nephritis", died: Soldier's Home, 19 Jun 1914, record (1914): 274.

John F. QUADE, age: 67 years, born: Philadelphia, single, paretns: not stated, death cause: "cystitis", died: Soldier's Home, 15 Jun 1914, record (1914): 275.

Violet A. PRICE, age: 2 years and 2 months, parents: John PRICE and Flora SAUNDERS, death cause: "cholera infantum", informant: mother (Johnson City), died: 23 Jun 1914, record (1914): 276.

Alice TAYLOR, negro, born: 7 Nov 1875, widow, parents: Jackson TAYLOR and Dolly HALL, death cause: "cirrhosis of liver, typhoid fever", informant: Obelia TAYLOR (Johnson City), buried: West Lawn, died: 29 Jun 1914, record (1914): 277.

Lula REDMAN, colored, age: 68 years, born: Virginia, married, parents: not stated, death cause: "paralysis and heart failure", buried: West Lawn, died: 27 Jan 1914, record (1914): 278.

Mary Alice CARTER, age: 3 months, parents: George F. CARTER and Lillie May (illegible), death cause: "ileo colitis", buried: Oak Hill, died: 25 Jun 1914, record (1914): 279.

Susie PICKENS, colored, age: 80 years, born: North Carolina, married, parents: Tom SHERRELL (NC) and Susie HYATT (NC), death cause: "heart disease", buried: Beta, NC., died: Johnson City, 25 Jun 1914, record (1914): 280.

Amanda Eva WEST, born: 20 Feb 1838, widow, parents: G.W. TELFORD and Amanda (illegible), death cause: "heart failure", informant: W.A. WEST (Telford), buried: Washington College, died: 30 Jul 1914, record (1914): 281.

Madison BARRON, born: 3 Apr 1877, married, parents: Madison BARRON and Mary Elizabeth LOVE, death cause: "pulmonary tuberculosis", informant: Lillian BARRON (Telford), died: 22 Jul 1914, record (1914): 282.

Mary Magdeline FOSTER, born: 24 Sep 1913, parents: Marion FOSTER (Unicoi County) and Dora ADAMS (Greene County), death cause: "meningitis", informant: John DUNN (Limestone), buried: Providence, died: 5 Jul 1914, record (1914): 283.

William HAMMET, born: 27 Jun 1887, married, well digger, parents: Joseph HAMMET and Nancy STORY, death cause: "overcome by gas in well", died: Limestone, 28 Jul 1914, record (1914): 284.

Sarah SEICLE, black, age: 85 years, widow, parents: not stated, death cause: "aortic regrugitation", informant: Alfred GALASPY (Washington College), died: 6 Jul 1914, record (1914): 285.

Infant BAGLEY, female, parents: Allen BAGLEY and Lena LITTLETON, death cause: "stillborn", informant: father (Fall Branch), buried: Baptist Cemetery, died: 20 Jul 1914, record (1914): 286.

Rosetta MCCLELLAN, born: __ Aug 1911, parents: Frank MCCLELLAN (Unicoi County) and Louise HICKS (NC), death cause: not stated, informant: father (Uncioi), died: 8 Aug 1914, record (1914): 287.

Doak COLLIER, born: __ Jan 1899, parents: G.T. COLLIER (Knox County) and Ellen NEAL (Greene County), death cause: "typhoid fever", informant: Martha COLLIER (Limestone), died: 1 Aug 1914, record (1914): 288.

Bonnie A. SAYLOR, born: 13 May 1913, parents: James SAYLOR and Beatrice MORRIS, death cause: "dysentery", informant: father (Johnson City), died: 13 Jul 1914, record (1914): 289.

Omer Clinton COLE, born: 17 Apr 1913, parents: Frank COLE and Mary GARLAND, death cause: "ptomaine poisoning", informant: J.H. COLE (Jonesboro), buried: Union Cemetery, died: 14 Jul 1914, record (1914): 290.

Ross COLE, born: 13 Jul 1900, parents: Frank COLE and Mary GARLAND, death cause: "ptomaine poisoning", informant: Sam SHIELDS (Jonesboro), buried: Union Cemetery, died: 13 Jul 1914, record (1914): 291.

Infant CLOYD, male, born: 27 May 1914, parents: Roy CLOYD and Fannie COLLINS, death cause: "cholera infantum", informant: J.P. MILES (Jonesboro), buried: Onks Cemetery, died: 6 Jul 1914, record (1914): 282.

James CHATMAN, age: about 80 years, widow, parents: Richard CHATMAN and Cassie FORD, death cause: "heart trouble", informant: J.A. CHATMAN (Jonesboro), buried: Boones Creek, died: 10 Jul 1914, record (1914): 293.

James M. BARKLEY, born: 2 Jun 1839, widower, parents: William T. BARKLEY and Mary Lou AIKEN, death cause: "heart disease", informant: J.C. AIKEN (Jonesboro), died: 7 Jul 1914, record (1914): 294.

John COPP, born: 14 Apr 1830, married, parents: Jacob COPP and Mary WALTER, death cause: "diarrhoea and age", informant: W.L. HOPE (Chuckey), buried: Philadelphia, died: 13 Jul 1914, record (1914): 295.

Infant FELLERS, male, parents: Harrison FELLERS and Mary BROYLES, death cause: "premature", buried: Liberty Cemetery, died: 5 Jul 1914, record: 296.

Bettie PENLEY, born: 15 Jan 1849, married, parents: John WATS and Sue MOORE, death cause: "paralysis", informant: Henry PENLEY (Chuckey), buried: Liberty, died: 18 Jun 1914, record (1914): 297.

Pauline WATSON, born: 20 Sep 1909, parents: P.E. WATSON and Mattie THOMPSON, death cause: "typhoid fever", buried: Bethasda, died: 6th District, 28 Jun 1914, record (1914): 298.

Cordelia Caroline HENDERSON, born: 20 Feb 1838, widow, parents: Allen STOUT and Sallie LINK (VA), death cause: "heart disease", informant: G.W. BALL (Telford), buried: Limestone, died: 26 Jul 1914, record (1914): 299.

James LANE, age: 69 years, parents: not stated, death cause: "stomach trouble and age", informant: David VAUGHN (Jonesboro), died: 15th District, 20 Jul 1914, record (1914): 300.

William Trappin PONDER, born: 10 May 1913, parents: Willaim PONDER and Lucy BROYLES, death cause: "cholera infantum", informant: father (Johnson City), buried: Oak Hill, died: 16 Jun 1914, record (1914): 301.

Goly M. THOMAS, age: not stated, married, merchant, parents: Samuel THOMAS and Elizabeth MASSENGILL,

death cause: "heart disease", informant: Joe THOMAS (Bluff City), died: Johnson City, 21 Jul 1914, record (1914): 307.
Mary L. HENSLEY, age: 56 years, born in Sullivan County, married, parents: James HICKS and Mary SMITH (Sullivan Co.), death cause: "heart disease", informant: John LACY (Johnson City), buried: Williams Cemetery, died: 22 Jul 1914, record: 306.
Willie Buford KITE, born: 19 Oct 1913 in Sullivan County, parents: Nimpson KITE (NC) and Vicie HYDER, death cause: "congestion of bowels", informant: Martha KITE (Johnson City), buried: Oak Grove Cemetery, died: 28 Jul 1914, record (1914): 305.
John Worley MILLARD, born: 2 Jun 1855 in Virginia, single, parents: Samuel H. MILLARD and Maria BLEVINS, death cause: "carcinoma of face", informant: Samuel T. TILLARD (Johnson City), buried: Oak Hill Cemetery, died: 25 Jul 1914, record: 304.
Infant WILSON, female, parents: D.G. WILSON and Emily BRIGGS (NC), death cause: "stillborn", informant: father (Johnson City), buried: Oak Grove Cemetery, died: 30 Jul 1914, record (1914): 303.
Daniel C. KITE, age: 69 years, born: Tennessee, widower, parents: not stated, death cause: "pulmonary tuberculosis", died: Soldier's Home, 1 Aug 1914, record (1914): 302.
George W. MCCORMICK, age: 68 years, born: Ohio, widower, parents: not stated, death cause: "interstitial nephritis", died: Soldier's Home, 4 Aug 1914, record (1914): 301.
Timothy HARTNETT, age: 69 years, born: Ireland, parents: not stated, death cause: "cerebral hemorrhage", died: Soldier's Home, 9 Jul 1914, record (1914): 300.
John R. BARRINGER, age: 80 years, born: Indiana, widower, parents: not stated, death cause: "nephritis", died: Soldier's Home, 18 Jul 1914, record (1914): 299.
Lane WRIGHT, age: 79 years, born: Tennessee, widower, parents: not stated, death cause: "arterio sclerosis", died: Soldier's Home, 19 Jul 1914, record (1914): 290.

Miles MCGREW, age: 82 years, born: Kentucky, widower, parents: not stated, death cause: influenza, died: Soldier's Home, 24 Jul 1914, record (1914): 279.

James J. CAMPBELL, age: 73 years, born: Pennsylvania, single, parents: not stated, death cause: "peritonitis", died: Soldier's Home, 28 Jul 1914, record (1914): 296.

James WILLIAMS, age: 78 years, born: Illinois, widower, parents: not stated, death cause: "asthma", died: Soldier's Home, 31 Jul 1914, record: 295.

Pauline HOSS, age: 1 year and 7 months, parents: Learry HOSS and Ella LONGMIRE, death cause: "indigestion", buried: Boones Creek, died: Johnson City, 1 Jul 1914, record (1914): 294.

Hugh RILEY, age: 67 years, born: Ireland, single, parents: not stated, death cause: "pulmonary tuberculosis", buried: Chicago, Illinois, died: Soldier's Home, 3 Jul 1914, record (1914): 293.

Thomas H. WORTON, age: 69 years, widower, parents: not stated, death cause: "bronchitis", died: Soldier's Home, 6 Jul 1914, record (1914): 292.

Sidney SMITH, age: 42 years, born: Virginia, single, parents: not stated, death cause: "pulmonary tuberculosis", died: Soldier's Home, 7 Jul 1914, record (1914): 291.

Anne Elizabeth King MAHONEY, born: 11 Jun 1845, widow, parents: Henry KING and Elizabeth TIPTON (Carter County), death cause: "heart disease", died: 6th District, 7 Jul 1914, record (1914): 290.

Josie BURCHFIELD, age: 24 years, born: Alabama, married, parents: John TODD and Sahra JOINER (NC), death cause: "lightning stroke", buried: Milligan, died: 9th District, 10 Jul 1914, record (1914): 289.

Julia EVANS, born: 11 Aug 1889, married, parents: Ed HAUN and Annie WALKER, death cause: "tuberculosis of bowels", informant: Will EVANS (Johnson City), buried: Buena Vista, died: 11 Jul 1914, record (1914): 288.

John MURPHY, age: 69 years, born: Ireland, widower, parents: not stated, death cause: "nephritis", buried: Dennison, Ohio, died: Soldier's Home, 13 Jul 1914, record (1914): 287.

George GEIER, age: 69 years, parents: not stated, death cause: "diarrhoea", buried: Grassland, Indiana, died: Soldier's Home, 13 Jul 1914, record (1914): 286.

Robert Theodore GALLOWAY, colored, born: 19 May 1914, parents: Theodore GALLOWAY and Lena BENTLEY (VA), death cause: "bronchitis", informant: father (Johnson City), buried: West Lawn, died: 14 Jul 1914, record (1914): 285.

E.P. SAYLER, age: 25 years, parents: Manuel TAYLOR and mother not stated, death cause: "killed by train, suicide", buried: Cameron, TN., died: 16 Jul 1914, record (1914): 284.

Dump SAYLOR, colored, born: 12 Mar 1846 in North Carolina, single, death cause: not stated, death cause: "heart disease", buried: West Lawn, died: 18 Aug 1914, record (1914): 369.

Delila M. STEVENSON, age: 49 years, born in Virginia, married, parents: John PHILLIPS (VA) and mother not stated, death cause: "nephritis", informant: J.W. STEVENSON (Johnson City), buried: Buena Vista, died: 11 Aug 1914, record (1914): 368.

Sallie CADE, born: 11 Sep 1809 (age: 104), born in Washington County, widow, parents: Jim HARMON and Betsy WATENBURGER (Germany), death cause: "apoplexy", buried: Lake Cemetery, died: Johnson City, 17 Aug 1914, record (1914): 367.

Marie JENKINS, born: 22 Apr 1910, parents: Fuston JENKINS and Pearl TITTLE (NC), death cause: "diptheria", informant: father (Johnson City), buried: Oak Hill, died: 11 Aug 1914, record: 366.

Landon GILLESPIE, colored, born: 7 Dec 1872, widower, parents: Harvy GILLESPIE and mother not stated, death cause: "pellagra, syphillis", informant: Martha GILLESPIE (Johnson City), buried: Hyder Cemetery, died: 7 Aug 1914, record: 365.

Nannie E. MILES, born: 22 May 18__, age: 53 years, 4 months and 14 days, married, parents: James FORD and Katie BARNES, death cause: "paralysis", buried: Onks

Cemetery, informant: William MILES (Johnson City), died: 5 Aug 1914, record (1914): 364.

Frank B. REID, age: 27 years, born in Virginia, married, parents: David N. REID (VA), buried: Abingdon, VA., died: Johnson City, 3 Aug 1914, record (1914): 363.

Infant TUSKIN, male, parents: Frank TUSKIN (Italy) and Jennie E. WITT (KY), death cause: "stillborn", informant: father (Johnson City), buried: Buena Vista, died: 3 Aug 1914, record (1914): 362.

Eva WEAVER, born: 10 Aug 1884, married, parents: Dan WHITE and Elizabeth ROSE, death cause: "dysentery and mitral regurgitation", informant: Charles E. WEAVER (Rt 5, Johnson City), buried: Oak Hill, died: 28 Aug 1914, record (1914): 361.

George H. CROUCH, born: 15 Jun 1840, married, optician, parents: Joseph CROUCH and mother not stated, death cause: "malignant tumor", informant: William B. CROUCH (Johnson City), buried: Oak Hill, died: 29 Aug 1914, record (1914): 360.

Clara Naoma JONES, born: 27 Jan 1914, parents: Joe H. JONES and Lura JUSTICE, death cause: "ptomaine poisoning", informant: father (Johnson City), buried: Greeneville, died: 27 Aug 1914, record (1914): 359.

Ramey E. SHOUP, born: 21 Jun 1914, parents: Andy J. SHOUP (VA) and Nora CAMPBELL (Texas), death cause: "diarrhoea", informant: father (Johnson City), buried: Buena Vista, died: 27 Aug 1914, record (1914): 358.

Rosa Lee WINBUSH, colored, born: 19 Mar 1914, parents: Lynn WINBUSH (VA) and Cinthie HALE, death cause: "cholera infantum", informant: mother (Johnson City), buried: West Lawn, died: 25 Aug 1914, record (1914): 357.

William Bufford PRINCE, born: 6 Jul 1912, parents: W.L. PRINCE and Mary E. COFFMAN, death cause: "cholera infantum", buried: Oak Hill, died: 22 Aug 1914, record (1914): 356.

Infant HORTON, female, parents: Doss HORTON and Mary TAYLOR, death cause: "asphyxia", informant: father

(Johnson City), buried: Hyder Cemetery, died: 21 Aug 1914, record (1914): 355.

George W. PRICHARD, age: 60 years, married, parents; James PRICHARD and Eliza (illegible), death cause: "locomotor ataxia", buried: Oak Hill, died: 9th District, 18 Aug 1914, record (1914): 354.

Mildred Louise OLIVER, born: 6 Feb 1912, parents: John OLIVER and Effie BAYLESS, death cause: "broncho pneumonia", informant: father (Johnson City), buried: Oak Hill, died: 19 Aug 1914, record: 353.

Joseph LAWSON, age: 46 years, born: Illinois, single, parents: not stated, death cause: "pulmonary tuberculosis", died: Soldier's Home, 25 Aug 1914, record (1914): 352.

George W. KOSTER, age: 67 years, born: Michigan, single, parents: not stated, death cause: "pulmonary tuberculosis", died: Soldier's Home, 23 Aug 1914, record (1914): 351.

James G. MARTIN, age: 76 years, born: New York, widower, parents: not stated, death cause: "gastritis", died: Soldier's Home, 22 Aug 1914, record (1914): 350.

Benjamin F. MOORE, age: 69 years, born: Pennsylvania, widower, parents: not stated, death cause: "gangrene", died: Soldier's Home, 20 Aug 1914, record (1914): 349.

Sandy ALEXANDER, colored, age: 80 years, born: North Carolina, single, parents: not stated, death cause: "arterio sclerosis, died: Soldier's Home, 20 Aug 1914, record (1914): 348.

Clancey BROWN, age: 72 years, born: New York, single, parents: not stated, death cause: "hemiplegia", died: Soldier's Home, 13 Aug 1914, record (1914): 347.

Paul THROUX, age: 41 years, born: Rhode Island, single, parents: not stated, death cause: "peritonitis", died: Soldier's Home, 9 Aug 1914, record (1914): 346.

Edwin D. HAYNES, age: 82 years, born: New Hampshire, married, civil engineer, parents: not stated, death cause: "cystitis", died: Soldier's Home, 10 Aug 1914, record (1914): 345.

Georgia Emma MORELOCK, born: 11 Oct 1899, parents: Jacob MORELOCK and Ollie MORELOCK, death cause: "typhoid fever and measles", died: Fall Branch, 11 Aug 1914, buried: M.E. Church, record (1914):: 344.

Anna Bradley KIPLINGER, born: 19 Dec 1895, married, parents: Bud BRADLEY and Mollie HYLTON, death cause: "pneumonia, pleurisy", buried: Bethesda, died: 4th District, 1 Sep 1914, record (1914): 343.

Hutson Martin BASKETTE, born: 1 Mar 1847, married, parents: John T. BASKETTE and Asenth HARTMAN, death cause: "pulmonary tuberculosis", informant: Charles STAFFORD (Limetone), died: 5 Aug 1914, record (1914): 342.

Cora FERGUSON, age: 47 years, married, parents: David DICKEMON and Martha HYSINGER, death cause: "tuberculosis", informant: G.W. FERGUSON (Telford), buried: Mt. Wesley, 15 Jul 1914, record (1914): 341.

Thomas HENLEY, age: 54 years, 6 months and 3 days, single, parents: Joseph HENLEY and Elizabeth BOYERS, death cause: "suicide, hanging", died: Jonesboro, 20 Aug 1914, record (1914): 340.

July Ann REED, born: 12 Nov 1829, widow, parents: John MILLER and Mary KELLEY, death cause: "carcinoma, mammary gland, age", informant: P.D. REED (Limestone), buried: Knob Creek, 28 Aug 1914, record (1914): 339.

Mahala GOBBLE, born: 20 Apr 1820 in West Virginia, widow, parents: not stated, death cause: "dysentery or flux", informant: M.N. DAVENPORT (Whitesburg, TN), buried: Onks Cemetery, died: 8 Aur 1914, record (1914): 338.

Mrs. Eliza Cahterine MURPHY, born: 31 Jan 1831, widow, parents: General A.E. JACKSON (Pennsylvania) and Sarafina Katherine TAYLOR, death cause: "paralysis", informant: Lilie H. STRICKLAND (Pittsburg, PA), buried: Jonesboro, died: 27 Aug 1914, record (1914): 337.

Margaret SALTS, born: 15 Dec 1856, married, parents: Jack TOMKINS (VA) and mother not stated, death cause: "tuberculosis", informant: Ida SALTS (Jonesboro), died: 5 Aug 1914, record (1914): 336.

Mrs. Julia Carver MATHIS, born: 12 Dec 1850 in Mobile, Alabama, parents: Robert CARVER (Mass) and Julia A. JONES (SC), death cause: "heart and kidney trouble", died: Jonesboro, 9 Aug 1914, record (1914): 335.
Mrs. Jane R. CUMMINGS, born: 29 Mar 1841 in Greene County, widow, parents: Isah STEWART (Greene Co.) and Lydia YEAKLY (Greene Co.), death cause: "typhoid fever", died: Jonesboro, 22 Aug 1914, record: 334.
Robert R. MCCLURE, born: 12 Aug 1882, married, parents: Francis M. MCCLURE (VA)[note: died of carcinoma of testicle] and Henrietta C. WILCOX (VA), death cause: "carcinoma of testicle, believed hereditary", informant: M.S. MCCLURE (Jonesboro), buried: Fordtown Church, died: 14 Aug 1914, record (1914): 333.
George Lincoln BARNES, born: 24 Aug 1884, single, parents: Allen BARNES and Elizabeth CARR, death cause: "gunshot wound", informant: H.H. BARNES (Jonesboro), buried: Hales Chapel, died: 13 Aug 1914, record (1914): 332.
Marie Elizabeth EMMERT, born: 22 Jul 1914, parents: Andrew Jackson EMMERT and Mary Eliza DYER (Hawkins County), death cause: "marasmus", buried: Emmert Cemetery, died: 10th District, 11 Aug 1914, record (1914): 331.
Loueffie BROWN, born: 26 Mar 1886, married, parents: John CARATHEN, and Lizzie NORTHINGTON, death cause: "typhoid fever, heart disease", informant: A.J. BROWN (10th District), buried: Brown Cemetery, died: 4 Sep 1914, record (1914): 330.
Richard C. BOWMAN, born: 20 Nov 1837, married, parents: Joseph BOWMAN and Sarah WHITE, death cause: "paralysis", informant: W.W. BOWMAN (Rt. 4, Johnson City), buried: Boones Creek, died: 28 Aug 1914, record (1914): 329.
Alice Greenway GRUBBS, born: 30 Mar 1852, married, parents: Eldridge GREENWAY and Sarah (illegible), death cause: "tuberuclosis of bowels", informant: A.S. GRUBBS (Limestone), buried: Asbury Cemetery, died: 3 Oct 1914, record (1914): 328.

Howard Thomas FERGUSON, age: 10 months and 29 days, parents: Courtney FERGUSON and Clara BALL, death cause: "bronchitis", informant: father (Telford), buried: Mt. Wesley, died: 24 Sep 1914, record (1914): 405.

Clarence CARTER, born: 23 Sep 1914, parents: Cloyd CARTER (Blue Springs, TN) and Cynthia PATTON, death cause: not stated, informant: father (Jonesboro), died: 1 Oct 1914, record (1914): 404.

Martha E. HEADRICK, born: 28 Feb __ in Hawkins County, age: 70 years, 6 months and 5 days, widow, parents: __ BALL and mother not stated, death cause: "consumption", informant: Dr. C.S. LOVE (Chuckey), buried: Midway, died: 2 Sep 1914, record: 403.

Sherman PAINTER, age: 48 years, married, parents: Jessie PAINTER and Cinthia SMITH, death cause: "tuberculosis", informant: Henry PENLEY (Chuckey), buried: Liberty, died: 1 Sep 1914, record: 402.

Sarah SPITZER, born: 15 Jun 1848 in Virginia, single, parents: Jessie SPITZER (VA) and Elizabeth HOOVER (VA), death cause: "hemorrhage of brain", informant: Dora SPITZER (Jonesboro), died: 20 Sep 1914, record (1914): 401.

Laura WINTON, born: 30 Jul 1869, married, parents: Jesse MOORE and Louisa GRAY (Hawkins County), death cause: "tuberculosis of bowels", informant: D.D. WINTON (Jeraldstown), buried: 17th District, died: 17 Sep 1914, record (1914): 400.

John YOKAM, age: 73 years, born in Germany, widower, parents: not stated, death cause: "cerebral hemorrhage", died: Soldier's Home, 29 Sep 1914, record (1914): 399.

John SAMPSON, age: 67 years, born in Michigan, single, parents: not stated, death cause: "cardiac dilatation", died: Soldier's Home, 22 Sep 1914, record (1914): 398.

William H. GULLIVER, age: 68 years, born in Pennsylvania, R.R. engineer, married, parents: not stated, death cause: "pulmonary tuberculosis", died: Soldier's Home, 22 Sep 1914, record (1914): 397.

Paul HOOK, age: 73 years, born: Germany, widower, parents: not stated, death cause: "curhossis of liver", died: Soldier's Home, 16 Sep 1914, record (1914): 396.

Charles KANE, age: 77 years, born: Ireland, single, parents: not stated, death cause: "nephritis", died: Soldier's Home, 16 Sep 1914, record (1914): 395.

Mollie E. TINER, born: 22 Jul 1874 in North Carolina, married, parents: Will GOOCH (NC) and Mary GIBSON (NC), death cause: "pulmonary tuberculosis", informant: L.R. TINER (New York), buried: Ashville, NC., died: 9th District, 30 Sep 1914, record: 394.

James BOOHER, colored, age: 19 years, single, parents: Runner BOOHER and Sallie BOOHER, death cause: "typhoid", buried: Hyder Cemetery, died: 29 Sep 1914, record (1914): 393.

William Albert ROSE, born: 26 Sep 1914, parents: Leslie ROSE and Fannie BAKAR, death cause: "intestinal disease", informant: father (Johnson City), buried: Union Cemetery, died: 27 Sep 1914, record (1914): 392.

Alice HUNTER, colored, age: 55 years, born: North Carolina, married, parents: William VALENTINE (NC) and mother not stated, death cause: "cancer of uterus", informant: Alferd HUNTER (Johnson City), buried: West Lawn, died: 25 Sep 1914, record: 391.

Joanna KEEN, born: 5 Aug 1848, married, parents: John BAYLESS and Adeline GOURLEY, death cause: "heart disease", informant: N.K. HUMPHREYS (Johnson City), buried: Vaughn Cemetery, died: 25 Sep 1914, record (1914): 390.

Georgia ERWIN, colored, age: 16 years, parents: Thomas ERWIN (NC) and Mary ERWIN (NC), death cause: "typhoid and tuberculosis", buried: Hyder Cemetery, died: 24 Sep 1914, record (1914): 389.

Adron Carson SNODGRASS, born: 12 Nov 1912, parents: Worley M. SNODGRASS and Buna SCOTT, death cause: "toxic poison", informant: Charles SNODGRASS (Johnson City), buried: Milligan College, died: 21 Sep 1914, record (1914): 388.

Sarah GUINN, colored, age: 87 years, widow, parents: not stated, death cause: "heart failure", informant: Mose DALTON (Johnson City), buried: Bulls Gap, died: 19 Sep 1914, record (1914): 387.

George MILLHORN, born: 22 Aug 1852, married, parents: Elkana MILLHORN (Ireland) and Bettie HODGES, death cause: "cerebral hemorrhage", informant: C.S. MILLHORN (Johnson City), buried: New Bethel Cemetery, died: 19 Sep 1914, record: 386.

Paul ANDERS, born: 6 Jul 1913 in Virginia, parents: Cleve ANDERS (VA) and Ethel BEDDELL (VA), death cause: "indigestion", informant: father (Johnson City), buried: Buena Vista, died: 19 Sep 1914, record (1914): 385.

George F. CAMPBELL, born: 15 Sep 1861 in Greene County, married, chief of police, parents: Archibald CAMPBELL and Susan DAVIS, death cause: "gunshot wound in head", informant: Mrs. F.P. BAXTER (Johnson City), buried: Greeneville, died: 16 Sep 1914, record (1914): 384.

Charles Henry GREENLEE, colored, born: 18 Dec 1912, parents: Will NAVE (VA) and Fannie GREENLEE, death cause: "typhoid fever", buried: Jonesboro, died: 16 Sep 1914, record (1914): 383.

William H. GEISLER, born: 30 Mar 1880, married, parents: Hugh GEISLER and Sarah THOMAS, death cause: "typhoid fever", informant: N.H. GEISLER (Elk Park, NC), buried: Bluff City, died: 14 Sep 1914, record (1914): 382.

Henry Arnsdon BROWN, lived 11 days, parents: Herbert BROWN and Olen BURGNER, death cause: "cyanosis", buried: Oak Hill, died: 13 Sep 1914, record: 381.

Infant LUNSFORD, male, parents: Andrew LUNSFORD and Minnie OWENS (VA), death cause: "heart disease", informant: father (Johnson City), buried: Oak Hill, born/died: 11 Sep 1914, record (1914): 380.

Wilson KENNEDY, age: 72 years, born: Pennsylvania, widower, parents: not stated, death cause: "syphilis", died: Soldier's Home, 7 Sep 1914, record (1914): 379.

John M. SOUTH, born: 27 Sep 1827, born: North Carolina, married, parents: Jessie SOUTH (NC) and Mary HOULDER (NC), death cause: "paralysis", informant: Harvy SOUTH (Johnson City), buried: Oak Hill, died: 7 Sep 1914, record (1914): 378.

Samuel W. ROE, Jr., born: 10 Aug 1914, parents: Samuel ROE and Lula WILLIAMS (VA), death cause: "marasmus", buried: Buena Vista, died: 8 Sep 1914, record (1914): 377.

Christopher ZANG, age: 69 years, born: Pennsylvania, married, parents: not stated, death cause: "asthma", buried: Pittsburg, PA., died: Soldier's Home, 11 Sep 1914, record (1914): 376.

Infant BROWN, male, parents: Herbert BROWN and Olen BURGNER, death cause: illegible, informant: father (Johnson City), buried: Oak Hill, born/died: 3 Sep 1914, record (1914): 375.

Infant POLLING, male, parents: W.R. POLLING (Ohio) and Nona SALINGER (Ohio), death cause: "stillborn", informant: father (Johnson City), buried: Oak Hill, died: 1 Sep 1914, record (1914): 374.

Rosie HAUK, born: 17 Aug 1914, parents: C.M. HAUK and Amanda BLAIN, death cause: "anaimia", informant: father (Johnson City), buried: Buena Vista, died: 7 Sep 1914, record (1914): 373.

Infant POLING, male, parents: W.B. POLING and Nora SALINGER (Ohio), death cause: "stillborn", informant: father (Johnson City), buried: Oak Hill, died: 1 Sep 1914, record (1914): 372.

Claud C. WATSON, age: 28 years, born: Virginia, single, parents: James W. WATSON (VA) and Elizabeth MOSER (VA), death cause: "pulmonary tuberculosis", informant: father (Johnson City), buried: Oak Hill, died: 6 Sep 1914, record (1914): 371.

Margaret ROE, lived 18 days, parents: Samuel W. ROE and Lula WILLIAMS, death cause: illegible, buried: Oak Hill, died: 4 Sep 1914, record (1914): 370.

Violet Vernis DECKER, born: 17 Jan 1914, parents: Thomas C. DECKER and Rhea THOMPSON, death cause: "bronchitis", informant: father (Jonesboro), died: 11 Oct 1914, record (1914): 393.

Sarah Ann AUSTIN, born: 5 Sep 1834, widow, parents: Soloman S. SHERFEY and (illegible) DEAKINS, death cause: "age and fracture femur", informant: B.F. AUSTIN (Telford), buried: Bowmantown, died: 25 Oct 1914, record (1914): 394.

Infant WILLIAMS, male, parents: Henry Harrison WILLIAMS and Anna Bell BOWMAN, death cause: "difficult labor", informant: father (Telford), buried: Fairview, born/died: 12 Oct 1914, record (1914): 395.

Mrs. Margie DOWNER, born: 19 Dec 1849 in Virginia, married, parents: Levi MCPEAK (VA) and mother not stated, death cause: "stomach trouble", informant: Josua MCPEAK (Johnson City), buried: Boones Creek, died: 1 Oct 1914, record (1914): 396.

Charles E. DILWORTH, born: 7 Jul 1837 in Virginia, single, music teacher, parents: James A. DILWORTH (Wales) and Charlotte WARTMANN (VA), death cause: "heart disease", informant: Fred MCPHERSON (Jonesboro), died: 6 Oct 1914, record (1914): 397.

James SHIPLEY, age: 67 years, 5 months and 27 days, born in Sullivan County, married, parents: Tollbert SHIPLEY (Sullivan Co.) and Bettie TROXELL (Sullivan Co.), death cause: "fell from wagon, died of injuries", informant: Renah SHIPLEY (Leesburg), buried: Fairview, died: 14 Oct 1914, record: 398.

Deborah KEEFAUVER, born: 10 Sep 1850, married, parents: not stated, death cause: "unknown", buried: Pleasant Valley, died: 14th District, 12 Oct 1914, record (1914): 399.

Mary Sue GRAY, born: 6 Aug 1914, parents: W. Boyd GRAY (VA) and Ollie CHASE, death cause: "malnutrition", informant: father (Jonesboro), buried: Fordtown, died: 10 Oct 1914, record: 400.

David G.W. BARNES, Jr., born: 5 Sep 1846, married, parents: A.S. BARNES and Sarah E. CARETHERS, death cause: "carcinoma of face", informant: F.H. BARNES (Jonesboro), buried: Buffalo Ridge, died: 17 Oct 1914, record (1914): 401.

Margaret Rebecca LOVE, born: 5 Jun 1836 in Washington County, VA., widow, parents: Dennis BRIDGES and Elizabeth DICKASON (VA), death cause: "Brights disease", informant: D. White LOVE (Bluff City), buried: Johnson City, died: 19 Oct 1914, record (1914): 402.

Caroline GILLESPIE, colored, age: 60 years, widow, parents: William BAYLESS and Nancy G. BAYLESS, death cause: "cardiac dropsy", informant: Ham BAILEY (Limestone), died: 14 Oct 1914, record (1914): 403.

Albert Kimmons RANGE, born: 4 May 1913 in Sullivan County, parents: William RANGE and Clandis PRICHETT, death cause: "ileo colitis", informant: J.A. PRICHETT (Rt. 3, Johnson City), buried: Boones Creek, died: 10 Oct 1914, record (1914): 404.

Infant WALKER, male, parents: James WALKER and Ethel KIPLINGER, death cause: "premature birth", informant: father (Jonesboro), born/died: 14 Oct 1914, record (1914): 405.

DAvid J.N. ERVIN, born: 10 Oct 1844, married, parents: David J.N. ERVIN and Sue JONES, death cause: "cerebral hemorrhage", informant: Thomas J. ERVIN (Jonesboro), buried: Unicoi County, died: 22 Sep 1914, record (1914): 406.

David MILLER, age: illegible, parents: Jerry MILLER and mother not stated, death cause: "pulmonary tuberculosis", died: 22 Oct 1914, record: 407.

Infant SIMMERMAN, (Zimmerman ?), male, born: 12 Oct 1914, parents: J.H. SIMMERMAN (VA) and Mollie DULANY, death cause: illegible, informant: father (Jonesboro), buried: Dulaney Cemetery, died: 14 Oct 1914, record (1914): 408.

Nathan H. KELLER, age: 38 years, born: Tennessee, married, parents: not stated, death cause: "mania following exhaustion", died: Soldier's Home, 23 Oct 1914, record (1914): 409.

John M. BAILS, age: 67 years, born: Tennessee, widower, parents: not stated, death cause: "gastritis", died: Soldier's Home, 19 Oct 1914, record (1914): 410.

Lyman A. RICH, age: 67 years, born: Pennsylvania, widower, parents: not stated, death cause: "cerebral hemorrhage", died: Soldier's Home, 17 Oct 1914, record (1914): 411.

Miguel MARTINEZ, age: 80 years, born: Spain, sailor, single, parents: not stated, death cause: "bronchitis", died: Soldier's Home, 15 Oct 1914, record (1914): 412.

Richard T. BALLARD, age: 67 years, born: Indiana, druggest, parents: not stated, death cause:

"alcoholism", died: Soldier's Home, 10 Oct 1914, record (1914): 413.

Washington MERNA, age: 71 years, born: Illinois, single, parents: not stated, death cause: "tarumatism from railroad accident", died: Soldier's Home, 10 Oct 1914, record (1914): 414.

Joseph N. LORIS, age: 69 years, born: New York, widower, parents: not stated, death cause: "carbuncle", died: Soldier's Home, 24 Oct 1914, record (1914): 415.

Collin MCLEOD, age: 82 years, born: Scotland, widower, parents: not stated, death cause: "traumatism from railroad accident", died: Soldier's Home, 12 Oct 1914, record (1914): 418.

William H. HAWK, age: 74 years, born: Iowa, widower, parents: not stated, death cause: "cardiac asthma", died: Soldier's Home, 3 Nov 1914, record: 417.

Jacob RAGLON, age: 40 years, born: Tennessee, married, parents: not stated, death cause: "pulmonary tuberculosis", died: Soldier's Home, 3 Nov 1914, record (1914): 418,

William C. ROBINSON, born: 13 Jul 1849 in London, England, married, parents: John ROBINSON (England) and Matilda BUNTING (England), death cause: "nephritis", informant: Mary ROBINSON (Johnson City), buried: Oak Hill, died: 29 Oct 1914, record (1914): 419.

C.E. SCOTT, age: 50 years, single, parents: Daniel SCOTT and B.V. BORING (VA), death cause: "paralysis", buried: Milligan Cemetery, died: 29 Oct 1914, record (1914): 420.

William A. SPARKS, age: 81 years, born: Virginia, married, printer, parents: Ruben SPARKS (VA) and __ MCCLELLAND (VA), death cause: "heart disease", buried: Oak Hill, died: 28 Oct 1914, record: 421.

Nannie J. ROBERTSON, age: 47 years, married, parents: Isaac HARVEY and Hannah LONGMIRE, death cause: "pellagra", buried: King Cemetery, died: Johnson City, 27 Oct 1914, record (1914): 422.

John William MORREL, parents: Worley Cox MORREL and Lelia Novela VANHUSS, death cause: "stillborn",

buried: Buena Vista, died: 27 Oct 1914, record (1914): 423.
John Samuel BROWN, colored, born: 23 Oct 1914 in North Carolina, parents: Benson BROWN (Ashe County, NC) and Ida YOUNG, death cause: illegible, buried: West Lawn, died: 24 Oct 1914, record (1914): 424.
Joseph B. SPENCER, age: 64 years, born: Tennessee, married, druggest, parents: not stated, death cause: "interstitial nephritis", buried: Greenville, died: Soldier's Home, 24 Oct 1914, record (1914): 425.
Helem Alma BRACE, age: 2 years and 6 months, born: Bristol, parents: H.P. BRACE (Bristol) and Alma MAUK (Bristol), death cause: "croup", buried: Bristol, died: 24 Oct 1914, record (1914): 426.
Cephas STOVER, age: 73 years, born: Salem, VA., parents: not stated, death cause: "unknown", buried: Dallas, Texas, died: Soldier's Home, 21 Oct 1914, record (1914): 427.
Jessie M. HAMPTON, age: 65 years, married, parents: Acie HAMPTON and Martha LAWS, death cause: "indigestion", informant: H.M. HAMPTON (Rt. 3, Johnson City), buried: Carr Cemetery, died: 22 Oct 1914, record (1914): 428.
Rebecca E. PIPPIN, born: 22 Jul 1864, married, parents: William ERWIN and Elizabeth ERWIN, death cause: "severe burns", informant: W.D. FORD (Johnson City), buried: Erwin, TN., died: 19 Oct 1914, record (1914): 429.
Katheren I. HOSS, born: 1 Sep 1856, married, parents: W.R. KING (NC) and Mary ARNOT, death cause: illegible, informant: A.F. HOSS (Johnson City), buried: Oak Hill, died: 19 Oct 1914, record: 430.
Infant FULLWOOD, Negro, female, parents: A.J. FULLWOOD (NC) and Delia OWEN (NC), death cause: "stillborn", buried: West Lawn, died: 19 Oct 1914, record (1914): 431.
Robert GODSEY, born: 24 Jul 1913, parents: John GODSEY and Bessie FIELDS, death cause: "diarrhoea", informant: father (Johnson City), buried: Buena Vista, died: 18 Oct 1914, record (1914): 432.
Lawrence DODSON, age: 3 years, born: Cripple Creek, VA., parents: Percy DODSON (VA) and Lucy ROSENBAUM

(VA), death cause: "typhoid fever", buried: Cripple Creek, VA., died: 14 Oct 1914, record (1914): 433.

Mollie LOUDY, born: __ Jul 1865, married, parents: Wash OWEN and Nancy LOUDY, death cause: "pneumonia following appendectomy", informant: R.L. LOUDY (Rt. 5, Johnson City), buried: Loudy Cemetery, died: 11 Oct 1914, record (1914): 434.

Robert Franklin WHITLOCK, age: 7 years, parents: Carl WHITLOCK and Mary (illegible), death cause: illegible, buried: Oak Hill, died: 6 Oct 1914, record (1914): 435.

John M. POSTLEWAIT, age: 77 years, born: Pennsylvania, single, parents: not stated, death cause: "shock from thigh injury", died: Soldier's Home, 2 Oct 1914, record (1914): 436.

Moses CRAPO, age: 77 years, born: Canada, single, parents: not stated, death cause: "nephritis", died: Soldier's Home, 1 Oct 1914, record (1914): 437.

Louis C. GERHART, age: 45 years, born: Ohio, single, parents: not stated, death cause: "pulmonary tuberculosis", died: Soldier's Home, 1 Oct 1914, record (1914): 438.

Edward Johnson MERRICK, born: 25 Oct 1914, parents: Charles MERRICK and Fannie GREENWAY, death cause: illegible, informant: D.E. FRANCE (Johnson City), buried: Onks Cemetery, died: 27 Nov 1914, record (1914): 439.

Edward BARRETT, age: 47 years, born: England, single, parents: not stated, death cause: "pulmonary tuberculosis", died: Soldier's Home, 25 Nov 1914, record (1914): 440.

William FISHER, age: 79 years, born: Ohio, widower, parents: not stated, death cause: "mitral insufficiency", died: Soldier's Home, 24 Nov 1914, record (1914): 441.

Jacob RUSSELL, age: not stated, born: Switzerland, single, parents: not stated, death cause: "cerebral hemorrhage", died: Soldier's Home, 17 Nov 1914, record (1914): 442.

Edward A. MARBLE, age: 73 years, born: New Yor, single, parents: not stated, death cause: "pulmonary tuberculosis", died: Soldier's Home, 15 Nov 1914, record (1914): 443.

Henry JORDAN, age: 48 years, born: England, married, parents: not stated, death cause: "pulmonary tuberculosis", died: Soldier's Home, 15 Nov 1914, record (1914): 443-A.

Anthony SCRUGGS, age: 74 years, born: Tennessee, single, parents: not stated, death cause: "mitral insufficiency", died: Soldier's Home, 10 Nov 1914, record (1914): 444.

John T. LANGSTAFF, age: 74 years, born: Pennsylvania, married, railroad engineer, parents: not stated, death cause: "asthma", died: Soldier's Home, 8 Nov 1914, record (1914): 445.

Sylvester A. WRIGHT, age: 73 years, born: New York, widower, parents: not stated, death cause: "dilitation of heart", died: Soldier's Home, 6 Nov 1914, record (1914): 446.

George C. MCNABB, born: 16 Feb 1914, parents: G.W. MCNABB and Edith STEVENSON, death cause: "meningitis", informant: father (Erwin), buried: Erwin, died: 29 Nov 1914, record (1914): 447.

Ella MURRAY, age: 68 years, married, parents: John MURRAY (Ireland) and Susie MURRAY (SC), death cause: "intestinal indigestion", buried: Oak Hill, died: 26 Nov 1914, record (1914): 448.

Gordon WILLIAMS, colored, age: 19 years, born: North Carolina, parents: Wash WILLIAMS and Cora MABRY (NC), death cause: "typhoid fever", informant: father (Johnson City), buried: West Lawn, died: 25 Nov 1914, record (1914): 449.

Lillie May COOK, age: 11 years, parents: James D. COOK and Lura J. PRICE, death cause: "pulmonary tuberuclosis", buried: Oak Hill, died: 26 Nov 1914, record (1914): 450.

Mrs. Margaret Toncray VANCE, age: 42 years, married, parents: George H. ANGEL and (illegible) ROBERTS, death cause: "Brights disease", informant: J.E. VANCE (Johnson City), buried: Oak Hill, died: 23 Nov 1914, record (1914): 451.

Mary E. DAY, age: 96 years, born: North Carolina, widow, parents: W.M. REED (NC) and mother not stated, death cause: "senility", informant: J.W. LOOPER (Johnson City), buried: Buena Vista, died: 23 Nov 1914, record (1914): 452.

George HOWINGTON, age: 39 years, single, parents: W.P. HOWINGTON (NC) and Martha UTSMAN (NC), death cause: "tuberculosis", buried: Mount Vista, died: 20 Nov 1914, record (1914): 453.

Mrs. Emma PATTON, age; 42 years, married, parents: Samuel BALL and Lucinda MITCHELL, death cause: "nephritis", buried: Telford, died: 9th District, 23 Nov 1914, record (1914): 454.

Carl Emmet POTEAT, born: 23 Sep 1914, parents: D.S. POTEAT (NC) and Angie DODSON, death cause: "bronchitis", informant: father (Johnson City), buried: Oak Hill, died: 19 Nov 1914, record: 455.

Infant HUMPHREY, male, born: 7 Nov 1914, parents: Charles HUMPHREY and Chessie HAUCK, death cause: "jaundice", inforant: J.E. HAUCK (Johnson City), buried: Leach Cemetery, died: 18 Nov 1914, record (1914): 456.

Infant WRIGHT, sex: not stated, parents: Charlie WRIGHT and Ollie MUSIC, death cause: "stillborn", informant: W.H. LEACH (Johnson City), buried: Oak Hill, died: 17 Nov 1914, record (1914): 457.

Infant KELLEY, male, parents: Taylor KELLEY and Sarah KELLEY, death cause: "born dead", buried: Hampton, TN., died: 11 Nov 1914, record (1914): 458.

John H. NAYLOR, age: 72 years, born: Maryland, single, parents: not stated, death cause: "Brights disease", buried: Oak Hill, died: Johnson City, 9 Nov 1914, record (1914): 459.

Robert LOWEY, age: 5 years, born: Carter County, parents: E.D. LOWEY and Amanda DUNN, death cause: "whooping cough", informant: D.H. GOOD (Johnson City), buried: Speedwell Cemetery, died: 9 Nov 1914, record (1914): 460.

Julia Ann MILLER, born: 11 Apr 1834, widow, parents: D. LEONARD (VA) and Ester LACY, death cause: "mitral insufficiency", informant: A.R. MILLER (Johnson City), buried: Unicoi, died: 5 Nov 1914, record (1914): 461.

Henry R. RATLIFF, born: 3 Nov 1914, parents: J.C. RATLIFF (Indiana) and Mary W. WHEELER, death cause: illegible, buried: Oak Hill, died: 5 Nov 1914, record (1914): 462.
David M. COFFMAN, age: 70 years, born: Ohio, married, coal mine owner, parents: not stated, death cause: "mitral insufficiency", buried: Rockwood, TN., died: Soldier's Home, 3 Nov 1914, record (1914): 463.
Bertha V. AUSTIN, born: 21 Oct 1914, parents: David A. AUSTIN and Edith STORY, death cause: "found dead in bed", died: 4th District, 18 Nov 1914, record (1914): 464.
Elizabeth MILLER, age: 33 years, married, parents: John DUNN (VA) and mother not stated, death cause: "tuberculosis of lungs", informant: J.H. JONES (4th District), buried: Union Cemetery, died: 23 Nov 1914, record (1914): 465.
Verna S. DEAKINS, born: 16 Jun 1891, married, parents: John MARTIN and Sarah BACON, death cause: "puerperal septicemia", informant: John KEEFAUVER (Jonesboro), buried: Sulphur Springs, died: 3 Dec 1914, record (1914): 466.
Ester Ann MARKWOOD, born: 11 Dec 1847, widow, parents: James NELSON and Margaret FERGUSON, death cause: "apoplexy", informant: Bertie MARKWOOD (Washington College), buried: Salem, died: 2 Nov 1914, record (1914): 467.
James M. HARRIS, born: 15 Nov 1880, single, parents: James Y. HARRIS (NC) and Mary NELSON (Sullivan County), death cause: "pneumonia", informant: Mary HARRIS (Jonesboro), died: 22 Nov 1914, record (1914): 468.
Mrs. Dicy Ann KINCHLOE, born: 22 Feb 1872, married, parents: Elija HUNT and Nancy DEVAULT, (Scott Co., VA), death cause: "pulmonary tuberculosis", informant: J.J. KINCHLOE (Jonesboro), died: 9 Nov 1914, record (1914): 469.
Sarah Ellen JONES, born: 13 Apr 1895, single, parents: Elbert JONES and Deborah HENSLEY, death cause: "pneumonia and typhoid", informant: father

(Limestone), buried: Pleasant Grove, died: 29 Nov 1914, record (1914): 470.

Cordia Francis SHEPHERD, born: 28 May 1861, married, parents: S.K.N. PATTON (Sullivan County) and Catherine WALL (Sullivan County), death cause: "cancer of kidney", informant: Oscar S. VINCENT (Fall Branch), died: 16 Oct 1914, record: 471.

Miss Millie WHETSEL, age: 82 years, single, parents: not stated, death cause: "old age", buried: Mt. Wesley, died: 2nd District, 29 Nov 1914, record (1914): 472.

Clyde Donal HUMPHREYS, born: 9 Oct 1912, parents: C.C. HUMPHREYS and Willie MCKEE, death cause: "tonsilitis, bronchitis", informant: father (Limestone), buried: New Salem, died: 20 Nov 1914, record (1914): 473.

Infant COPP, female, parents: Walt COPP and Eva FELLERS, death cause: "born dead", informant: father (Chuckey), buried: Liberty, died: 27 Nov 1914, record (1914): 474.

Jane CAMPBELL, age: about 70 years, born: Greene County, married, parents: John RICHARD (VA) and mother not stated, death cause: "heart disease", informant: Thomas LYTLE (Jonesboro), buried: Fairview, died: 4 Nov 1914, record (1914): 475.

Robert Houston KEEBLE, born: 19 Nov 1914, parents: H.K. KEEBLE (Blount, TN) and Lizzie SCHAVER (VA), death cause: "meningitis", informant: father (Jonesboro), died: 28 Nov 1914, record (1914): 476.

Abraham CAMPBELL, born: 17 Nov 1831, widower, parents: William CAMPBELL and Sallie RICHARDS (VA), death cause: "heart disease", informant: S.B. CAMPBELL (Jonesboro), buried: Fairview, died: 14 Nov 1914, record (1914): 477.

Brazelton MOORE, born: 26 Apr 1840 in Greene County, parnets: William MOORE and Mary BRANDON, death cause: "illegible.. fractured femur", informant: Lucinda MOORE (Fall Branch), died: 18 Dec 1914, record (1914): 478.

William MOSELY, born: 17 Mar 1838 in Sullivan County, married, parents: not stated, death cause: "uremia and cystitis", informant: Nicy MOSELY (Fall

Branch), buried: Oak Glen, died: 21 Dec 1914, record (1914): 479.

Clarence SMITH, born: 16 Jun 1911, parents: Lafayette SMITH (Sullivan Co.) and Virginia JONES (Sullivan Co.), death cause: "bronchitis, tuberculosis", informant: Virgie SMITH (Jonesboro), died: 28 Nov 1914, record (1914): 480.

Iva Lee Virginia GRILLS, born: 25 Jul 1914 in Greene County, parents: W.T. GRILLS (Sullivan Co.) and Lena KELSEY (Roane Co.), death cause: "acute indigestion", informant: John W. HARRISON (Fall Branch), buried: Clover Bottom, TN., died: 25 Nov 1914, record (1914): 481.

Ramon B. ARNOLD, born: 26 Aug 1913, parents: J.C. ARNOLD (Hawkins Co.) and Mable DYKES (Greene Co.), death cause: "measles, pneumonia", buried: Lovelace Cemetery, died: Fall Branch, 10 Dec 1914, record (1914): 482.

Robert Elmer COX, born: 16 Mar 1910, parents: Matthew COX and Julia BROWN, death cause: "diptheria", informant: mother (Jonesboro), buried: Bethany Church, died: 28 Dec 1914, record: 483.

Marry PETERSON, age: 32 years, born: North Carolina, married, parents: S.S. MCCURRY (NC) and Dortha STAMPTON (NC), death cause: "abortion, septicemia", informant: D.M. PETERSON (Limestone), buried: New Salem, died: 7 Dec 1914, record (1914): 484.

Samuel B. ERWIN, born: 12 Feb 1844 in Unicoi County, married, parents: Samuel ERWIN and mother's name illegible, death cause: "heart disease", buried: Liberty Cemetery, died: 1st District, 24 Nov 1914, record (1914): 485.

Infant DUNBAR, male, parents: M.F. DUNBAR and Unna MCINTURFF (Erwin), death cause: "born dead", informant: father (Chcukey), buried: Liberty Cemetery, died: 5 Dec 1914, record (1914): 486.

Nathaniel T. BUCK, born: 18 Sep 1845 in Carter County, married, parents: Johnathon BUCK and Susie MORELAND, death cause: "paralysis", buried: Union Church, died: 8th District, 3 Dec 1914, record (1914): 487.

Paul T. DUGGER, born: 22 Dec 1914, parents: Thomas DUGGER and Ella May PAUL, death cause: illegible, informant: James MCINTURFF (Johnson City), buried: France Cemetery, died: 28 Dec 1914, record: 488.

J.C. PROPST, Jr., parents: J.C. PROPST and Elizabeth SLONAKER, death cause: "stillborn", buried: Payne Cemetery, died: 7 Dec 1914, record (1914): 489.

Lucinda FEATHERS, born: 3 Dec 1844, widow, parents: Samuel HUNT and Litia ELLIS, death cause: "heart truouble", buried: Barnes Cemetery, died: 10th District, 30 Dec 1914, record (1914): 490.

Sarah MATHERLY, age: 76 years, born: Johnson County, widow, parents: not stated, death cause: not stated, informant: John MATHERLY (Jonesboro), buried: Boones Creek Church, died: 10 Dec 1914, record (1914): 491.

Ida M. HAMILTON, born: 11 Aur 1877, married, parents: L.M. JACKSON and Martha COPAS, death cause: "tuberculosis of lungs", informant: R.D. JACKSON (Jonesboro), buried: Hales Chapel, died: 13 Dec 1914, record (1914): 492.

Amanda Fadora KIRKPATRICK, born: 11 May 1847, widow, parents: Henry HOSS and Anna SEVIER, death cause: "clothing caught fire, burned to death", informant: S (illebible) KIRKPATRICK (Jonesboro), died: 28 Dec 1914, record (1914): 493.

Niles Byrd INGLE, born: 21 Apr 1914, parents: S.W. INGLE and Jennie BARLOW, death cause: "pneumonia", informant: father (Jonesboro), buried: New Victory Cemetery, died: 24 Dec 1914, record (1914): 494.

Mary PATTON, born: 1 Nov 1900, parents: Samuel F. PATTON (Carter Co.) and Ida MILLION, death cause: "tuberculosis of spine", informant: father (Limestone), died: 12 Dec 1914, record (1914): 495.

Stella Mare PLEASANT, born: 9 Apr 1909, parents: Samuel PLEASANT and Lizzie COLLET, death cause: "mastoid abscess", informant: father (Limestone), buried: Mt. Bethel, died: 17 Dec 1914, record (1914): 496.

George WILSON, colored, age: 76 years, born: North Carolina, married, parents: Jake WILSON and Matilda WILSON, death cause: "disease kidney and heart",

buried: Hyder Cemetery, died: 2 Dec 1914, record (1914): 497.
Adoline HARRIS, colored, age: 75 years, born: Arkansas, death cause: "organic heart disease", informant: G.A. FITZGERALD (Johnson City), buried: West Lawn, died: 13 Dec 1914, record: 498.
James P. DYER, age: 43 years, married, merchant, parents: John H. DYER and Mary M. ALLISON, death cause: "cerebral hemorrhage", buried; Oak Hill, died: 9th District, 5 Dec 1914, record (1914): 499.
William CHINOUTH, born: 22 Jun 1838, married, carpenter, parents: Richard CHINOUTH and Martha ELLIS, death cause: "brain concussion from accident", informant: C.W. CHINOUTH (Johnson City), buried: Oak Hill, died: 6 Dec 1914, record: 500.
Cherry Aldridg SWIFT, age: 9 years, born: Nashville, parents: R.W. SWIFT and Matilda POWELL (KY), death cause: "gunshot wound in heart, killed accidently by brother", buried: Buena Vista, died: 8 Dec 1914, record (1914): 501.
Arthur OLIVER, Jr., born: 9 Dec 1914, parents: Arthur OLIVER and Florence (illegible), death cause: "premature", informant: P.P. GIBSON (Johnson City), buried: Onks Cemetery, died: 13 Dec 1914, record (1914): 502.
Sarah L. ROMINGER, born: 22 Mar 1859, widow, parents: __ HUX (Ireland) and mother not stated, death cause: "heart disease", informant: Sidney GURVIN (Johnson City), buried: Oak Hill, died: 14 Dec 1914, record (1914): 503.
Mollie DOUGLAS, age: 28 years, married, parents: E. (illebible) TOMPSON and __ GIBSON, death cause: "tuberculosis", buried: Erwin, died: 15 Dec 1914, record (1914): 504.
George E. SWADLEY, born: 26 Feb 1838, married, parents: Henry SWADLEY (VA) and Elizabeth ROADCAFF (VA), death cause: "heart disease", informant: Hunter SWADLEY (Johnson City), buried: Oak Hill, died: 16 Dec 1914, record (1914): 505.
Walter H. BROWN, age: 35 years, married, parents: Anderw S. BROWN and Agnes WILDS, death cause:

"appendicitis", buried: Greenville, died: 17 Dec 1914, record (1914): 506.

Matilda E. GARK, born: 6 Nov 1839 in Michigan, father illegible and Luavin A. THOMAS (NY), death cause: "lagrippe", buried: Millington, Michigan, died: 17 Dec 1914, record (1914): 507.

Infant HICE, male, father not stated and Gertrude HICE, death cause: "premature birth", informant: mother (Johnson City), buried: Buena Vista, born/died: 22 Dec 1914, record (1914): 508.

Annabell ASHBY, born: 25 Aug 1914, parents: Charles ASHBY and Ella ASHBORN (VA), death cause: "whooping cough", informant: W.J. ASHBY (Johnson City), buried: Buena Vista, died: 22 Dec 1914, record (1914): 509.

Jeremiah LANG, age: 36 years, born: Maine, single, parents: not stated, death cause: "pulmonary tuberculosis", buried: Portland, Maine, died: Soldier's Home, 24 Dec 1914, record (1914): 510.

Jacob STAUDEMAYER, age: 66 years, born: Pennsylvania, married, parents: not stated, death cause: "carcinoma of stomach", buried: Chicago, Illinois, died: Soldier's Home, 22 Dec 1014, record (1914): 511.

Emily COLLETTE, born: 1 Jul 1913, parents: Charles COLLETTE and Laura M. DARDEN, death cause: "whooping cough", informant: father (Johnson City), buried: Oak Hill, died: 28 Dec 1914, record (1914): 512.

Infant KILGORE, male, parents: Thomas KILGORE and Virgie MUSE, death cause: "premature birth", informant: J.D. HUFFINE (Johnson City), buried: Whitesburg, TN., died: 28 Dec 1914, record: 513.

Thomas LOWDY, born: 25 Dec 1886, married, parents: Jake ORREN and Maggie LOWDY, death cause: "pulmonary tuberculosis", informant: Jake ORREN (Johnson City), died: 28 Dec 1914, record (1914): 514.

Allen W. MONROE, age: 82 years, born: Kentucky, married, clergyman, parents: not stated, death cause: "interstitial nephritis", died: Soldier's Home, 10 Dec 1914, record (1914): 515.

James D. WARREN, age: 69 years, born: Michigan, married, parents: not stated, death cause: "cardiac dilatation", died: Soldier's Home, 12 Dec 1914, record (1914): 516.

Hugh B. MCNEILL, age: 70 years, born: Virginia, single, death cause: "mitral insufficiency", died: Soldier's Home, 14 Dec 1914, record: 517.

Walter CRESWICK alias William HICKMAN, age: 70 years, born: England, married, gunsmith, parents: not stated, death cause: "traumatism from railroad accident on 24 Dec 1914", died: Soldier's Home, 28 Dec 1914, record (1914): 518.

Antonio LOPEZ, age: 69 years, born: Spain, single, parents: not stated, death cause: "myocarditis", died: Soldier's Home, 31 Dec 1914, record: 519.

David DAVENPORT, born: 13 Mar 1834 in Russell County, VA., married, parents: Isom DAVENPORT (NC) and __ MILLION, death cause: "heart disease", buried: Onks Cemetery, died: 25 Dec 1914, record (1914): 322.

Luna DAVIS, born: 17 Feb 1879 in Greene County, single, parents: Phillip DAVIS (Greene Co.) and Sarah E. CRAWFORD (Greene Co.), death cause: "diptheria", informant: father (Limestone), died: 17 Dec 1914, record (1914): 323.

Woodson, T. MILLER, age: 30 years, born: Tennessee, single, parents: not stated, death cause: "pulmonary tuberculosis", buried: Russleville, TN., died: Soldier's Home 2 Jan 1915, record (1915): 20.

Infant WHITE, male, parents: Frank WHITE and Elizabeth ELLER, death cause: "stillborn", informant: father (Johnson City), buried: Union Cemetery, died: 4 Jan 1915, record (1915): 21.

Roberta Mae BARNETT, born: 3 Jan 1915, parents: Walter BARNETT (NC) and Minnie WHALEY, death cause: "hives", informant: T.N. BARNETT (Johnson City), buried: McInturff Cemetery, died: 4 Jan 1915, record (1915): 22.

John W. MCINTURFF, born: 3 Apr 1841 in Carter County, married, parents: John MCINTURFF and Mary MCINTURFF, death cause: "apoplexy", buried: Unicoi, TN., died: 9th District, 5 Jan 1915, record: 23.

Infant GARDNER, black, female, born: 13 Dec 1914, parents: father not stated and Katheline GARDNER, death cause: "hives and spasms", informant: Ader HOWELL (Johnson City), buried: West Lawn, died: 5 Jan 1915, record (1915): 24.

Infant REDWINE, male, parents: James Waller REDWINE and Margaret O'BRIEN, death cause: "stillborn", buried: Union Cemetery, died: 5 Jan 1915, record (1915): 25.

Robert BLAIR, age: 79 years, born: Ohio, parents: not stated, death cause: "aortic insufficiency", died: Soldier's Home, 3 Jan 1915, record (1915): 26.

Michael FITZGERALD, age: 71 years, born: Ireland, parents: not stated, death cause: "cerebral hemorrahage", buried: New York City, died: Soldier's Home, 3 Jan 1915, record (1915): 27.

Charles HERMAN, age: 71 years, born: Germany, parents: not stated, death cause: "nephritis", died: Soldier's Home, 4 Jan 1915, record (1915): 28.

Bordie M. COLLINS, born: 29 Jun 1879 in Sullivan County, single, parents: J.M. COLLINS (Sullivan Co.) and Malissa MILLER (Sullivan Co.), death cause: illegible, informant: D.E. DIDDLE (Johnson City), buried: Oak Hill, died: 7 Jan 1915, record: 29.

John PENDLETON, colored, age: 74 years, born : Virginia, widower, parents: father not stated and Hariet JOHNSON (VA), death cause: illegible, informant: Lula HARRIS (Johnson City), buried: Roan Hill Cemetery, died: 9 Jan 1915, record (1915): 30.

Ralph WISHONG, born: 8 Jan 1915, parents: Henry WISHONG and Melvina GRAYBILL (VA), death cause: "unknown", informant: J.S. MORRELL (Johnson City), buried: Buena Vista, died: 9 Jan 1915, record (1915): 31.

Etta Cornelia CAUVINS (?), age: 36 years, born: Yancey County, NC., single, parents: W.M. (illegible) (NC) and Sarah E. WILLIS (NC), death cause: "pulmonary tuberculosis", buried: Oak Hill, died: 14 Jan 1915, record (1915): 32.

William Howard RADFORD, born: 13 Mar 1909, parents: W.C. RADFORD (NC) and Mattie C. LACEY, death cause: "accident, gunshot wound in abdomen", informant: father (Hampton, TN), buried: Blevins Cemetery, died: Memorial Hospital, 16 Jan 1915, record: 33.

Lillie BRIDGES, colored, born: 4 Jul 1892, married, parents: George CAMERON and Hattie ERVIN, death cause: "fractured rib resulting in (illegible)", informant: Hattie CAMERON (Johnson City), buried: Elizabethton, died: 18 Jan 1915, record (1915): 34.

Mary CLARK, age: 62 years, 6 months and 6 days, single, parents: Jacob CLARK (VA) and Sarah BOWMAN, death cause: "heart lesion", buried: Knob Creek, died: 9th District, 18 Jan 1915, record (1915): 35.

Nancy PERSELL, born: 11 Oct 1854 in North Carolina, married, parents: John R. WILBORNE (NC) and Nancy NAYLOR (NC), death cause: "tuberculosis", informant: H.H. PERSELL (Johnson City), buried: Oak Hill, died: 19 Jan 1915, record (1915): 36.

Mrs. Sabery FRY, age: 54 years, married, parents: __ CADE and mother not stated, death cause: "peritonitis", informant: T.W. MOSIER (Johnson City), buried: Buena Vista, died: 21 Jan 1915, record (1915): 37.

Leon BROWN, age: 38 years, born: Texas, single, cowboy, parents: not stated, death cause: "pulmonary tuberculosis", buried: Ardmore, Oklahoma, died: Soldier's Home, 22 Jan 1915, record (1915): 38.

Dennis H. DUNN, age: 69 years, born: Wisconsin, married, nurseryman, death cause: "pulmonary tuberculosis", buried: Milwaukee, Wisconsin, died: Soldier's Home, 19 Jan 1915, record (1915): 39.

Luther NELSON, born: 11 Jan 1915, parents: John W. NELSON (Hamilton County) and Callie Ann NELSON, death cause: "bold hives", buried: Providence Church", died: 17th District, 18 Jan 1915, record (1915): 1.

Henry W. SHERFEY, age: 68 years, single, parents: Joseph SHERFEY and Susan MILLER (VA), death cause: "mitral regurgitation", buried: Limestone, died: 17th District, 12 Jan 1915, record (1915): 2.

Hannah BAKER, born: 5 Jan 1834, married, parents: Sam LYMER and Susan KRAUSE, death cause: "myocarditis", died: 10th District, 13 Jan 1915, record (1915): 3.

George Una HARDIN, born: 17 Sep 1914 in Greene County, parents: George W. HARDIN and Hannah BROWN

(Greene Co.), death cause: "whooping cough", informant: father (Chuckey), buried: Philadelphia, died: 11 Jan 1915, record (1915): 4.

Martha Ellen HALL, born: 3 Oct 1909, parents: Joseph HALL and Carie Mae FORD, death cause: "meningitis", informant: father (Jonesboro), buried: Tom Ford Cemetery, died: 25 Jan 1915, record (1915): 5.

Bettie W. BROWNING, age: 76 years, 1 month and 14 days, married, parents: John H. CARR and Myra CROUCH, death cause: "influenza", informant: J.W. BROWNING (Gray), buried: Dunkard Church Cemetery, died: 5 Jan 1915, record (1915): 6.

Hannah BAKER, born: 5 Jan 1834, widow, parents: Hiram LARIMER and Susan KRAUSE, death cause: "heart trouble", informant: Chrisley LARIMER (Rt. 4, Johnson City), buried: Krause Cemetery, died: 13 Jan 1915, record (1915): 7.

Infant GIBSON, black, parents: Starling GIBSON (SC) and Bertha RHEA, death cause: "stillborn", informant: Jenny RHEA (Jonesboro), died: 1 Jan 1915, record (1915): 8.

Lucinda HARRISON, born: __ Jul 1875, married, parents: Tom MORGAN (Greene County) and Sarah HARRIS (Unicoi County), death cause: "Brights disease", informant: J.M. HARRISON (Jonesboro), died: 14 Jan 1915, record (1915): 9.

James LISENBY, age: 59 years, widower, parents: not stated, death cause: "kidney disease", buried: County, Farm, died: Jonesboro, 14 Jan 1915, record (1915): 10.

Sophia HEUES, colored, age: 78 years, widow, parents: Jack BIRCH and mother not stated, death cause: "pneumonia", informant: Frank BUHR (Jonesboro), died: 21 Jan 1915, record (1915): 11.

Sam EDWARD, colored, born: 14 Aug 1870, married, parents: Sam EDWARDS and mother not stated, death cause: "bronchial pneumonia", died: Jonesboro, 25 Jan 1915, record (1915): 12.

John T. BROWN, colored, born: 1 Aug 1887, married, parents: James BROWN (NC) and Sophia YANCEY (NC), death cause: "pulmonary tuberculosis", informant:

Nola C. BROWN (Jonesboro), died: 25 Jan 1915, record (1915): 13.

Rachel MARSHAL, colored, widow, parents: Richard CHESTER and Lucy ROBERTS, death cause: "heart disease", informant: Ella M. CARTER (Jonesboro), died: 25 Jan 1915, record (1915): 14.

Sarah Ann AUSTIN, age: 75 years and 8 days, born: North Carolina, married, parents: Clem ARWOOD (GA) and Sarah Ann ARWOOD (NC), death cause: "pneumonia", informant: Clem AUSTIN (Limestone), buried: New Salem, died: 20 Jan 1915, record (1915): 15.

Francis Cornelia CHAPEL, born: 1 Dec 1856 in Wilkes County, NC., married, parents: Nelson JOHNSON (NC) and mother not stated, death cause: "pneumonia", informant: J.L. CHAPEL (Limestone), buried: New Salem, died: 27 Jan 1915, record (1915): 16.

Alice Francis LOYD, age: 4 months and 29 days, parents: R.B. LOYD and Bertha SLIGER, death cause: "meningitis", informant: Y.N. KYKER (Telford), buried: New Victory, died: 30 Jan 1915, record (1915): 17.

Ivon Wallis BAILEY, born: 27 Dec 1914, parents: I.N. BAILEY (NC) and Anna L. WALLER, death cause: "lung congestion", buried: New Victory, died: 3 Jan 1915, record (1915): 18.

Infant GRIMES, colored, male, born: 1 Jan 1915, parents: Guy GRIMES and Aurolia JOHNSON, death cause: "congenital deformity", informant; father (Johnson City), buried: West Lawn, died: 4 Jan 1915, record (1915): 19.

Rachel A. SAYLOR, born: 3 Dec 1854, widow, parents: James PRICE and Maggie CORNELL, death cause: illegible, informant: J.W. SAYLOR (Johnson City), buried: Lowdy Cemetery, died: 24 Jan 1915, record (1915): 40.

Infant MILLER, male, born: 19 Jan 1915, parents: E.H. MILLER and Marion FREBERG, death cause: illegible, buried: Monte Vista, died: 27 Jan 1915, record (1915): 41.

Infant MORRISON, male, parents: H.G. MORRISON (VA) and Lucile BARKER (VA), death cause: "premature", buried: Gate City, born/died: 29 Jan 1915, record (1915): 42.

Horace L. FARMER, age: 66 years, born: Tennessee, married, shoemaker, parents: not stated, death cause: "mitral insufficiency", died: Soldier's Home, 11 Jan 1915, record (1915): 43.

Frank METZ, age: 73 years, born: Germany, single, parents: not stated, death cause: "alcoholism and exposure", died: Soldier's Home, 11 Jan 1915, record (1915): 44.

William DWYER, age: 78 years, born: "on the ocean", widower, blacksmith, death cause: "cardiac dilatation", died: Soldier's Home, 16 Jan 1915, record (1915): 45.

Zachary T. COLE, age: 70 years, born: Missouri, widower, parents: not stated, death cause: "cardiac dilitation", died: Soldier's Home, 11 Jan 1915, record (1915): 46.

Alfred BRADLEY, age: 77 years, born: New York, widower, railroad conductor, parents: not stated, death cause: "gangrene of foot", died: Soldier's Home, 12 Jan 1915, record (1915): 47.

Harrison V. MILLER, age: 78 years, born Pennsylvania, widower, book keeper, death cause: "cystitis", died: Soldier's Home, 15 Jan 1915, record (1915): 48.

George W. REID, age: 58 years, born: Iowa, single, parents: not stated, death cause: "pulmonary tuberculosis", died: Soldier's Home, 24 Jan 1915, record (1915): 49.

John W. NEVILLE, age: 79 years, born: Virginia, widower, cattle dealer, parents: not stated, death cause: "myo carditis", died: Soldier's Home, 28 Jan 1915, record (1915): 50.

William L. MAULFAIR, age: 72 years, born: Pennsylvania, widower, druggest, parents: not stated, death cause: "nephritis", died: Soldier's Home, 28 Jan 1915, record (1915): 51.

Miss Andy BAKER, born: 2 Jan 1911, parents: W.P. BAKER and Minnie WILSON (NC), death cause: "clothing caught fire, burned", buried: Union Cemetery, died: 2 Jan 1915, record (1915): 52.

Polly Marinda FERGUSON, age: 82 years, widow, parents: Robert HALE and mother not stated, death cause: "unknown", buried: Pleasant Grove, died: 13th District, 16 Jan 1915, record (1915): 53.

Walter Preston SHIPLEY, born: 17 Dec 1891, single, parents: C.F. SHIPLEY (Sullivan County) and Julia SHORT, death cause: "measles", informant: Tom Shipley (Fall Branch), buried: M.E. Church, died: 11 Jan 1915, record (1915): 54.

Nancy Ellen HARTMAN, age: about 59 years, married, parents: Franklin FURGUSON and Margaret IRVIN, death cause: illegible, died: 13th District, 6 Feb 1915, record (1915): 55.

Viola WHITTAKR, born: 21 Nov 1866, married, parents: Thomas BRANDON and __ RINEHART (NC), death cause: "catarral occlusion of bile duct", informant: A.R. BRANDON (Fall Branch), died: 15 Feb 1915, record (1915): 56.

Joseph BOOTH, born: 26 Feb 1830, married, parents: not stated, death cause: "old age", informant: J.W. BOOTH, buried: Cherokee, died: 4th District, 26 Feb 1915, record (1915): 57.

Ellen DURHAM, age: about 78 years, born: North Carolina, widow, parents: J. SHOEMAKER (NC) and mother not stated, death cause: not stated, informant: T.N. DURHAM (Jonesboro), buried: Boones Creek, died: 5 Feb 1915, record (1915): 58.

Sallie CHARLTON, born: 11 Sep 1871 in Greene County, married, parents: Abraham DYKES (Hawkins County) and __ MARSHALL (Hawkins County), death cause: "pulmonary tuberculosis", informant: E.T. CHARLTON (Fall Branch), buried: Lovelace Cemetery, died: 9 Feb 1915, record (1915): 59.

Ambrose D. BURGER, age: 52 years, born: Pennsylvania, married, steel worker, parents: not stated, death cause: "diabetes", buried: Harriman, TN., died: Soldier's Home, 1 Feb 1915, record (1915): 60.

Elias W. SMITH, age: 70 years, born: Kentucky, widower, dentist, parents: not stated, death cause: "cerebral hemorrhage", died: Soldier's Home, 1 Feb 1915, record (1915): 61.

George W. NEWBRAND, age: 37 years, born: Ohio, stenographer, parents: not stated, death cause: "pulmonary tuberculosis", died: Soldier's Home, 4 Feb 1915, record (1915): 62.
Henry L. ADDISON, age: 88 years, born: Maine, widower, civil engineer, parents: not stated, death cause: "arterio sclerosis", died: Soldier's Home, 8 Feb 1915, record (1915): 63.
John Calvin FORD, age: about 40 years, married, parents: J.R. FORD and Elvisa COX, death cause: "tuberculosis of lungs", informant: Henry FORD (Jonesboro), died: 7 Feb 1915, record (1915): 64.
John W. DULANEY, age: 67 years, married, parents: Milton DULANEY and Orpia FINE, death cause: "diabetes and heart failure", informant: E.D. DULANEY (Jonesboro), buried: Eaden Cemetery, died: 1 Feb 1915, record (1915): 65.
Monroe F. KIRBY, age: 40 years, born: Illinois, single, parents: not stated, death cause: "pulmonary tuberculosis", died: Soldier's Home, 27 Feb 1915, record (1915): 66.
James W. LONG, age: 79 years, born: Indiana, widower, coal miner, parents: not stated, death cause: "lobar pneumonia", died: Soldier's Home, 24 Feb 1915, record (1915): 67.
Charles ASHLEY, age: 66 years, born: Georgia, married, parents: not stated, death cause: "cerebral hemorrhage", died: Soldier's Home, 19 Feb 1915, record (1915): 68.
Jacob CROPF, age: 43 years, born: Germany, blacksmith, single, parents: not stated, death cause: "acute pericarditis", died: Soldier's Home, 16 Feb 1915, record (1915): 69.
Fritz THAYER, age: 47 years, born: Canada, single, parents: not stated, death cause: "pulmonary tuberculosis", died: Soldier's Home, 16 Feb 1915, record (1915): 70.
Christopher DIPPRE, age: 63 years, born: Pennsylvania, single, parents: not stated, death cause: "mitral insufficiency", died: Soldier's Home, 15 Feb 1915, record (1915): 71.

Henry CLAY, age: 76 years, born: Virginia, married, blacksmith, parents: not stated, death cause: "perilonites", died: Soldier's Home, 10 Feb 1915, record (1915): 72.

Spero A. SVORONAS, age: 47 years, born: Greece, single, florist, parents: Analtaie SVORONAS (Greece) and Penelope COURI (Greece), death cause: "Brights, uremia", informant: Danepisos SVORONAS (Chicago, Illinois), buried: Oak Hill, died: 27 Feb 1915, record (1915): 73.

Charles W. HESTER, born: __ Feb 1890 in North Carolina, married, parents: John HESTER and Susie WILSON (NC), death cause: "injuries from railroad accident", informant; J.M. HESTER (Cranberry, NC), buried: Cranberry, died: 26 Feb 1915, record: 74.

Infant ANDERS, male, parents: Cleve ANDERS (VA) and Ethel BEDWELL (VA), death cause: "stillborn", informant: father (Johnson City), buried: Buena Vista, died: 23 Feb 1915, record (1915): 75.

Emily NELSON, colored, age: 75 years, born: Georgia, widow, parents: Sam AERTERE (GA) and mother not stated, death cause: "pneumonia", buried: West Lawn Cemetery, died: 17 Feb 1915, record (1915): 76.

Jocie Bramlett BUCK, born: 25 Jun 1846 in Mississippi, widow, parents: John BRAMLETT (Alabama) and __ FORTSON (Alabama), death cause: "pneumonia", informant: P.L. GREGORY (Johnson City), buried: Oak Hill, died: 17 Feb 1915, record (1915): 77.

Dave MCINTURFF, born: 6 Mar 1876, married, parents: Will MCINTURFF and Mattie DANIELS, death cause: "tuberculosis and heart disease", informant: James MCINTURFF (Johnson City), buried: Simerly Cemetery, died: 16 Feb 1915, record (1915): 78.

Mildred BUCHANAN, born: 5 Oct 1898 in North Carolina, parents: Stokes BUCHANAN and Nola BROYLES, death cause: "nephritis", informant: father (Johnson City), buried: Oak Hill, died: 15 Feb 1915, record (1915): 79.

Sallie GARRON, age: 37 years, married, parents: Jake SMITH and Nancy BENNETT, death cause: "heart disease", buried: Oak Hill, died: 9th District, 15 Feb 1915, record (1915): 80.

John Calvin FORD, age: 40 years, married, parents: Robert FORD and Laura COX, death cause: "tuberculosis", buried: Buffalo Ridge, died: 7 Feb 1915, record (1915): 81.

Sarah C. TOMLINSON, born: 1 Aug 1887, single, teacher, parents: John W. TOMLINSON and Mary E. SMITH, death cause: "pneumonia", informant: father (Johnson City), buried: Gunning Cemetery, died: 5 Feb 1915, record (1915): 82.

Infant HORTON, colored, male, parents: Arthur HORTON and Lannie KELLY, death cause: "stillborn", informant: father (Johnson City), buried: Hyder Cemetery, died: 2 Feb 1915, record (1915): 83.

Rufus JONES, age: 2 years, parents: Robert F. JONES (NC) and __ CRUMM, death cause: "whooping cough", informant: R.F. JONES (Chuckey), buried: Greene County, died: 14 Feb 1915, record (1915): 84.

John W. DULANEY, age: 67 years, married, parents: Milton DULANEY and Orpha FINE, death cause: "diabetes and heart failure", informant: E.D. DULANEY (Jonesboro), buried: Eden Cemetery, died: 1 Feb 1915, record (1915): 85.

Infant MILLER, female, parents: Moses MILLER and Nellie TYREE, death cause: "stillborn", informant: Zacharias TYREE (Johnson City), buried: Carather Creek, died: 17 Feb 1915, record (1915): 86.

Robert Franklin VANCE, born: 7 Feb 1915, parents: Calvin VANCE and Emeline STORY, death cause: "asphixiation", died: 16 Feb 1915, record: 87.

Mary Pauline DAVIS, born: 9 Feb 1915, parents: Charles DAVIS (Greene County) and Lucretia DOBBINS (Greene County), death cause: "premature birth", informant: father (Limestone), died: 12 Feb 1915, record (1915): 88.

Lewana BAIR, age: 25 years, born: Carter County, married, parents: Joe WALKER (Carter Co.) and Eliza LYON (Carter Co.), death cause: "pulmonary tuberculosis", informant: W.H. BAIR (Jonesboro), died: 8 Feb 1915, record (1915): 89.

Hyawatha SHADE, colored, born: 20 Aug 1912, parents: Henry SHADE (NC) and Pearl RUSSELL, death cause:

"memingitis", informant: father (Jonesboro), died: 4 Feb 1915, record (1915): 90.
David HULSE, born: 3 Nov 1913, parents: S.B. HULSE (Sullivan County) and Ise (illegible) (Johnson County), death cause: "pneumonia", informant: father (Jonesboro), buried: Cherokee, died: 6 Feb 1915, record (1915): 91.
Infant HEAD, female, parents: father not stated and Carrie HEAD, death cause: "stillborn", informant: Walter HEAD (Jonesboro), died: 21 Feb 1915, record (1915): 92.
Mary LANE, age: 63 years, widow, parents: Ezekiel HAMMETT (NC) and mother not stated, death cause: "tuberculosis of lungs", informant: Byrd REED (Jonesboro), buried: 8th District, died: 28 Feb 1915, record (1915): 93.
Laura Hassie WADDELL, born: 5 Feb 1878, married, parents: James W. SMITH and Roina BROWN, death cause: "pulmonary tuberculosis", informant: Clyde WADDELL (Limestone), buried: Asbury Cemetery, died: 11 Feb 1915, record (1915): 94.
John SALTS, age: 70 years, widower, parents: Isaac SALTS and Emeline MCCARTY, death cause: "lobar pneumonia", informant: Steve BOVELL, buried: Asbury Cemetery, died: 6 Mar 1915, record (1915): 95.
Rutheuer TOWNSEND, female, age: 93 years, born: North Carolina, parents: Andy HOLLER and mother not stated, death cause: "cerebral hemorrhage", informant: Moses BAILEY (Telford), died: 30 Mar 1915, record (1915): 96.
Lilly Belle WILSON, born: 11 Mar 1915, parents: Ed WILSON (Sullivan County) and Ella STUART, death cause: "weakness", informant: J.H. JONES, died: 4th District, 11 Mar 1915, record (1915): 97.
William A. GARBER, born: 17 Dec 1846, depot agent, parents: Isaac GARBER (VA) and Rachel BROWN, death cause: "heart and kidney disease", buried: Cherokee, died: 5 Mar 1915, record (1915): 98.
Infant EDENS, male, parents: Eugene EDENS and Carrie STOUT (Carter County), death cause: "stillborn", informant: R.W. DULANEY (Jonesboro), buried: Cherokee, died: 16 Mar 1915, record (1915): 99.

Absolom Lowry SCOTT, born: 6 Sep 1831, married, stone mason, parents: David SCOTT, and Nancy B. LOWRY (Sullivan County), death cause: "old age and uremia", informant: D.J. FINE (Johnson City), buried: Union Cemetery, died: 21 Mar 1915, record (1915): 100.

Zachariah Taylor LEE, born: 29 Aug 1851 in Virginia, married, parents: not stated, death cause: "heart disease", buried: Lee Cemetery, died: 8th District, 2 Mar 1915, record (1915): 101.

James Wade BURGESS, born: 21 Sep 1871 in Greene County, married, parents: Aden H. BURGESS (Haywood Co., NC) and Catherine M. REEVES (Greene Co.), death cause: "carcinoma of liver", informant: J.S. BURGESS (Chuckey), buried: Liberty Cemetery, died: 29 Mar 1915, record (1915): 102.

Noah VINES, born: 24 Jul 1828 in Johnson County, widower, parents: William VINES and Rosanna DUNCAN, death cause: "diarrhoea", informant: Phil S. TAYLOR (Jonesboro), buried: New Salem, died: 1 Mar 1915, record (1915): 103.

Nancy BROOKS, born: 19 Dec 1859 in North Carolina, widow, parents: Moses MILLER (NC) and Ruth Ellen ENSOR (NC), death cause: "pernicious anemia", informant: James M. BROOKS (Jonesboro), buried: Simpson Cemetery, died: 2 Mar 1915, record: 104.

Harris FERGUSON, age: 5 years and 6 months, parents: Joe FERGUSON and mother's name illegible, death cause: illegible, informant: J.F. FERGUSON (Jonesboro), buried: Cherokee Cemetery, died: 2 Mar 1915, record (1915): 105.

Infant KEYS, born: 28 Feb 1915, parents: John T. KEYS and Jessie BABB, death cause: "meningitis", informant: father (Jonesboro), died: 3 Mar 1915, record (1915): 106.

John SAYLOR, born: 6 Mar 1841, widower, parents: William SAYLOR and __ GARBER, death cause: "arterio sclerosis", informant: J.R. SAYLOR (Jonesboro), buried: Pleasant Valley, died: 4 Mar 1915, record (1915): 107.

Martha Isabel CARTER, born: 28 May 1861 in Greene County, married, parents: Dr. G.N. BAILEY, Sr.,

(Greene Co.) and Sarah MCAMIS (Greene Co.), death cause: "asthma and heart failure", informant: Mrs. C.W. MCCOLLUM (Bulls Gap), buried: Greeneville, died: 15 Mar 1915, record (1915): 108.
Ruben D. NANCE, born: 5 Apr 1848 in Grainger, TN., married, parents: Prior NANCE (Grainger) and Mary VINYARD (Grainger), death cause: "arterio sclerosis", informant: J.W. WHITLOCK (Joesboro), died; 19 Mar 1915, record (1915): 109.
Ratchel Anita ANDERSON, born: 15 Dec 1881, single, parents: Sam H. ANDERSON (Sullivan County) and E. Everton MASON, death cause: "pneumonia", informant: J.H. ANDERSON (Jonesboro), died: 22 Mar 1915, record (1915): 110.
Samuel B. HOWARD, born: 6 Aug 1877, married, parents: James HOWARD (Johnson County) and Nancy C. MORELAND (Johnson County), death cause: "alcoholism and pneumonia", informant: Lula HOWARD (Jonesboro), buried: Fairview, died: 23 Mar 1915, record: 111.
James K. LITTLE, born: 19 Apr 1836, married, parents: John LITTLE and Ruth BOREN, death cause: "arterio sclerosis", informant: Mrs. Amanda LITTLE (Limestone), buried: Dunkard Church Cemetery, died: 26 Mar 1915, record (1915): 112.
Infant LOCKNER, female, parents: James LOCKNER and Mary J. LOCKNER (NC), death cause: "stillborn", informant: Joseph LOCKNER (Embreeville), buried: Tucker Cemetery, died: 2 Mar 1915, record: 113.
Andrew M. ZELL, born: 27 Mar 1915, parents: Robert L. ZELL (Minn) and Delia B. CURTIS, death cause: "premature", informant: A.M. CURTIS (Jonesboro), buried: Buffalo Ridge, died: 28 Mar 1915, record (1915): 114.
Daniel FOUST, born: 16 Sep 1830, married, parents: not stated, death cause: "arterio sclerosis", informant: C.H. FOUST (Greeneville), buried: South Watauga, died: 25 Mar 1915, record (1915): 115.
J. Montie PATTON, born: 6 Jun 1838, divorced, parents: George PATTON and Jane PITMAN, death cause: "lagrippe", informant: H.N. DILLOW (Limestone), buried: Asbury Cemetery, died: 10 Mar 1915, record (1915): 116.

Delia Taylor BALL, born: 17 Dec 1843, parents: Bailey COLLINS and Susan MCGHECHAN, death cause: "aortic regurgitation", informant: D.L. MILLION (Knoxville), buried: Mt. Wesley, died: 16 Mar 1915, record (1915): 117.

Susan LEADFORD, born: 29 Apr 1843 in Unicoi County, married, parents: Joseph TIPTON (NC) and Caroline HONEYCUTT (NC), death cause: "carcinoma of pancreas", informant: G.B. LEDFORD (Jonesboro), buried: Pleasant Valley, died: 18 Mar 1915, record (1915): 118.

Infant GRAY, female, parents: John L. GRAY (Greene County) and Mattie ARCHER, death cause: "stillborn", informant: father (Jonesboro), died: 20 Mar 1915, record (1915): 119.

Martha DROKE, born: 30 Apr 1842, widow, parents: David WOOD (Sullivan Co.) and Jennie ALEXANDER (Sullivan Co.), death cause: "pulmonary tuberculosis", informant: James SMITH (Jonesboro), buried: Fairview, died: 23 Mar 1915, record: 120.

Daniel F. MCHENRY, age: 70 years, born: New Jersey, widower, saylor, parents: not stated, death cause: "cardiac dilitation", died: Soldier's Home, 28 Mar 1915, record (1915): 121.

Howard P. SMITH, age: 37 years, born: Louisiana, parents: not stated, death cause: "pulmonary tuberculosis", died: Soldier's Home, 27 Mar 1915, record (1915): 122.

Thomas H. SHARP, age: 50 years, born: New Jersey, widower, candy maker, parents: not stated, death cause: "morphine poisoning", died: Soldier's Home, 23 Mar 1915, record (1915): 123.

William REMINGTON, age: 50 years, born: New York, single, parents: not stated, death cause: "pulmonary tuberculosis", died: Soldier's Home, 23 Mar 1915, record (1915): 124.

John BRITT, age: 61 years, born: Indiana, widower, painter, parents: not stated, death cause: "pulmonary tuberculosis", died: Soldier's Home, 16 Mar 1915, record (1915): 125.

Herbert L. SALLIE, age: 41 years, born: Arkansas, parents: not stated, death cause: "pulmonary

tuberculosis", died: Soldier's Home, 15 Mar 1915, record (1915): 126.
Richard ALEXANDER, colored, age: 78 years, born: Alabama, widower, parents: not stated, death cause: "cerebral hemorrhage", died: Soldier's Home, 14 Mar 1915, record (1915): 127.
Ira S. HATCHER, age: 80 years, born: Maine, widower, parents: not stated, death cause: "interstitial nephritis", died: Soldier's Home, 13 Mar 1915, record (1915): 128.
Sidney A. ALLEN, age: 70 years, born: Maine, widower, druggist, parents: not stated, death cause: "mitral insufficiency", died: Soldier's Home, 9 Mar 1915, record (1915): 129.
Mary Elizabeth WEAVER, born: 29 Aug 1912, parents: J.D. WEAVER and Bessie SHORT, death cause: "meningitis", informant: father (Johnson City), buried: Buena Vista, died: 28 Mar 1915, record (1915): 130.
Will JOHNSON, colored, age: 29 years, born: Virginia, married, parents: not stated, death cause: "consumption", informant: Nannie JOHNSON (Johnson City), buried: West Lawn, died: 28 Mar 1913, record (1915): 131.
Martha C. SNODGRASS, born: 14 Apr 1854, married, parents: William SMITH (NC) and Julia BORING, death cause: "tuberculosis", informant: T.Y. SNODGRASS (Johnson City), buried: Milligan, died: 27 Mar 1915, record (1915): 132.
Cora Gracie YOUNG, colored, age: 20 years, married, parents: John WALTON (VA) and Maggie REED (NC), death cause: "pneumonia", informant: Tom YOUNG (Johnson City), buried: West Lawn, died: 25 Mar 1915, record (1915): 133.
Jacob VANDENBURG, age: 69 years, born: New York, widower, Railroad engineer, parents: not stated, death cause: "cerebral hemorrhage", buried: St. Cloud, FL, died: Soldier's Home, 23 Mar 1915, record (1915): 134.
J.H. RENGLEY, born: 20 Aug 1964 in Virginia, married, parents: James H. RENGLEY (VA) and Alice VILE (VA), death cause: "diabolic coma", informant;

Mrs. J.H. RANGLEY (Johnson City), buried: Stewart, VA., 23 Mar 1915, record (1915): 135.

Lilcie L. LOVE, colored, born: __ May 1895, single, parents: Henry LOVE and Eva LOVE, death cause: illegible, informant: father (Johnson City), buried: West Lawn, died: 21 Mar 1915, record (1915): 136.

John William PICKLE, born: 6 Jan 1913, parents: William PICKLE and Bell DENSMORE, death cause: "indigestion", informant: W.W. PICKLE (Johnson City), buried: Oak Hill, died: 28 Mar 1915, record (1915): 137.

Laura M. HILBERT, born: 14 Oct 1872 in Carter County, single, parents: William SHIPLEY and Emma MCKINNEY, death cause: "asthma and pneumonia", buried: Boones Creek, died: 20 Mar 1915, record (1915): 138.

John P. SCHWAB, age: 67 years, born: New Jersey, widower, parents: not stated, death cause: "mitral insufficiency", died: Soldier's Home, 2 Mar 1915, record (1915): 139

Almira WHITESIDE, born: 2 Jul 1847 in Pennsylvania, married, parents: William REEDLER (PA) and Irabela HENDERSON (PA), death cause: "paraplegia and cardiac (illegible)", informant: W.B. WHITESIDE (Johnson City), buried: Oak Hill, died: 19 Mar 1915, record (1915): 140.

Dewy DRAIN, age: 16 years, parents: James DRAIN and Ida DAVIS, death cause: "epilepsy", buried: Greene County, died: 18 Mar 1915, record (1915): 141.

J.T. WHITE, age: 2 years and 4 months, born: Sullivan County, parents: N.M. WHITE (Roane Co.) and Ada BERRY (Sullivan Co.), death cause: "lagrippe", buried: White Cemetery, Boones Creek, died: 18 Mar 1915, record (1915): 142.

Alfred Stewart TREADWAY, born: 29 Oct 1894 in Carter County, single, parents: J.H. TREADWAY and Jane INGRAM, death cause: "appendicidal abscess", informant: G.E. TREADWAY (Johnson City), buried: Patton Simmons Cemetery, died: 17 Mar 1915, record (1915): 143.

Maggie M. ELLIS, colored, born: 21 Apr 1891 in Bristol, VA., single, parents: Frank ELLIS and Mary

WALKER (VA), death cause: "tuberculosis", informant: father (Johnson City), buried: West Lawn, died: 15 Mar 1915, record (1915): 144.

Teddy MOODY, age: 1 year and 10 days, parents: Ben MOODY and Nora BUTLER (VA), death cause: "malnutrition", buried: Oak Hill, died: 15 Mar 1915, record (1915): 145.

John R. THOMPSON, born: 14 Aug 1843 in Louisiana, widower, parents: James W. THOMPSON (LA) and mother not stated (Mississippi), death cause: "myo carditis, uremia", informant: M.W. THOMPSON (Johnson City), buried: Oak Hill, died: 13 Mar 1915, record (1915): 146.

John William WILLIS, born: 27 Jan 1915, parents: John WILLIS (Washington Co., VA) and Lou Emma May VANHOY (Carter Co.), death cause: "broncho pneumonia", buried: Windale, VA., died: 7 Mar 1915, record (1915): 147.

William GRANT, age: 82 years, born: England, single, seaman, parents: not stated, death cause: "arterio sclerosis", died: Soldier's Home, 4 Mar 1915, record (1915): 148.

Thomas MURPHY, age: 64 years, born: New York, single, parents: not stated, death cause: "pulmonary tuberculosis", buried: Peoria, Illinois, died: Soldier's Home, 3 Mar 1915, record (1915): 149.

John MURRAY, age: 48 years, born: Louisiana, married, parents: not stated, death cause: "pulmonary tuberculosis", died: Soldier's Home, 2 Mar 1915, record (1915): 150.

George W. MOORE, colored, age: 74 years, born: Alabama, married, parents: Sims MOORE (Ala) and Delia DIXON (Ala), death cause: "pneumonia fever", informant: George MOORE (Johnson City), buried: West Lawn, died: 1 Mar 1915, record (1915): 151.

Mrs. O.A. SMITH, born: 15 DEc 1838 in Hanover County, VA., married, parents: C.C. BUTLER (VA) and Judy LAWRENCE (VA), death cause: "pneumonia and grip", buried: Bristol, VA., died: 9th District, 1 Mar 1915, record (1915): 152.

Louise GOOD, born: 7 Mar 1915, parents: Charles GOOD and Virgie C. HAMMETT, death cause: not stated, informant: J.A. CHATMAN (Jonesboro), buried: Boones Creek, died: 7 Mar 1915, record (1915): 153.

Joseph ARCHER, born: 1 Jun 1836, widower, parents: Hany HALE and Rachel ARCHER, death cause: "cancer", informant: D.W. ARCHER (Piney Flats), buried: Oak Hill, died: 2 Mar 1915, record (1915): 154.

Sarah Ellen STANTON, born: 4 Jun 1851, married, parents: Jacob TEMPLIN and Sarah BOOTHE, death cause: "broncho pneumonia", informant: Ida Grace STANTON (Limestone), died: 25 Mar 1915, record (1915): 155.

Carmel SHERFEY, born: 7 Apr 1915, parents: John SHERFEY (Sullivan Co.) and Mattie GIBSON, death cause: "unknown", informant: father (Jonesboro), buried: Double Springs, Sullivan County, died: 20 Apr 1915, record (1915): 156.

Nancy FULWILER, born: 2 Jan 1846 in Virginia, single, parents: John FULWILER (VA) and mother not stated, death cause: "cancer of (illegible)", informant: Alvin FULWILER, buried: Baptist Church, Fall Branch, died: 25 Apr 1915, record (1915): 157.

Danl POORE, parents: James POORE and Lottie WILSON (SC), death cause: "lived 15 minutes", buried: Dry Creek Cemetery, born/died: 20 Apr 1915, record (1915): 158.

Hannah LOCKNER, age: 73 years, widow, parents: Philip WILHOITT and Mary TUCKER, death cause: "mitral regurgitation", died: 6th District, 6 Apr 1915, record (1915): 159.

Johnathan Hyder BEALS, born: 23 Dec 1868, married, parents: William BEALS and Elizabeth NELSON, death cause: "paralysis", died: 19 Apr 1915, record (1915): 160.

Emma Sue DURHAM, born: 26 Jan 1915, parents: Charles DURHAM (NC) and Nora SMITH, death cause: "whooping cough", informant: Roan DURHAM (Jonesboro), buried: Boones Creek, died: 16 Apr 1915, record (1915): 161.

Infant BROYLES, female, parents: Burney BROYLES and Lena PAINTER, death cause: "premature birth", informant: C.W. BRABSON (Chuckey), buried: Liberty Cemetery, born/died: 8 Apr 1915, record (1915): 162.

Mrs. Mary F. PICKLEY, born: 3 Feb 1841 in Carol County, TN., widow, parents: Jessie HARDIE (NC) and Hannah GIST (Carrol Co. TN), death cause: "pneumonia", informant: Mrs. L.H. HODGE (Bristol), buried: Clarenton, Arkansas, died: 5 Apr 1915, record (1915): 163.

William Wilson JORDAN, African, born: 28 Jul 1876 in Blountville, married, parents: Henry JORDAN and Heldie WASHINGTON, death cause: "pulmonary tuberculosis", informant: Lewis WALKER (Jonesboro), died: 10 Apr 1915, record (1915): 164.

Robert HELTON, born: 1 Mar 1830, widower, parents: not stated, death cause: "old age, heart disease", informant: Bird REED (Jonesboro), buried: County Farm, died: 13 Apr 1915, record (1915): 165.

James A. FEBUARY, born: 13 Sep 1845 in Sullivan County, married, parents: A.D. FEBUARY (France) and Mariah SNEED (England), death cause: "pneumonia", informant: L.W. FEBUARY (Jonesboro), died: 17 Apr 1915, record (1915): 166.

Nellie WALKER, colored, age: 98 years, widow, parents: father not stated and Sophia MAXWELL, death cause: "paralysis", died: Jonesboro, 20 Apr 1915, record (1915): 167.

M. Ellen CONLEY, age: 54 years, married, parents: Elsee RUPE (VA) and Sophia BRIDGEWATER (VA), death cause: "paralysis", informant: Charles RUPE (Jonesboro), buried: Fairview, died: 23 Apr 1915, record (1915): 168.

Florence Boring MORRIS, born: 23 Sep 1857, widow, parents: Montgomery BORING and Anna LEIBER (VA), death cause: "cancer, gall bladder", informant: P.L. PATTERSON (Jonesboro), buried: Urile Cemetery, died: 11 Apr 1915, record (1915): 169.

Mrs. Ettie MITCHELL, age: 28 years and 2 days, married, parents: Henry WALKER and Jane BASON, death cause: "pulmonary tuberculosis", died: Fall Branch, 19 Apr 1915, record (1915): 170.

Mary Elizabeth JACKSON, born: 20 Apr 1837 in Sullivan County, married, parents: George BOUSER and Betsy COX, death cause: "lagrippe, mitral regurgitation", informant: George JACKSON (Jonesboro), died: 19 Apr 1915, record (1915): 171.

<u>Elizabeth CHANDLER</u>, age: 62 years, single, parents: Zachariah CHANDLER and Malinda WILBURN, death cause: "heart and kidney disease", buried: D.L. Ford Cemetery, died: 12th District, 11 Apr 1915, record (1915): 172.

<u>Gentry HODGES</u>, born: 10 Dec 1877, married, school teacher, parents: George W. HODGES and Mary E. JENKINS, death cause: "brain tumor", informant: R.L. HODGES (Jonesboro), buried: Hodges Cemetery, died: 9 Apr 1915, record (1915): 173.

<u>John C. BASHOR</u>, born: 27 Dec 1846 in Virginia, married, parents: Carroll BASHOR (VA) and Suseanna WHETSEL (VA), death cause: "gall stone, rupture gall bladder", informant: John HILBERT (Jonesboro), buried: Pleasant Valley, died: 16 Apr 1915, record (1915): 174.

<u>Infant BRADLEY</u>, male, parents: Matthew BRADLEY and Ana Lee KEPLINGER, death cause: "still born", buried: Bethesda Cemetery, died: 24 Apr 1915, record (1915): 175.

<u>Ella WILSON</u>, born: 26 Sep 1841 in Missouri, widow, parents: not stated, death cause: "pneumonia", informant: Bruce WILSON (Garbers), died: 4th District, 29 Apr 1915, record (1915): 176.

<u>Anna Lee BRADLEY</u>, born: 5 Apr 1893, married, parents: Matt KEPLINGER and Sue BARRING, death cause: "difficult labor", informant: J.T. BRADLEY (Garbers), buried: Bethesda, died: 24 Apr 1915, record (1915): 177.

<u>Carol Wade BARNES</u>, born: 10 Apr 1915, parents: J.S. BARNES and Julia TUCKER, death cause: "malnutrition", informant: G.W. TUCKER (Telford), buried: Mt. Wesley, died: 16 Apr 1915, record (1915): 178.

<u>Nellie CLOYD</u>, lived: 7 days, parents: J.M. CLOYD and Maggie PHILLIPS, death cause: not stated, informant: father (Telford), buried: Mt. Wesley, died: 11 Apr 1915, record (1915): 179.

<u>William Henry MAY</u>, born: 1 Aug 1860, married, parents: William MAY and Eliza KING (VA), death

cause: "typhoid fever", informant: Mrs. W.H. MAY (Limestone), buried: Asbury Cemetery, died: 24 Apr 1915, record (1915): 180.

John CHRIST, Jr., age: 47 years, born: New York, widower, parents: not stated, death cause: "mitral insufficiency", died: Soldier's Home, 28 Apr 1915, record (1915): 181.

Thomas MCCAVAN, age: 63 years, born: Pennsylvania, widower, parents: not stated, death cause: "mitral insufficiency", died: Soldier's Home, 26 Apr 1915, record (1915): 182.

Westall P. SHAFFER, age: 66 years, born: Pennsylvania, widower, parents: not stated, death cause: "nephritis", died: Soldier's Home, 26 Apr 1915, record (1915): 183.

John SIMONS, age: 77 years, born: Germany, married, butcher, parents: not stated, death cause: "nephritis", died: Soldier's Home, 25 Apr 1915, record (1915): 184.

Nelson A. WOOD, age: 55 years, born: Connecticut, single, cotton spinner, parents: not stated, death cause: "pulmonary tuberculosis", died: Soldier's Home, 21 Apr 1915, record (1915): 185.

Aaron MOYER, age: 68 years, born: Pennsylvania, single, shoe maker, parents: not stated, death cause: "pulmonary tuberculosis", died: Soldier's Home, 20 Apr 1915, record (1915): 186.

John CARR, age: 52 years, single, steam fitter, parents: not stated, death cause: "pulmonary tuberculsis", died: Soldier's Home, 15 Apr 1915, record (1915): 187.

Alexander R. DAVIS, age: 81 years, born: Tennessee, single, parents: not stated, death cause: "nephritis", died: Soldier's Home, 14 Apr 1915, record (1915): 188.

Infant JOHNSON, male, parents: Charles HAYSE and Viola JOHNSON, death cause: "died at birth", informant: Sarah KELLEY (Johnson City), buried: Oak Hill, died: 1 Apr 1915, record (1915): 189.

Lewis GENTILE, age: 80 years, born: Louisiana, married, parents: not stated, death cause: "lobar pneumonia", died: Soldier's Home, 2 Apr 1915, record (1915): 190.

Horace Sidney MCCLURE, age: 6 months, parents: W.S. MCCLURE and Mattie LEONARD, death cause: "heart disease", informant: Jacob LEONARD (Jonesboro), buried: Boones Creek, died: 2 Apr 1915, record (1915): 191.

Mrs. Martha J. PEARCE, born: 29 Jul 1952, married, parents: Thomas C. CROW and Elva MCQUEEN, death cause: "tuberculosis", informant: John T. PEARCE (Johnson City), buried: Buena Vista, died: 2 Apr 1915, record (1915): 192.

Bertha E. PARNELL, born: 16 Aug 1892 in Selma, NC., married, parents: D.T. MASSEY (Selma, NC) and Millie MUNS (NC), death cause: "septicemia following miscarriage", buried: Selma, NC., died: 9th District, 3 Apr 1915, record (1915): 193.

Mildred Francis PRICE, born: 24 Sep 1914, parents: James PRICE (VA) and Edna DUGGER, death cause: "physis pulmonatis", informant: father (Johnson City), buried: Wofford Cemetery, died: 5 Apr 1915, record (1915): 194.

Clarence J. MERRIWEATHER, colored, born: 4 Apr 1882 in Alabama, married, parents: Clarence MERRIWEATHER (KY) and mother not stated, death cause: "syphilis", informant: Walter REEVES (Johnson City), buried: West Park Cemetery, died: 7 Apr 1915, record: 195.

Charles B. ROGERS, age: 73 years, born: New Jersey, widower, fruit grower, parents: not stated, death cause: "mitral insufficiency", buried: Plainfield, NJ., died: Soldier's Home, 7 Apr 1915, record (1915): 196.

Texas HAMLER, female, age: 52 years, married, parents: not stated, death cause: "lagrippe and pneumonia", buried: Oak Hill, died: 9 Apr 1915, record (1915): 197.

Hiram BLEDSOE, colored, age: 60 years, born: North Carolina, married, parents: Andy DOBBINS (NC) and Hannah DOBBINS (NC), death cause: "pneumonia fever", informant: Lizzie CUNNINGHAM (Johnson City), buried: West Park Cemetery, died: 10 Apr 1915, record (1915): 198.

Infant LYONS, male, parents: J.R. LYONS (Watauga, TN) and Minnie CANNON (Elizabethton), death cause: "stillborn", buried: Watauga, died: 12 Apr 1915, record (1915): 199.

Lena BAILEY, age: 1 year and 4 months, parents: David BAILEY and Malinda ARWOOD, death cause: "obstructed bowels", informant: father (Johnson City), buried: Buena Vista, died: 13 Apr 1915, record (1915): 200.

James QUILLEN, age: 10 years, parents: James QUILLEN and Minnie LEE, death cause: "killed by trolley car accident", buried: Knoxville, died: Johnson City, 13 Apr 1915, record (1915): 201.

Nelson A. MCFAUL, born: 7 Apr 1835 in Canada, widower, parents: John MCFAUL (Canada) and Catherine E. ELLSWORTH (Canada), death cause: "cardiac dilatation", informant: Mrs. J.A. RUBLE (Johnson City), buried: Oak Hill, died: 14 Apr 1915, record: 202.

Anita D. DIEMENLLE, born: 29 Feb 1888 in Louisiana, married, parents: Henry DEARMOND (Kingston, TN) and Sallie DIXON (Mississippi), death cause: "asthma and illegible", buried: Oak Hill, died: 17 Apr 1915, record (1915): 204.

Mrs. Bessie STOUT, age: 26 years, married, parents: S.G. SAYLOR and Maggie RANGE, death cause: "tuberculosis", buried: Longmire Cemetery, died: 16 Apr 1915, record (1915): 203.

Infant SOUTH, male, parents: George SOUTH (VA) and Ella LOWE (VA), death cause: "stillborn", informant: father (Johnson City), buried: Oak Hill, died: 20 Apr 1915, record (1915): 205.

John WOODS, colored, age: 65 years, born: North Carolina, married, parents: not stated, death cause: illegible, informant: George FITZGERALD (Johnson City), buried: West Lawn, died: 19 Apr 1915, record (1915): 206.

Infant ALLISON, male, parents: John Wallace ALLISON (Washington Co., VA) and Lucille MCCOWN, death cause: "unknown", buried: Oak Hill, died: Johnson City date not stated, buried: 22 Apr 1915.

Infant MCPEAK, male, parents: Levy M. PEAK and Fronia FEATHERS, death cause: "stillborn", buried: Boones Creek, died: 21 Apr 1915, record (1915): 208.

Hildred WILSON, colored, born: 5 Aug 1908 in North Carolina, parents: A.H. WILSON (NC) and Dona WELLS (NC), death cause: "pulmonary tuberculosis", informant: Rev. A.H. WILSON (Johnson City), buried: West Park, died: 24 Apr 1915, record (1915): 209.

Mrs. Mary C. FEATHERS, age: 67 years, divorced, parents: Thomas BRANCH (VA) and __ KELLY (VA), death cause: "grippe and heart trouble", died: 9th District, 23 Apr 1915, record (1915): 210.

James JOHNSON, age: 62 years, widower, parents: Steve JOHNSON and mohter not stated, death cause: "colitis and gangrene", informant: W.R. JOHNSON (Johnson City), buried: Kingsport, died: 25 Apr 1915, record (1915): 211.

Willie Picket RUFFIN, born: 19 Apr 1880 in Virginia, single, parents: W.N. RUFFIN (VA) and Mary B. HARVEY (VA), death cause: "tuberculosis", informant: J.M. FEATHERSTONE (Johnson City), buried: Danville, VA., died: 24 Apr 1915, record (1915): 212.

George W. LOCKWOOD, age: 63 years, born: Virginia, married, parents: not stated, death cause: "gastritis", buried: Birmingham, Alabama, died: Soldier's Home, 23 Apr 1915, record (1915): 213.

William Pond HARRIS, born: 12 Feb 1846 in Worchester, Massachusetts, married, parents: William H. HARRIS (Connecticut) and Mary POND (New Hampshire), death cause: "pneumonia", buried: Brooklyn, NY., died: 24 Apr 1915, record: 214.

Infant BISHOP, male, parents: Joseph C. BISHOP and Mary CARMICHAEL, death cause: "died at birth", buried: Snows Chapel, died: 25 Apr 1915, record (1915): 215.

Mary Elizabeth BOSBURY, age: 46 years, born: Marietta, Ohio, single, parents: Charles J. BOSBURY (England) and Mary E. WILLOUGHBY (Maryland), death cause: "brain abscess", buried: Oak Hill, died: 20 Apr 1915, record (1915): 216.

Joseph ENGOMAR, age: 75 years, widower, glass blower, parents: not stated, death cause: "acute alcoholism", died: Soldier's Home, 9 Apr 1915, record (1915): 217.

Joseph C. DONNELLY, age: 43 years, born: New Jersey, married, book keeper, parents: not stated, death cause: "pulmonary tuberculosis", died: Soldier's Home, 12 Apr 1915, record (1915): 218.

Hazel Virginia GIBSON, born: 18 Nov 1886, single, parents: John E. GIBSON (Sullivan County) and Susie L. HICKS, death cause: "pulmonary tuberculosis", informant: Mrs. J.E. GIBSON (Limestone), buried: Fairviev, died: 17 Apr 1915, record (1915): 219.

Mary Essa EVANS, born: 24 Nov 1877, married, parents: Taylor PAYNE and Rebecca MCCURRY, death cause: "nephritis and uremia following childbirth", informant: A.J. EVANS (Limestone), died: 3 Apr 1915, record (1915): 220.

Henry CAREY, born: 10 Oct 1838, widower, parents: Joseph CAREY and Catherine SHERFEY, death cause: "organic heart disease", informant: J.M. CAREY (Jonesboro), buried: Pleasant Valley, died: 5 Apr 1915, record (1915): 221.

Dililah MALONEY, born: 8 Oct 1849, married, parents: Albert TAYLOR (VA) and Sarah DUN (VA), death cause: "mitral regurgitation, angina pectoris", informant: Will MALONEY (Fall Branch), died: 9 Apr 1915, record (1915): 222.

Mrs. Hattie Boring JOHNSON, born: 13 Apr 1849, widow, parents: Vinson BORING and __ LITTLE, death cause: "tumor of bowels", informant: Richard JOHNSON (Johnson City), buried: Longmires Cemetery, died: 9 Apr 1915, record (1915): 223.

Henry L. ZELL, born: 27 Mar 1915, parents: Bob L. ZELL (Minnisota) and Dellia B. CURTIS, death cause: "premature", informant: A.M. CURTIS (Jonesboro), buried: Buffalo Ridge, died: 2 Apr 1915, record (1915): 224.

Infant JOHNSON, male, parents: Alfred JOHNSON and Etter WHALEY, death cause: "born dead", died: 4th District, 9 Apr 1915, record (1915): 225.

Edward STUART, age: 62 years, married, parents: not stated, death cause: "heart disease" died: Jonesboro, 18 May 1915, record (1915): 226.

Sam R. PETERS, born: 1 Apr 1915, parents: John W. PETERS and Nora MICHELL, death cause: not stated, informant: father (Jonesboro), buried: Dry Creek, died: 13 May 1915, record (1915): 227.

Ula HENSLEY, age: 10 years, 9 months and 8 days, born: Greene County, parents: Matthew HENSLEY (NC) and Lisse BULLMAN, death cause: "tuberculosis of spine", informant: Lissa HENSLEY (Chuckey), buried: Philadelphia, died: 6 May 1915, record (1915): 228.

Martha M. MOORE, born: 15 Nov 1830, widow, parents: Henry RUBLE and Phebe HUNTER, death cause: "cerebral hemorrhage", informant: Daniel MOORE (Jonesboro), buried: Philadelphia, died: 9 May 1915, record (1915): 229.

Maggie CLOYD, age: 39 years and 3 days, married, parents: John PHILLIPS and Sarah WOODRUFF, death cause: "pulmonary tuberculosis", informant: James CLOYD (Telford), buried: Mt. Wesley, died: 6 May 1915, record (1915): 230.

Lena May Houston COX, born: 26 Aug 1885, married, parents: James M. HOUSTON and L.W. WILLIAMS, death cause: "septicemia", informant: E.L. COX (Washington College), died: 24 May 1915, record (1915): 231.

Infant BOGART, female, parents: William A. BOGART and Bessie WHALEY, death cause: "stillborn", died: 5th District, 21 May 1915, record (1915): 232.

Mathas Daniel LOCKNER, born: 1 Jan 1969, married, miner, parents: Mathas LOCKNER (Germany) and Hannah WILHOIT, death cause: "accidental, mine fell in", died: 6th District, 12 May 1915, record (1915): 233.

Mrs. Eliza Jane BOLTON, age: near 45, widow, parents: James CASSADY and Mary VINES, death cause: "tuberculosis", informant: A.S. VINES (Jonesboro), buried: Vines Cemetery, died: 24 May 1915, record (1915): 234.

Ralph PAUL, born: 12 Sep 1914, parents: John PAUL (KY) and Fannie HAMMET, death cause: "pneumonia", informant: father (Johnson City), buried: Price Cemetery, died: 15 May 1915, record (1915): 235.

Infant WHITAKER, female, parents: Charlie WHITAKER and Sabrie DUNN, death cause: "stillborn", buried:

Speedwell cemetery, died: 17 May 1915, record (1915): 236.

John HINES, age: 73 years, born: Ireland, single, cotton spinner, parents: not stated, death cause: "acute alcoholism", died: Soldier's Home, 4 May 1915, record (1915): 237.

Elbert J. CLARK, age: 26 years, born: Kentucky, single, hotel waiter, parents: not stated, death cause: "pulmonary tuberculosis", died: Soldier's Home, 3 May 1915, record (1915): 238.

Henry W. BELDEN, age: 72 years, born: Wisconsin, married, merchant, parents: not stated, death cause: "nephritis", died: Soldier's Home, 30 May 1915, record (1915): 239.

George A. CLARK, age: 77 years, born: England, married, sailor, parents: not stated, death cause: "nephritis". died: Soldier's Home, 24 May 1915, record (1915): 240.

William H. KING, age: 75 years, born: New York, married, parents: not stated, death cause: "cerebral hemorrhage", died: Soldier's Home, 13 May 1915, record (1915): 241.

Patrick WILLIAMS, age: 68 years, bonr: Ireland, widower, cigar maker, parents: not stated, death cause: "nephritis", died: Soldier's Home, 23 May 1915, record (1915): 242.

Frank FINE, colored, age: 73 years, born: Tennessee, married, parents: not stated, death cause: "cardiac dilitation", died: Soldier's Home, 12 May 1915, record (1915): 243.

Charles H. ELLIOTT, age: 68 years, born: Illinois, coal miner, parents: not stated, death cause: "cardiac dilitation", died: Soldier's Home, 7 May 1915, record (1915): 244.

Laura ORR, age: 27 years, married, parents: Jim BUTLER and Mary BUTLER, death cause: "lobar pneumonia", buried: Oak Hill, died: Johnson City, 29 May 1915, record (1915): 245.

Mary BUTLER, age: 64 years, born: Virginia, married, parents: Jeff MCCROCKIN (VA) and Mary HILLARD, death cause: "lobar pneumonia", buried: Oak Hill, died: 27 May 1915, record (1915): 246.

Martha Jane LAMONS, age: 37 years, born: Greene County, married, parents: W.H. DENSMORE (Greene Co.) and Sarah DENSMORE, death cause: "pellagra", buried: Greeneville, died: 26 May 1915, record (1915): 247.

Josephine TAYLOR, age: 36 years, married, parents: James P. TAYLOR and Mary GEORGE, death cause: "septicemia following childbirth", informant: Charles L. TAYLOR (Johnson City), buried: Oak Hill, died: 25 May 1915, record (1915): 248.

Sarah Alice CROSS, age: 57 years, married, parents: Noah GALLOWAY and Mary CARTWRIGHT, death cause: "tuberculosis of bowels", buried: Oak Hill, died: 24 May 1915, record (1915): 249.

Infant HAYES, female, parents: G.C. HAYES and Ella BLAIR, death cause: "stillborn", buried: Oak Hill Cemetery, died: Johnson City, 21 May 1915, record (1915): 250.

James KIRBY, born: 16 Dec 1875 in Wilkes County, NC., married, parents: not stated, death cause: "heart disease", informant: G.L. SMITH (Johnson City), buried: Oak Hill, died: 28 May 1915, record (1915): 251.

John Sidney HUMPHREY, born: 21 Aug 1838, married, parents: Jessie HUMPHREY and Eliza SMITH, death cause: "catarrh and illegible", informant: J.N. HUMPHREY (Johnson City), buried: Oak Hill, died: 20 May 1915, record (1915): 252.

Audrey Ruth DAWSON, age: not stated, single, parents: Capt. E.S. DAWSON (VA) and Mary HUGHES, death cause: "asphixia", buried: Oak Hill, died: Johnson City, 19 May 1915, record (1915): 253.

Adie Elizabeth HORTON, colored, born: 4 Feb 1915, parents: Bradis HORTON (NC) and Virginia BAKER (VA), death cause: "gastritis", informant: father (Johnson City), buried: West Lawn, died: 16 May 1915, record (1915): 254.

William C. SMITHPETERS, born: 19 Jun 1848, widower, shoe maker, parents: William M. SMITHPETERS and mother not stated, death cause: "paralysis", informant: Mike SMITHPETERS (Johnson City), buried: Knob Creek, died: 16 May 1915, record (1915): 255.

Anna L. YOUNG, born: 26 Oct 1886, married, parents: James C. FISHER and Lizzie DOBBINS, death cause: "tuberculosis", informant: W.R. YOUNG (Johnson City), buried: Chuckey, died: 8 May 1915, record (1915): 256.

Margaret WILSON, colored, age: 75 years, married, parents: not stated, death cause: "tuberculosis", informant; George FITZGERALD (Johnson City), buried: Roan Hill, died: 14 May 1915, record (1915): 257.

Sarah SPROLES, age: 68 years, married, parents: __ TURNER and mother not stated, death cause: "dysentery", informant: M.S. CANNON (Johnson City), buried: Oak Hill, died: 6 May 1915, record: 258.

Infant GUNTER, male, born: 1 May 1915, parents: James GUNTER and Hannah WATSON (VA), death cause: "premature", informant: mother (Johnson City), buried: Oak Hill, died: 4 May 1915, record: 259.

Mrs. Blanch REGAN, born: 16 Sep 1883 in Pennsylvania, married, parents: Edward J. ARNEY (PA) and Susan MCGETTIGEN (Ireland), death cause: "nephritis and heart disease", informant: father (Johnson City), buried: Oak Hill, died: 3 May 1915, record (1915): 260.

Infant CAMPBELL, born: 16 Apr 1915, parents: Dave CAMPBELL and Neta WILLIAMSON, death cause: "specific infection", informant: father (Johnson City), buried: Jonesboro, died: 1 May 1915, record: 261.

Margie WILLIN, born: 22 Sep 1914, parents: Martin WILLIN (Sullivan County) and Lula CAGLE (Sullivan County), death cause: "whooping cough", informant: Dr. F.T. MASSINGILL (Jonesboro), buried: Union Cemetery, died: 10 May 1915, record (1915): 262.

Martha HALL, born: 1 Jan 1839, widow, parents: Ben FORD and mother's name illegible, death cause: "heart disease", informant: R.C. HAMILTON (Fordtown), buried: Fordtown B. Church, died: 28 May 1915, record (1915): 263.

William CROCKETT, colored, age: "unknown", widower, parents: not stated, death cause: "heart complications", informant: Columbus RINER (Jonesboro), died: 16 May 1915, record (1915): 264.

Edward STUART, colored, age: 62 years, married, parents: not stated, death cause: not stated, informant: Lettie STUART (Jonesboro), died: 18 May 1915, record (1915): 265.

Sarah SALTS, born: 27 May 1862, single, parents: not stated, death cause: "cancer of breast", informant: J.B. REED (Jonesboro), buried: County Farm, died: 28 May 1915, record (1915): 266.

Charles Allen GILLESPIE, born: 12 Apr 1865, married, parents: Robert GILLESPIE and Maria BROWN, death cause: "diabetes and gangrene", informant: Harry GILLESPIE (Limestone), died: 26 May 1915, record (1915): 267.

Katherine BROYLES, born: 19 Jun 1913 in Missouri, parents: Rex BROYLES and Johnnie WALKER, death cause: "cholera infantum", informant: father (Limestone), died: 12 Jun 1915, record (1915): 268.

Sarah Phine C. GRAHAM, born: 11 Jan 1835, married, parents: Joshua HENLEY (VA) and Sarah CLARK (NC), death cause: "dierrhoea", informant: J.S. GRAHAM (Jonesboro), buried: Mt. Wesley, died: 15 Jun 1915, record (1915): 269.

Sarah May MILLER, born: 13 May 1915, parents: Herman MILLER and Grace COPP, death cause: "colitis", informant: O.J. FOX (Chuckey), buried: Philadelphia, died: 3 Jun 1915, record (1915): 270.

Infant FILLER, female, lived: 5 hours, parents: Harrison FILLER and Mary BROYLES, death cause: not stated, informant: Dr. C.S. LOVE (Chuckey), buried: Liberty, died: 2 Jun 1915, record (1915): 271.

Landeen S. LEACH, age: 68 years, married, parents: John LEACH and Sarah PARKER, death cause: "heart disease", informant: John LEACH (Johnson City), buried: Leach Cemetery, died: 9 Jun 1915, record (1915): 272.

Infant LIPPS, male, parents: Charles LIPPS and Mollie DAVIS, death cause: "stillborn", died: 11th District, 26 Jun 1915, record (1915): 273.

Sue LIPPS, born: 13 Aug 1911, parents: Charles LIPPS and Mollie DAVIS, death cause: "whooping cough", informant: father (Jonesboro), buried: Flowersville, died: 23 Jun 1915, record (1915): 274.

Infant ELLIS, male, parents: Wiley ELLIS and Martha (illegible) (Greene County), death cause: "strangulation", informant: J.A. HAMILTON (Jonesboro), buried: Boones Creek, born/died: 14 Jun 1915, record (1915): 275.

James H. MITCHELL, age: 80 years, born: Maryland, widower, parents: not stated, death cause: "mitral insufficiency", died: Soldier's Home, 3 Jun 1915, record (1915): 276.

Edward J. NIEMAN, age: 35 years, born: Wisconsin, married, engineer, death cause: "pulmonary tuberculosis", died: Soldier's Home, 1 Jun 1915, record (1915): 277.

Albion W. TEFFETTS, age: 77 years, born: Massachusetts, widower, soldier, parents: not stated, death cause: "nephritis", buried: Washington, D.C., died: Soldier's Home, 4 Jun 1915, record (1915): 278.

John D. REEVES, born: 25 Mar 1839, married, parents: Peter REEVES and Matilda DEVAULT, death cause: "softening of brain and heart disease", informant: Mrs. John D. REEVES (Rt 3, Johnson City), buried: Reeves Cemetery, died: 2 Jun 1915, record: 279.

Helen SHEARER, colored, born: 1 Mar 1914, parents: William SHEARER (NC) and Bell HAYES, death cause: "cholera infantum", informant: father (Johnson City), buried: West Lawn, death date not recorded, record (1915): 281.

Julia MOORE, age: 63 years, married, parents: Nick SARRON (?) and Marry TOPLINS, death cause: "stomach and liver disease", buried: Oak Hill, died: Johnson City, 4 Jun 1915, record (1915): 281.

Infant WILLIAMS, female, born: 3 Jun 1915, parents: Hop WILLIAMS (VA) and Sallie CAMPBELL (Texas), death cause: "hives", informant: father (Johnson City), buried: Monte Vista, died: 5 Jun 1915, record (1915): 282.

Ira Nepoleon CLARK, born: 16 Sep 1836 in North Carolina, married, parents: Ely CLARK (NC) and Elizabeth CLARK (NC), death cause: "nephritis", informant: C.E. BIRCHFIELD (Knoxville), buried: Buena Vista, died: 11 Jun 1915, record (1915): 283.

Melvina LILLY, age: 65 years, 1 month and 15 days, born: Carter County, married, parents: Stephen HOUSTON and Emaline BARNES, death cause: "heart disease and gastric carcinoma", buried: Houston Cemetery, died: 14 Jun 1915, record (1915): 284.

Charlie MOORE, age: 35 years, single, parents: David MOORE and Julia (illegible), death cause: "tuberculosis and dysentery", buried: Oak Hill, died: 19 Jun 1915, record (1915): 285.

Infant SWINGLE, male, parents: Allie SWINGLE and Mary DENT, death cause: not stated, informant: father (Johnson City), buried; Hunt Cemetery, born/died: 19 Jun 1915, record (1915): 286.

Charles H. JONES, born: 2 Sep 1883, married, parents: William JONES and Kathern WOODY (NC), death cause: "ruptured bladder, peritonitis", informant: father (Jonesboro), buried: Sulphur Springs, died: 20 Jun 1915, record (1915): 287.

Infant FISHER female, parents: H.C. FISHER (Greene County) and Cloe M. CROUCH, death cause: not stated, buried: Boones Creek, born/died: 20 Jun 1915, record (1915): 288.

Eva MURRELL, colored, age: 46 years, 5 months and 16 days, widow, parents: George HALE and Julia DAY (VA), death cause: "pellagra", informant: Julia HALE (Johnson City), buried: West Lawn, died: 21 Jun 1915, record (1915): 289.

Lillie DURHAM, age; 29 years, married, parents: George W. FORD and Mary (illegible), death cause: "leukemia", informant: E.M. DURHAM (Johnson City), buried: Boones Creek, died: 24 Jun 1915, record (1915): 290.

Infant TIPTON, female, parents: Mose TIPTON and Clara ARWOOD (NC), death cause: "stillborn", informant: father (Johnson City), buried: Buena Vista, died: 25 Jun 1915, record (1915): 291.

Infant WEAVER, male, parents: Clarence WEAVER and Lizzie CARRIGER, death cause: illegible, informant: father (Johnson City), buried: Kings Cemetery, born/died: 27 Jun 1915, record (1915): 292.

Frederick G. SHAMBERG, age: 45 years, born: Pennsylvania, single, coal miner, parents: not stated, death cause: "pulmonary tuberculosis", buried: Titusville, PA., died: Soldier's Home, 26 Jun 1915, record (1915): 293.

Theodore MUNGEN, age: 70 years, born: Ohio, widower, lawyer, parents: not stated, death cause: "gangrene of foot", died: Soldier's Home, 2 Jun 1915, record (1915): 294.

Charles O. MASON, age: 71 years, born: Virginia, widower, parents: not stated, death cause: "cerebral hemorrhage", died: Soldier's Home, 8 Jun 1915, record (1915): 295.

Tony FRYS alias Tony FRIESON, age: 63 years, born: Tennessee, siggle, parents: not stated, death cause: "senile dementia", died: Soldier's Home, 17 Jun 1915, record (1915): 296.

Charles W. COX, age: 36 years, born: Tennessee, single, musician, parents: not stated, death cause: "pulmonary tuberculosis", died: Soldier's Home, 17 Jun 1915, record (1915): 297.

Micajah SCARBOROUGH, age: 73 years, born: Massachusetts, married, shoe maker, parents: not stated, death cause: "nephritis", died: Soldier's Home, 26 Jun 1915, record (1915): 298.

John Henry KELLER, born: 22 Nov 1852, married, parents: Alexander KELLER and Elizabeth LOVEL (VA), death cause: "diabetes", informant: W.R. FOSTER (Telford), buried: New Victory, died: 26 Jun 1915, record (1915): 299.

Thomas S. HENSLEY, born: 14 Apr 1840 in Sullivan County, widower, parents: William HENSLEY (Sullivan Co.) and Barbara WOLF (Sullivan Co.), death cause: "artero sclerosis", informant: H.H. HUMPHREY (Telford), buried: Johnson City, died: 30 Jun 1915, record (1915): 300.

Samuel MCCRACKEN, born: 17 Dec 1831, widower, parents: John MCCRACKEN and Nancy Elizaabeth RUTH, death cause: "pulmonary tuberculosis", informant: Mahaloa MCCRACKEN (Limestone), died: 1 Jun 1915, record (1915): 301.

Mary Ann MOULTON, born: 8 Nov 1830, widow, parents: David F. HALL and Lydia ROBINSON, death cause: "old age, cerebral softening", informant: J.W. MOULTON

(Fall Branch), buried: Hopper Cemetery, died: 10 Jun 1915, record (1915): 302.

William P. JOBE, born: 5 Jul 1875 in Roan County, married, parents: J.P. JOBE and M.A. HUDNALL (Roan Co.), death cause: illegible, informant: J.P. JOBE (Jonesboro), buried: 12th District, died: 5 Jun 1915, record (1915): 303.

Mrs. Mary Dillworth EASTRIDGE, born: 12 Jun 1873, married, parents: Oscar F. DILLWORTH (Rockingham Co., VA) and Mary KIRKPATRICK, death cause: "atrophic cirrhosis of liver", informant: Fred MCPHERSON (Jonesboro), died: 10 Jun 1915, record (1915): 304.

Francis G. FINLEY, colored, born: 22 Aug 1914, single, parents: James JOHNSON and Hattie FINLEY, death cause: "whooping cough", informant: Florence FINLEY (Jonesboro), died: 15 Jun 1915, record (1915): 305.

S.M. BROYLES, born: 12 Aug 1860, married, parents: James BROYLES and Margaret PRESNELL, death cause: "tuberculosis of left hip", informant: James BROYLES (Limestone), buried: New Salem, died: 28 Jun 1915, record (1915): 306.

Cleo REED, parents: Roy REED and Virgie FERGUSON, death cause: "premature birth", informant: father (Telford), buried: Mt. Wesley, born/died: 12 Jun 1915, record (1915): 307.

John HAMMETT, age: about 70 years, single, parents: Ezekiel HAMMETT (NC) and mother not stated, death cause: "heart disease", buried: Blair Cemetery, died: 4th District, 15 Jun 1915, record (1915): 308.

Mattie Pauline ROGERS, born: 10 Nov 1914, parents: Samuel ROGERS and Ada Pearl RIDDLE, death cause: "brain fever", died: 6th District, 30 Jun 1915, record (1915): 309.

Tolbert THOMPSON, age: 14 years, 11 months and 28 days, parents: A.B. THOMPSON and Alzenia HENLEY, death cause: "typhoid fever", informant: father (Jonesboro), died: 21 Jun 1915, record (1915): 310.

William Henry ALLISON, born: 20 Sep 1868, married, parents: Watson BACON and Hannah Eliza ALLISON, death cause: "typhoid fever", informant: J.B.

ALLISON (Rheatown), buried: New Hope, died: 30 Jun 1915, record (1915): 311.

Nancy Carter GILTON, born: 11 Jan 1835 in Greene County, widow, parents: William CARTER and Fannie CARTER, death cause: "flux", informant: Dr. C.L. LOVE (Chuckey), buried: Liberty Cemetery, died: 24 Jul 1915, record (1915): 312.

Mark L. SEATON, age: 74 years, widower, parents: David SEATON and ___ GREENE, death cause: "enteritis", informant: Fird SEATON (Jonesboro), died: 25 Jul 1915, record (1915): 313.

Carl PAINTER, born: 10 Oct 1914, parents: Otto J. PAINTER and Meda BROYLES, death cause: "cholera infantum", informant: father (Chuckey), buried: Liberty, died: 11 Jul 1915, record (1915): 314.

Mrs. Julia WALLER, age: 58 years, widow, parents: G.W. STANTON and Mary Ann JOHNSON (Greene County), death cause: "hypertrophy of heart", informant: W.E. WEST (Washington College), buried: Liberty, died: 2 Jul 1915, record (1915): 315.

Bessie Guinn HURT, age: 23 years, born: North Carolina, married, parents: J.M. GUINN (NC) and mother not stated, death cause: "toxemia of pregnancy", informant: H.G. GUINN (Jonesboro), buried: Bethesda, died: 6 Jul 1915, record (1915): 316.

Infant HURT, male, parents: Stuart HURT and Bessie GUINN, death cause: "premature birth", informant: father (Jonesboro), buried: Bethesda, born/died: 5 Jul 1915, record (1915): 317.

Vernia CARROLL, age: 58 years, housewife, parents: Dave BRITT and mother not stated, death cause: "asthma", buried: Union Church, died: 4th District, 23 Jul 1915, record (1915): 318.

Rosie STORY, born: 19 Dec 1906, parents: Tom STORY and Martha FRANCIS, death cause: "typhoid fever", informant: father (Garbers), died: 2 Jul 1915, record (1915): 319.

Martha Ellen MILLER, age: 20 years, parents: Munro MILLER (NC) and Becky MCCURRY (NC), death cause: "tuberculosis", informant: John LEWIS (Jonesboro), buried: Dry Creek, died: 19 Jul 1915, record: 320.

Jettie HALE, born: 1 Oct 1895 in Johnson County, parents: Cane POTTER (Johnson Co.) and Nancy JOHNSON, death cause: "typhoid fever", informant: P.C. RASH (Jonesboro), buried: Cherokee Cemetery, died: 22 Jul 1915, record (1915): 321.

J.C. GLOVER, born: 9 Nov 1854 in Virginia, single, railroad conductor, parents: William J. GLOVER (Sullivan County) and Susan MCCALLY (VA), death cause: "dibestos cystitis", informant: Jake SAULTS (Jonesboro), died: 5 Jul 1915, record (1915): 322.

Sarah WATTS, born: 24 Jan 1880, single, parents: Sam WATTS and Lizzie BEALS, death cause: "arotic regurgitation", died: 6th District, 29 Jul 1915, record (1915): 323.

William GIBSON, born: 23 Feb 1849, married, parents: George GIBSON and __ MCCAULEY (VA), death cause: "dropsy", informant: Thomas GIBSON (Fall Branch), died: 2 Jul 1915, record (1915): 324.

George Rice DUNCAN, born: 9 Feb 1848, widower, parents: Rice DUNCAN and Eleanor SNAPP, death cause: "gunshot wound left lung, probably suicide, ulcer and nephritis", informant: E.P. MORGAN (Fall Branch), buried: Baptist Church Cemetery, died: 28 Jul 1915, record (1915): 325.

Walter Hoorce VINES, born: 19 May 1908, parents: N.A. VINES and Mattie B. HOPPER, death cause: illegible, informant: father (Jonesboro), buried: Vines Cemetery, died: 1 Jul 1915, record (1915): 326.

Katherine DISHNER, age: 80 years, born: Kingsport, widow, parents: Jack CLICK (Kingsport) and Mary HESS (Kingsport), death cause: "old age", informant: G.K. DISHNER (Johnson City), buried: Kingsport, died: 17 Jul 1915, record (1915): 327.

Franklin HULSE, born: 28 Jan 1826, married, parents: John HULSE and Sarah CRAFT (Washington Co., VA), death cause: "rheumatism of heart", informant: Mattie HULSE (Jonesboro), died: 31 Jul 1915, record (1915): 328.

John ORR, age: 71 years, born: Ohio, widower, parents: not stated, death cause: "interstitial nephritis", died: Soldier's Home, 29 Jul 1915, record (1915): 329.

Frank CAMBERT, age: 43 years, born: Ohio, single, parents: not stated, death cause: "pulmonary tuberculosis", died: Soldier's Home, 27 Jul 1915, record (1915): 330.

Carl GREGRAN, age: not stated, born: Georgia, single, parents: not stated, death cause: "cardiac dilitation", died: Soldier's Home, 17 Jul 1915, record (1915): 331.

Charles H. CUNNINGHAM, age: 60 years, born: West Virginia, single, parents: not stated, death cause: "cystitis", died: Soldier's Home, 5 Jul 1915, record (1915): 332.

Isaac HARRIS, age: 75 years, born: England, widower, peddler, parents: not stated, death cause: "nephritis", died: Soldier's Home, 3 Jul 1915, record (1915): 333.

Michael SHAFFER, age: 69 years, born: Tennessee, married, parents: not stated, death cause: "hemiplegia", died: Soldier's Home, 13 Jul 1915, record (1915): 334.

David DUGAN, age: 64 years, born: Maryland, single, carpenter, parents: not stated, death cause: "hemiplegia", died: Soldier's Home, 12 Jul 1915, record (1915): 335.

George W. STANLEY, age: not stated, born: Alabama, single, parents: not stated, death cause: "mitral insufficiency", died: Soldier's Home, 11 Jul 1915, record: 336.

Hugo GOLTZ, age: 86 years, born: Germany, single, florist, parents: not stated, death cause: "gangrene of foot", died: Soldier's Home, 9 Jul 1915, record (1915): 337.

Infant ARWOOD, born: 22 Jul 1915, parents: J.N. ARWOOD and Elizabeth ADAMS, death cause: "premature birth", informant: father (Johnson City), buried: Longmire Cemetery, died: 23 Jul 1915, record: 338.

William Jay NEURATH, age: 64 years, born: Germany, married, lumber inspector, parents: William NEURATH (Germany) and Elizabeth __ (Germany), death cause: "run over by train", informant: Miss Maud NEURATH (Johnson City), buried: Oak Hill, died: 22 Jul 1915, record (1915): 339.

Catherine WAGNER, colored, age: 33 years, married, parents: James MALONE (NC) and Sarah DUGGER, death cause: illegible, informant: Alfred MALONE (Johnson City), buried: West Lawn, died: 19 Jul 1915, record (1915): 340.

Infant CARROLL, female, parents: J.W. CARROLL and Maud AKERS, death cause: "stillborn", buried: Buena Vista, died: 19 Jul 1915, record (1915): 341.

William J. MILES, born: 22 May 1871 in Virginia, widower, parents: Mark MILES and Melvina FELTY (VA), death cause: "typhoid fever", informant: J.F. BULLOCK (Soldier's Home), buried: Onks Cemetery, died: 15 Jul 1915, record (1915): 342.

Thomas DOYLE, age: 40 years, married, railroader, parents: not stated, death cause: "diarrhoea", buried: Oak Hill Cemetery, died: 8 Jul 1915, record (1915): 343.

Edeline MOSLEY, age: 25 years, born: Clinchport, VA., single (?), housewife, parents: J.A. HALE (VA) and Eliza TAYLOR (VA), death cause: "tuberculosis", buried: Clinchport, VA., died: 9 Jul 1915, record (1915): 344.

T.E. BOWMAN, born: 28 Feb 1884, married, parents: C.C. BOWMAN and Elizabeth KEEN, death cause: "gastritis", buried: Okalona Cemetery, died: 7 Jul 1915, record (1915): 345.

Elbert CARROLL, age: 64 years, married, parents: George CARROLL (VA) and mother not stated, death cause: "cancer of some internal organ", informant: Mat CARROLL (Kingsport), buried: Harrison Cemetery, died: 22 Jul 1915, record (1915): 346.

James O. AKERS, born: 15 Sep 1850, married, blacksmith, parents: Will AKERS (VA) and Eliza SMITH (VA), death cause: "cerebral hemorrhage", informant: Mrs. Roda AKERS (Johnson City), buried: Buena Vista, died: 24 Jul 1915, record (1915): 347.

Edna SNYDER, age: 1 year and 4 months, parents: A.E. SNYDER (Johnson County) and mother not stated (Johnson County), death cause: "marasmus", buried: Mountain City, died: Johnson City, 26 Jul 1915, record (1915): 348.

Hannah Ellen BRUMITT, born: 3 Mar 1878, married, parents: John W. FULMER and Trephenia HARVEY, death cause: "pellagra", buried: Fulmer Cemetery, died: Johnson City, 30 Jul 1915, record (1915): 349.
William H.H. MCCOLLUM, age: 48 years, born: Kentucky, married, parents: not stated, death cause: "hemiplegia", died: Soldier's Home, 19 Jul 1915, record (1915): 350.
D.A. AKARD, born: 23 Mar 1858, married, parents: William AKARD and mother not stated, death cause: "Brights disease", buried: Beelers Chapel, died: 10th District, 29 Jul 1915, record (1915): 351.
Nancy CASH, age: 90 years, married, parents: father not stated and Nancy WAGNER, death cause: "organic heart disease", buried: Union Church, died: 10th District, 24 Jul 1915, record (1915): 352.
Susan A. LAWSON, born: 22 May 1868, married, parents: Samuel G. KING and Susan C. MORRELL (VA), death cause: "heart disease", informant: S.S. KING (Johnson City), buried: King Cemetery, died: 24 Jul 1915, record (1915): 353.
Carmel Lee DEPEW, lived: 6 hours, parents: William DEPEW and Lauria FORD, death cause: "premature birth", informant: E.C. COPASS (Jonesboro), buried: Boones Creek, died: 8 Jul 1915, record (1915): 354.
Sallie FOX, born: 2 Jul 1849, married, parents: Nathaniel EDEN and Barbara EDEN, death cause: "tuberculosis", informant: Daniel FOX (Jonesboro), buried: Hales Chapel, died: 4 Jul 1915, record (1915): 355.
Pearl Tennie GIBSON, born: 26 Aug 1898, parents: William GIBSON and Matilda MURRAY (Buffalo Ridge), death cause: "typhoid fever", informant: mother (Fall Branch), buried: Logans Chapel, died: 9 Jul 1915, record (1915): 356.
John F. NELSON, born: 3 Mar 1843, married, parents: John NELSON and Ester Ann FERGUSON, death cause: "tuberculosis of lungs", informant: Jack N. NELSON (Jonesboro), buried: Sulphur Springs, died: 2 Jul 1915, record (1915): 357.
John WALKER, colored, age: 41 years, divorced, parents: Monroe WALKER (Johnson County) and Nellie

YANCEY, death cause: "nephritis", informant: Howell YANCEY (Jonesboro), died: 30 Jul 1915, record (1915): 358.

Mary Evans DILLWORTH, born: 15 Aug 1850, married, parents: __ KIRKPATRICK (Ireland) and Louisa EVANS, death cause: "rheumatism", informant: James O. DILLWORTH (Jonesboro), died: 31 Jul 1915, record (1915): 359.

Frankie BENNETT, born: 9 Jun 1915 in Poplar, NC., parents: George BENNETT (Poplar, NC) and Minie GOFORTH (NC), death cause: not stated, buried: Poplar, NC., died: 7 Jul 1915, record (1915): 360.

J. Coson SMITH, born: __ Aug 1833, widower, parents: Thomas SMITH and mother not stated, death cause: "injured hip", informant; A.J. SMITH (Jonesboro), buried: Fairview, died: 12 Jul 1915, record: 361.

Harrem W. KEYS, born: 29 Oct 1854, married, parents: James M. KEYS and Mary J. (illegible), death cause: "heart disease", informant: S.B. CAMPBELL (Jonesboro), buried: Fairview, died: 12 Jul 1915, record (1915): 362.

Clarence C. KEYS, born: 30 Jul 1912, parents: Bob KEYS and Maggie CLINEAS, death cause: "dysentery", informant: T.S. JONES (Limestone), buried: Pleasant Grove, died: 29 Jul 1915, record (1915): 363.

Elizabeth SHEPHERD, father not stated and Bessie Margaret SHEPHERD, death cause: "born dead", buried: Limestone Cemetery, died: 30 Jul 1915, record (1915): 364.

John Bowman KLEPPER, born: 6 Nov 1824, widower, parents: Jacob KLEPPER (VA) and Catherine BOWMAN (VA), death cause: "heart failure", informant: T.B. KLEPPER (Limestone), died: 6 Jul 1915, record (1915): 365.

Glena C. CASEDAY, born: 26 Feb 1913, parents: James CASEDAY and Maud WILLIS, death cause: "meningitis", informant: father (Jonesboro), buried: Sulphur Springs, died: 2 Sep 1915, record (1915): 366.

Lillian HENSLEY, born: 13 Oct 1914, parents: Eirett HENSLEY and Bettie HUGHES, death cause: "gastr .. illegible", informant: father (Johnson City), buried: Bluff City, died: 7 Aug 1915, record: 367.

M.L. CRUMLEY, age: 65 years, married, parents: Daniel CRUMLEY and Dorothy HARKLEROAD, death cause: "paresis", buried: Miller Cemetery, died: 9th District, 12 Aug 1915, record (1915): 368.

Samuel GALLOWAY, age: 77 years, parents: Thomas GALLOWAY and mother not stated, death cause: "Brights disease", died: 13th District, 10 Aug 1915, record (1915): 369.

Mrs. Ida HICE, age: 47 years and 7 months, widow, parents: Isaac SAYLOR and mother's name illegible, death cause: illegible, informant: Charles G. ISBEL (Johnson City), buried: Hice Cemetery, died: 13 Aug 1915, record (1915): 370.

Susan NEAD, born: 14 Dec 1832, single, parents: Daniel NEAD (Maryland) and Barbara ROADCAP (VA), death cause: "dropsy", informant: Daniel C. NEAD (Jonesboro), buried: Greenwood Cemetery, died: 14 Aug 1915, record (1915): 371.

John CAIN, age: 81 years, born: North Carolina, widower, parents: Anderson CAIN (NC) and mother not stated, death cause: "cancer of bowels", informant: Jesse COLLINS (Johnson City), buried: Onks Cemetery, died: 20 Aug 1915, record (1915): 372.

William SMITH, born: 12 May 1915, parents: Walter SMITH and Anie LILLEY, death cause: "convulsions", informant: S.J. HYDER (Jonesboro), buried: Onks Cemetery, died: 25 Aug 1915, record (1915): 373.

Vergie REED, born: 13 Sep 1895, married, parents: G.W. FERGUSON and Cora DICKMAN, death cause: "pulmonary tuberculosis", informant: Lucy FERGUSON (Telford), buried: Mt. Wesley, died: 17 Aug 1915, record (1915): 374.

Martie Frank BALL, born: 17 Jul 1915, parents: J.H. BALL and Eva BOLTON, death cause: not stated, informant: Noah MCKEE (Telford), buried: Mt. Wesley, died: 1 Aug 1915, record (1915): 376.

Maria L. STUART, born: 17 May 1847, married, parents: A.L. GARMAN and Mira ANDERSON, death cause: "nephritis", informant: G.G. STUART (Limestone), buried: Old Salem, died: 27 Aug 1915, record: 375.

Jeremiah BOOTH, age: 74 years, single, parents: John BOOTH (VA) and mother not stated, death cause: "old age", buried: Cherokee Cemetery, died: 4th District, 14 Aug 1915, record (1915): 377.

Opal Margie LOUIS, born: 27 Aug 1915, parents: Will LOUIS and Lettie VAUGHN, death cause: illegible, informant: father (Garbers), buried: Mayberry Cemetery, died: 28 Aug 1915, record (1915): 378.

Hattie FINLEY, colored, born: 23 Nov 1894, single, parents: John FINLEY (Carol Co., VA) and Florence MILLER (Knoxville), death cause: "tuberculosis", informant: mother (Jonesboro), died: 4 Aug 1915, record (1915): 379.

Joseph MURRAY, age: 45 years, married, parents: not stated, death cause: "accident fractured ribs, complications", informant: J.B. SHOUN (Hampton, TN), buried: Elizabethton, TN., died: 28 Aug 1915, record: 380.

Ross R. FLEMING, born: 10 Feb 1892, married, parents: David B. FLEMING and Alice LEACH, death cause: "tuberculosis", informant: father (Johnson City), buried: Oak Hill, died: 30 Aug 1915, record: 381.

Mary Emeline LOUDY, born: 25 Oct 1847 in Carter County, married, parents: Samuel TAYLOR (Carter Co.) and P. (illegible) TAYLOR (Carter Co.), death cause: "heart and kidney trouble", informant: Thad LOUDY (Johnson City), buried: Sinking Creek, died: 28 Aug 1915, record (1915): 382.

Arthur MARRON alias William A. THORNTON, age: 33 years, born: England, single, laborer, parents: not stated, death cause: "pulmonary tuberculosis", died: Soldier's Home, 9 Aug 1915, record (1915): 383.

Owen E. BRYSON, age: 40 years, born: Indiana, single, miller, parents: not stated, death cause: "pulmonary tuberculosis", died: Soldier's Home, 10 Aug 1915, record (1915): 384.

Alexander SMITH, age: 66 years, born: Russia, single, fireman, parents: not stated, death cause: "cerebral hemorrhage", died: Soldier's Home, 11 Aug 1915, record (1915): 385.

Urban C. SHEATS, age: 68 years, born: Pennsylvania, laborer, parents: not stated, death cause: "unknown", died: Soldier's Home, 11 Aug 1915, record (1915): 386.

Edward DEMPSEY, age: 69 years, born: Wisconsin, married, parents: not stated, death cause: "cerebral hemorrhage", died: Soldier's Home, 13 Aug 1915, record (1915): 387.
Henry CAFFERY, age: 88 years, born: Maine, widower, parents: not stated, death cause: "diarrhoea", died: Soldier's Home, 15 Aug 1915, record (1915): 388.
Clarence C. INGRAM, age: 73 years, born West Virginia, widower, parents: not stated, death cause: "cerebal hemorrhage", died: Soldier's Home, 17 Aug 1915, record (1915): 389.
Earl E. WILLIAMS, born: 16 Mar 1892, single, parents: Reese J. WILLIAMS (VA) and Flora E. MCADAMS, death cause: "accidentally drowned in Holston River at Bluff City, buried: Oak Hill, died: 1 Aug 1915, record (1915): 390.
Hester M. COX, born: 20 Dec 1879 in Greene County, married, parents: J.N. HAYES (Greene Co.) and Etta REED (Greene Co.), death cause: "brain hemorrhage", informant: I.W. COX (Fall Branch), buried: Logan Chapel, died: 25 Aug 1915, record (1915): 391.
John Wesley YOUNG, colored, born: 25 Dec 1844, widower, parents: father not stated and Jessie GAMMON, death cause: "heart failure", informant: Albert YOUNG (Johnson City), buried: West Lawn, died: 1 Aug 1915, record (1915): 392.
Docie Hildred PICKERING, born: 9 Feb 1915, parents: Sam PICKERING and Lucie SHEETS, death cause: "stomach and bowel disease", informant: father (Johnson City), buried: Buena Vista, died: 2 Aug 1915, record (1915): 393.
James Ira MCLAIN, born: 23 Sep 1914, parents: J.I. MCLAIN and Geneva DANIEL, death cause: "whooping cough", informant: M.S. CANNON (Johnson City), buried: Sinking Creek, died: 3 Aug 1915, record (1915): 394.
Coleman MOORES, age: 69 years, born: Kentucky, widower, parents: not stated, death cause: "pulmonary tuberculosis", buried: Louisville, KY., died: Soldier's Home, 11 Aug 1915, record (1915): 395.
Allen James HURLBUT, Jr., born: 1 Mar 1915, parents: Alen HURLBUT (NY) and Corine SIBLEY (PA), death

cause: "ptomaine poisoning", informant: father (Johnson City), buried: Buena Vista, died: 12 Aug 1915, record (1915): 396.

May Bell DENNEY, colored, born: __ Mar 1893, married, parents: William BLEDWSOW (NC) and Louise VAUGHT, death cause: "dysentery and tuberculosis", informant: father (Johnson City), buried: West Lawn, died: 12 Aug 1915, record (1915): 397.

Manson GREEN, colored, born: 21 Aug 1913, parents: William GREEN and Addie BLEDSOW, death cause: "meningitis", informant: father (Johnson City), buried: West Lawn, died: 9 Aug 1915, record (1915): 398.

William E. DEVAULT, born: 2 Jun 1849 in Kingsport, married, parents: James M. DEVAULT and Margaret EVERET, death cause: "tuberculosis", buried: Oak Lawn, died: Johnson City, 9 Aug 1915, record: 399.

Geldra E. HALE, colored, born: 24 Jul 1909, parents: Charles HARRIS (VA) and Glenore ANDERSON (VA), death cause: "appendicitis", informant: mother (Johnson City), buried: Bristol, died: 18 Aug 1915, record (1915): 400.

Sam RAY, colored, age: 74 years, born: North Carolina, widower, parents: not stated, death cause: "paralysis", informant: Ed RAY (Johnson City), buried: Shell Creek, TN., died: 24 Aug 1915, record (1915): 401.

James C. SINGLETON, age: 45 years, born: Kentucky, single, death cause: "alcoholic gastritis", buried: Barborsville, died: Soldier's Home, 24 Aug 1915, record (1915): 402.

Joseph Millard STOUT, born: 1 Aug 1915, parents: Millard STOUT and Susan GLOVER, death cause: "indigestion", informant: father (Johnson City), buried: Buena Vista, died: 25 Aug 1915, record (1915): 403.

Leona SELLERS, born: 30 Mar 1908, parents: Arthur SELLERS and Elizabeth CROSS, death cause: "typhoid fever", informant: mother (Rt 3, Johnson City), buried: Harrison Chapel, died: 4 Sep 1915, record (1915): 404.

James Jacob Brown REED, born: 10 Aug 1842, married, parents: G.W. REED (VA) and Catherine GUYER, death cause: "stomach and bowel trouble, hypertrophic cirrhosis of liver", informant: William LOYD (Telford), buried: Mt. Wesley, died: 25 Sep 1915, record (1915): 405.

Elias ARTERBUM, age: about 80 years, born: Sullivan County, married, parents: Elias ARTERBUM (Sullivan Co.) and Mary PROPHET (Sullivan Co.), death cause: "nephritis, heart disease", died: 13th District, 1 Sep 1915, record (1915): 406.

John RATTIGAN, age: 43 years, born: Ireland, parents: not stated, death cause: "unknown", died: Soldier's Home, 15 Sep 1915, record (1915): 407.

Martha Covington BURTON, born: 17 Feb __, age: 82 years and 7 months, maried, parents: Wiley COVINGTON (Rockingham, VA) and Martha COVINGTON, death cause: "fracture femur, nervous exhaustion", informant: W.S. BURTON (McKinzie, TN), died: 6 Sep 1915, record (1915): 408.

Conley BURGNER, age: 9 months, parents: Clarence BURGNER and Myrtle CORATHURS, death cause: "cholera infantum", buried: Snow Chapel, died: 12 Sep 1915, record (1915): 409.

Laura GOLDEN, colored, age: 48 years, born: Virginia, widow, parents: James TRENT (VA) and Sallie HUGHES (VA), death cause: "paralysis", informant: James TRENT (Johnson City), buried: West Lawn, died: 12 Sep 1915, record (1915): 410.

William A. KITE, age: 69 years, widower, civil engineer, parents: Hickman A. KITE and Eliza __, death cause: illegible, informant: H.R. KITE (Persia, TN), buried: Mohawk, TN., died: 5 Sep 1915, record (1915): 411.

Norman RHEA, colored, born: 8 Jan 1904, parents: John RHEA and Lena FORD, death cause: "crushed by railroad car", informant: father (Johnson City), buried: Buena Vista, died: 7 Sep 1915, record (1915): 412.

Mary Jane CRUMLEY, age: 45 years, married, parents: Calvin WHITAKER (VA) and Nancy CRUTSINGER, death cause: "cerebral hemorrhage", informant: William

CRUMLEY (Johnson City), buried: Oak Hill, died: 8 Sep 1915, record (1915): 413.

Mrs. M.V. KEENE, age: 54 years, married, parents: Christy BAKER (VA) and Eliza SMITH, death cause: "intestinal obstruction", buried: Poplar Grove, died: 9th District, 24 Sep 1915, record (1915): 414.

Miles Vincent AMMONS, born: 29 Jul 1914, parents: C.F. AMMONS and Lucy Lee HOWERN, death cause: "diarrhoea", buried: Tucker Cemetery, died: 6th District, 24 Sep 1915, record (1915): 415.

Lela LOYD, born: 3 Jan 1915, parents: Thomas LOYD and Eliza TITTLE, death cause: "accidentally took mercury tablet", informant: Ben LOYD (Embreeville), died: 28 Sep 1915, record (1915): 416.

Infant CLEMONS, female, parents: Roy CLEMONS and Dora (illegible), informant: father (Johnson City), buried: Snow Chapel, died: 16 Sep 1915, record (1915): 417.

Laura CORBY (?), age: 32 years, married, parents: Reese HAMMET and __ CHANDESS, death cause: "intestinal cararrh", buried: Philadelphia, died: 3 Sep 1915, record (1915): 418.

Elizabeth BROYLES, born: 16 Mar 1835, married, parents: Henry PAROT and __ YETT, death cause: "nephritis", informant: Jesse BROYLES (Chuckey), buried: Liberty Cemetery, died: 29 Sep 1915, record (1915): 419.

Harry MCFALL, born: 14 Jul 1915, parents: W.K. MCFALL and Texie MCALISTER (Fall Creek, NC), death cause: "spinal meningitis", informant: Dr. F.T. MASSENGILL (Jonesboro), buried: Boones Creek, died: 21 Sep 1915, record (1915): 420.

Arley Ray LOVEGROVE, born: 9 Feb 1910, parents: J.R. LOVEGROVE and Jodie CROYAL, death cause: "appendicitis", informant: J.F. LOVEGROVE (Jonesboro), buried: 5th District, died: 27 Sep 1915, record (1915): 421.

Mary J. SIMMERMAN, born: 7 Aug 1853, married, parents: Russell FINE and Marinda SCOTT, death cause: "pulmonary tuberculosis", informant: D.S. MILLER (Jonesboro), buried: 8th District, died: 3 Sep 1915, record (1915): 422.

Texana BAYLEY, born: 2 Sep 1868 in North Carolina, married, parents: not stated, death cause: "paralysis", informant: Hampton WILLIAMS (Johnson City), buried: Union Church, died: 25 Sep 1915, record (1915): 423.

Andrew J. LEARY, age: 74 years, born: Canada, widower, parents: not stated, death cause: "lobar pneumonia", died: Soldier's Home, 19 Sep 1915, record (1915): 424.

Louis G. TROTTER, age: 44 years, born: Illinois, single, shoe maker, parents: not stated, death cause: "peritonitis", died: Soldier's Home, 20 Sep 1915, record (1915): 425.

William J. KOGER, age: 77 years, born: Tennessee, widower, photographer, parents: not stated, death cause: "cystitis", died: Soldier's Home, 13 Sep 1915, record (1915): 426.

Charles F. BECKER, age 40 years, born: New York, single, iron moulder, parents: not stated, death cause: "pulmonary tuberculosis", died: Soldier's Home, 19 Sep 1915, record (1915): 427.

James MURPHEY, age: 77 years, born: Maryland, widower, parents: not stated, death cause: "cardiac dilitation", died: Soldier's Home, 25 Sep 1915, record (1915): 428.

William CLIFT, age: 83 years, born: Indiana, married, parents: not stated, death cause: "nephritis", died: Soldier's Home, 18 Sep 1915, record: 429.

Gustav A. BLANK, age: 73 years, single, parents: not stated, death cause: "lobar pneumonia", died: Soldier's Home, 21 Sep 1915, record (1915): 430.

Angia ELLIS, age: 5 years, parents: James ELLIS and Lula LOWERY, death cause: "endo carditis", buried: Oak Hill, died: Johnson City, 27 Sep 1915, record (1915): 431.

Nellie Blanch HAYES, born: 26 Sep 1907 in Virginia, parents: Charles A. HAYES and Claudie CRAWFORD, death cause: "meningitis", informant: father (Johnson City), buried: Fall Branch, 27 Sep 1915, record (1915): 432.

Edgar Earl EAKIN, born: 27 Aug 1913, parents: Harry EAKIN and Annie ARCHER, death cause: "cholera infantum", informant: father (Johnson City), buried: Archer Cemetery, died: 25 Sep 1915, record: 433.

Thomas MCGILL, age: 48 years, born: Ireland, parents: Patrick MCGILL (Ireland) and Mary MCGILL (Ireland), death cause: "tuberculosis", buried: Oak Hill, died: 9th District, 23 Sep 1915, record (1915): 434.

Lauretta KINDLE, colored, born: 7 Jul 1891, married, parents: M.G. CRAWFORD and Cardelia JACKSON, death cause: "tuberculosis", informant: father (Johnson City), buried: West Lawn, died: 25 Sep 1915, record (1915): 435.

Clarence HENSON, born: 7 Apr 1910, parents: J.J. HENSON and Lockie DAVENPORT, death cause: "diptheria", informant: father (Johnson City), buried; Buena Vista, died: 19 Sep 1915, record (1915): 436.

Clyde MILLER, born: 15 Sep 1915, parents: Sam MILLER and Lizzie BOWMAN, death cause: "found dead in bed", informant: father (Garbers), buried: Union Cemetery, died: 15 Oct 1915, record (1915): 437.

Martin N. DUNHAM, age: 78 years, born: Vermont, widower, tin smith, parents: not stated, death cause: "cardiac dilatation", died: Soldier's Home, 24 Nov 1915, record (1915): 438.

Eva Josephine RUBLE, born: 11 Aug 1915, parents: David H. RUBLE and Josie THOMPSON, death cause: "pneumonia", died: Jonesboro, 12 Oct 1915, record (1915): 439.

Julia HONEYCUTT, born: 8 Dec 1914, parents: Julius HONEYCUTT (NC) and Mary FRY (NC), death cause: "pertussus", died Embreeville, 18 Oct 1915, record (1915): 440.

James Franklin RIDDLE, born: 7 Sep 1911, parents: Nelson RIDDLE and Nora PRICE, death cause: "pertussis", died: Embreeville, 7 Oct 1915, record (1915): 441.

John MILBURN, age: about 65 years, married, parents: father not stated, and Mary MILBURN, death cause: "tuberculosis of bowels", buried: Buffalo Ridge, died: 12th District, 20 Oct 1915, record: 442.

Jeamie W. STOUT, born: 6 Jun 1847 in West Virginia, married, parents: James DEEN (W.VA), and __ LIGGETT (W.VA), death cause: "carcinoma of breast", informant: Charles E. STOUT (Johnson City), buried: Oak Hill, died: 9 Oct 1915, record (1915): 443.

Milo M. ALGER, age: 77 years, born: New York, widower, parents: not stated, death cause: "myo carditis", buried: Jackson, Michigan, died: Soldier's Home, 9 Oct 1915, record (1915): 444.

George W. WILLETT, age: 73 years, single, parents: George W. WILLETT and Eliza M. CROOKSHANK, death cause: "indigestion", informant: Maynard CANNON (Johnson City), buried: Oak Hill, died: 6 Oct 1915, record (1915): 445.

Infant PRICE, female, age: 2 months, parents: Henry PRICE and Cordia DAVIS, death cause: "unknown", buried: Sulphur Springs, died: 11th District, 4 Oct 1915, record (1915): 446.

Helen KEGLEY, born: 18 Jul 1812, parents: Earnest KEGLEY (VA) and Elizabeth ALLISON (NC), death cause: "anemia", buried: Oak Hill, died: 4 Oct 1915, record (1915): 447.

Susan STOUT, born: 17 Sep 1879, married, parents: F.M. GLOVER and Mary A. TILLIE, death cause: "tuberculosis", informant: M.E. STOUT, buried: Buena Vista, died: 4 Oct 1915, record (1915): 448.

Ethan M. LEONARD, age: 82 years, born: North Carolina, widower, parents: Thomas LEONARD (NC) and mother not stated, death cause: "gangrene of foot", buried: Leonard Cemetery, died: Johnson City, 3 Oct 1915, record (1915): 449.

Mary Ann HYDER, colored, born: 22 Sep 1845, widow, parents: father not stated and Peggie OSBORNE, death cause: "probably carcinoma of stomach", informant: F.M. HYDER (New York City), buried: West Lawn, died: 2 Oct 1915, record (1915): 450.

Green F. WILSON, age: 79 years, widower, parents: Larkin WILSON and mother not stated, death cause: "railroad accident, shock etc.", buried: Bluff City, died: Johnson City, 1 Oct 1915, record (1915): 451.

Kennard H. WILSON, age: 77 years, born: Pennsylvania, widower, parents: not stated, death cause: "cerebral hemorrhage", buried: Philadelphia, PA., died: Soldier's Home, 1 Oct 1915, record (1915): 452.

Henry GRIFFITH, age: 72 years, born: Indiana, single, parents: not stated, death cause: "nephritis", died: Soldier's Home, 28 Oct 1915, record: 453.

Ralph MOORE, age: 10 months, parents: Arthur MOORE and Ella CALLOWAY, death cause: illegible, informant: M.D. ONKS (Johnson City), buried: Oak Hill, died: 27 Oct 1915, record (1915): 454.

William Thadore MILLER, age: 13 years, born: Unicoi, parents: J.M. MILLER (Unicoi) and Polly GARLAND (Unicoi), death cause: "cerebral tumor", buried: Unicoi, died: 29 Oct 1915, record (1915): 455.

James WATS, colored, born: 13 Jun 1915, parents: Ernes WATS (GA) and Gay COLE, death cause: "bronchitis", informant: Gay COLE (Johnson City), buried: West Lawn, died: 25 Oct 1915, record: 456.

Neil Albert MERRITT, born: __ Jul 1905, parents: W.F. MERRITT and Rachel CURTIS, death cause: "tuberculosis and Brights disease", informant: A.E. MERRITT (Johnson City), buried: Onks Cemetery, died: 23 Oct 1915, record (1915): 457.

James B. CLAWSON, born: 22 Mar 1862, married, parents: William CLAWSON and __ DUGGER, death cause: "appendicitis", buried: Snow Chapel, died: 9th District, 24 Oct 1915, record (1915): 458.

Infant MORRISON, male, parents: H.G. MORRISON (VA) and Lucil BAKER, death cause: "stillborn", buried: Gate City, VA., died: 9th District, 20 Oct 1915, record (1915): 459.

Evie MATHENSON, age: 8 months, parents: Finley MOATHENSON (NC) and Winnie ROBERTS, death cause: "indigestion", informant: W.F. OWENS (Johnson City), buried: Buena Vista, died: 20 Oct 1915, record (1915): 460.

Mrs. Judith Evans BLACKWELL, born: 27 Nov 1831 in Carolina County, VA., married, parents: David EVANS (VA) and __ BULWARS (VA), death cause: "paralysis", buried: Shelbyville, TN., died: 9th District, 19 Oct 1915, record (1915): 461.

Glen Elmore HOSS, age: 5 months, parents: Olerry HOSS and Ellen LONGMIRE, death cause: "enteritis", buried: Boones Creek, died: 18 Oct 1915, record (1915): 462.

Garfield GREENLEE, colored, born: 13 Sep 1896, single, parents: Sam GREENLEE (SC) and Maggie MCDOW (SC), death cause: "overdose of morphane", informant: Sherman GREENLEE (Johnson City), buried: West Lawn, died: 17 Oct 1915, record (1915): 463.

Infant GOAD, male, parents: Nath GOAD and Lula SELLIS, death cause: "stillborn", informant: Maynard CANNON (Johnson City), buried: Buena Vista, died: 15 Oct 1915, record (1915): 464.

Woodrow STOUT, born: 22 Dec 1912, parents: Millard STOUT and Susan GLOVER, death cause: "diptheria", informant: M.F. SCOTT (Johnson City), buried: Buena Vista, died: 12 Oct 1915, record (1915): 465.

Juliah MCINTURFF, born: 28 Mar 1902, parents: father not stated and Lucy MCINTURFF, death cause: "dysentery", informant: James MCINTURFF (Johnson City) buried: France Cemetery, died: 9 Oct 1915, record (1915): 466.

Infant SCOTT, male, parents: William G. SCOTT (New Jersey) and Margaret MCLUTZ, death cause: "stillborn", buried: Knoxville, died: 9 Oct 1915, record (1915): 467.

Orland TADLOCK, born: 15 Oct 1915, parents: Samuel H. TADLOCK and Sarah M. FERGUSON, death cause: not stated, buried: Sulphur Springs, died: 15 Oct 1915, record (1915): 468.

Mary Jane KINCHLOE, born: 11 Feb 1833 in Greene County, widow, parens: Hale BAXTER (Greene Co.) and Mary CRAWFORD (Greene Co.), death cause: "endo carditis", informant: George E. KINCHLOE (Fall Branch), died: 12 Oct 1915, record (1915): 469.

Cora WALTERS, age: 43 years and 4 months, single, parents: William WALTERS and Mary Ellen GRAHAM, death cause: "tuberculosis of lungs", buried: Speedwell, 8th District, died: 15 Oct 1915, record (1915): 470.

John R. LAWS, born: 10 Jun 1910, parents: Isaac LAWS and Mary DUNN, death cause: "croup", informant:

father (Joneboro), buried: Union Church, died: 23 Oct 1915, record (1915): 471.

Jane BROYLES, born: 9 Aug 1843, widow, parents: Johnathan COPP and Francis HENSLEY, death cause: illegible, informant: B.B. BROYLES (Chuckey), buried: Philadelphia, died: 3 Oct 1915, record (1915): 471.

John KEEBLER, colored, born: 4 May 1852, married, parents: Jake DEADRICK and mother not stated, death cause: "Brights disease", informant: Will KEEBLER (Washington College), buried: Limestone, died: 7 Oct 1915, record (1915): 473.

Hannah BEARD, born: 18 Jan 1833 in Virginia, married, parents: John STEPP and Mary HAGA, death cause: "debility, fractured thigh", died: Telford, 20 Oct 1915, record (1915): 474.

Evelyn RIDLEY, born: 9 Jun 1911, parents: R.C. RIDLEY and Katie BOWDEN, death cause: illegible, died: 23 Oct 1915, record (1915): 475 (note: this is a Carroll County record)

E.E. CROCKER, born: 23 Mar 1838, widower, parents: not stated, death cause: "general debility", buried: New Hope Cemetery, died: 13 Oct 1915, record (1915):: 476 (note: this is a Carroll County record)

Harold Sylvester MOSIER, born: __ Dec 1914, parents: Arthur MOSIER and Lizzie PICKINGS, death cause: "diptheria", informant: father (Johnson City), buried: Buena Vista, died: 31 Oct 1915, record (1915): 477.

Ethel WEAVER, born: 20 Sep 1913, parents: E.C. WEAVER and Lizzie CARIGAR, death cause: "diptheria", informant: father (Johnson City), buried: King Cemetery, died: 31 Oct 1915, record (1915): 478.

Clifton L. SITTON, age: 38 years, born: Georgia, machinist, parents: not stated, death cause: "diarrhoea", died: Soldier's Home, 29 Oct 1915, record (1915): 479.

John KOCH, age: 77 years, born: Germany, single, parents: not stated, death cause: "peritonitis", died: Soldier's Home, 23 Oct 1915, record: 480.

John THOMPSON, age: 39 years, born: Tennessee, single, carpenter, parents: not stated, death cause:

"pulmonary tuberculosis", died: Soldier's Home, 21 Oct 1915, record (1915): 481.
Henry DIMON, age: 73 years, born: Ohio, married, laborer, parents: not stated, death cause: "hemorrhage of lungs", died: Soldier's Home, 24 Oct 1915, record (1915): 482.
John P. JONES, age: 33 years, born: Washington D.C., married, soldier, parents: not stated, death cause: "pulmonary tuberculosis", died: Soldier's Home, 13 Oct 1915, record (1915): 483.
Francis A. MASON, age: 73 years, born: Massachusetts, married, painter, parents: not stated, death cause: not stated, died: Soldier's Home, 13 Oct 1915, record (1915): 484.
Bessie ADAMS, born: 18 Oct 1915, parents: Mallison ADAMS and Bessie TYREE (SC), death cause: "premature", informant: father (Johnson City), buried: Onks Cemetery, died: 31 Oct 1915, record (1915): 485.
Dee Mitchell FORD, born: 20 Sep 1915, parents: John T. FORD and Sallie MITCHELL, death cause: "inanition", informant: father (Jonesboro), died: 3 Oct 1915, record (1915): 486.
Jerry MCQUEEN, age: 77 years, born in Virginia, married, shoe maker, parents: not stated, death cause: "pneumonia", died: Soldier's Home, 3 Oct 1915, record (1915): 487.
Foster M. HASKELL, age: 74 years, born: Massachusetts, widower, painter, parents: not stated, death cause: "cardiac dilatation", died: Soldier's Home, 2 Oct 1915, record (1915): 488.
Mary A. MILLER, age; 75 years, parents: not stated, death cause: "heart lesion", died: 5th District, 6 Oct 1915, record (1915): 489.
Jesse CARROLL, age: 25 years, single, parents: father not stated, and Vina CARROLL (KY), death cause: illegible, informant: R.N. BROWN (Jonesboro), buried: Fordtown, died: 4 Nov 1915, record: 490.
Rev. R.E. DEAKIN, born: 2 Jul 1871, married, parents: John DEAKIN and Nancy Caroline DEAKIN, death cause: "typhoid fever", buried: Bacon Cemetery, died: 5 Nov 1915, record (1915): 491.

James HIX, born: 4 Jul 1841, married, parents: Eli HIX (NC) and Susanah WALKER, death cause: "heart disease", informant: Susan GIBSON (Limestone), died: 1 Nov 1915, record (1915): 492.

Mrs. Bessie C. ADAMS, born: 3 Nov 1896 in South Carolina, married, parents: Richard TINER (SC) and Mollie GOOCH (SC), death cause: "pulmonary tuberculosis", informant: M.A. ADAMS (Johnson City), buried: Onks Cemetery, died: 4 Nov 1915, record (1915): 493.

Gardner C. DURRELL, age: 72 years, born: New Hampshire, single, parents: not stated, death cause: "facial erysipelas", buried: Laconia, NH., died: Soldier's Home, 5 Nov 1915, record (1915): 494.

Infant FULKERSON, female, born: 26 Sep 1915, parents: M. FULKERSON and Martha CARTER, death cause: "found dead in bed", buried: Snow Chapel, died: 10 Nov 1915, record (1915): 495.

Malissa COLLINS, age: 64 years, born: Sullivan County, married, parents: __ MILLER and mother not stated, death cause: "heart and kidney disease", buried: Oak Hill, died: 9th District, 13 Nov 1915, record (1915): 496.

Infant PRICE, born: 8 Nov 1915, parents: J.H. PRICE (VA) and Maude CASPER (Alabama), death cause: "disease of heart", buried: Buena Vista, died: 11 Nov 1915, record (1915): 497.

Troy Edward CARDWELL, born: 27 May 1912 in Virginia, parents: T.W. CARDWELL (VA) and Effie HURLEY (NC), death cause: "diptheria", informant: father (Johnson City), buried: Saltville, VA., died: 16 Nov 1915, record (1915): 498.

William P. WORLEY, age: 69 years, born: Tennessee, widower, parents: not stated, death cause: "pyemia", buried: Calhoun, TN., died: Soldier's Home, 16 Nov 1915, record (1915): 499.

Cassie TROXELL, age: 19 years, married, parents: David TROXELL and (illegible) FAIR, death cause: "pellegra", buried: Mottern Cemetery, died: 9th District, 17 Nov 1915, record (1915): 500.

Kemper FIELDS, age: 30 years, born: Sullivan County, married, parents: Charlie FIELDS (VA) and Eliza

EVANS (VA), death cause: "tuberculosis", died: 9th District, 19 Nov 1915, record (1915): 501.

Elizabeth MCCRACKEN, age: 69 years, born: Virginia, married, parents: Daniel ELKENS and __ MILLARD (VA), death cause: "pulmonary tuberculosis", buried: Oak Hill, died: 9th District, 22 Nov 1915, record (1915): 502.

Mary C. GIBSON, born: 19 Jul 1875, married, parents: William LEWIS (NC) and Nancy SCALF, death cause: "acute indigestion", informant: H.M. GIBSON (Johnson City), buried: Longmire Cemetery, died: 24 Nov 1915, record (1915): 503.

Mrs. Elizabeth TAUGHY (?), born: 10 May 1864 in Virginia, married, parents: Alfred DOUGHERTY (VA) and Mary PHILLIPS, death cause: "dysentery", informant: M.S. CANNON (Johnson City), buried: Kelley Cemetery, died: 26 Nov 1915, record (1915): 504.

Jacob M. GOOD, age: 84 years, born: Tennessee, married, parents: not stated, death cause: "cerebral hemorrhage", died: Soldier's Home, 9 Nov 1915, record (1915): 506.

J. Ada COX, age: 52 years, married, parents: F.L. BUMGARDNER (Wytheville, VA) and Edna TIPTON, death cause: "cerebral hemorrhage", buried: Blundville (Blountville ?), TN., died: 27 Nov 1915, record (1915): 505.

James BARNETT, age: 70 years, born: New York, married, plasterer, parents: not stated, death cause: "asthma and pneumonia", died: Soldier's Home, 11 Nov 1915, record (1915): 507.

John W. KEYS, born: 16 Apr 1855, married, parents: Aaron KEYS and Mary HUSTMAN, death cause: "nephritis, pleurisy", buried: Providence, died: Limestone, 24 Nov 1915, record (1915): 509.

Bricen H. PRESLEY, age: 72 years, born: Tennessee, married, parents: not stated, death cause: "cancer of stomach", died: Soldier's Home, 27 Nov 1915, record (1915): 508.

Infant TREADWAY, female, parents: John TREADWAY and Sallie MCGEE, death cause: "stillborn", informant: father (Telford), died: 30 Nov 1915, record: 510.

Infant STORY, female, born: 25 Nov 1915, parents: Hubert STORY and Rebecca (illegible), death cause: "premature", informant: father (Garbers), buried: Keplinger Cemetery, died: 27 Nov 1915, record (1915): 511.

Florence Etta PATRICK, born: 8 Oct 1915, parents: Doris PATRICK (VA) and Lula B. GREEN, death cause: not stated, informant: father (Johnson City), buried: Union Cemetery, died: 4 Nov 1915, record (1915): 512.

Margaret Emaline STRICKLAND, born: 5 Nov 1915, parents: William STRICKLAND and Julia BROCKWELL, death cause: not stated, informant: Joseph FINE (Johnson City), buried: Slagle Cemetery, died: 28 Nov 1915, record (1915): 513.

___ MURR, female, age: 8 years, parents: Charley MURR and Ida CRAWFORD, death cause: "diptheria", informant: Huston MURR (Telford), died: 17 Nov 1915, record (1915): 514.

Mary Elizabeth SMITH, born: 13 May 1832 in Virginia, widow, parents: James PATTERSON (VA) and Sarah BYLEY (VA), death cause: "carcinoma .. (illegible)", informant: J.B. BUCK (Jonesboro), died: 11 Nov 1915, record (1915): 515.

Infant WALKER, male, parents: Lute WALKER and Bonisie WILHOIT, death cause: "stillborn", informant: father (Chuckey), buried: Philadelphia, died: 19 Nov 1915, record (1915): 516.

Infant BROYLES, male, parents: Rolla BROYLES and (illegible) WALKER, death cause: "stillborn", informant: father (Chuckey), buried: Philadelphia, died: 12 Nov 1915, record (1915): 517.

George W. TAYLOR, black, born: ___ Jul 1886, single, parents: J.W. TAYLOR and Mary Jane CARMICLE, death cause: "pulmonary tuberculosis", informant: father (Jonesboro), buried: Little Brick, died: 6 Nov 1915, record (1915): 518.

Catherine MOYERS, age: not stated, widow, parents: not stated, death cause: "heart and Brights disease", died: 14th District, 13 Nov 1915, record (1915): 519.

S.W. FURCHES, born: 20 Jul 1835 in North Carolina, married, parents: not stated, death cause: "pneumonia", died: 6th District (Unicoi County), 13 Nov 1915, record (1915): 520.

Amandah MONTGOMERY, age: 77 years, married, parents: father not stated, mother's name illegible, death cause: "hemorrhage from bowels", informant: Wilson MONTGOMERY (Fall Branch), died: 22 Nov 1915, record (1915): 521.

Samuel B. GRAHAM, born: 4 Oct 1848, widower, parents: John GRAHAM (VA) and Polly BAYLESS, death cause: "broncho pneumonia", buried: Mt. Wesley, died: Jonesboro, 21 Dec 1915, record (1915): 522.

Walter Henry BAYLESS, born: 29 Nov 1911, parents: E.B. BAYLESS and Fannie B. CARR, death cause: "scarlet fever", informant: father (Johnson City), buried: Bayless Cemetery, died: 21 Dec 1915, record (1915): 523.

Infant RIDDLE, male, parents: Guss RIDDLE and Hassie LOWERY, death cause: "premature birth", died: 6th Disrict, 21 Dec 1915, record (1915): 524.

Laura Alice TUCKER, born: 25 Jan 1857, single, parents: Johnathan TUCKER and Mary Jane HAYNES, death cause: "tuberculosis of lungs", died: 21 Dec 1915, record (1915): 525.

Johnie BLEVINS, born: 24 Mar 1915, parents: Frank BLEVINS and Levis WHITE, death cause: "pertussis", informant: J.P. LOCKNER (Embreeville), died: 19 Dec 1915, record (1915): 526.

Charlie GREEN, born: 21 Apr __, age: 1 year and 7 months, parents: Harrison GREEN (NC) and Julie FRY, death cause: "perussis", died: Embreeville, 9 Dec 1915, record (1915): 527.

John O'BRIEN, age: 81 years, born: Ireland, parents: not stated, death cause: "perionitis", died: Soldier's Home, 16 Dec 1915, record (1915): 528.

Walter A. NEWCOMB, age: 45 years, born: New York, married, decorator, parents: not stated, death cause: "pellagra", died: Soldier's Home, 12 Dec 1915, record (1915): 529.

William A. MCINTURFF, age: 60 years, 11 months and 21 days, married, parents: Israel MCINTURFF and

Darkis BAILEY, death cause: "lobar pneumonia", informant: M.F. DUNBAR (Chuckey), buried: Liberty Cemetery, died: 21 Dec 1915, record (1915): 530.

Joe GRIFFEN, colored, age: 37 years, single, parents: not stated, death cause: "syphillis", died: Soldier's Home, 16 Dec 1915, record (1915): 531.

Benjamin K. REED, age: 71 years, born: Ohio, widower, parents: not stated, death cause: "shock following fractured hip, died: Soldier's Home, 11 Dec 1915, record (1915): 532.

Jasper B. GRIFFITH, age: 75 years, widower, parents: not stated, death cause: "pulmonary tuberculosis", buried: Ethridge, TN., died: Soldier's Home, 2 Dec 1915, record (1915): 533.

Earle Edward CAMPBELL, born: 24 Aug 1915, parents: W.F. CAMPBELL (Texas) and Minnie COALY, death cause: "found dead in bed", informant: J.F. CAMPBELL (Johnson City), buried: Buena Vista, died: 5 Dec 1915, record (1915): 534.

Ward CROSBY, born: 1 May 1859 in Canada, married, chief engineer, parents: O.K. CROSBY (Canada) and Martha V. DEMARY (Vermont), death cause: "Brights disease and asthma", informant: Mrs. Ward CROSBY (Johnson City), buried: Tolley, Massachusetts, died: 5 Dec 1915, record (1915): 535.

Zora May GIBSON, age: 1 month and 12 days, parents: J.F. GIBSON and Bertha MCQUEREY (NC), death cause: illegible, buried: Sinking Creek Cemetery, died: 8 Dec 1915, record (1915): 536.

George Henderson BERRY, born: 18 Apr 1855, married, dentist, parents: L.C. BERRY (VA) and Mary FOLSOM (NC), death cause: "cancer of stomach", informant: Mrs. George BERRY (Johnson City), buried: Buena Vista, died: 13 Dec 1915, record (1915): 536.

Fannie May CLAUSON, age: 8 years, parents: James B. CLAUSON and Margaret DUNN, death cause: not recorded, buried: Snow Chapel, died: 9th District, 14 Dec 1915, record (1915): 537.

Isaac P. PRICE, age: 73 years, born: Pennsylvania, married, carpenter, parents: not stated, death cause: "nephritis", buried: Philadelphia, PA., died: Soldier's Home, 16 Dec 1915, record (1915): 538.

Mrs. Nanie E. HENDRIX, born: 30 May 1861, widow, parents: James SCOTT and Christine MOTTERN, death cause: "pulmonary tuberculosis", informant: Blain HENDRIX (Johnson City), buried: Oak Hill, died: 16 Dec 1915, record (1915): 539.

George Bushon O'BRIEN, born: 29 Dec 1849, married, parents: William O'BRIEN (PA) and Lavina GARLAND (NC), death cause: "apoplexy", informant: Will O'BRIEN (Johnson City), buried: Oak Hill, died: 20 Dec 1915, record (1915): 540.

Mrs. W.A. CAMPBELL, age: 32 years, married, parents: Dr. Samuel ANDERSON and Margaret DOPE (?), death cause: "pellagra", informant: W.A. CAMPBELL (Johnson City), buried: Greenville, TN., died: 20 Dec 1915, record (1915): 541.

Isaac P. HOPSON, age: 65 years, born: North Carolina, married, parents: William HOPSON (NC) and Sallie HONEYCUTT (NC), death cause: "heart lesion", informant: J.P. HOPSON (Johnson City), buried: Hicks (?) Chapel, died: 22 Dec 1915, record (1915): 542.

Ruth Ala RICHARDSON, born: 25 Dec 1895, married, parents: R.F. SWIFT and Matilda POWELL (KY), death cause: "pellagra", informant: M.S. CANNON (Johnson City), buried: Buena Vista, died: 24 Dec 1915, record (1915): 543.

Glennie DULANEY, born: 31 Mar 1911, parents: C.D. DULANEY and Julia HICKS, death cause: "diptheria", informant: father (Johnson City), buried: Buena Vista, died: 25 Dec 1915, record (1915): 544.

Dabncey (?) B. SELTON, age: 14 years, parents: G.W. SELTON (GA) and Florence LOYALL (VA), death cause: "shock, traumatic amputation of legs and arm", informant: father (Johnson City), buried: Oak Hill, died: 26 Dec 1915, record (1915): 545.

George WEST, age: 72 years, born: Pennsylvania, parents: not stated, death cause: "cystitis", buried: Philadelphia, PA., died: Soldier's Home, 24 Dec 1915, record (1915): 546.

Hettie CANNON, born: 15 Sep 1863, widow, parents: not stated, death cause: "anemia and indigestion", informant: Wilmer CANNON (Johnson City), buried: Greenville, TN., died: 31 Dec 1915, record: 547.

Jerry AVARY alias Jerry AVERY, colored, age: 72 years, born: Tennessee, widower, parents: not stated, death cause: "cardiac dilatation", died: Soldier's Home, 23 Dec 1915, record (1915): 548.

Infant ERWIN, colored, male, parents: Emery ERWIN (Sullivan County) and Charlotte STUART, death cause: not stated, informant: father (Jonesboro), born/died: 9 Dec 1915, record (1915): 549.

Mrs. Virginia Bachman COX, born: 11 Sep 1846 in Sullivan County, widow, parents: Nathan W. BACHMAN (Sullivan Co.) and Emeline BIRDWELL (Sullivan Co.), death cause: "apoplexy", informant: John D. COX (Jonesboro), died: 13 Dec 1915, record (1915): 550.

Arthor James STORIE, born: 25 Jan 1896 in Johnson County, married, parents: James STORIE (Johnson Co.) and Eliza WILKERSON (NC), death cause: "tuberculosis of lungs", informant: James STORIE (Jonesboro), buried: Mt. Bethel, died: 14 Dec 1915, record (1915): 551.

Berty SERCY, born: 15 Dec 1910, parents: Burran SERCY and Ira CASH, death cause: "burned", informant: David SERCY (Jonesboro), buried: Boones Creek, died: 15th District, 15 Dec 1915, record: 552.

Lonie RAMEY, born: 20 Dec 1914 in Ohio, parents: Charles RAMEY (Kansas City, MO.) and Louise GIBSON (VA), death cause: "croup and indigestion", informant: father (Johnson City), buried: Oak Hill, died: 30 Dec 1915, record (1915): 553.

Hazel Elizabeth OLLIVER, born: 2 Mar 1910, parents: John OLLIVER and Maggie WHITAKER, death cause: "diptheria", informant: F.T. MASSINGILL (Johnson City), buried: New Bethel Cemetery, died: 11 Dec 1915, record (1915): 554.

Margaret MELVIN, born: 17 Mar 1848, single, parents: James R. MELVIN and Eliza WHITE, death cause: "ulcer of stomach", informant: William MELVIN (Johnson City), buried: Duncan Cemetery, died: 25 Dec 1915, record (1915): 555.

Lavina STORY, age: 28 years, married, parents: Melvin CROSSWHITE and Rebecca __, death cause: "tuberculosis", informant: Thomas STORY (Jonesboro), died: 10 Dec 1915, record (1915): 556.

Louise WHITE, age: 35 years, married, parents: James MURDOCK and mother not stated, death cause: "pulmonary tuberculosis", informant: D.K. WHITE (Jonesboro), buried: Fairview, died: 11 Dec 1915, record (1915): 557.
Isac Lewis FLEENOR, born: 13 Dec 1828 in Washington County, VA., widower, parents: not stated, death cause: "nephritis", informant: Pierce FLEENOR (Limestone), buried: Washington Co., VA., died: 15 Dec 1915, record (1915): 558.
Katherine J. BRABSON, born: 15 Oct 1850, married, parents: D.B. BARKLEY and Mary A (illegible), death cause: "cancer of .. (illegible)", informant: E.D. BRABSON (Telford), buried: Oakland Cemetery, died: 11 Dec 1915, record (1915): 559.
Grace SMITH, age: 4 years, parents: W.H. SMITH and Fannie LOVEGROVE, death cause: "diptheria", informant: J.H. SLONAKER (Jonesboro), died: 8 Dec 1915, record (1915): 560.
Vina CARROLL, age: about 59 years, born: Kentucky, single, parents: George CARROLL (KY) and Nancy HALL, death cause: "uterine cancer", informant: Charles BOWMAN (Jonesboro), buried: Fordtown Church, died: 2 Dec 1915, record (1915): 561.
Elizabeth COX, born: 17 Aug 1841, widow, parents: Johnathan BACON and Deborah BARNES, death cause: "cerebral apoplexy", informant: J. Mat COX (Jonesboro), buried: Range Cemetery, died: 3 Dec 1915, record (1915): 562.
Martha TUCKER, born: 6 Nov 1844, single, parents: James TUCKER and Susan BROWN, death cause: "nephritis", informant: Isac TUCKER, buried: Mt. Wesley, died: Telford, 11 Dec 1915, record: 563.
William M. BOLTON, age: 67 years, born: Virginia, married, parents: Samuel BOLTON (VA) and mother not stated, death cause: "nephritis", informant: Nannie BOLTON (Telford), buried: Mt. Wesley, died: 4 Dec 1915, record (1915): 564.
Alzata RINES, born: __ Mar 1980, parents: Shadrack RINES and Creacy CARSON, death cause: "diptheria", informant: father (Jonesboro), died: 21 Jan 1916, record (1916): 1.

Infant DICKINSON, female, parents: Garfield DICKINSON and Ethel MCNICHOLS, death cause: "stillborn", informant: father (Jonesboro), died: 16 Jan 1916, record (1916): 3.
William H.H. DENTON, age: 75 years, widower, parents: Henry DENTON (VA) and Delithia STEVENS, death cause: "heart trouble", informant: D.B. DENTON (W. VA.), buried: 8th District, died: Jonesboro, 8 Jan 1916, record (1916): 2.
Skelton TAYLOR, born: 19 Aug 1831, widower, parents: A.P. TAYLOR and Elizabeth MCCRAY, death cause: "grippe", informant: Ed S. BOYD (Jonesboro), died: 12 Jan 1916, record (1916): 4.
James Anderson DAY, born: 9 Feb 1874, married, parents: Anderson DAY and Nancy HAMIT, death cause: "lagrippe and pneumonia", informant: Maggie DAY (Johnson City), buried: Union Cemetery, died: 1 Jan 1916, record (1916): 5.
Matthew SPRING, age: 71 years, born: New York, widower, parents: not stated, death cause: "myo carditis", died: Soldier's Home, 1 Jan 1916, record (1916): 6.
Wilham Jacob DEAKINS, born: 19 Feb 1878, married, school teacher, parents: J.J. DEAKINS and Laura HUDDLE, death cause: "pulmonary tuberculosis", buried: Sulphur Springs, died: 4 Jan 1916, record (1916): 7.
R.C. METCALF, born: 15 Jan 1884 in Unicoi County, married, parents: Harrison METCALF (NC) and Eliza REED (NC), death cause: "pneumonia", informant: Joseph P. LOCKNER (Embreeville), died: 28 Jan 1916, record (1916): 8.
Albert W. LINDSEY, age: 71 years, born: Ohio, married, parents: not stated, death cause: "mitral insufficiency", died: Soldier's Home, 18 Jan 1916, record (1916): 9.
Isaac D. COKELET, age: 68 years, born: New York, single, parents: not stated, death cause: "pulmonary tuberculosis", died: Soldier's Home, 14 Jan 1916, record (1916): 10.
Daniel B. THACHER, age: 70 years, born: Ohio, married, parents: not stated, death cause: "aortic

stenosis", died: Soldier's Home, 14 Jan 1915, record (1916): 11.

Edwin WOOD, age: 72 years, born: New York, single, parents: not stated, death cause: "pulmonary tuberculosis", died: Soldier's Home, 9 Jan 1916, record (1916): 12.

William RICE alias William JOHNSON, age: 72 years, single, parents: not stated, death cause: "rheumatism", died: Soldier's Home, 8 Jan 1916, record (1916): 13.

Mrs. J.M. BROWN, age: 34 years, born: Hawkins County, married, parents: father's name illegible and mother not stated, death cause: illegible, informant: J.M. BROWN (Johnson City), buried: Buena Vista, died: 25 Jan 1916, record (1916): 14.

Eliza CADE, born: 21 Aug __, age: 58 years, 5 months and 4 days, single, parents: Louis CADE (NC) and Sallie HARMON, death cause: "Brights and heart disease", informant: E.C. CADE (Johnson City), buried: Buena Vista, died: 26 Jan 1916, record (1916): 15.

Hattie PICKENS, colored, born: 9 Oct 1906 in North Carolina, parents: James PICKENS (NC) and Margaret FREEMAN (NC), death cause: "lobar pneumonia", informant: father (Johnson City), buried: Shelbyville, NC., died: 21 Jan 1916, record (1916): (not numbered).

Evaline KITE, born: 3 Sep 1915, parents: T.E. KITE and Laura MORRELL, death cause: "lung congestion", informant: Howard KITE (Johnson City), died: 19 Jan 1916, record (1916): 16.

Mable HAWS, age: 7 years, parents: Charlie HAWS and Sudie BACON, death cause: "diptheria", buried: Pleasant Valley, died: 9th District, 14 Jan 1916, record (1916): 17.

John C. HEUBRICK, age: 72 years, born: Germany, single, cattle dealer, parents: not stated, death cause: "cerebral hemorrhage", buried: Louisville, KY., died: Soldier's Home, 14 Jan 1916, record (1916): 18.

Harrison EDWARDS, born: 2 Mar 1914, parents: Allen EDWARDS and Martha FLETCHER, death cause: "ileo colitis", informant: father (Johnson City), buried: Buena Vista, died: 11 Jan 1916, record (1916): 19.

Mrs. Anna Lee GEORGE, born: 26 Oct 1873 in Ohio, married, parents: Horola NELSON (Ireland) and Carie LEE (NY), death cause: "pregnancy and uremia", informant: J.F. GEORGE (Johnson City), buried: Knoxville, died: 10 Jan 1016, record (1916): 20.

Agnes HORTON, colored, born: 3 Dec 1915, parents: Arthur HORTON and Lena KELLEY, death cause: "tubeculosis of bowels", buried: Hyder Cemetery, died: 10 Jan 1916, record (1916): 21.

Infant CLOYD, colored, female, parents: Will CLOYD and Grace VAUGHT, death cause: "stillborn", informant: G.A. FITZGERALD (Johnson City), buried: West Lawn, died: 5 Jan 1916, record (1916): 22.

Susan E. ARNEY, born: 29 Dec 1856 in Ireland, married, parents: John MCGETTIGAN (Ireland) and mother not stated, death cause: "malignancy of stomach and gall bladder", informant: E.J, ARNEY (Johnson City), buried: Oak Hill, died: 4 Jan 1916, record: 23.

Sallie PHIPP, born: __ Aug 1870 in Virginia, parents: Freeman TATE and Mary MINNICK (VA), death cause: "pellagra", buried: Buena Vista, died: Johnson City, 3 Jan 1916, record (1916): 24.

Infant BROWN, female, parents: J.M. BROWN and Nancy MAWS (Hawkins County), informant: father (Johnson City), buried: Buena Vista, born/died: 3 Jan 1916, record (1916): 25.

Mrs. Martha EDWARDS, age: 37 years, married, parents: Dave FLETCHER and Mary MCAFEE, death cause: "pulmonary tuberculosis", informant: Allen EDWARDS (Johnson City), buried: Buena Vista, died: 2 Jan 1916, record (1916): 26.

Henry GIBSON, born: 8 Apr 1852, married, parents: Braswell GIBSON and Emeline CURTIS, death cause: "neuralgia of stomach and heart", informant: Anna GIBSON (Rt 4, Johnson City), buried: Vaughn Cemetery, died: 15 Jan 1916, record (1916): 27.

Samantha FIELDS, age: 67 years, born: Hawkins County, single, parents: Leonard FIELDS and Polly FISH, death cause: "uremic poisoning", informant:

G.H. DISHNER (Johnson City), buried: 15th District, died: 20 Jan 1916, record (1916): 28.

Ethel AIKEN, born: 30 Jul 1890, single, parents: James AIKEN and Elizabeth GUIRE, death cause: "careous tuberculosis", informant: Dennie GRAY (Telford), buried: Oakland Cemetery, died: 14 Jan 1916, record (1916): 29.

Elizabeth Catherine MCKAY, born: 18 Jan 1846, widow, parents: Jesse ARMENTROUT (VA) and Rachael ZIMMERMAN (VA), death cause: "cancer of piloris", informant: Hellen STONIES (Limestone), buried: Oakland Cemetery, died: 20 Jan 1916, record (1916): 30.

James Richard RAMSEY, born: __ Aug 1915, parents: James RAMSEY (NC) and Cordie RAMSEY (NC), death cause: "worms", informant: J.M. STORY (Garbers), died: 6 Jan 1916, record (1916): 31.

John FLEMING, born: 18 Mar 1852 in Detroit, Michigan, widower, parents: not stated, death cause: "uremic coma", informant: Martha YONKEY (Edgar, Wisconsin), buried: Fordtown, died: 23 Jan 1916, record (1916): 32.

Earl DOVE, born: 18 Mar 1915, parents: C.E. DOVE and Mary MARRION, death cause: "diptheria", informant: father (Jonesboro), buried: Hales Chapel, died: 1 Jan 1916, record (1916): 33.

Wade HODGES, born: 11 Jun 1914, parents: R.L. HODGES and Maud BOLTON (Greene County), death cause: "burns, paralysis of muscles and respiration", infomant: mother (Jonesboro), died: 17 Jan 1916, record (1916): 34.

Lafayette CONLEY, age: 45 years, married, parents: J.A. CONLEY and Elizabeth KEEBLER, death cause: "lagrippe and pneumonia", informant: S.B. CAMPBELL (Jonesboro), buried: Keebler Institute, 14th District, died: 1 Jan 1916, record (1916): 35.

George WHITE, age: 66 years, born: Virginia, married, parents: not stated, death cause: "paralysis", buried: County Farm, died: 11 Jan 1916, record (1916): 36.

Lou HAMMER, colored, age: 53 years, born: Morganton, NC., married, parents: __ CONLEY and Lydia CONLEY (Morganton, NC.), death cause: "pneumonia", informan: Nola HAMMER (Johnson City), buried: Jonesboro, died: 8 Jan 1916, record (1916): 36.

Mrs. Bettie BAILEY, born: 1 Aug 1833, widow, parents: __ COOPER and mother not stated, death cause: "(illegible) of stomach", informant: B.H. HUFFMAN (Jonesboro), buried: Deakins Cemetery, died: 16 Jan 1916, record (1916): 38.

Infant HUMPHREYS, male, parents: Fred HUMPHREYS and Bell BLAKELEY (Greene County), death cause: "stillborn", informant: father (Jonesboro), died: 16 Jan 1916, record (1916): 39.

Mary Ann Amelia DOSSER, age: 89 years, born: Virginia, widow, parents: William H. ATKINSON (Baltimore, MD.) and Mary CARTER (VA), death cause: "cerebral .. (illegible)", informant: James E. DOSSER (Knoxville), died: Jonesboro, 24 Jan 1916, record (1916): 40.

Thomas B. SAULTS, born: 20 Jan 1828, widower, parents: Daniel SAULTS and Rebecca BALL, death cause: "organic heart trouble", informant: Ida SAULTS (Jonesboro), died: 26 Jan 1916, record (1916): 41.

Bessie LUTTRELL, born: 4 Sep 1915, parents: W.F. LUTTRELL and Pearl STORY, death cause: "whooping cough", informant: father (Jonesboro), buried: Union Church Cemetery, died: 6 Jan 1916, record: 42.

Nannie DULANEY, age: 60 years, married, parents: Madison PATTON and Elizabeth PATTON, death cause: "tuberuclosis of bowels", informant: E. DULANEY (Jonesboro), buried: Cherokee, 8th District, died: 25 Jan 1916, record (1916): 43.

Gaston Powell LOWE, age: 72 years, 4 months and 2 days, born: Johnson County, married, parents: John A LOW and Millie ARLINGTON (NC), death cause: "diarrhoea and heart disease", buried: Liberty Cemetery, died: 9th District, 23 Jan 1916, record (1916): 44.

William KANEY, age: 78 years, born: Ireland, widower, railroad engineer, parents: not stated, death cause: "nephritis", died: Soldier's Home, 29 Jan 1916, record (1916): 45.

William M. IRELAND, age: 71 years, born: Kentucky, widower, cattle dealer, parents: not stated, death cause: "mitral insufficiency", died: Soldier's Home, 27 Jan 1916, record (1916): 46.

Robert DRUIT, age: 69 years, born: New York, widower, tin smith, parents: not stated, death cause: "mitral insufficiency", died: Soldier's Home, 18 Jan 1916.

Julia A. MANGOLD, born: 12 Nov 1869, married, parents: Soloman G. ARNOLD (VA) and Jane ARMENTROUT (VA), death cause: "bowel obstruction and fatty degeneraton of heart", informant: J.M. MANGOLD (Telford), died: 17 Jan 1916, record (1916): 48.

George Nathan LOYD, born: 22 Sep 1867 at Baileyton, TN., married, parents: Robert LOYD and Lucinda WALLER, death cause: "influenza and pneumonia", informant: Vesta LOYD (Fall Branch), buried: Lovalace Cemetery, died: 13 Jan 1916, record (1916): 49.

Charles HOLMES, born: 8 Mar 1845, married, parents: Samuel D. MCADAMS and Jane HOLMES, death cause: "gastric cancer", informant: wife, Matilda HOLMES (Jonesboro), died: 14 Jan 1916, record (1916): 50.

Adaline ADAMS, age: 70 years, widow, parents: Soloman COLE and __ MALONEY, death cause: "gastro enteritis", informant: J.E. ADAMS (Chuckey), buried: Liberty Cemetery, died: 16 Jan 1916, record: 51.

Mrs. Luce HUFFMAN, born: 5 Oct 1852, married, parents: Joseph E. REESER (Greene County) and Mary E. MATHES, death cause: "carcinoma of breast", informant: S.G. LEWIS (Telford), buried: Mt. Wesley, died: 5 Jan 1916, record (1916): 52.

Polly Elmira MASTERS, born: 2 Sep 1852 in North Carolina, married, parents: John PATTERSON (NC) and Suckey BRYANT (NC), death cause: "lobar pneumonia", buried: Mt. Wesley, died: 12 Jan 1916, record (1916): 53.

Mrs. Hannah Mary MASTERS, born: 19 Jan __, age: 32 years and 5 months, born: Mitchell County, NC., single, parents: T.D. MASTERS (Mitchell Co.) and Polly PATTERSON (Yancey County, NC.), death cause: "lobar pneumonia", buried: Mt. Wesley, died: 11 Jan 1916, record (1916): 54.

William Earl LOVE, colored, born: 15 Mar 1894, single, miner, parents: Marion LOVE (NC) and Peachie

MEVENICK, death cause: "tuberculosis of lungs", informant: Dr. A.J. WILLIS (Embreeville), died: 27 Jan 1916, record (1916): 55.

James TAYLOR, age: 70 years, born: Pennsylvania, single, parents: not stated, death cause: "mitral insufficiency", died: Soldier's Home, 25 Feb 1916, record (1916): 56.

Marcure R. THOMPSON, age: 79 years, born: Pennsylvania, widower, carpenter, parents: not stated, death cause: "mitral insufficiency", died: Soldier's Home, 26 Feb 1916, record (1916): 57.

John B. JONES, age: 60 years, born: Tennessee, widower, stone mason, parents: not stated, death cause: "cystitis", died: Soldier's Home, 29 Feb 1916, record (1916): 58.

Raymond Lee WHITE, born: 4 Aug 1914, parents: Thomas WHITE and Mary GOOD, death cause: "bronchial pneumonia", informant: George SHIPLEY (Jonesboro), buried: Boones Creek, died: 13 Feb 1916, record (1916): 59.

Nancy BERRY, age: 89 years, widow, parents: Isaac MILLER and mother not stated, death cause: "heart trouble", informant: W.E. WHITE (Jonesboro), died: 15 Feb 1916, record (1916): 60.

Mary D. CRUMP, born: 7 Sep 1841, married, parents: Elie STANFIELD and (illegible) ADAMS, death cause: "heart trouble", informant: J.P. CRUMP (Jonesboro), buried: Hodges Cemetery, died: 12 Feb 1916, record (1916): 61.

William BLACK, age: 77 years, parents: not stated, death cause: "natural causes", informant: Sam INGLE (Jonesboro), buried: New Victory, died: 2 Feb 1916, record (1916): 62.

Barbery BAIRFIELD, age: 65 years, born: North Carolina, married, parents: Daniel GLASS (NC) and __ SCHUB (NC), death cause: "spinal disease of several years", informant: J.M. BARFIELD (Jonesboro), buried: Boones Creek, died: 7 Feb 1916, record (1916): 63.

Virginia SELLERS, age: about 62 years, single, parents: Jacob SELLERS (VA) and Priscilla ARMENTROUT (VA), death cause: "heart failure", informant: S.C. BALL (Telford), died: 15 Feb 1916, record: 64.

Louise MCCRACKEN, born: 24 Aug 1914, parents: J.A. MCCRACKEN and Estell PICKENS, death cause: "bronchitis", informant: father (Jonesboro), buried: Boones Creek, died: 5 Feb 1916, record (1916): 65.

H. HOLDER, female, age: 1 year and 4 months, parents: Steve HOLDER and Sarah ESTEP, death cause: "whooping cough", informant: J.C. LEACH (Johnson City), died: 29 Feb 1916, record (1916): 66.

Infant BROYLES, female, parents: Burney BROYLES and Lena PAINTER, death cause: "stillborn", informant: C.W. BRABSON (Chuckey), buried: Liberty Cemetery, died: 28 Feb 1916, record (1916): 67.

Simeon BELL, born: 8 Jan 1838, parents: Briahes (?) BELL (VA) and Elizabeth BROYLES, death cause: "dropsy", informant: C.S. LOVE (Chuckey), buried: Liberty Cemetery, died: 7 Feb 1916, record: 68.

Bell DAVIS, born: 1 Mar 1915, parents: John DAVIS and Sarah TREADWAY, death cause: "whooping cough", died: Embreeville, 21 Feb 1916, record (1916): 69.

Nathan COGGINS, age: 76 years, born: North Carolina, widower, parents: not stated, death cause: "nephritis", died: Jonesboro, 3 Feb 1916, record (1916): 70.

Jasper KING, born: 3 Feb 1916, parents: Charley FURCHESS (NC) and Janie WHITE, death cause: "bronchitis", informant: Ira W. BAXTER (Washington College), died: 6 Feb 1916, record (1916): 71.

Hester E. GREENWAY, born: 26 ov 1844, married, parents: Samuel MCCRACKEN and mother not stated, death cause: "ileo colitis", died: 3rd District, 2 Feb 1916, record (1916): 72.

Maggie Bell DUNCAN, born: 24 Mar 1914, parents: Nelse DUNCAN and Bertie MCKEE, death cause: "bronchitis", informant: father (Washington College), died: 7 Feb 1916, record (1916): 73.

James Henry PROPST, born: 1 Jun 1912, parents: John Calvin PROPST and Mary Elizabeth SLONAKER, death cause: "lobar pneumonia", informant: father (Telford), died: 23 Feb 1916, record (1916): 74.

Letie G. MULLINS, age: 14 days, parents: Roy ROSE and Lettie G. MULLINS, death cause: "pneumonia", informant: N.J, MULLINS (Johnson City), buried: Ellis Cemetery, died: 12 Feb 1916, record (1916): 75.

Bessie GODSEY, age: 19 years, married, parents: Charles FIELDS and Eliza (illegible), death cause: "diarrhoea", buried: Buena Vista, died: Johnson City, 11 Feb 1916, record (1916): 76.

Montgomery SCOTT, born: 11 Dec 1866, married, parents: Don SCOTT and Beuna BORING, death cause: "paralysis", informant: Richard SCOTT (Johnson City), buried: Speedwell Cemetery, died: 9 Feb 1916, record (1916): 77.

James ROBINSON, colored, age: 57 years, married, parents: not stated, death cause: "heart disease", informant: John MIKELS (Johnson City), buried: West Lawn, died: 15 Feb 1916, record (1916): 78.

Nellie Gertrude HILL, colored, born: 9 Apr 1904, parents: Mose HILL (VA) and Carrinth THOMAS, death cause: "diabetes", informant: father (Johnson City), buried: West Lawn, died: 21 Feb 1916, record: 79.

Maud WAGNER, colored, age: 14 years, parents: J.C. WAGNER and Kate MALONE, death cause: "pulmonary tuberculosis", buried: West Lawn, died: 22 Feb 1916, record (1916): 80.

Maggie ROYSTER, colored, age: 51 years, born: Virginia, married, parents: not stated, death cause: "cancer of bladder", informant: Dock MCMILLEN (Johnson City), buried: West Lawn, died: 23 Feb 1916, record (1916): 81.

Maxie BLEVINS, age: 32 years, born: Kingsport, married, parents: J.M. COLLINS (Kingsport) and Malissa MILLER (Kingsport), death cause: "tuberculosis", buried: Oak Hill, died: 9th District, 24 Feb 1916, record (1916): 82.

Mrs. Mary ELMENDORF, age: 84 years, born: New York, widow, parents: Ruben WILDER (Massachusetts) and Mary MERRETT (NY), death cause: "senility", informant: Mrs Mary MALIER (Rhone Mt., TN), buried: Chattanooga, died: 9th District, 26 Feb 1916, record (1916): 83.

Joe CARSON, colored, age: 68 years, born: North Carolina, married, parents: Robert CARSON (NC) and mother not stated, death cause: "hemorrhage", informant: Ed. CARSON (Johnson City), buried: West Lawn, died: 27 Feb 1916, record (1916): 84.

Henry GOBLE, age: 70 years, born: Tennessee, widower, parents: not stated, death cause: "cardiac dilitation", died: Soldier's Home, 12 Feb 1916, record (1916): 85.

William JOHNSON, age: not stated, born: Vermont, widower, parents: not stated, death cause: "cerebral hemorrhage", died: Soldier's Home, 17 Feb 1916, record (1916): 86.

Michael KANE, age: 71 years, born: Pennsylvania, married, policeman, parents: not stated, death cause: "nephritis", died: Soldier's Home, 19 Feb 1916, record (1916): 87.

Thomas J. WOOD, age: 70 years, born: England, widower, theatrical manager, parents: not stated, death cause: "cirrhosis of liver", died: Soldier's Home, 1 Feb 1916, record (1916): 88.

David Thomas BOWMAN, born: 19 Oct 1878 in Greene County, single, parents: Sparling BOWMAN (Greene Co.) and Caroline MORELOCK (Greene Co.), death cause: "pulmonary tuberculosis", informant: F.T. MASSINGILL (Johnson City), buried: Greeneville, died: 5 Feb 1916, record (1916): 89.

Anna Glodina WITHLOCK, parents: George E. WHITLOCK and Mary E. ELSEA, death cause: "stillborn", buried: Fall Branch, died: 24 Feb 1916, record (1916): 90.

Infant BROYLES, female, parents: Burney BROYLES and Lena PAINTER, death cause: "premature, lived 30 minutes", informant: C.W. BRABSON (Chuckey), buried: Liberty Cemetery, died: 28 Feb 1916, record: 91.

Daisey HARDIN, born: 29 Dec 1915, parents: Hooker HARDIN and Elen ESTEP, death cause: "whooping cough", died: 8th District, 17 Feb 1916, record (1916): 92.

William Harrison POOR, age: not stated, married, parents: Sam POOR and Emeline HUSKINS, death cause: "typhoid fever", died: 6th District, 27 Feb 1916, record (1916): 93.

A.L. MCNABB, age: 56 years and 1 day, married, miller, parents: not stated, death cause: "nephritis and gall bladder infection", informant: Ben MCNABB

(Elizabethton), buried: Elizabethton, died: Hospital, Johnson City, 26 Feb 1916, record: 94.

Marriah Agnes GILLESPIE, born: 5 Mar 1837, widow, parents: Enoch BROWN and mother not stated, death cause: "gastritis, possible carcinoma of stomach", informant: F.A. CARTER (Sweetwater, TN), buried: Limestone, died: 19 Feb 1916, record (1916): 95.

Mildred WETHERBY, born: 26 Jun 1895 at Magnetic City, TN., single, parents: Albert C. WETHERBY (Ohio) and Mary F. VOORHES (Ohio), death cause: "sarcoma", buried: Oak Hill, died: 3 Feb 1916, record (1916): 96.

Ida HELTON, age: 35 years, married, parents: William BATCHLEY and Amanda ALLEN, death cause: "tuberculosis", informant: J.H. HELTON (Johnson City), buried: Oak Hill, died: 2 Feb 1916, record (1916): 97.

William Martin ROBERTS, born: 10 Aug 1915, parents: S.A. ROBERTS (NC) and Julia BRASWELL (NC), death cause: "intestinal toxemia, pneumonia", informant: father (Johnson City), buried: Oak Hill, died: 2 Feb 1916, record (1916): 98.

James F. VENABLE, born: 29 Jan 1852, married, florist, parents: Daniel VENABLE (NC) and mother not stated, death cause: "grippe and pellagra", informant: J.F. VENABEL, Jr. (Johnson City), buried: Buena Vista, died: 6 Feb 1916, record (1916): 99.

Mrs. Susie WOOLWINE, colored, age: 44 years, born: Virginia, married, parents: John SALES (VA) and mother not stated, death cause: "pelagra", informant: P.A. WOOLWINE (Johnson City), buried: Wytheville, VA., died: 7 Feb 1916, record: 100.

Infant GILLIS, male, parents: William GILLIS and Lula (?) BROYLES (Greene Co.), death cause: "premature birth", informant: Dr. C.S. LOVE (Chuckey), buried: Liberty, born/died: 1 Mar 1916, record (1916): 101.

Mrs. John F. PAINE, born: 2 Feb 1850 in Stokes County, VA., married, parents: Winston POWERS (NC) and Polly GLASS (NC), death cause: "paralysis", buried: Abingdon, VA., died: Johnson City, 27 Mar 1916, record (1916): 102.

Mrs. Sarah PHILLIPS, born: 9 Jun 1821 in North Carolina, widow, parents: not stated, death cause: "bronchitis", informant: Cass PHILLIPS (Johnson City), buried: North Carolina, died: 29 Mar 1916, record (1916): 103.

Amanda HAUK, born: __ Jan 1875 in Kentucky, married, parents: John BLAINE and Louisa WEALEN, death cause: "pneumonia", informant: C.M. HAUK (Johnson City), buried: Buena Vista, died: 30 Mar 1916, record (1916): 104.

William PATTERSON, colored, born: 24 May 1867, married, parents: Rufus PATTERSON (NC) and Susan CHAVER (NC), death cause: "nervous breakdown", informant: Clara PATTERSON (Abingdon, VA), buried: Abingdon, died: 30 Mar 1916, record (1916): 105.

Tom BROWN, colored, age: 37 years, single, coal miner, parents: not stated, death cause: "crushed by coal falling on him", buried: West Lawn Cemetery, died: 30 Mar 1916, record (1916): 106.

Frank FERRIN, age; 68 years, born: Maine, married, sailor, parents: not stated, death cause: "pulmonary tuberculosis", died: Soldier's Home, 9 Mar 1916, record (1916): 107.

Jerome B. ALLISON, age: 69 years, born: Tennessee, widower, parents: not stated, death cause: "pulmonary tuberculosis", died: Soldier's Home, 11 Mar 1916, record (1916): 108.

Joseph O. PICHE, age: 79 years, born: Canada, single, carpenter, parents: not stated, death cause: "ulcer of rectum", died: Soldier's Home, 11 Mar 1916, record (1916): 109.

Nathan H. DORNEY, age: 83 years, born Pennsylvania, single, machinist, parents: not stated, death cause: "mitral insufficiency", died: Soldier's Home, 20 Mar 1916, record (1916): 110.

Jacob IRVIN alias Jacob ERVAN, age: 74 years, born: Tennessee, married, parents: not stated, death cause: "cardiac dilitation", died: Soldier's Home, 21 Mar 1916, record (1916): 111.

James H. JOHNSON, age: 84 years, married, parents: not stated, death cause: "pneumonia", died: Soldier's Home, 22 Mar 1916, record (1916): 112.

Joseph HARRIS, age; 74 years, born: England, married, parents: not stated, death cause: "nephritis", died: Soldier's Home, 23 Mar 1916, record (1916): 113.

Herman JUSTE, age: 44 years, born: Kentucky, single, musician, parents: not stated, death cause: "pulmonary tuberculosis", died: Soldier's Home, 27 Mar 1916, record (1916): 114.

John COFFMAN, age; 40 years, born: Tennessee, married, parents: not stated, death cause: "pellagra", died: Soldier's Home, 25 Mar 1916, record (1916): 115.

Leroy C. HOLT, age; 80 years, born: Tennessee, married, parents: not stated, death cause: "nephritis", died: Soldier's Home, 30 Mar 1916, record (1916): 116.

William E. MORRISON, age; 76 years, born: New York, widower, parents: not stated, death cause: "cardiac dilitation", buried: Ramsey, Illinois, died: Soldier's Home, 3 Mar 1916, record (1916): 117.

Stephen COLLINS, age; 72 years, born: Ireland, widower, parents: not stated, death cause: "pneumonia", died: Soldier's Home, 6 Mar 1916, record (1916): 118.

William Amison JONNARD, age: 1 year, parents: Rev. W.A. JONNARD (Nashville) and Ann DUBASE (Sewanee, TN), death cause: "convulsions, intestinal toxemia", informant: father (Johnson City), buried: Sewanee, TN., died: 1 Mar 1916, record (1916): 119.

Sarah ARRANTS, age: 60 years, married, parents: Ben HURTY and Bessie CHURCH, death cause: "pneumonia", informant: M.S. CANNON (Johnson City), buried: Oak Hill, died: 1 Mar 1916, record (1916): 120.

Jesse J. MARTIN, born: 19 Jul 1876, married, parents: James Mat MARTIN and Sarah COX, death cause: "gastro enteritis", informant: C.C. MAUPIN (Johnson City), buried: Boones Creek, died: 4 Mar 1916, record (1916): 121.

Viola E. BAINES, age: 2 years, parents: Walter BAINES and Laura BARRON, death cause: "whooping cough", buried: Fairview Cemetery, died: 5 Mar 1916, record (1916): 122.

Mrs. Harrison COOK, born: 13 Feb 1897, married, parents: J.M. DEPEW and Minnie KEYS, death cause: "pellagra", buried: Oak Hill, died: 5 Mar 1916, record (1916): 123.
Luke S. BAYLESS, born: 23 Mar 1846 in Greene County, married, parents: not stated, death cause: "cancer of liver", informant: Mrs. Luke S. BAYLESS (Johnson City), buried: Oak Hill, died: 7 Mar 1916, record (1916): 124.
Infant WIDNER, female, parents: William WIDNER (VA) and Florence GIBSON, death cause: "stillborn", informant: father (Johnson City), buried: Buena Vista, died: 7 Mar 1916, record (1916): 125.
M.J. ARCHER, age: 62 years, married, paretns: Joseph WILCOX and mother not stated, death cause: "heart disease", buried: Archer Cemetery, died: 9th District, 12 Mar 1916, record (1916): 126.
Mary Smith MCDONALD, age: 53 years, born: Raleigh, NC., married, parents: __ SMITH (Raleigh, NC) and mother not stated, death cause: "ptomaine poison", buried: Roanoke, VA., died: 9th District, 12 Mar 1916, record (1916): 127.
George MCNEAL, colored, age: 52 years, born: North Carolina, married, parents: Daublin MCNEAL (NC) and mother not stated, death cause: "grippe", informant: Thomas C. MCNEAL (Johnson City), buried: West Lawn, died: 13 Mar 1916, record (1916): 128.
Mrs. Louisa KELLEY, born: 23 Aug 1844 in Virginia, widow, parents: __ DUARTY and mother not stated, death cause: "lagrippe", informant: John KELLEY (Johnson City), buried: E. Carnega, died: 16 Mar 1916, record (1916): 129.
Paul MOREFIELD, born: 15 Feb 1915 in Cushing, Oklahoma, parents: E.D. MOREFIELD (Ashe County, NC.) and Mattie COPELAND (Sullivan County), death cause: "pneumonia", buried: Bristol, VA., died: 16 Feb 1916, record (1916): 130.
Mrs. Bertha WILLIAMS, age: 36 years, married, parents: J.C. CRUMLEY and Jesie ARMSTEAD, death cause: "tuberculosis", informant: Eli WILLIAMS (Johnson City), buried: Washington College, died: 9 Mar 1916, record (1916): 131.

Frank Landon GIBSON, born: 4 Sep 1915, parents: J. Pierce GIBSON and Sallie Elizabeth CARR, death cause: "marasmus", informant: T.J. GIBSON (Watauga), buried: Carr Cemetery, Watauga, TN., died: 24 Mar 1916, record (1916): 132.

Will NASH, colored, age: 55 years, born: Virginia, married, parents: Joe NASH (VA) and mother not stated, death cause: "oldema and asthma", informant: Wallace TRENT (Johnson City), buried: West Lawn, died: 24 Mar 1916, record (1916): 133.

Charlie EVANS, age: 10 years, parents: George EVANS and Laura EVANS, death cause: "lobar pneumonia", buried: Buena Vista, died: 9th District, 24 Mar 1916, record (1916): 134.

Joseph PHILLIPS, age: 59 years, 2 months and 24 days, born: Sullivan County, married, parents: not stated, death cause: "pulmonary tuberculosis", informant: Pierce FLEENOR (Limestone), buried: Cedar Lane, died: Telford, 24 Mar 1916, record: 135.

Melinda BERRY, age: 70 years, widow, parents: not stated, death cause: "pneumonia", informant: J.W. JONES (Garbers), died: 4th District, 13 Mar 1916, record (1916): 136.

Ella BOOTH, born: 8 Oct 1848, widow, parents: Johnathan WRIGHT and father not stated, death cause: "heart disease", died: 4th District on 19 Mar 1916, record (1916): 137.

Hannah Lizzie MCNEAR, age: 79 years, widow, parents: Isaac WHITE and Hannah Liza WHITE, death cause: "pneumonia", died: 4th District, 19 Mar 1916, record (1916): 138.

Doney H. ADAMS, born: 2 Jan 1916, parents: Elijah S. ADAMS and Jennie B. ADAMS, death cause: "dyptheria", informant: father (Jonesboro), buried: Buffalo Ridge, died: 25 Mar 1916, record (1916): 139.

Loucinda HALL, age: 73 years, widow, parents: Anson HODGE and Harriett GRAY, death cause: "cancer of stomach", buried: Hall Cemetery, died: 11th District on 17 Mar 1916, record (1916): 140.

James A. SMALLWOOD, age: 81 years, born: England, widower, parents: not stated, death cause:

"unknown", died: Soldier's Home, 1 Mar 1916, record (1916): 141.
Joseph MURPHY, age: 77 years, born: Ireland, single, parents: not stated, death cause: "hemeplegia", died: Soldier's Home, 2 Mar 1916, record: 142.
Isaac COOPER, age: 71 years, born: Kentucky, single, parents: not stated, death cause: "pellagra", died: Soldier's Home, 3 Mar 1916, record (1916): 143.
Cora Lee HOLMES, born: 10 Sep 1896, single, parents: Arthur OLIVER and Mary HOLMES, death cause: "Brights and heart disease", informant: J.E. HOLMES (Jonesboro), buried: Onks Cemetery, died: 2 Mar 1916, record (1916): 144.
Elizabeth D. CORNETT, born: 25 Sep 1847 in Virginia, widow, parents: Montgomery CORNETT (VA) and Margaret CORNETT, death cause: "cerebral hemorrhage", informant: D.S. MORRELL (Jonesboro), buried: Fair View, died: 3 Mar 1916, record (1916): 145.
Moore STRICKLAND, age: 73 years, born: North Carolina, married, parents: Daniel STRICKLAND (NC) and __ SEFFORD (Germany), death cause: "lagrippe", informant: J.T. LEACH (Jonesboro), buried: Fine Cemetery, died: 9 Mar 1916, record (1916): 146.
Nora MILLER, born: 10 Sep 1892, single, parents: D.J. MILLER and Julia H. MILLER, death cause: "tuberculosis", informant: G.W. MILLER (Jonesboro), buried: Onks Cemetery, died: 9 Mar 1916, record (1916): 147.
Sarah L. WHITE, born: 20 Jul 1857, single, parents: Isaac WHITE (Erwin) and Mariah SALTS (Embreeville), death cause: "pneumonia", informant: J.G. HAWOOD (Johnson City), buried: Embreeville, died: 24 Mar 1916, record (1916): 148.
James William KEEN, born: 24 Aug 1915, parents: Clive KEEN and Jina PATRICK (VA), death cause: "dropsy of brain", buried: Pleasant Valley, died: 23 Mar 1916, record (1916): 149.
Infant PAINTER, born: 13 Mar 1916, parents: Bertice PAINTER and Bettie HAMMER, death cause: "asthma", informant: father (Limestone), buried: Liberty Cemetery, died: 17 Mar 1916, record (1916): 150.

Crinny CHASE, born: 1 Aug 1913 in Atchison County, MO., parents: John CHASE (Greene Co.) and Bell MCMACKIN (Greene Co.), death cause: "broncho pneumonia", informant: father (Limestone), buried: Milbertown, died: 5 Mar 1916, record (1916): 151.

Mrs. Leptitia, HUMPHREYS, born: 11 Jul 1837 in Sullivan County, minister's wife, parents: William HENSLEY (Sullivan Co.) and Barbie WOLF (Sullivan Co.), death cause: "lobar pneumonia", informant: G.W. HUMPHREYS (Telford), buried: Liberty Cemetery, died: 2 Mar 1916, record (1916): 152.

Infant TYREE, male, parents: Moses MILLER and Nellie TYREE, death cause: "born dead", buried: Caruthers Cemetery, died: 3 Mar 1916, record (1916): 153.

Sarah J. BOLTON, born: 25 Sep 1826, married, parents: Joe WILLETT and __ STANT, death cause: "cholera and paralysis", died: 3rd District, 26 Mar 1916, record (1916): 154.

W.A. BROWNING, born: 18 Nov 1839, widower, parents: __ W. BROWNING and __ WAGNER, death cause: "influenza", informant: S. BROWNING (Knoxville), buried: Dunkard Church Cemetery, died: 18 Mar 1916, record (1916): 155.

Alferd GELASPY. black, born: 26 Jan 1868, widower, parents: Preston GELASPY and Manerva __, death cause: "heart disease", informant: George GILLESPIE (Washington College), died: 15 Mar 1916, record (1916): 156.

Lola Beatrice CRAWFORD, born: 20 Feb 1916, parents: Florida CRAWFORD and Georgia CRAWFORD, death cause: "premature birth", died: 7th District, 4 Mar 1916, record (1916): 157.

David Franklin WISHON, born: 11 Feb 1916, parents: Hunter WISHON and Bertha MILLER, death cause: "hives", buried: Buena Vista, died: 26 Mar 1916, record (1916): 158.

Hillard MATHIS, age: not known, married, parents: Lawson MATHIS (NC) and Lucinda LOWE (NC), death cause: "paralysis", informant: Mrs. Maggie LAWS (Johnson City), buried: Liberty, died: 17 Mar 1916, record (1916): 159.

Annie GREENLEE, colored, age: about 36 years, born: North Carolina, married, parents: father not stated and Angeline ROGERS, death cause: "heart trouble", informant: Howell YANCEY (Jonesboro), died: 30 Mar 1916, record (1916): 160.

W.S. MITCHELL, age: 63 years and 5 months, married, parents: Hiram MITCHELL (Maryland) and Mira ELLIOTT (SC), death cause: "heart disease", buried: Oak Hill, died: 9th District, 18 Apr 1916, record (1916): 161.

Flora E. DICKSON, age: 23 years, single, parents: N.H. DICKSON and Mattie DEVAULT, death cause: "suicide, cut throat with razor", informant: S.C. DICKSON (Johnson City), buried: Kingsport, died: 21 Apr 1916, record (1916): 162.

Infant RANGE, male, parents: Harry RANGE and Reta SMITH, death cause: "stillborn", informant: Mrs. J.J. RANGE (Johnson City), buried: Oak Hill, died: 26 Apr 1916, record (1916): 163.

Blain GOBBLE, age: 1 year and 4 months, parents: Grover GOBBLE and Rosie GILES, death cause: illegible, informant: father (Johnson City), buried: Giles Cemetery, died: 29 Apr 1916, record: 164.

Samuel E. SMITH, born: 15 Jan 1897, single, parents: David H. SMITH and Rillie JONES, death cause: "killed by train", informant: father (Blountville), buried: Bristol, died: 29 Apr 1916, record: 165.

John MITCHELL, age: 81 years, born: New York, widower, actor, parents: not stated, death cause: "nephritis", died: Soldier's Home, 9 Apr 1916, record (1916): 166.

James B. FINNELL, age: 74 years, born: Virginia, married, parents: not stated, death cause: "mitral insufficiency", died: Soldier's Home, 17 Apr 1916, record (1916): 167.

William H. LETSINGER, age: 76 years, born: Tennessee, widwer, parents: not stated, death cause: "unknown", died: Soldier's Home, 28 Apr 1916, record (1916): 168.

Charles M. STEBBINS, age: 63 years, born: Alabama, single, parents: not stated, death cause:

"nephritis", died: Soldier's Home, 29 Apr 1916, record (1916): 169.
Charles H. FOSDICK, age: 66 years, born: New York, single, musician, parents: not stated, death cause: "cystitis", died: Soldier's Home, 30 Apr 1916, record (1916): 170.
Infant ARCHER, female, parents: W.J. ARCHER and Janie STEEN (Abingdon, VA), death cause: "stillborn", buried: Archer Cemetery, Jonesboro, died: 5 Apr 1916, record (1916): 171.
Thomas Nadison STORY, born: 22 Mar 1869, married, parents: George STORY and Armenta WILLIAMS, death cause: "pneumonia", died: 4th District, 15 Apr 1916, record (1916): 172.
Alexander BROWN, born: 11 Mar 1844, married, parents: Hiram BROWN and Cintha CARROLL, death cause: "heart disease", informant: Tom BROWN (Jonesboro), died: 19 Apr 1916, record (1916): 173.
Vista EDWARDS, born: 6 Jan 1878 in North Carolina, married, parents: Robert HOWELL (NC) and Finetta ELLIOTT, death cause: "abortion, septicemia", buried: Mt Bethel Cemetery, died: Limestone, 4 Apr 1916, record (1916): 174.
Anna BROWN, born: 27 Nov 1848, married, parents: W.H. HUMPHREYS and Matilda (illegible), death cause: "nephritis and paralysis", informant: A.J. HUMPHRIES (Limestone), died: 3 Apr 1916, record (1916): 175.
Munroe JOHNSON, colored, born: 15 Jan 1914, parents: Munroe JOHNSON and Lena COLLINS (NC), death cause: "burn", informant: father (Jonesboro), died: 1 Apr 1916, record (1916): 176.
Bernie DICKISON, born: 2 Jun 1915, parents: Garfield DICKISON and Ethel MCNICHOLS, death cause: illegible, informant: father (Jonesboro), died: 10 Apr 1916, record (1916): 177.
Orlena SLAUGHTER, age: 61 years, single, parents: Louis T. MARTIN and Deborah REGISTER, death cause: "illegible, (looks like cancer)", buried: Oak Hill, died: 8 Apr 1916, record (1916): 178.
Infant CRUMLEY, male, parents: B.M. CRUMLEY and Bertha KEEN, death cause: "stillborn", informant:

father (Johnson City), buried: Keen Cemetery, died: 5 Apr 1916, record (1916): 179.

Sarah ESTES, colored, born: 3 Dec 1829 in North Carolina, widow, parents: Wilson SCOTT (NC) and Mahalia MATTHEWS (NC), death cause: illegible, informant: Lula HULL (Johnson City), buried: West Lawn, died: 9 Apr 1916, record (1916): 180.

Elenor Sarah TAYLOR, born: 10 Feb 1916 in Bristol, VA., parents: Robert Lee TAYLOR (Mt. Ariey, NC) and Lillian Elenor HOWARD (Mt. Airey, NC), death cause: "marasmus", buried: Oak Hill, died: 9 Apr 1916, record (1916): 181.

Frederick SMITH, born: 10 Apr 1916, parents: John W. SMITH (NC) and Maggie ELLIS, death cause: "suppose, indigestion", buried: Boones Creek, died: 12 Apr 1916, record (1916): 182.

Joseph Crouch ARCHER, age: 60 years, married, parents: Thomas ARCHER and mother not stated, death cause: "lung abscess", buried: Archer Cemetery, Jonesboro, died: 9th District, 13 Apr 1916, record (1916): 183.

Henry David BAILEY, born: 11 Mar 1916, parents: David R. BAILEY and Malinda ARWOOD, death cause: "hives", informant: father (Johnson City), buried: Buena Vista, died: 17 Apr 1916, record (1916): 184.

William J. CHAPPELLE, age: 51 years, born: Virginia, married, boiler maker, parents: not stated, death cause: "pulmonary tuberculosis", buried: Norfolk, VA., died: Soldier's Home, 19 Apr 1916, record (1916): 185.

Henry P. DURANT, age: 73 years, born: Massachusetts, widower, parents: not stated, death cause: "atrophic cirrhosis of liver", died: Soldier's Home, 2 Apr 1916, record (1916): 186.

Johnson MAPLES, age: 70 years, born: New Jersey, single, parents: not stated, death cause: "unknown", died: Soldier's Home, 5 Apr 1916, record: 187.

James W. SHERFEY, born: 20 Dec 1855, married, parents: Samuel D. SHERFEY and __ DEAKINS, death cause: "Brights disease and tuberculosis", buried; Harmony Cemetery, died: Jonesboro, 4 Apr 1916, record (1916): 188.

John Howard HELTON, parents: William Carson HELTON (NC) and Bessie Marie STARNES, death cause: "weak infant", informant: F.D. HILL (Garbers), buried: Dry Creek, born/died: 1 Apr 1916, record (1916): 189.

Jacob Morelock BOWMAN, born: 17 Sep 1873, single, parents: Sparling BOWMAN and Caroline MORELOCK, death cause: "kidney .. (illebible)", buried: Greenville, died: Johnson City, 9 Apr 1916, record (1916): 190.

Carrie Willie TYREE, born: 12 May 1906, parents: Sam TYREE and Mary CANTER, death cause: "diptheria", informant: Mose MILLER (Johnson City), buried: Hunts Cemetery, died: 8 Apr 1916, record (1916): 191.

Martin K. HODGE, born: 19 Jul 1828, married, parents: James HODGE (NC) and Polly KITZMILLER, death cause: "old age", informant: J.A. HAMILTON (Jonesboro), buried: Boones Creek, died: 10 May 1916, record (1916): 192.

George CLARK, age: 60 years, widower, parents: not stated, death cause: "pellagra", informant: Mrs. W.A. WHITE (Johnson City), buried: Fall Branch, died: 27 May 1916, record (1916): 193.

Mary KILLINGSWORTH, born: 1 Aug 1892, married, parents: L. ADAMS and Susan GOOD, death cause: "tuberculosis", buried: Buena Vista, died: Johnson City, 3 May 1916, record (1916): 194.

Samuel Allison CARDER, born: 22 Apr 1916, parents: Sam CARDER and Nannie GLOVER, death cause: "hives", informant: Sam CARDER, Sr. (Johnson City), buried: Oak Hill, died: 4 May 1916, record (1916): 195.

Willie Eola WELLS, colored, age: 24 years, married, parents: Benson ARNETT and Texie RAWLINGS, death cause: "heart trouble", informant: Roy SCHOWEN (Johnson City), buried: West Lawn, died: 4 May 1916, record (1916): 196.

Marget Ruth PICKENS, born: 1 Jul 1915, parents: James B. PICKENS and Nannie SHEPLEY, death cause: "indigestion", buried: Oak Hill, died: 5 May 1916, record (1916): 197.

Mrs. Mary C. WEAVER, born: 23 Apr 1850, widow, parents: Benjamin PATTON and mother not stated, death cause: "cancer of liver and heart disease",

informant: J.D. WEAVER (Johnson City), buried: Watauga Point, died: 5 May 1916, record (1916): 198.
William C. MILLER, age: 75 years, born: Pennsylvania, married, stone mason, parents: not stated, death cause: "cirrhosis of liver", died: Soldier's Home, 5 May 1916, record (1916): 199.
Martha A. TOWNSEND, age: 88 years, born: Pennsylvania, widow, parents: not stated, death cause: "general debility", informant: Maggie BLAIR (Johnson City), buried: Oak Hill, died: 6 May 1916, record (1916): 200.
Frank ZIMMERMAN, born: 11 May 1896, single, parents: J.C. ZIMMERMAN and Sarah LUNSFORD, death cause: "tuberculosis", buried: Fordtown, died: Johnson City, 8 May 1916, record (1916): 201.
Charles F. CAMP, age: 61 years, born: Pennsylvania, single, parents: not stated, death cause: "cirrhosis of liver", buried: Oak Hill, died: Johnson City, 9 May 1916, record (1916): 202.
J.M. MALONEE, age: 57 years, married, parents: not stated, death cause: "paralysis", buried: Oak Hill, died: Johnson City, 10 May 1916, record (1916): 203.
Mrs. Cordia WATSON, born: 3 Sep 1872 in Carter County, married, parents: Jacob LEONARD (VA) and Lydia RANGE (Carter Co.), death cause: "tuberculosis", buried: Leonard Cemetery, died: Rt. 5, Johnson City, 10 May 1916, record (1916): 204.
Aletha ESTEP, born: 4 May 1916, parents: John ESTEP and Tennessee TIPTON, death cause: "pneumonia", buried: Marbleton, died: Johnson City, 10 May 1916, record (1916): 205.
John Thomas SMITH, colored, born: 10 Jan 1866 in Virginia, married, parents: Dick ROBINSON (VA) and Amelia SMITH (VA), death cause: "pulmonary tuberculosis", informant: Alice BELL (Johnson City), buried: West Lawn, died: 12 May 1916, record: 206.
W.A. FORD, age: 42 years, married, parents: George FORD and Mary COURTES, death cause: "ordema of .. (illegible)", buried: Harrison Chapel, died: Johnson City, 12 May 1916, record (1916): 207.
Mable HOUCK, born: 12 Feb 1894, parents: J.E. HOUCK (NC) and Laura PACKER (NC), death cause: "automobile

accident", informant: C.K. METCALF (Johnson City), buried: Limestone, died: 14 May 1916, record: 208.

John COLE, colored, age: 76 years, married, parents: not stated, death cause: illegible, informant: Mattie COLE (Johnson City), buried: Cole Cemetery, died: 18 Mary 1916, record (1916): 209.

Infant CROW, born: 25 Apr 1916, parents: R.B. CROW and Minnie MILES, death cause: "hives", informant: father (Johnson City), buried: Onks Cemetery, died: 21 May 1916, record (1916): 210.

Mrs. Elander ALLEN, born: 3 Mar 1832, born: North Carolina, widow, parents: Abram FRISBEE (NC) and Tamer HUNTER (NC), death cause: "heart disease", informant: J.L. ALLEN (Johnson City), buried: Buena Vista, died: 21 May 1916, record (1916): 211.

Carle C. BOWMAN, born: 5 Jan 1911, parents: W.B. BOWMAN (NC) and Annie NUCKLES (VA), death cause: "bronchitis", informant: father (Johnson City), buried: Oak Grove Cemetery, died: 21 May 1916, record (1916): 212.

Mildred LUNSFORD, age: 4 years, parents: A.J. LUNSFORD and Minnie OWEN, death cause: "pneumonia", buried: Oak Hill, died: 23 May 1916, record: 213.

Howard E. MCMACKIN, born: 11 Mar 1916, parents: J.D. MCMACKIN and Mollie PERKINS, death cause: "indigestion", buried: Speedwell, TN., died: 27 May 1916, record (1916): 214.

Terry HOBSON, age: 30 years, born: Carter County, married, parents: Coleman HOBSON (Mitchell Co., NC) and Mary E. FORBES (Mitchell Co., NC), death cause: "tonsilitis, septicemia", buried: Cranberry, NC., died: Johnson City, 28 May 1916, record (1916): 215.

Thomas PUGH, colored, born: __ Oct 1846 at Sumpter, SC., widower, parents: father not stated and Jennice BISHOP, death cause: "influenza and pneumonia", informant: James GOSSETT (Johnson City), buried: West Lawn, died: 26 May 1916, record (1916): 216.

Carl E. FEATHERS, Jr., born: 16 Jun 1915, parents: Carl E. FEATHERS and Bessie Lou BUCHANAN, death cause: "intestinal toxemia", informant: father (Johnson City), buried: Knob Creek, died: 27 May 1916, record (1916): 217.

D.J. WISHONG, age: 57 years, married, parents: Leonard WISHONG and Becky WALKER, death cause: "bronchitis and heart failure", buried: Buena Vista, died: Johnson City, 11 May 1916, record (1916): 218.
Samuel J.W. BYRD, age: 53 years, born: Louisiana, single, parents: not stated, death cause: "carcinoma of stomach", died: Soldier's Home, 7 May 1916, record (1916): 219.
Finley FOSTER, age: 73 years, born: Pennsylvania, widower, parents: not stated, death cause: "nephritis", died: 13 May 1916, record (1916): 220.
William P. SMITH, age: 76 years, born: Deleware, married, parents: not stated, death cause: "cirrhosis of liver", died: Soldier's Home, 23 May 1916, record (1916): 221.
James CRAFT, age: 71 years, born: Illinois, married, parents: not stated, death cause: "nephritis", died: Soldier's Home, 18 May 1916, record (1916): 222.
George W. CREACY, age: 75 years, born: Virginia, married, parents: not stated, death cause: "mitral insufficiency", died: Soldier's Home, 25 May 1916, record (1916): 223.
Henderson CLARK, age: 76 years, born: Missouri, married, parents: not stated, death cause: "cardiac dilatation", died: Soldier's Home, 29 May 1916, record (1916): 224.
Infant MILLER, male, parents: J.L. MILLER and Martina J. MOORE, death cause: "stillborn", informant: father (Telford), born/died: 29 May 1916, record (1916): 225.
Robert B. REED, age: 79 years, married, parents: G.W. REED and Katie GUYRE (Greene Co.), death cause: "catarrhal enteritis", informant: J.K. BYERLY (Telford), died: 29 May 1916, record (1916): 226.
Infant KICKER, male, parents: Ernest KICKER and Eva YOUNG, death cause: illegible, informant: J. REED (Jonesboro), buried: Cherokee Cemetery, born/died: 17 May 1916, record (1916): 227.
John Joseph Samuel HOWARD, born: 22 Oct 1851 in Johnson County, married, parents: Samuel B. HOWARD (Johnson Co.) and Lou KENSEY (Johnson Co.), death cause: "pneumonia", informant: Robert T. HOWARD

(Jonesboro), buried: Fairview, died: 10 May 1916, record (1916): 228.

James W. OLIVER, born: 1 Jan 1880, married, parents: Joseph OLIVER and Jane SHAW, death cause: "was shot", informant: Frank C. FINE (Jonesboro), died: 14 May 1916, record (1916): 229.

Minnie COLLIER, colored, age: 40 years, born: Ohio, married, parents: __ JACKSON and mother not stated, death cause: "disease of spine", informant: George COLLIER, buried: Jonesboro, died: 22 May 1912, record (1916): 230.

Mrs. Lizzie HALE, born: 19 Jan 1889, married, parents: Frank HITE and Jane COX, death cause: "pulmonary tuberculosis", informant: William HALE (Johnson City), buried: Union Cemetery, died: 21 May 1916, record (1916): 231.

Pansy Jenette MCNICHOLS, age: 14 days, parents: Albert MCNICHOLS and Ida LISTER, death cause "hives", died: Embreeville, 21 May 1916, death record (1916): 232.

Sol SHELTON, age: 23 years, single, parents: Arch SHELTON (NC) and Ida LOYD (NC), death cause "pneumonia", died: Embreeville, 4 May 1916, death record (1916): 233.

Corra Lee PETERSON, born: 11 Feb 1878 in Unicoi County, divorced, parents: Sam WATE and Lizzie BAHR, death cause "huntington's corea, informant: Sam PETERSON (Embreeville), died: 30 May 1916, death record (1916): 234.

Leona MCINTOSH, age: 3 months and 5 days, born: North Carolina, parents: W.P. MCINTOSH (NC) and Nora SHELTON (NC), death cause "ptomane poison", informant: DR. A.J. WILLIS (Embreeville), died: 16 May 1916, death record (1916): 235.

Aaron PAINTER, age: about 78 years, married, parents: Samuel PAINTER and mother not stated, death cause "heart failure", informant: A.C. SEATON (Chuckey), buried: Liberty Cemetery, died: 29 May 1916, death record (1916): 236.

Alice PATTERSON, born: 12 Mar 1859, married, parents: Jefferson BURLESON (NC) and Sarah Belle __, death cause "myo carditis", informant: M.S.

PATTERSON (Johnson City), buried: Burleson Cemetery, died: 20 May 1916, death record (1916): 237.

Lillie Grace LEACH, born: 13 May 1880, married, parents: Mike ELLIOTT and mother not stated, death cause "tuberculosis", informant: Will LEACH (Johnson City), buried: Leach Cemetery, died: 23 May 1916, death record (1916): 238.

Mary Jane TRUMAN, born: 15 Nov 1831 in North Carolina, married, parents: Allen HAMBY (NC) and mother not stated, death cause "senility", informant: Sam TRUMAN (Rt 1, Johnson City), buried: Snow Chapel, died: 21 May 1916, death record: 239.

Jane WHITAKER, age: 73 years and 7 months, widow, parents: John (illegible) and Barbry MURRAY, death cause "nephritis", died: Limestone, 1 May 1916, death record (1916): 240.

Martha Ford KING, born: 2 Dec 1897, married, parents: R.R. FORD and Allie BROWN, death cause "pulmonary tuberculosis", informant: R.N. BROWN (Jonesboro), buried: Fordtown Church, died: 7 May 1916, death record (1916): 241.

Joseph STRICKLER, age: about 50 years, married, parents: Rubin STRICKLER and Lennie BOWERY, death cause "dispencia and bronchitis", buried: Boones Creek, died: 11th District, 2 May 1916, death record (1916): 242.

R.M. GALLOWAY, born: 20 Feb 1876 in Virginia, married, parents: G.W. GALLOWAY and Susan WHITE, death cause "heart disease", buried: Weaver Cemetery, died: 11th District, 7 May 1916, death record (1916): 243.

Fannie HEATON, born: 18 Feb 1915 in Johnson County, parents: J.S. HEATON (Johnson Co.) and Maggie FIZER (Sullivan Co.), death cause "croup and measles", informant: father (Johnson City), buried: Buena Vista, died: 8 Jun 1916, death record (1916): 244.

Samuel T. DIEHL, born: 11 Dec 1844 in Virginia, married, parents: David DIEHL (VA) and Elizabeth HARTMAN (VA), death cause "heart disease", informant: C.H. DIEHL (Jonesboro), buried: Pleasant Valley, died: 4 Jun 1916, death record (1916): 245.

William VANCE, born: 14 Feb 1835, married, parents: George VANCE and Margaret MCNABB, death cause "diarrhoea", buried: Dry Creek, died: 8th District, 12 Jun 1916, death record (1916): 246.

Infant WALTER, born: 9 Jun 1916, parents: Franklin WALTER and Viola MILLER, death cause "premature birth", informant: father (Jonesboro), died: 10 Jun 1916, death record (1916): 247.

Jacob KINNICK, born: 1 Mar 1850, married, parents: John KINNICK and Mary CULBERT, death cause "heart trouble", buried: Longmire Cemetery, died: 10th District, 13 Jun 1916, death record (1916): 248.

Mrs. Mollie SLIGER, age: 56 years, parents: not stated, death cause "lobar pneumonia", informant: John SLIGER (husband, Jonesboro), buried: New Victory, died: 24 Jun 1916, death record: 249.

Nellie Garfield TUCKER, born: 7 Aug 1881, single, parents: Isaac N. TUCKER and Dora SMITH, death cause "pulmonary tuberculosis", informant: father (Jonesboro), buried: Mt. Wesley, died: 21 Jun 1916, death record (1916): 250.

Mary Elizabeth BAILEY, age: 70 years, widow, parents: J.M. MAUK and mother's name illegible, death cause "heart disease", informant: H.M. MOORE (Chuckey), buried: Philadelphia Cemetery, died: 21 Jun 1916, death record (1916): 251.

Teddy HARRIS, age: 7 years, born: Virginia, parents: E.B. HARRIS and mother not stated, death cause "accidentally shot by Stuart KELLY", informant: Henry BAILEY (Johnson City), buried: Onks Cemetery, died: 21 Jun 1916, death record (1916): 252.

Charles F. PATTERSON, born: 2 Mar 1892, single, parents: S.L. PATTERSON and Alice BURLESON, death cause "typhoid fever", buried: Burleson Cemetery, died: 12 Jun 1916, death record (1916): 253.

Charles E. ALLEN, born: 30 Mar 1840, widower, parents: Isaac ALLEN and mother not stated, death cause "kidney disease", informant: S.C. ALLEN (Jonesboro), buried: Union Church, died: 6 Jun 1916, death record (1916): 253.

Infant MORROW, male, parents: James Franklin MORROW and Nora Ethel CORSON, death cause "convulsions", informant: A.B. MORELOCK (Limestone), born/died: 10 Jun 1916, death record (1916): 254.

Nora Ethel MORROW, age: 31 years, 6 months and 20 days, married, parents: Brookins CARSON and Ellen CAMPBELL, death cause "uremic coma", informant: John MORROW (Telford), buried: Leesburg Cemetery, died: 10 Jun 1916, death record (1916): 255.

Riley B. DANIEL, born: 20 Jun 1861, married, R.R. conductor, parents: Greenberry DANIEL (NC) and Elizabeth FOSTER (NC), death cause "malorial poisoning", buried: Sinking Creek, died: Johnson City, 1 Jun 1916, death record (1916): 257.

Infant FAIN, black, male, parents: father not stated and Mary FAIN, death cause "stillborn", buried: Hyder Cemetery, died: 1 Jun 1916, death record (1916): 258.

Infant FAIN, black, male, parents: father not stated and Mary FAIN, death cause "stillborn", buried: Hyder Cemetery, died: 1 Jun 1916, death record (1916): 259.

Glen Fulton SEAVER, born: 28 Mar 1915, parents: George F. SEAVER (Hawkins Co.) and Suda STEFFEY (Hawkins Co.), death cause "cholera infantum", buried: Oak Hill, died: 3 Jun 1916, death record (1916): 260.

Adrout Kyle WILSON, age: 3 weeks, born: Ashville, NC., parents: A.K. WILSON (NC) and Dora MCINTYRE (NC), death cause "premature birth", buried: Buena Vista, died: 3 Jun 1916, death record (1916): 261.

John MAUPIN, born: 21 Mar 1861, married, parents: George MAUPIN and Rahcel HILBERT, death cause "softening of brain", informant: G.H. MAUPIN (Johnson City), buried: Boones Creek, died: 12 Jun 1916, death record (1916): 262.

Mrs. Mary SMITH, age: 42 years, married, parents: not stated, death cause "tuberculosis", buried: Oak Hill, died: 9th District, 12 Jun 1916, death record (1916): 263.

Toney POPE, age: 39 years, married, parents: not stated, death cause "lung hemorrhage", buried: Rogersville, TN, died: 12 Jun 1916, death record (1916): 264.

Effie Augusta CASH, born: 1 Oct 1897, single, parents: father not stated and Adie CASH, death cause "cardiac (illegible)", buried: Union Cemetery, died: Johnson City, 12 Jun 1916, death record (1916): 265.

Paul RICHARDSON, age: 15 months, parents: Alsin RICHARDSON and Ruth SWIFT, death cause: "whooping cough and measles", informant: Matilda SWIFT (Johnson City), buried: Buena Vista, died: 7 Jun 1916, record (1916): 266.

Mrs. M.E. CHUNEWTH, born: 18 Jun 1848, widow, parents: G.W. BOWERING and Elizabeth KING, death cause: "tuberculosis", informant: Charles CHUNEWTH (Johnson City), buried: Oak Hill, died: 21 Jan 1916, record (1916): 267.

Teddy HARRIS, age: 7 years, parents: Ed HARRIS and Sallie BAILEY (VA), death cause: "gunshot wound in abdomen", informant: Toy ROMMES (Johnson City), buried: New Bethel Cemetery, died: Memorial Hospital, 21 Jun 1916, record (1916): 268.

Infant ELSWICK, female, age: 6 months, parents: Will ELSWICK and mother not stated, death cause: "cholera infantum", informant: Sam RUSSELL (Johnson City), buried: Buena Vista, died: 22 Jun 1916, record (1916): 269.

Marshall T. BURTON, age: 62 years, born: Indiana, widower, parents: not stated, death cause: "nephritis", buried: Mitchell, Indiana, died: Soldier's Home, 27 Jun 1916, record (1916): 270.

Amanda ZIMMERMAN, born: 27 Oct 1848, married, parents: William S. SMITH (KY) and Mary STRICKLER, death cause: "heart disease", buried: Pactolus, TN., died: Johnson City, 23 Jun 1916, record (1916): 271.

Edgar DUFFIELD, age: 36 years, born: England, married, parents: not stated, death cause: "pulmonary tuberculosis", buried: Philadelphia, PA., died: Soldier's Home, 23 Jun 1916, record: 272.

Captolia GUINN, female, age: 11 months, parents: George GUINN and Rosa STOUT, death cause: "anaemia", buried: Oak Hill, died: 26 Jun 1916, record: 273.

Susan B. TALBUTT, age: 64 years, born: __ Apr 1852 in Washington County, VA., married, parents: Russell B. ROGERS (VA) and (illegible) HAIL (Grayson County,

VA), death cause: "typhoid fever", buried: Wyndale, VA., died: 26 Jun 1816, record (1916): 274
Lessie May HOUSTON, born: 16 Sep 1915, parents: J.H. HOUSTON (VA) and Ettie GREER (NC), death cause: "gastro enteritis", buried: Oak Hill, died: 26 Jan 1916, record (1916): 275.
William MITCHELL, age: 80 years, born: Scotland, widower, harness maker, parents: not stated, death cause: "diearrhoea", buried: Morganton, NC., died: Soldier's Home, 28 Jun 1916, record (1916): 276.
Sarah LEDFORD, born: 25 Apr 1865 in North Carolina, married, parents: John Wesley CONNELY (NC) and Margaret BATY (NC), death cause: "tuberculosis", buried: Sinking Creek, died: Johnson City, 29 Jun 1916, record (1916): 277.
Rev. William C. MAUPIN, age: 76 years, born: Virginia, married, parents: George MAUPIN and Rebecca __, death cause: "enlarged prostate", informant: W.H. MAUPIN (Johnson City), buried: Boones Creek, died: 30 Jun 1916, record (1916): 278.
Leon DEGLETTE, age: 75 years, born: Canada, single, parents: not stated, death cause: "cerebral hemorrhage", died: Soldier's Home, 12 Jun 1916, record (1916): 279.
Henry I. WILKINS, age: 71 years, born: Illinois, married, parents: not stated, death cause: "nephritis", died: Soldier's Home, 17 Jun 1916, record (1916): 280.
Frederick D. FULKERSON, age: 77 years, born: Virginia, widower, parents: not stated, death cause: "shock following hip injury", died: Soldier's Home, 23 Jun 1916, record (1916): 281.
Henry C. CONNOR, age: 84 years, born: Massachusetts, married, parents: not stated, death cause: "pneumonia", died: Soldier's Home, 24 Jun 1916, record (1916): 282.
Edward STTTIN alias SUTTON, age: 72 years, born: Ireland, widower, parents: not stated, death cause: "nephritis", died: Soldier's Home, 25 Jun 1916, record (1916): 283.
Walace Willis PEARSON, born: 23 May 1916, parents: David PEARSON (NC) and Edith COLLETTE, death cause:

"found dead in bed", infomant: father (Limestone), buried: New Salem, died: 7 Jun 1916, record: 284.

Mrs. Mary NICODEMAS, born: 4 Sep 1835 in Pennsylvania, widow, parents: Philip WEISEL and Mary NICHOM (PA), death cause: "nephritis", buried: Jonesboro, died: 15th District, 10 Jun 1916, record (1916): 285.

Jane Elizabeth HEAD, age: 76 years, married, parents: Allen OLIVER and Katherine STORNES, death cause: "cerebral hemorrhage", informant: Frank FINE (Jonesboro), buried: Oliver Cemetery, died: 11 Jun 1916, record (1916): 286.

Sue MORRELL, born: 15 Oct 1900, parents: D.C. MORRELL and Mary BASHOR, death cause: "spinal meningitis", informant: Roy E. MORRELL (Jonesboro), buried: Pleasant Valley, died: 19 Jun 1916, record (1916): 287.

Tabitha PEOPLES, born: 12 May 1834 in Carter County, widow, parents: William TAYLOR (Carter Co.) and __ HYDER (Carter Co.), death cause: "dysentery", informant: W.R. PEOPLES (Jonesboro), buried: Cherokee Cemetery, died: 4th District, 23 Jun 1916, record (1916): 288.

Mrs. Martha E. ROSENBAUM, born: 25 Dec 1852 in Washington County, VA., married, parents: J.D. BUCHANAN (Washington Co., VA) and Sarah E. MOREFIELD (Johnson County), death cause: "heart clot from glans of neck", informant: Abraham ROSENBAUM (Jonesboro), buried: Damascus, VA., died: 29 Jun 1916, record (1916): 289.

Jacob WHALEY, age: 72 years, married, parents: mother not stated, father's name illegible, death cause: "mitral insufficiency", died: 3rd District, 14 Jun 1816, record (1916): 290.

J.C. FORD, age: 1 year and 6 months, parents: James FORD and Eliza SFFORD, death cause: "accidentally scalded to death", informant: father (Jonesboro), died: 20 Jul 1916, record (1916): 291.

Ruby Lee BARNES, born: 18 May 1816, parents: Argel BARNES and Minnie HALE, death cause: "measles", informant: Bessie J. BARNES (Jonesboro), died: 15 Jul 1916, record (1916): 292.

Eva CONNOR, born: 27 Apr 1888, married, parents: Henry CONNER and Annie BRANCH, death cause: "tuberculosis of lungs", buried: Buffalo Ridge, died: Jonesboro, 15 Jul 1916, record (1916): 293.
Jacob G. CRUMLEY, born: 28 Oct 1859, single, parents: James CRUMLEY and mother not stated, death cause: "heart failure", informant: T.K. CRUMLEY (Rt 3, Johnson City), buried: Crumley Cemetery, died: 15 Jul 1916, record (1916): 294.
Bettie WHITLOCK, born: 9 Feb 1869 in Sullivan County, married, parents: Nathan HICKMAN (Sullivan Co.) and __ CRAWFORD (Sullivan Co.), death cause: "pulmonary tuberculosis", informant: George WHITLOCK (Jonesboro), died: 7 Jul 1916, record (1916): 295.
Eloise MORRISON, born: 21 Jul 1916, parents: Alonzo MORRISON and Ilie DILLOW (Sullivan County), death cause: "unknown", informant: Lonnie MORRISON (Jonesboro), buried: Fall Branch, died: 24 Jul 1916, record (1916): 296.
Alva Maxine WARD, born: 12 Jun 1916, parents: William Bruce WARD and Nellie Kate BOWMAN, death cause: "malnutrition, nephritis in mother", informant: S.B. MORELOCK (Limestone), died: 15 Jul 1916, record (1916): 297.
Barsha Ann RANGE, born: 20 Jul 1828, widow, parents: Johnathan RANGE and Fartha KELLEY, death cause: "heart disease", informant: G.E. RANGE (Jonesboro), buried: Sulphur Springs, died: 3 Jul 1916, record (1916): 298.
J.C. FORD, born: 22 Dec 1914, parents: James FORD and Eliza SIFFORD, death cause: "severe burn from scalding", informant: George SIFFORD (Jonesboro), buried: Buffalo Ridge, died: 20 Jul 1916, record (1916): 299.
Mrs. Rebecca Dooley HOSS, born: 30 May 1862 in Sullivan County, widow, parents: William DOOLEY (Sullivan Co.) and Martha NEWLAND (Scott County, VA), death cause: illegible, died: Jonesboro, 14 Jul 1916, record (1916): 300.
Dortha PURCELL, born: 3 Mar 1915, parents: Samuel PURCELL and Clara Bell ADAMS, death cause:

"diptheria", informant: father (Jonesboro), died: 11 Jul 1916, record (1916): 301.

Mary Elizabeth BOWMAN, born: 11 Jul 1835 in Carter County, married, parents: Enic KEEN (Carter Co.) and mother not stated, death cause: "fell down stairs", informant: W.C. BOWMAN (Jonesboro), buried: Taylor Chapel, died: 9 Jul 1916, record (1916): 302.

Georgia Rhe HASHBERGER, born: 25 Aug 1915, parents: C.E. HASHBERGER and Mattie ARMSTRONG, death cause: "cholera infantum", buried: Logan Chapel, died: Jonesboro, 11 Jul 1916, record (1916): 303.

Anna Bell JOHNSON, colored, born: 27 Aug __, age: 8 years, parents: Thomas SCOTT and Julia Ellen SCOTT, death cause: "tuberculosis", informant: Henry JOHNSON (Jonesboro), died: 31 Jul 1916, record (1916): 304.

Amanda BISHOP, born: 5 May 1841, widow, parents: Joseph HAMMETT and Sarah COUDLER, death cause: "heart failure", informant: J.F. CLARK (Jonesboro), buried: Boones Creek, died: 17 Jul 1916, record (1916): 305.

Henry COFFEY, age: 28 years, born: Tennessee, parents: not stated, death cause: "pulmonary tuberculosis", died: Soldier's Home, 29 Jul 1916, record (1916): 306.

Frederick H. CUSHING, age: 70 years, born: Ireland, widower, R.R. engineer, parents: not stated, death cause: "carcinoma of inferior maxillary", died: Soldier's Home, 27 Jul 1916, record (1916): 307.

Luman FRINK, age: 80 years, born: Michigan, single, parents: not stated, death cause: "nephritis", died: Soldier's Home, 27 Jul 1916, record (1916): 308.

John H. BECKER, age: 80 years, born: Germany, widower, shoe maker, parents: not stated, death cause: "cerebral hemorrhage", died: Soldier's Home, 23 Jul 1916, record (1916): 309.

Richard E. MICHAEL, age: 70 years, born: Maryland, single, physician, parents: not stated, death cause: "mitral insufficiency", died: Soldier's Home, 16 Jul 1916, record (1916): 310.

Arthur BROWN, age: 48 years, born: England, married, parents: not stated, death cause: "pulmonary tuberculosis", died: Soldier's Home, 16 Jul 1916, record (1916): 311.

James P. BROWN, age: 80 years, born: Missouri, single, stone cutter, parents: not stated, death cause: "pulmonary tuberculosis", died: Soldier's Home, 15 Jul 1916, record (1916): 312.

J.M. SCOTT, born: 5 Apr 1837 in Carter County, single, parents: father not stated and Elizabeth SCOTT (NC), death cause: "bronchitis since Civil War", inforant: J.M. GARVIN (Telford), died: 18 Jul 1916, record (1916): 313.

Infant SLIGER, female, parents: William SLIGER and Sallie SAULTS, death cause: "born dead", informant: Enoch SLIGER (Jonesboro), buried: Cherokee Cemetery, died: 15 Jul 1916, record (1916): 314.

Patrick HEALY, age: 56 years, born: Illinois, single, livery man, parents: not stated, death cause: "pulmonary tuberculosis", died: Soldier's Home, 10 Jul 1916, record (1916): 315.

Lee CALLOWAY, age: not stated, born: North Carolina, parents: not stated, death cause: "gastro enteritis", informant: Robert CALLOWAY (Johnson City), buried: Oak Hill, died: 30 Jul 1916, record: 316.

Mrs. Lucy ESTES, colored, age: 55 years, born: Caldwell County, NC., widow, parents: Jack ESTES (NC) and Sarah SCOTT (NC), death cause: "lobar pneumonia", informant: Mrs. Lucy HALL (Johnson City), buried: West Lawn, died: 28 Jul 1916, record: 317.

Eugene WOOD, born: 17 Nov 1915, parents: M.C. WOOD (NC) and Etta CAUDILL (NC), death cause: "whooping cough and colitis", buried: Buena Vista, died: 27 Jul 1916, record (1916): 318.

Andy Jackson JONES, age: 5 months and 2 days, parents: Bert JONES and Janie ANDES, death cause: "cholera infantum", buried: Snow Chapel, died: 26 Jul 1916, record (1916): 319.

Dora Jannett GREER, born: 14 Oct 1914 in Johnson County, parents: S.C. GREER (NC) and Susa CAMPBELL (Johnson Co.), death cause: "cholera infantum", buried: Doeville, TN., died: Johnson City, 25 Jul 1916, record (1916): 320.

Infant SHAVER, colored, female, parents: Albert SHAVER and Gertrude SHAVER, death cause: "stillborn", informant: father (Johnson City), buried: Roan Hill Cemetery, died: 24 Jul 1916, record (1916): 321.

Paul KILBY, born: 5 Feb 1895, parents: J.W. KILBY and Julia DOUGLAS, death cause: "carcinoma following testicle injury", buried: Oak Hill, died: 22 Jul 1916, record (1916): 322.

Mamie COLLINS, born: 8 Jul 1916, parents: Will J. COLLINS (VA) and Effie BURKETT, death cause: "premature", informant: father (Johnson City), buried: Oak Hill, died: 17 Jul 1916, record: 323.

Herman JONES, age: 6 months, parents: Isaac JONES (Greene County) and Flora HOLT (VA), death cause: "colitis", buried: Snow Chapel, died: 14 Jul 1916, record (1916): 324.

Henry C. ROHRBACH, age: 68 years, born: Pennsylvania, widower, parents: not stated, death cause: "cardiac dilitation", buried: Reding, PA., died: Soldier's Home, 12 Jul 1916, record: 325.

Ida BANNER, colored, age: 52 years, born: North Carolina, widow, parents: William WEBB (NC) and Martha WEBB (NC), death cause: "hemorrhage of brain", informant: Jerry BANNER (Johnson City), buried: West Lawn, died: 14 Jul 1916, record: 326.

Infant DUNN, male, parents: Clinton DUNN and Jane BUCHANAN, death cause: "heart lesion", buried: Speedwell Cemetery, born/died: 15 Jul 1916, record (1916): 327.

Margaret A. SIZEMORE, born: 5 May 1861 in North Carolina, married, parents: Morgan RANDOLPH (NC) and Sarah MCCURRY (NC), death cause: "nephritis", buried: Oak Hill, died: Johnson City, 11 Jul 1916, record (1916): 328.

Mrs. Hylie KITE, born: 6 Apr 1835, widow, parents: not stated, death cause: "dysentary and age", buried: Mohawk, TN., died: Johnson City, 9 Jul 1916, record (1916): 329.

Henrietta EVANS, colored, born: 26 Feb 1873, married, parents: Ruth TAYLOR and; Alica LOAL, death cause: "hepatitis", informant: Alice THOMAS (Johnson

City), buried: Hyder Cemetery, died: 7 Jul 1916, record (1916): 330.

Melda GUINN, age: 5 years and 5 months, parents: George GUINN and Rosa STOUT, death cause: illegible, buried: Oak Hill, died: 5 Jul 1916, record: 331.

Lue SCOTT, colored, age: 66 years, married, parents: Marshall JACKSON and Eliza JACKSON, death cause: "influenza", buried: Hyder Cemetery, died: 5 Jul 1916, record (1916): 332.

Sarah May TAYLOR, born: 24 May 1915, parents: Lyons R. TAYLOR and Blanch HYDER, death cause: "colitis", informant: father (Johnson City), buried: Oak Hill, died: 4 Jul 1916, record (1916): 333.

Homer F. EARP, born: 16 Sep 1914, parents: J.W. EARP (NC) and Bertha TRIVETT (Colorado), death cause: "whooping cough", informant: father (Johnson City), buried: Buena Vista, died: 2 Jul 1916, record (1916): 334.

Emma Isabell KING, born: 2 Aug 1894, married, parents: J.E. WADE (VA) and Virginia BERRY, death cause: "heart disease", informant: Ed KING (Johnson City), buried: Oak Hill, died: 1 Jun 1916, record (1916): 335.

Mary A. COX, born: 23 Apr 1898 in North Carolina, single, parents: Sam F. COX (NC) and Carolina HILL (NC), death cause: "heart disease", informant: father (Johnson City), buried: Marbleton, TN., died: 1 Jul 1916, record (1916): 336.

Infant ILLEGIBLE, female, parents: father's name illegible and Julia ROBINS, death cause: "premature", born/died: 1 Jul 1916, record: 337.

Josie Alice ADAMS, born: 8 Sep 1888, parents: John L. CAMPBELL and Mollie ORR, death cause: "tuberculosis", buried: Oak Hill, died: 17 Jul 1916, record (1916): 338.

Miss Julia Edna BUTLER, born: 2 Jul 1859, school teacher, parents: R. Ellis BUTLER (Sullivan Co.) and Sauana THOMAS (Sullivan Co.), death cause: "Brights disease", informant: J.A. BUTLER (Jonesboro), died: 6 Jul 1916, record (1916): 339.

John SLIGER, age: 54 years, parents: Adam SLIGER and mother not stated, death cause: "pneumonia", informant: Jim SLIGER (Jonesboro), buried: New Victory, died: 2 Jul 1916, record (1916): 340.

Mary Francis BAILEY, born: 14 Mar 1916, parents: Mose BAILEY and Mary (illegible), death cause: "meningitis", informant: Floyd BERRY (Jonesboro), died: 1 Jul 1916, record (1916): 341.

Nora BAILEY, age: 8 months, parents: Henry BAILEY (KY) and Clary (illegible), death cause: "cholera infantum", informant: father (Johnson City), buried: Onks Cemetery, died: 3 Aug 1916, record (1916): 342.

Mrs. Sarah YOUNG, age: 80 years, born: North Carolina, married, parents: George TUCKER and Harriett MCCAREY (NC), death cause: "septicemia, gall bladder infection", buried: Toe Cane, NC., died: 6 Aug 1916, record (1916): 343.

Mary FEATHERS, born: 8 Mar 1854, married, parents: (illegible) TAYLOR and Sallie PALLET, death cause: "cancer of liver", died: Johnson City, 7 Aug 1916, record (1916): 344.

L.A. ELLIS, age: 32 years, married, parents: Joseph ELLIS and Amanda HATLEY, death cause: "gun shot wound in thigh and infection", informant: H.G. ELLIS (Athens, TN), buried: Oak Hill, died: 12 Aug 1916, record (1916): 345.

John REAVES, colored, age: 3 months, born: Virginia, parents: Charles REAVES and Venie HORTON, death cause: "malnutrition", buried: Hyder Cemetery, died: 13 Aug 1916, record (1916): 346.

Bulah REEVES, colored, age: 3 years, parents: Charles REEVES and Venie HORTON, death cause: "measles", buried: Hyder Cemetery, died: 15 Aug 1916, record (1916): 347.

Ula REEVES, colored, age: 3 years, parents: Charles REEVES and Venie HORTON, death cause: "measles", buried: Hyder Cemetery, died: 15 Aug 1916, record (1916): 348.

Charles Riley CREWS, born: 12 May 1916, parents: C.R. CREWS (NC) and Juanita YOUNG (NC), death cause: "diarrhoea", informant: father (Kingsport), buried: Oak Hill, died: 16 Aug 1916, record (1916): 349.

Hiram G. GARDNER, age: 63 years, born: Pennsylvania, married, death cause: "accidentally killed by log

fracturing skull", buried: Pennsylvania, died: 15 Aug 1916, record (1916): 350.
Will CLARK, age: 28 years, married, parents: Bob CLARK and Nancy Ann BRITT, death cause: "gastro enteritis", informant: father (Johnson City), buried: Buck Cemetery, died: 16 Aug 1916, record (1916): 351.
William Raymon WEAVER, born: 16 May 1893, single, parents: W.R. WEAVER and Alice SAYLOR, death cause: "pellagra", informant: father (Johnson City), buried: Gourley Cemetery, died: 16 Aug 1916, record (1916): 352.
William H. BUCHER, born: 22 Feb 1843 in Wooster, Ohio, widower, parents: John BUCHER (PA) and Mary (illegible), death cause: "lobar pneumonia", buried: Cincinatti, Ohio, died: Soldier's Home, 19 Aug 1916, record (1916): 353.
Taylor KELLY, age: 56 years, married, pns, death cause: "Brights disease", informant: Sarrah KELLY (Johnson City), buried: Hampton, TN., died: 10 Aug 1916, record (1916): 359.
Sallie TAYLOR, colored, age: 70 years, widow, parents: Alfred HUNT and Jennie GAMBLIN, death cause: "cholera", informant: Alex MILLER (Johnson City), buried: Roan Hill, died: 20 Aug 1916, record (1916): 355.
Mary Abigail HUTCHENS, born: 27 Nov 1914, parents: O.D. HUTCHENS (Indiana) and Carrie Celia ROLFE (Indiana), death cause: "dysentery", informant: father (Johnson City), buried: Oak Hill, died: 23 Aug 1916, record (1916): 356.
Lodie James MITCHEL, born: 2 Feb 1901, parents: George MITCHEL (VA) and Jane BOUNER, death cause: "typhoid fever", informant: Henry MITCHEL (Johnson City), buried: Snow Chapel, died: 24 Aug 1916, record (1916): 357.
M.G. CURTIS, age: 60 years, married, parents: Henry CURTIS and mother not stated, death cause: "tuberculosis", informant: E.C. CURTIS (Johnson City), buried: Boones Creek, died: 21 Aug 1916, record (1916): 358.

Guy Vincent BARNES, born: 3 Apr 1893, single, parents: N.D. BARNES and Sallie ESTEP, death cause: "typhoid fever", informant: father (Fall Branch), died: 18 Aug 1916, record (1916): 359.

Terry Soloman EVANS, born: 21 Apr 1855 in North Carolina, married, parents: Eliot EVANS (NC) and Mary FRANKLIN (VA), death cause: "pulmonary tuberculosis", informant: Julina EVANS (Fall Branch), died: 16 Aug 1916, record (1916): 360.

Hamilton BAYLESS, black, age: about 86 years, widower, parents: Charles DEMICHAEL and Phebe DEMICHAEL, death cause: "dysentery", informant: Fanny STEPHESON (Limestone), died: 3 Aug 1916, record (1916): 361.

W.E. RANGE, born: 17 Jul 1884, married, parents: Thomas RANGE and Jennie SHERFY, death cause: "typhoid fever", buried: Barnes Cemetery, died: Johnson City, 25 Aug 1916, record (1916): 362.

Nancy Jane COLLINS, born: 25 Aug 1855, married, parents: Frank FRASIER and Martha CASH, death cause: "disentery", informant: Susana CRITSINGER (Piney Flats), buried: Pleasant Hill, died: 10th District, 28 Aug 1916, record (1916): 363.

James COLLINS, born: 18 Apr 1839, married, parents: Isaac COLLINS and Sarah RINEHART, death cause: "disentery", informant: Susana CRITSINGER (Piney Flats), buried: New Bethel Cemetery, died: 10th District, 18 Aug 1916, record (1916): 363.

Sarah TAYLOR, born: 2 Apr 1844 in South Carolina, married, death cause: "cancer of breast", informant: John TAYLOR (Jonesboro), buried: Jackson Cemetery, died: 2 Aug 1916, record (1916): 365.

Raymond GOOD, born: 1 Jul 1916, parents: Agil GOOD and Ethel GREENE (NC), death cause: "meningitis", buried: Milburton Cemetery, died: 22 Aug 1916, record (1916): 366.

Charles BLEVINS, age: 58 years, married, parents: Walter BLEVINS and Mary HENSLEY, death cause: "typhoid fever", died: 6th District, 10 Aug 1916, record (1916): 367.

Myrtie H. AMMONS, born: 4 Jun 1899, single, parents: Lee AMMONS (NC) and Rachel JOHNSON, death cause:

"measles", died: 6th District, 19 Aug 1916, record (1916): 368.
Sarah CONNER, born: 11 Oct 1849, married, parents: father not stated and Mary F. FOX, death cause: "arthritis", informant: John CONNOR (Jonesboro), buried: Buffalo Ridge, died: 8 Aug 1916, record (1916): 369.
Mary E. BACON, born: 27 Apr 1848, married, parents: John F. GRESHAM and Matilda CARROLL (Alabama), death cause: "measles", informant: Joseph L. CLARK (Jonesboro), buried: Buffalo Ridge, died: 1 Aug 1916, record (1916): 370.
Mrs. Francis HENLEY, age: 74 years, born: Sullivan County, widow, parents: not stated, death cause: "heart disease", buried: Asbury Cemetery, died: Limestone, 25 Aug 1916, record (1916): 371.
Elen FOYSTER, age: 72 years, born: Johnson County, widow, parents: Wash SNYDER (Johnson Co.) and mother not stated, death cause: "heart disease", informant: T.F. FOYSTER, son (Trade, TN), died: 5th District, 25 Aug 1916, record (1916): 372.
Mrs. Nellie Elizabeth GARVIN, born: 12 Sep 1845 in Unicoi, County, widow, parents: not stated, death cause: "enteritis", informant: J.M. GARVIN (Telford), buried: Mount Wesley, died: 8 Aug 1916, record (1916): 373.
Infant CERCY, male, lived 6 hours, parents: Buran CERCY and Fry CASH, death cause: "strangulation", informant: David CERCY (Johnson City), died: 30 Aug 1916, record (1916): 374.
Ollie Bell MARTIN, born: 21 May 1890, married, parents: W.R. WEAVER and Alice SAYLOR, death cause: "tuberculosis", buried: Boones Creek, died: 11th District, 25 Aug 1916, record (1916): 375.
Eliza CERCY, born: 22 Oct 1915 in Virginia, parents: James CERCY and Monie MATHERLY, death cause: "catarrh fever", informant: David CERCY (Jonesboro), buried: Boones Creek, died: 22 Aug 1916, record (1916): 376.
John CAMPBELL, born: 14 Sep 1874, married, parents: Jack CAMPBELL and Bettie JENKINS, death cause: "pulmonary tuberculosis", informant: Mrs. John

CAMPBELL (Jonesboro), died: 23 Aug 1916, record (1916): 377.

Ed ALLISON, age: about 53 years, married, parents: John ALLISON and Mariah WHITEHORN, death cause: "tuberculosis of lungs", informant: S.B. CAMPBELL (Jonesboro), buried: Little Brick Cemetery, died: 11 Aug 1916, record (1916): 378.

Thomas Martin ARNOLD, born: 1 Jan 1901, parents: Thomas Jefferson ARNOLD and Martha Jane BROWN, death cause: "foot and leg crushed in sawmill accident, shock", informant: William F. ARNOLD (Jonesboro), buried: Fair View, died: 15 Aug 1916, record: 379.

Alice E. WHITAKER, born: 18 Aug 1866, married, parents: Martain HUNT and Nannie COGGINS, death cause: "fractured skull, thrown from buggy", died: 3th District, 27 Aug 1916, record (1916): 380.

Seinthia Jane BACON, born: 24 Oct 1845, widow, parents: Robert FERGUSON and Acksie DEAKINS, death cause: "diabetes", informant: Thomas P. FERGUSON (Jonesboro), died: 25 Aug 1916, record (1916): 381.

N.C. WALKER, age: 41 years, married, parents: F.M. WALKER (Johnson City) and Mary DYER, death cause: "paralysis", informant: J.B. WALKER (Johnson City), buried: Longmire Cemetery, died: 3 Aug 1916, record (1916): 382.

Dan WHITE, Jr., age: 17 years, parents: Dan WHITE and Bettie ROSE, death cause: "typhoid", informant: C.C. WHITE (Erwin), buried: Buena Vista, died: 11 Aug 1916, record (1916): 383.

Sadie CARTER, born: __ Sep 1910, parents: Frank CARTER and Jannie BOND, death cause: "typhoid fever", informant: father (Johnson City), buried: Oak Hill, died: 25 Aug 1916, record (1916): 384.

Mrs. Mollie G__ (illegible), age: 56 years, married, parents: Mr. __ ORR and mother not stated, death cause: "tuberculosis", buried: Oak Hill, died: 27 Aug 1916, record (1916): 385.

Benjamin J. SITTON, age: 73 years, born: Dalton, GA., widower, death cause: "locomotor ataxia", buried: Dalton, GA., died: 28 Aug 1916, record (1916): 386.

Amanda BIDDLE, age: 60 years, born: Woodbury, PA., married, parents: Dr. Charles OELLIG and Susanna WEITZ, death cause: "heart disease", buried: Buena Vista, died: 28 Aug 1916, record (1916): 387.

John CLARK, age: 42 years, single, parents: Robert CLARK and Anna BRITT, death cause: "gunshot wound", buried: Buck Cemetery, died: 26 Aug 1916, record (1916): 388.

Nellie WEAVER, age: 18 years, single, parents: Wilson WEAVER and Alice SAYLOR, death cause: "tuberculosis", informant: W.R. WEAVER (Johnson City), buried: Hughes Cemetery, died: 28 Aug 1916, record (1916): 389.

Infant ODOM, black, female, parents: Will ODOM and Virgie FILOX, death cause: "premature", informant: George FITZGERALD (Johnson City), buried: West Lawn, born/died: 11 Aug 1916, record (1916): 390.

Hugh DUGAN, age: 70 years, born: Pennsylvania, single, parents: not stated, death cause: "cerebral hemorrhage", died: Soldier's Home, 5 Aug 1916, record (1916): 391.

Thomas BOND, age: 82 years, born: Indiana, widower, parents: not stated, death cause: "nephritis", died: Soldier's Home, 19 Aug 1916, record (1916): 292.

Christian OWEN, age: 75 years, born: Ohio, married, parents: not stated, death cause: "cirrhosis of liver", died: Soldier's Home, 23 Aug 1916, record (1916): 393.

Walter L. ROLFS, age: 38 years, born: Louisiana, single, parents: not stated, death cause: "pulmonary tuberculosis", died: Soldier's Home, 19 Aug 1916, record (1916): 394.

George Edward HARRELL, age: 2 years, parents: Waits HARRELL and Elvia THOMPSON, death cause: "diarrhoea", buried: Leonard Cemetery, died: Johnson City, 25 Aug 1916, record (1916): 395.

Bettie BUCHANAN, colored, age: 65 years, widow, parents: not stated, death cause: "paralysis", informant: Henry HALE (Johnson City), buried: Hyder Cemetery, died: 27 Aug 1916, record (1916): 396.

William D.B. ZELL, age: 47 years, born: Louisiana, single, parents: not stated, death cause: "pulmonary tuberculosis", died: Soldier's Home, 14 Aug 1916, record (1916): 397.

Nellie DYKES, born: 1 Jun 1916, parents: G__ (illegible) DYKES and L. Dora HENSLEY (Unicoi), death cause: "spasms", informant: J.A. MCNEESE (Jonesboro), died: 5 Aug 1916, record (1916): 398.

Lizzie HODGE, age: 51 years, married, parents: William TRENT (VA) and Amada MARTIN (VA), death cause: "typhoid fever", informant: Arch HODGE, died: 6 Aug 1916, record (1916): 399.

Infant GRAY, female, parents: Fred GRAY and Sarah Ellen HULSE, death cause: "stillborn", buried: Milburton, died: 14 Aug 1916, record (1916): 400.

Maud TINKER, born: 26 Apr 1911, parents: B.R. TINKER and Eliza ERWIN, death cause: "diptheria", informant: father (Chuckey), died: 29 Sep 1916, record (1916): 401.

William Valentine DEVAULT, born: 10 Sep 1847, married, parents: Jacob DEVAULT and mother not staed, death cause: "paralysis", buried: Devault Cemetery, died at Austin Springs on 12 Sep 1916, record (1916): 402.

Susana KROUSE, born: 21 Dec 1824 in Virginia, widow, parents: Chrisley WINE (VA) and Barbara BRAN (VA), death cause: "dysentery", buried: Krouse Cemetery, died: 10th District, 28 Sep 1916, record: 403.

Infant FELLERS, male, parents: Frank FELLERS and Allie BROYLES, death cause: "stillborn", informant: father (Chuckey), buried: Liberty Cemetery, died: 27 Sep 1916, record (1916): 404.

Absolom HUFFINE, born: 10 Oct 1845, married, parents: Daniel HUFFINE (NC) and Achsah DULANEY, death cause: "gastro intestinal cararrh", informant: Walter S. HUFFINE (Jonesboro), died: 18 Sep 1916, record (1916): 405.

Mary JOLLY, age: 79 years, widow, parents: William VINES and Rosa DUNCAN (VA), death cause: "diarrhoea and bronchitis", informant: A.S. VINES (Johnson City), buried: Vines Cemetery, died: 17 Sep 1916, record (1916): 406.

W.T. LEACH, age: 78 years, married, parents: Johnie LEACH and Fhibe FINE, death cause: "general break down, age", buried: Leach Cemetery, died: Jonesboro, 6 Sep 1916, record (1916): 407.

John W. MATTACK, age: 78 years, born: Illinois, parents: not stated, death cause: "mitral insufficiency", died: Soldier's Home, 28 Sep 1916, record (1916): 408.

William C. LEDFORD, age: 77 years, born: North Carolina, widower, parents: not stated, death cause: "cerebral hemorrhage", died: Soldier's Home, 28 Sep 1916, record (1916): 409.

George TYLER, age: 60 years, born: Missouri, widower, parents: not stated, death cause: "pneumonia", died: Soldier's Home, 27 Sep 1916, record: 410.

Albert H. STRIBLING, age: 36 years, born: South Carolina, single, parents: not stated, death cause: "pulmonary tuberculosis", died: Soldier's Home, 24 Sep 1916, record (1916): 411.

James M. WINSTEAD, age: 75 years, born: Kentucky, widower, parents: not stated, death cause: "mitral insufficiency", died: Soldier's Home, 18 Sep 1916, record (1916): 412.

Alfred LANPHER, age: 67 years, born: Vermont, married, parents: not stated, death cause: "hemiplegia", died: Soldier's Home, 15 Sep 1916, record (1916): 413.

W.B. JOHNSON, Jr., age: 6 years, parents: W.B. JOHNSON and Ethel AKIN, death cause: "dysentery", buried: Oak Hill, died: 30 Sep 1916, record: 414.

Charles H. CAMBRIDGE, age: 73 years, widower, parents: not stated, death cause: illegible, buried: Oak Hill, died: Johnson City, 28 Sep 1916, record (1916): 415.

Mary Elizabeth ROGERSON, born: 16 Jul __, age: 57 years and 3 months, married, parents: John COLEMAN and Martha Ann SMITH, death cause: "nephritis and mitral insufficiency", informant: Mrs. Emma MILLER (Johnson City), buried: Oak Hill, died: 27 Sep 1916, record (1916): 416,

Jake JACKSON, colored, age: 50 years, married, parents: not stated, death cause: "pulmonary tuberculosis", buried: West Lawn, died: Johnson City, 22 Sep 1916, record (1916): 417.

Glenn WIDENER, age: 7 months, parents: Will WIDENER (VA) and Florence GIBSON, death cause: "cholera infantum", informant: father (Johnson City), buried: Longmire Cemetery, died: 25 Sep 1916, record: 418.

John Raymond APPLEGATE, born: __ Jul 1914, parents: John Raymond APPLEGATE and Pearl YOUNCE, death cause: "illeo colitis", buried: Oak Hill, died: 24 Sep 1916, record (1916): 419.

Mrs. F.S. DAUGHERTY, age: 21 years, married, parents: John WHETSELL and Ida SPARKS, death cause: "suicide, -- illegible", informant: T.S. DAUGHERTY (Johnson City), buried: Oak Hill, died: 23 Sep 1916, record (1916): 420.

George W. TABOR, born: 19 Aug 1916, parents: Robert C. TABOR and Mary LONGMIRE, death cause: "intestinal toxemia", buried: Clark Cemetery, died: Johnson City, 25 Sep 1916, record (1916): 421.

Commadore GOBBLE, born: 6 May 1916, parents: John GOBBLE and Pearl GILES, death cause: "pneumonia", informant: J.W. GILES (Johnson City), died: 20 Sep 1916, record (1916): 422.

William TEMPLIN, age: 87 years and 3 months, married, parents: John TEMPLIN and Hannah BROWN, death cause: "dysentery", buried: Oak Hill, died: 15 Sep 1916, record (1916): 423.

Infant FRANCE, female, born: 20 Aug 1916, parents: Chester FRANCE and Mary HOPPER, death cause: "premature birth", informant: D.E. FRANCE (Johnson City), buried: 8th District, died: 12 Sep 1916, record (1916): 424.

James Matthew FORD, Negro, age: 36 years, married, railroad brakeman, parents: Jess FORD (Fordtown) and Kissey JACKSON, death cause: "accident, killed under train", buried: Hyder Cemetery, died: 3 Sep 1916, record (1916): 425.

George W. AVERY, colored, age: 31 years, born: Morganton, NC., married, parents: Joseph AVERY (NC) and Hattie BURTON (NC), death cause: "fractured skull, meningitis", informant: Robert AVERY (Morganton), buried: NC., died: 8 Sep 1916, record (1916): 426.

Marilla MCFALL, born: 22 Sep 1862, married, parents: E.S. PAINTER and May J. WALTERS, death cause: "gastritis, possible carcinoma of stomach", buried: Boones Cree, died: 22 Sep 1916, record (1916): 427.

Sarah Elizabeth MAHONEY, born: 4 Nov 1838, widow, parents: Eli SWINEY and Jane COOPER, death cause: "diarrhoea", informant: David Newton MCADAMS (Limestone), died: 2 Sep 1916, record (1916): 428.

Joseph HOWARD, black, age: about 60 years, born: North Carolina, widower, parents: not stated, death cause: "pulmonary tuberculosis", informant: Fred HOWARD (Limestone), died: 29 Sep 1916, record (1916): 429.

Nancy Ann SWINEY, born: 11 Jun 1844, single, parents: Eli SWINEY and Jane COOPER, death cause: "probably, paralysis", informant: D.N. MCADAMS (Limestone), died: 29 Sep 1916, record (1916): 430.

Burnie BEALS, age: 16 years, parents: Luck BEALS and __ MORRELL, death cause: "peritonitis", informant: Elbert MORRELL (Jonesboro), died: 5 Sep 1916, record (1916): 431.

Ellie SUSONG, age: about 35 years, single, parents: David SUSONG and __ BOWERY, death cause: "carcinoma of stomach", informant: J.A. CONNOR (Jonesboro), buried: Buffalo Ridge, died: 2 Sep 1916, record (1916): 432.

Paul CROUCH, born: 28 Apr 1916, parents; Robert CROUCH and Alice B__ (illegible), death cause: "intestinal toxemia", informant: R.H. CROUCH (Jonesboro), died: 8 Sep 1916, record (1916): 433.

Selma DICKENSON, born: 18 Jun 1911, parents: Garfield DICKENSON (Greene Co.) and Ethel MCMICHALS, death cause: "diptheria", informant: father (Jonesboro), died: 29 Sep 1916, record (1916): 434.

Minervey MCMILLEN, colored, age: about 80 years, born: Virginia, widow, parents: not stated, death cause: "cardiac lesion", informant: Florence FINLEY (Jonesboro), died: 19 Sep 1916, record (1916): 435.

Charles HOWERN, born: 18 Jun 1914, parents: David HOWERN and Bell HOSKINS, death cause: "measles", informant: C.F. AMMONS (Embreeville), died: 8 Sep 1916, record (1916): 436.

Ben CLAWSON, born: 15 Dec 1915, parents: Jim CLAWSON and Becky SMITH, death cause: "croup", informant: Dr. A.J. WILLIS, died: Embreeville, 30 Sep 1916, record (1916): 437.

James Robert SHEPHERD, born: 16 Feb 1916, parents: Robert Howey SHEPHERD and Effie May WHITE, death cause: "ileo colitis", informant: Howey SHEPHERD (Fall Branch), died: 20 Sep 1916, record: 438.

Jesse Lee BAINES, born: 16 Sep 1915, parents: Tom C. BAINES and Mary Elizabeth SELLS, death cause: "ileo colitis", informant: father (Fall Branch), died: 18 Sep 1916, record (1916): 439.

Clyde ISENBERG, born: 24 Jul __, age: 1 year, 1 month and 8 days, parents: B.U. ISENBERG and Mary HAWK, death cause: "pupura hemorrhage", informant: D.P. BARNES (Jonesboro), buried: Fordtown, died: 1 Sep 1916, record (1916): 440.

Martha Jane KROUSE, born: 10 May 1852, married, parents: John PRITCHETT and Mary SELLS, death cause: "pneumonia fever", informant: Jacob KROUSE (Rt 3, Johnson City), buried: Snow Chapel, died: 12 Oct 1016, record (1916): 441.

Mrs. Rena COLE, age: 42 years, widow, parents: Jerry PEAKS and Nancy Jane SCALF, death cause: "peritonitis", informant: Mrs. Alie MAUPIN (Johnson City), buried: Elizabethton, died: 2 Oct 1916, record (1916): 442.

George BEALS, age: 34 years, born: Friendsville, TN., single, parents: Hoary BEALS and Belle HACKNEY, death cause: "fracture of skull", buried: Friendsville, TN., died: 4 Oct 1916, record: 443.

Mrs. Mary Elizabeth SPARKS, born: 11 Feb 1834 in Virginia, widow, parents: James A. DILLWORTH and Charlotte WARTMAN, death cause: "paralysis", buried: Oak Hill, died: 14 Oct 1916, record (1916): 444.

James M. KEEN, born: 11 Feb 1850 in Carter County, married, parents: Jonas KEEN and Mary ORR, death cause: "nephritis", buried: Taylor Chapel, died: Johnson City, 15 Oct 1916, record (1916): 445.

Infant COLLINS, female, born: 15 Oct 1916, parents: Sam COLLINS and Mamie BULLIS, death cause:

"premature birth", buried: Oak Hill, died: 16 Oct 1916, record (1916): 446.

Will GILLESPIE, colored, age: 50 years, born: Virginia, married, parents: not stated, death cause: "heart disease", informant: Mrs. Cora GILLESPIE, buried: West Lawn, died: 9 Oct 1916, record: 447.

Jack SHUMATE, age: about 4 years, born: Virginia, parents: H.M. SHUMATE (VA) and Nannie BURGS (VA), death cause: "dysentery", buried: Oak Hill, died: 4 Oct 1916, record (1916): 448.

Fred Herman HUGHES, born: 19 Mar 1834, married, parents: Thomas R. HUGHES, and Josephine MCPEAK, death cause: "tuberculosis", informant: Josephine HUGHES (Johnson City), buried: Oak Hill, died: 25 Oct 1916, record (1916): 449.

Gorden EVERETT, age: 41 years, born: Lumpkin, GA., married, parents: M.L. EVERETT (GA) and Elizabeth BRYON (GA), death cause: "tuberculosis", buried: Portsmouth, VA., died: 25 Oct 1916, record: 450.

Infant SHELL, female, born: 26 Oct 1916, parents: Carson SHELL and Martha MILLER, death cause: "premature birth", died: Embreeville, 30 Oct 1916, record (1916): 451.

Carmon WHITE, age: 16 years, parents: B.F. WHITE and Charlotte Francis BASS (NC), death cause: "bus ran over his body", buried: Buena Vista, died: 25 Oct 1916, record (1916): 452.

James Arthur RUBLE, born: 4 Nov 1844, married, parents: Epram RUBLE and Malinda ORR, death cause: "cirrhosis of liver", buried: Maryville, TN, died: 29 Oct 1916, record (1916): 453.

Virgil CHURCH, age: 1 year and 4 months, parents: Lee CHURCH and Minnie FIELDS, death cause: "marasmus", buried: Oak Hill, died: 29 Oct 1916, record (1916): 454.

Nellie CASH, lived 1 day, parents: father not stated and Jessie CASH, death cause: "inanition", buried: Union Cemetery, died: 28 Oct 1916, record: 455.

Mrs. S.M. BROYLES, age: 71 years, parents: John PRESNELL (NC) and mother not stated, death cause: "aortic insufficiency", buried: Oak Hill, died: 29 Oct 1916, record (1916): 456.

Henry HARR, colored, age: 30 years, born: Rockwood, SC., married, parents: not stated, death cause: illegible, informant: Leo WHITTINGTON (Johnson City), buried: West Lawn, died: 30 Oct 1916, record (1916): 457.

Guy GOINS, colored, age: 2 years, parents: Richard GOINS and Dicea HAINES (Carter Co.), death cause: "dysentery", buried: Hyder Cemetery, died: 30 Oct 1916, record (1916): 458.

George R. PEARSON, age: 77 years, born: England, married, parents: not stated, death cause: "nephritis", died: Soldier's Home, 7 Oct 1916, record (1916): 459.

George C. KILGORE, age: 73 years, born: New York, single, parents: not stated, death cause: "cerebral hemorrhage", died: Soldier's Home, 9 Oct 1916, record (1916): 460.

Owen HANNAGAN, age: 71 years, born: New York, single, parents: not stated, death cause: "lobar pneumonia", died: Soldier's Home, 17 Oct 1916, record (1916): 461.

Peter SHERIDAN, age: 78 years, born: Ireland, single, parents: not stated, death cause: "nephritis", died: Soldier's Home, 19 Oct 1916, record: 462.

John W. POTTS, age: 35 years, born: Illinois, single, soldier, death cause: "pulmonary tuberculosis", died: Soldier's Home, 23 Oct 1916, record: 463.

Thomas M. MORAN, age: 77 years, born: England, widower, book binder, parents: not stated, death cause: "nephritis", died: Soldier's Home, 27 Oct 1916, record (1916): 464.

Benage SPROLES, age: 82 years, born: Virginia, widower, parents: not stated, death cause: "nephritis", died: Soldier's Home, 27 Oct 1916, record: 465.

Rev. James A. RUBLE, age: 76 years, born: Tennessee, married, chaplain, parents: not stated, death cause: "cardiac dilatation", buried: Maryville, TN., died: Soldier's Home, 29 Oct 1916, record: 466.

Haywood DUDLEY, colored, age: 76 years, born: Arkansas, widower, parents: not stated, death cause: "nephritis", died: Soldier's Home, 31 Oct 1916, record (1916): 467.

Mary Elza RICE, born: 19 Sep 1916, parents: Will RICE and Rebecca CAMPBELL (Sullivan County), death cause: "suffocation", buried: New Salem, died: 19 Oct 1916, record (1916): 468.

S.E. SAMS, age: not stated, parents: not stated, death cause: "broncho pneumonia", buried: New Salem, died: 30 Oct 1916, record (1916): 469.

Sarah Edith KEYS, born: 2 Jan 1909, parents: William W. KEYS and Ana E. TAYLOR, death cause: "diptheria", informant: father (Telford), buried: Pleasant Grove, died: 29 Oct 1916, record (1916): 470.

Elvae MURR, born: 6 Feb 1915, parents: Houston MURR and Eliza HARRISON (Greene County), death cause: "diptheria", informant: W.A. MILLER (Telford), died: 23 Oct 1916, record (1916): 471.

Harrich GRIMES, colored, born: 11 Apr 1835 in Virginia, parents: not stated, death cause: "natural causes", informant: Etta RAY (Jonesboro), died: 21 Oct 1916, record (1916): 472.

Preston SHIPLEY, born: 23 Aug 1916, parents: J.D. SHIPLEY (Sullivan Co.) and Virgie OLIVER, death cause: "marasmus", informant: father (Jonesboro), died: 16 Oct 1916, record (1916): 473.

Paul B. HILBERT, age: 19 years, single, parents: John B. HILBERT and Sue E. BASHOR, death cause: "pulmonary tuberculosis", buried: Pleasant Valley Cemetery, died: 16th District, 8 Oct 1916, record (1916): 474.

Mary Alta TAYLOR, born: 18 Mar 1813, parents: C.E. TAYLOR and Beulah MARTIN, death cause: "tuberculosis", informant: W.E. TAYLOR (Jonesboro), died: 8 Oct 1916, record (1916): 475.

Philip Jackson CARTER, born: 5 Jun 1831 in Henry County, VA., married, parents: Eliga CARTER (VA) and Amelia SPRANCE (VA), death cause: "uremic poison and enlarged prostate", informant: M.J. SANDERS (Jonesboro), buried: Wheeler Chapel, died: 27 Oct 1916, record (1916): 476.

Mahlow Harvey COX, born: 4 May 1852, widower, parents: Ezeke COX and Nancy Jane JACKSON, death cause: "cerebral hemorrhage", buried: Sulphur Springs, died: 11 Oct 1916, record (1916): 477.

Mrs. Mary TADLOCK, born: 24 Jun 1836, widow, parents: John NELSON and Ester FERGUSON, death cause: "tuberculosis and heart disease", informant: Arthur TADLOCK (Jonesboro), died: 12 Oct 1916, record (1916): 478.

Lindsey Pauline SHIPLEY, born: 7 Apr 1912 in Sullivan County, parents: Eugene SHIPLEY (Sullivan Co.) and Lula CHANDLER, death cause: "whooping cough", buried: Muddy Creek, died: 12th District, 27 Oct 1916, record (1916): 479.

Joseph E. SHIPLEY, born: 1 Jan 1857, single, physician, parents: Elkana SHIPLEY and Susana HALE, death cause: "diabetes", informant: M.C. JONES (Jonesboro), buried: Shipley Cemetery, died: 20 Oct 1916, record (1916): 480.

Jesse Kate LYNCH, born: 26 Apr 1914, parents: Rosco R. LYNCH (Greene Co.) and Dora BAINES, death cause: "suffocation from swallowing apple peel", informant: father (Jonesboro), died: 1 Oct 1916, record: 481.

William Gibson LONG, born: 25 Jul 1858 in Russell County, VA., married, parents: Harvey G. LONG (VA) and Cynthia D. GIBSON (VA), death cause: "laceration wound on neck, suspect homicide", informant: R.A. LONG (Johnson City), buried: Union Cemetery, died: 1 Oct 1916, record (1916): 482.

Benjamin F. MCKEY, age: 77 years, born: Indiana, widower, parents: not stated, death cause: "pneumonia", died: Soldier's Home, 6 Oct 1916, record (1916): 483.

Thomas LARKINS, age: 71 years, born: Pennsylvania, widower, parents: not stated, death cause: "cardiac diliation", died: Soldier's Home, 5 Oct 1916, record (1916): 484.

Infant SHELL, male, parents: Carson SHELL and Martha MILLER, death cause: "sillborn", died: 26 Oct 1916, record (1916): 485.

Infant BOOHER, colored, male, parents: Henry BOOHER and Magnolia RAY, death cause: "stillborn", buried: Hyder Cemetery, died: 13 Oct 1916, record: 486.

Infant LAINGHAM, male, parents: R.L. LAINGHAM and Bertie SHEETS, death cause: "stillborn", informant:

father (Johnson City), buried: Buena Vista, died: 19 Oct 1916, record (1916): 487.
Infant LAWS, female, parents: Alexander LAWS and Sallie MITCHELL, death cause: "stillborn", informant: father (Chuckey), buried: Philadelphia Cemetery, died: 27 Oct 1916, record (1916): 488.
Jesse MAUPIN, age: 12 years, parents: Sam MAUPIN and Alice BARNES, death cause: "nephritis", died: Jonesboro, 23 Nov 1916, record (1916): 489.
Terry KEEFAUVER, born: 2 Nov 1893, single, parents: S.U. KEEFAUVER and Nora CROUCH, death cause: "typhoid fever", informant: father (Jonesboro), buried: Boones Creek, died: 27 Nov 1916, record (1916): 490.
Lee Monroe BACON, born: 13 Aug 1914, parents: Enoch B. BACON and Stella FULKERSON, death cause: "tonsilitis, pneumonia fever", informant: Montgomery BACON (Jonesboro), died: 8 Nov 1916, record: 491.
Infant BROWN, male, born: 15 Oct 1916, parents: Oscar BROWN and Elsie BAILEY, death cause: illegible, informant: father (Chuckey), buried: Liberty Cemetery, died: 15 Nov 1916, record: 492.
Pearl MITCHELL, born: 9 Oct 1916, parents: C.E. MITCHELL and Lora ADAMS, death cause: "bronchitis", informant: father (Jonesboro), buried: Brothern Church Cemetery, died: 4 Nov 1916, record: 493.
Jessie DURHAM, colored, age: about 23 years, single, parents: father not stated and Mary DURHAM (NC), death cause: "tuberculosis of lungs", informant: mother (Jonesboro), buried: Brothern Church, died: 4 Nov 1916, record (1916): 494.
Mary A. HOPPER, born: 17 Dec 1831, widow, parents: William CROUCH and Delcenia HUNT, death cause: "senile decay", informant: J.H. HOPPER (Fall Branch), died: 7 Nov 1916, record (1916): 495.
Infant SLIGER, male, parents: Charles SLIGER and Minnie GROSS, death cause: "unknown", informant: Frank SLIGER (Telford), buried: New Victory, born/died: 15 Nov 1916, record (1916): 496.
Mary Ann DOTSON, born: 16 Feb 1836 in Virginia, widow, parents: __ CLARK and __ WRIGHT, death cause:

"mitral insufficiency", informant: M.E. CLARK (Limestone), died: 6 Nov 1916, record (1916): 497.

Fred Haines PILB, born: 27 Nov 1916, parents: John PILB and Mattie MOODY, death cause: "stillborn", informant: J.R. MCCRARY (Fall Branch), died: 29 Nov 1916, record (1916): 498.

Katherine CROSS, born: 2 Aug 1832 in Sullivan County, widow, parents: Jacob GOODMAN (VA) and Artie WOLFORD (Sullivan Co.), death cause: "heart disease", informant: J.W. CROSS (Rt 4, Johnson City), buried: Boones Creek, died: 14 Nov 1916, record (1916): 499.

Infant HANEY, male, parents: G.A. HANEY (NC) and Ella MCCOURRY (NC), death cause: "asphixia", born/died: 29 Nov 1916, record (1916): 500.

John B. RICHARDSON, born: 15 Mar 1915, parents: Robert RICHARDSON and Rosey RODGERS, death cause: "croup", died: 6th District, 27 Nov 1916, record (1916): 501.

John MITCHELL, age: 81 years, born: Ireland, single, parents: not stated, death cause: "nephritis", died: Soldier's Home, 20 Nov 1916, record (1916): 502.

Leroy BARLOW, age: 41 years, born: New Hampshire, married, parents: not stated, death cause: "nephritis", died: Soldier's Home, 18 Nov 1916, record (1916): 503.

William DAUGHERTY, age: 69 years, born: Kentucky, single, parents: not stated, death cause: "gangrene of foot", died: Soldier's Home, 13 Nov 1916, record (1916): 504.

John FORREST, age: 74 years, born: Pennsylvania, single, parents: not stated, death cause: "alcoholism", died: Soldier's Home, 9 Nov 1916, record (1916): 505.

Unknown INFANT, male, about 4 month fetus, found at Mountain Home, buried: Buena Vista Cemetery, record (1916): 506.

John W. SHELTON, age: 16 years, born; Virginia, parents: John F. SHELTON (VA) and Jestan F. BURTON (VA), death cause: "hemorrhage from gun shot wound", buried: Watauga, TN., died: 28 Nov 1916, record (1916): 507.

Timothy HERRIGTON, age: 47 years, married, parents: Kern HERRIGTON and mother not stated, death cause: "pulmonary tuberculosis", buried: Oak Hill, died: Johnson City, 27 Nov 1916, record (1916): 508.
Deborah WHITLOW, born: 19 Jun __, age: 75 years, widow, parents: Samuel HARRISON and mother not stated, death cause: "apoplexy", died: Johnson City, 25 Nov 1916, record (1916): 509.
Flora SILVERS, colored, born: 1 Jul 1916, parents: M.T. SILVERS and Hattie KENNELL, death cause: "pneumonia", informant: father (Johnson City), buried: West Lawn, died: 24 Nov 1916, record: 510.
Worley GREGG, born: 14 Oct 1916, parents: Will GREGG and Bettie HEATON, death cause: illegible, buried: Buena Vista, died: 24 Nov 1916, record (1916): 511.
Elizabeth J. LEONARD, age: 73 years, born: Washington County, VA., married, parents: Thomas CUNNINGHAM (Indiana) and Mary Jane (illegible) (VA), buried: Oak Hill, died: Johnson City, 19 Nov 1916, record (1916): 512.
Henry T. SLIGERLAND, age: not stated, born: Missouri, single, parents: not stated, death cause: "myo carditis", died: Soldier's Home, 21 Nov 1916, record (1916): 513.
Antonio ALSINA, age: 81 years, born: Spain, widower, parents: not stated, death cause: "cystitis", died: Soldier's Home, 21 Nov 1916, record (1916): 514.
Arthur PRICE, age: 70 years, born: England, widower, parents: not stated, death cause: "pellagra", died: Soldier's Home, 24 Nov 1916, record (1916): 515.
Amos L. GRIFFITH, age: not stated, born: Tennessee, widower, parents: not stated, death cause: "cystitis", died: Soldier's Home, 26 Nov 1916, record (1916): 516.
Mike CRANE, age: 52 years, born: Ireland, single, parents: not stated, death cause: "myo carditis", died: Soldier's Home, 28 Nov 1916, record: 517.
Henry HANGLETER, age: 76 years, born: Germany, widower, parents: not stated, death cause: "arterio sclerosis", died: Soldier's Home, 29 Nov 1916, record (1916): 518.

Mildred HALE, colored, born: 12 Apr 1915, parents: Eliga HALE and Sarah CHASE, death cause: "croup and bronchitis", informant: father (Johnson City), buried: West Lawn, died: 16 Nov 1916, record: 519.

Infant HENSON, female, parents: Clyde HENSON and Bertha MYERS (VA), death cause: "stillborn", buried: Buena Vista, died: 14 Nov 1916, record (1916): 520.

Lula Blanch MILLHORN, born: 3 Dec 1875 in Georgia, married, parents: Marahall MCCAMEY and Francis MCCAMEY, death cause: "heart disease", informant: C.E. MILLHORN (Johnson City), buried: Oak Hill, died: 12 Nov 1916, record (1916): 521.

Will LONG, colored, age: 22 years, married, parents: Jim LONG and mother not stated, death cause: "amputation middle of thigh, gangrene", buried: Elizabethton, died: 10 Nov 1916, record (1916): 522.

George LISENBERRY, age: about 39 years, married, parents: James LISENBERRY and mother not stated, death cause: "brain infection", informant: G.W. JACKSON (Jonesboro), buried: Fall Branch, died: 9 Nov 1916, record (1916): 523.

David GUMP, age: 85 years and 6 months, born: Germany, married, parents: Abraham GUMP (GE) and Rosa LEITER (GE), death cause: "arterio sclerosis", buried: Jewish Cemetery, died: 8 Nov 1916, record (1916): 524.

Mrs. Annie RICHARDSON, age: 84 years, born: North Carolina, widow, parents: John JACKSON (NC) and mother no stated, death cause: "lagrippe and age", informant: C.C. RICHARDSON (Johnson City), buried: Elk Park, NC., died: 7 Nov 1916, record (1916): 525.

Infant WILSON, male, born: 4 Nov 1916, parents: Horace C. WILSON (Blount County) and Maude MOODY, death cause: illegible, buried: Monte Vista, died: 6 Nov 1916, record (1916): 526.

Gicy GAINS, colored, age: 44 years, married, parents: George HAINES and Easter PENGH, death cause: "dysentery", informant: Richard GAINS (Johnson City), buried: West Lawn, died: 4 Nov 1916, record (1916): 527.

Axie Day COPASS, born: 7 Nov 1906, parents: John H. COPASS and Elmira SHERFEY (Sullivan County), death

cause: "heart failure and nephritis", informant: father (Fall Branch), died: 13 Nov 1916, record (1916): 528.
Jesse W. HALE, born: 14 Aug 1844, married, parents: McCagey B. HALE (Sullivan Co.) and Ludice COPASS (Sullivan Co.), death cause: "heart failure", informant: wife (Jonesboro), died: 20 Nov 1916, record (1916): 529.
Henry SELLS, born: 13 Feb 1846, divorced, parents: Johnathan SELLS and Rebecca STANFIELD, death cause: "organic heart trouble", informant: Josh MILLHORN (Jonesboro), died: 29 Nov 1916, record (1916): 530.
Patrick CHANNAFIN, born: 17 Mar 1832 in Ireland, married, stone mason, parents: not stated, death cause: not stated, informant: H.A. CHANNIFIN (Jonesboro), died: 21 Nov 1916, record (1916): 531.
Estella Kate CAMPBELL, born: 11 Aug 1913, parents: Arthur C. CAMPBELL and Ella RICE, death cause: "pneumonia", informant: S.B. CAMPBELL (16th District), buried: Maupin Cemetery, died: 3 Nov 1916, record (1916): 532.
James Allison MORRELL, born: 18 May 1863, married, parents: E.S. MORRELL (Sullivan County) and Susan ALLISON, death cause: "heart trouble", informant: Claude S. MORRELL (Jonesboro), buried: 11th District, died: 5 Nov 1916, record (1916): 533.
Frank MURRAY, age: 46 years, single, County Farm Resident, parents: not stated, death cause: "peritonitis", informant: Bird REED (Jonesboro), buried: County Farm, died: 12 Nov 1916, record (1916): 434.
Henderson C. CAMPBELL, born: 9 May 1834, widower, tanner, parents: William CAMPBELL and Sallie RICHARDS, death cause: "heart trouble", informant: S.B. CAMPBELL (Jonesboro), buried: Fairview, died: 14 Nov 1916, record (1916): 535.
Julia MOORE, age: about 71 years, married, parents: David MOORE and mother not stated, death cause: "heart trouble", buried: Cherokee Cemetery, died: 15th District, 25 Nov 1916, record (1916): 536.
Coy Lee RYAN, born: 31 Aug 1915, parents: Walter RYAN and Grace KITZMILLER, death cause: "indigestion

and pneumonia", informant: Earnest CARROLL (Jonesboro), buried: Fordtown, died: 18 Nov 1916, record (1916): 537.

Mrs. Kate E. MYERS, age: 51 years, married, parens: not stated, death cause: "organic heart lesion", buried: Onks Cemetery, died: 8th District, 18 Nov 1916, record (1916): 538.

John F. DENTON, born: 8 Aug 1850, married, parents: Henry DENTON and mother not stated, death cause: "dropsy", buried: Union Church Cemetery, died: 17 Nov 1916, record (1916): 539.

Richard Carr MOORE, born: 22 Sep 1841, married, parents: Thomas MOORE (NC) and Mary HAMPTON, death cause: "prosalitis, uremia", informant: Mrs. Mary MOORE (Limestone), died: 3 Nov 1916, record: 540.

Infant PETERSON, male, born: 30 Oct 1916, parents: (illegible) PETERSON (NC) and Bettie WISEMAN (NC), death cause: "found dead in bed", died: 2nd District, 19 Nov 1916, record (1916): 541.

Joseph Daniel DUNCAN, born: 26 Aug 1912, parents: John DUNCAN and Martha SHELL (Unicoi County), death cause: "tonsilitis and bronchitis", buried: New Salem, died: 10 Nov 1916, record (1916): 542.

William MITCHELL, born: 7 Jan 1872, married, parents: John M. MITCHELL and Elvira BROWN, death cause: "pneumonia", informant: S.B. MORELOCK (Limestone), buried: Fairview, died: 30 Nov 1916, record (1916): 543.

Mary Eva LOYD, born: 28 Ul 1916, parents: Robert C. LOYD and Ida BAILEY (NC), death cause: "broncho pneumonia", died: Telford, 18 Nov 1916, record (1916): 544.

Liddie Margaret WOODFIN, born: 3 Apr 1863 in Hawkins County, married, parents: Calvin BALDWIN and Axcia MILLER (NC), death cause: "pneumonia", buried: Martains Creek, TN., died: 6th District, 18 Dec 1916, record (1916): 545.

John GIPSON, born: 10 Nov 1865, married, parents: David GIPSON and Kizzie TRIVETT, death cause: "neuralgia of heart", informant: George WHITLOCK (Fall Branch), died: 13 Dec 1916, record: 546.

Homer JONES, born: 6 Dec 1916, parents: Herbert JONES and Oma P. EVANS, death cause: "premature birth", informant: Sam GOOD (Fall Branch), died: 13 Dec 1916, record (1916): 547.

Isacher Franklin YEAGER, born: 22 Nov 1845, married, parents: Joseph J. YEAGER and Mariah COLLET, death cause: "nephritis", died: Limestone, 13 Dec 1916, record (1916): 548.

Minnie Pearl MATHERLY, born: 17 Dec 1902, parents: John MATHERLY and Blanch CERCY, death cause: "typhoid and brain fever", informant: Blanch MATHERLY (Jonesboro), buried: White Cemetery, died: 7 Dec 1916, record (1916): 549.

John HUTCHINSON, age: 80 years, born: Scotland, widower, parents: not stated, death cause: "cerebral hemorrhage", died: Soldier's Home, 2 Dec 1916, record (1916): 550.

John MCCLAIN, age: 72 years, born: New Jersey, widower, parents: not stated, death cause: "cardiac dilitation", died: Soldier's Home, 29 Dec 1916, record (1916): 551.

Joseph H. HILLS, age: 74 years, born: England, single, school teacher, parents: not stated, death cause: "cerebral hemorrhage, died: Soldier's Home, 24 Dec 1916, record (1916): 552.

John STEWART, age: 79 years, born: Pennsylvania, single, parents: not stated, death cause: "cerebral hemorrhage", died: Soldier's Home, 8 Dec 1916, record (1916): 553.

Carter BLANKENSHIP, age: 73 years, born: Kentucky, single, parents: not stated, death cause: "diarrhoea", died: Soldier's Home, 7 Dec 1916, record (1916): 554.

G (illegible) ROBINSON, age: 3 years, parents: Sam ROBINSON (Russia) and Rachel OTTALOU (Russia), death cause: "premature", buried: Knoxville, died: 24 Dec 1916, record (1916): 555.

Infant HAWES, male, parents: Charlie HAWES and Sudie HAWES, death cause: "prematrue birth", buried: Jonesboro, died: 23 Dec 1916, record (1916): 556.

Ruth FORD, born: 8 Dec 1913, parents: Curtis FORD and Lucile HENSON, death cause: "croup", buried: Buena Vista, died: 19 Dec 1916, record (1916): 557.

William Thomas PHIPPS, born: 28 Apr 1899, parents: J.T. PHIPPS (VA) and Sarah TATE (VA), death cause: "pellagra", informant: O.W. PHIPPS (JOHNSON CITY), buried: Monte Vista, died: 20 Dec 1916, record (1916): 558.

Arthur MILLS, colored, born: 20 Dec 1916, parents: Will MILLS (NC) and Gracy SEE (Dayton, Ohio), death cause: "premature birth", buried: Hyder Cemetery, died: 20 Dec 1916, record (1916): 559.

Lucile MURRAY, born: 7 Apr 1913, parents: Lee MURRAY (Fordtown) and Francis BOOHER, death cause: "burns", buried: Fordtown, died: 16 Dec 1916, record: 560.

Hazel June PRIVETT, born: 27 Jun 1914, parents: G.W. PREVETT (VA) and Gertrude WEAVER, death cause: "lagrippe", informant: father (Johnson City), died: 12 Dec 1916, record (1916): 561.

Mrs. Julia A. SMITH, born: 24 Feb 1834 in West Virginia, widow, parents: Joseph BROWN (VA) and Mary ROBERTS (VA), death cause: "old age", informant: G.L. SMITH (Johnson City), buried: Chattanooga, died: 7 Dec 1916, record (1916): 562.

Roy JOHNSON, age: 9 years, born: North Carolina, parents: E.M. JOHNSON (NC) and Nora VANCE (NC), death cause: "tuberculosis of bowels", buried: Onks Cemetery, died: 5 Dec 1916, record (1916): 563.

Dr. E.L. DEADRICK, born: 16 Aug 1843, single, physician, parents: John F. DEADRICK and Rebecca WILLIAMS (NC), death cause: "diarrhoea", buried: Jonesboro, died: 4 Dec 1916, record (1916): 564.

Lucile Virginia OWEN, age: 7 months, parents: A.A. OWENS and Laura SHARRETT (VA), death cause: "meningitis", buried: Bristol, died: 3 Dec 1916, record (1916): 565.

Rosa GOAD, age: 2 months and 5 days, parents: Nate GOAD and Lula SELLS, death cause: not stated, buried: Buena Vista, died: 1 Dec 1916, record (1916): 566.

David Filmore DEPEW, born: 12 Apr 1852, married, parents: John DEPEW and Mary PAXTON, death cause:

"pneumonia", informant: E.S. DEPEW (Jonesboro), buried: Douglas Shed, died: 15 Dec 1916, record (1916): 567.

Mrs. Julia DENTON, age: 38 years, born: North Carolina, married, parents: John JONES (NC) and Margaret RIDDLE (NC), death cause: "tuberculosis", buried: Slagle Cemetery, died: 10 Dec 1916, record (1916): 568.

Susan CHANNIFIN, born: 10 Oct 1840, widow, parents: Frank BOWERY and __ COX, death cause: "lagrippe", informant: Andrew CHANNIFIN (Jonesboro), died: 12 Dec 1916, record (1916): 569.

Alvah MCPHERSON, female, born: 26 Oct 1858 in Bedford County, VA., widow, parents: T.R. WILLIAMSON (Bedford Co.) and Mary ST CLAIR, death cause: "tuberculosis", informant: A.A. MCPHERSON (Jonesboro), died: 1 Dec 1916, record (1916): 570.

Hugh L. BOYD, born: 29 Jan 1844 in Elizabethton, TN., married, parents: John BOYD (NC) and Jane TIPTON (NC), death cause: "pneumonia", informant: Ed S. BOYD (Jonesboro), died: 27 Dec 1916, record (1916): 571

Mrs. Manervia HARTMAN, age: 90 years, 6 months and 29 days, widow, parents: Robert G. HALE and __ KEEN, death cause: "arterio sclerosis", informant: J.W.S. HARTMAN (Jonesboro), buried: Sulphur Springs, died: 25 Dec 1916, record (1916): 572.

Infant GILLIAM, colored, born: 19 Dec 1916, parents: J.M. GILLIAM (SC) and Ella HAWKINS (SC), death cause: "stillborn", informant: father (Johnson City), buried: Watauga Point, died: 21 Dec 1916, record (1916): 573.

Infant SUMMERS, female, parents: father not stated and Estell SUMMERS (VA), death cause: "stillborn", informant: Mike ARNETT (Johnson City), died: 21 Dec 1916, record (1916): 574.

Robert E. DUNN, parents: Will DUNN and Dora SEATON, death cause: "stillborn", buried: Speedwell Cemetery, died: 20 Dec 1016, record (1916): 575.

Infant PIERCE, male, parents: John Ed PIERCE and Kathlene (illegible) (VA), death cause: "premature birth", died: 9 Dec 1916, record (1916): 576.

Index

Abel, William H. 91
Able, Tenie 114
Adams, __ 212
  __ Bessie 197
  Adeline 211 Clara B
  237 Doney H. 220 Dora
  119 Elijah S. 220
  Elizabeth 181 George T.
  47 Jennie B. 220
  John (Rev) 109 Josie A.
  241 J.E. 211 Lora 257
  L. 226 Mallison 197
  M.A. 198 Robert 62
Adard, D.A. 183
Addison, Henry L. 152
Aertere, Sam 153
Aiken, Ethel 209 James
  209 J.C. 120 Mary L 120
Akard, William 183
Akers, James O. 182
  Maud 182 Roda 182
  Will 182
Akin, Ethel 249
Aldrich, David B. 116
Alexander, Jennie 158
  Richard 159 Sandy 125
Alfred, Cilbert 88
  James 25
Alger, Milo M. 193
Alison, Ortie 72
  Sallie 72
Allen, Amanda 216
  Charles E. 232 Elander
  228 George 29 Isaac
  232 J.L. 238

Allen (continued)
  Sidney A. 159 S.C. 232
  Thomas M. 92 T.O. 87
Allison, Adolphus 113
  Ed 246 Elizabeth 193
  Ellen 10 Hannah E. 178
  Infant 167 Jerome B.
  217 John 246 John W.
  167 J.B. 179 Mary M.
  143 Susan 261
  William H. 178
Almany, John 88
Alsina, Antonio 259
Ammons, C.F. 190 251
  Lee 244 Miles V. 190
  Myrtie H. 244
Anders, Cleve 130 153
  Infant 153 Paul 130
Anderson, Finnie D. 67
  Glenore 188 Infant 97
  Joseph M. 97 J.H. 157
  Lizzie 45 Mary 66
  Mira 185 Ratchel A. 157
  Sallie 76 Sam H. 157
  Samuel (Dr) 203
  William H. 11
Andes, Janie 239
Angel, George H. 137
Applegate, John R. 250
  Raymond 250
Archer, Annie 191 Atta
  82 D.W. 162 Earl 56
  Infant 224 Joseph 162
  Joseph C. 225 Lillie 67
  Louise 10 Mary Sue 81

Archer (continued)
  Mattie 158 M.J. 219
  Nora D. 93 Rachel 162
  Thomas 225 W.J. 224
Arlington, Millie 210
Armatrout, R.L. 40
Armentrout, Cora E. 71
  Jane 211 Jesse 209
  Preston 71
  Priscilla 212
Armntrant, Hollie 6
Armstead, Jesie 219
Armstrong, Mattie 238
  Samuel A. 64
Arnett, Benson 226
  Clarence 87 Mike 265
Arney, Edward J. 173
  E.J. 208 Susan E. 208
Arnold, J.C. 141 Ramon B.
  141 Soloman G. 211
  Thomas J. 52 246
  Thomas M. 246
  William F. 246
Arnot, Mary 135
Aron, Sallie 21
Arrants, Sarah 218
Arterbum, Elias 189
Arwood, Clara 176 Clem
  149 Frank 88 Infant 88
  181 John 22 J.N. 181
  Malinda 167 225
  Sarah A. 149
Ashborn, Ella 144
Ashby, Annabell 144
  Charles 144 W.J. 144
Ashley, Charles 152
Atkinson, William H. 210
Austin, Bertha V. 139
  B.F. 131 Clem 149
  David A. 139
  Infant 2 68 J.K. 41

Austin (continued)
  Sarah A. 131 149
Avary, Jerry 204
Avery, George W. 250
  Jerry 204 Joseph 250
  Robert 250
Ayers, Alex 94
  James M. 22
Babb, I.U. 113
  Jessie 156
Bachman, L.H. 84
  Nathan W. 204
Bacon, Amanda 82 Dice 97
  Enoch B. 257 Era G. 39
  Fannie 93 James 10
  Jessie 108 John C. Jr.
  90 Johnathan 90 205
  Joseph 90 Julia 68
  J.C. 108 Lee M. 257
  Martha E. 52 Mary E.
  245 Minnie 95
  Montgomery 257
  Robert 10 R.H. 108
  Sarah 139 Senthia J.
  246 Watson 178
Bagley, Allen 119
  Infant 119
Bahr, Lizzie 230
Bailes, Marthy E. 110
Bailey, Addie 111
  Archey 30 Bettie 210
  Clary 242 Daniel H. 104
  Darkis 202 David 76 167
  David R. 225 Elsie 257
  George 66 George B. 104
  G.N. Sr. (Dr) 156
  Ham 133 Henry 232 242
  Henry D. 225 H.F. 69
  Ida 262 Infant 2 65 76
  Ivon W. 149 I.N. 149
  John 6 Joseph 108

Bailey (continued)
 Lee 54 Lena 167
 Lynn D. 108 Martha 8
 Martha A. 72 Mary 2 242
 Mary E. 232 Mary F. 242
 Mose 242 Moses 155
 Nancy A. 66 Neely 111
 Nora 242 Richard 7
 Sallie 234 T. 110
 Wesley 65
Bails, John M. 133
Baines, Bertie L. 65
 Dora 256 Jesse L. 252
 Mary A. 5 Sally 65
 Tom C. 252 Viola E. 218
 Walter 218
Bair, Lewana 154 W.H. 154
Bairfield, Barbery 212
Bakar, Fannie 129
Baker, Andy 150
 Bertha 28 31 Bessie 31
 Christy 190 Hannah 147
 148 Lucil 194 Lucy 31
 Nancie 117 Virginia 172
 W.P. 150
Baldwin, Calvin 262
Bales, Luck B. 10
Ball, __ 128
 Amantha J. 65 Clara 128
 Clarence 9 Delia T. 158
 G.W. 120 J.H. 185
 Martie F. 185
 Rebecca 210 Samuel 138
 S.C. 212
Ballard, Richard T. 133
Banner, Ida 240 Jerry 240
Barfield, Daniel 72
 J.M. 212
Barker, Lucile 149
Barkley, D.B. 205
 Isaac 17 James M. 120

Barkley (continued)
 Lula B. 66 Mary A. 205
 Melvina 9 Tessie 17
 William T. 120
Barlow, Infant 62
 Emily 43 Jennie 142
 Leroy 258
Barnes, Alice 257
 Allen 127 Argel 236
 A.M. 109 A.S. 132
 Bessie J. 236 Carol W.
 164 Celil E. 109
 Charles 91 David G. Jr.
 132 Deborah 205
 D.P. 252 Emaline 176
 F.H. 132 George L. 127
 Guy V. 244 J.S. 164
 Katie 123 M.W. 51
 N.D. 244 Rebecca A. 61
 Ruby Lee 236 R.H. 127
 Sarah E. 91
Barnett, Berrencia 79
 James 199 Roberta M.
 145 T.N. 145 Walter 145
Barrett, Bernica 79
 Edward 136
Barring, Sue 164
Barringer, John R. 121
Barron, Bell 81 Laura 218
 Lillian 118 Madison 118
Barry, Mary 105
Bashor, Carroll 164
 D.G. 12 Infant 97
 John C. 164 Mary 236
 Orsa 97 Sue E. 255
Basket, Sarah A. 36
Baskett, Efie 5
Baskette, Hutson M. 126
 John T. 126
Bason, Jane 163
Bass, Charlotte F. 253

Bass (continued)
  Martha 57 Mary E. 15
Batchley, William 216
Baty, Margaret 235
Baxter, F.P. (Mrs) 130
  Hale 195 Ira W. 213
  Joseph 17 May 87
Bayless, Effie 125
  E.B. 201 Hamilton 244
  Jessie 16 John 129
  Luke S. 219
  Luke S. (Mrs) 219
  Margaret 17 Nancy G.
  132 Polly 201 Rena 19
  Walter H. 201
  William 132
Bayley, Texana 191
Beach, Elsie M. 90
  John 90
Beals, Berine 251
  George 252 Hoary 252
  John 110 Johnathan H.
  162 Lizzie 180 Luke 251
  William 162
Bear, William H. 112
Beard, Dewitt 78
  Hannah 196 N.L. 19
  R.D. 2
Beasley, Catherine 55
Beckelhimer, Henrietta 93
  Warren P. 93 W.D. 93
Becker, Charles F. 191
  John H. 238
Beddell, Ethel 130 153
Belden, Henry W. 171
Beldsow, Ethel 90
Bell, Alice 227
  Briahes 213
  Chester H. 110 John 93
  Simeon 213 Thomas 110
Belton, Fred 24

Bennett, Frankie 184
  George 184 Nancy 153
Bentley, Lena 123
Berkhart, Mary 74
Berkhatz, Clara M. 80
Berry, Ada 160
  George H. 202
  George (Mrs) 202
  L.C. 202 Melinda 220
  Nancy 212 Virginia 241
Bibb, Eliza 98
Biddle, Amanda 247
Binkley, Sarah 115
Binnix, George W. 100
Birch, Jack 148
Birchfield, C.E. 175
  John 112 John Jr. 112
  Josie 112
Birdwell, Emeline 204
Bisbing, Albert H. 99
Bishop, Amanda 238
  Infant 168 Jennice 228
  Joseph C. 168 O.S. 86
  Rebecca 106
Black, J.E. (Mrs) 115
  R.B. 23 William 212
Blackwell, Judith E. 194
Blain, Amanda 131
Blaine, John 217
Blair, Ella 172
  Maggie 227 Robert 146
  Robert L. 106
  Robert W. 106
  Samuel C. 106
Blakeley, Bell 210
Blank, Gustav A. 191
Blankenship, Carter 263
Bledsoe, Hiram 166
Bledsow, Addie 188
  William 188
Blevins, ___ M. 86

Blevins (continued)
  Bessie 104 Charles 244
  Frank 201 Johnie 201
  Maria 121 Maxie 214
  Pearl 34 Robert 31
  Walter 244
Boaz, W.M. 111
Bodenheimer, Robert E. 57
Bogart, Infant 170
  James 48 William A. 170
Bolton, Eliza J. 170
  Eva 185 Maud 209
  Nannie 205 Samuel 205
  Sarah J. 222
  William M. 205
Bond, C.H. 116 Janie 246
  Thomas 247
Booher, Francis 264
  Henry 256 Infant 256
  James 32 129 Runner 129
  Sallie 129
Booth, Ana 18 Ella 220
  Eva B. 1 Ira 7
  Jeremiah 185 John 185
  Joseph 151 J.W. 151
  M.E. 1
Boothe, Sarah 162
Boreing, Ruth 103 157
Boring, Araline 32
  Beuna 214 B.V. 134
  Ellen 105 Julia 159
  Montgomery 163
  Vinson 169
Bosbury, Charles J. 168
  Mary E. 168
Bosenbaum, Lucy 135
Bouner, Jane 243
Bouser, George 163
Bouton, Ollie 85
Bovell, Steve 155
Bowden, Katie 196

Bowering, G.W. 234
Bowery, __ 251 Frank 265
  Lennie 231
Bowling, J.B. 91 J.W. 91
  Tennessee 91
Bowman, Anna B. 132
  Benjamin 42 Carle C.
  228 Catherine 184
  Charles 205 C.C. 182
  David T. 215 Henry E.
  97 Homer 110 Infant 109
  Jacob M. 226 John 36
  John B. 109 Joseph 35
  127 J.K.P. 110 J.R. 30
  Lizzie 192 Margaret 115
  Mary E. 238 Mollie C. 8
  Nellie E. 31 Nellie K.
  237 Richard C. 127
  Sam 110 Sarah 147
  Sparling 97 215 226
  Susanna 89 T.E. 182
  Willie 56 W.B. 13 228
  W.C. 238 W.W. 127
Boyd, Bertha 15
  Ed S. 206 265 Hugh L.
  265 John 265 Kate 52
  Tula F. 45
Boyer, James 79
  Joseph C. 19
Boyers, Elizabeth 126
Brabson, C.W. 162 213 215
  E.D. 205 Katherine 205
  T.A. 54
Brace, Helem A. 135
  H.P. 135
Bradley, Alfred 150
  Anna L. 164 Bud 126
  Daisy 106 Infant 164
  J.T. 164 Mary F. 48
  Matthew 164
Bramlett, John 153

Bran, Barbara 248
Branch, Annie 237
  Howard 26 Thomas 168
Brandon, A.R. 151
  Mary 140 Thomas 151
Braswell, Callie 38
  Julia 216
Breeding, Loyd C. 4
Bricker, Sallie 68
Bridges, Dennis 132
  Lillie 147
Bridgewater, Sophia 163
Briggs, Emily 121
Bright, Ananda C. 15
Brigman, Nina 51
  Rachel 54
Britt, Anna 247 Dave 179
  Flora 55 John 158
  Nancy A. 243
Brobeck, Lizzie 16
Brodrick, Levicy A. 5
Brooks, A.W. 101
  David 101 James M. 156
  Mose 101 Nancy 62 156
  Paul 46
Brown, Alexander 224
  Allen F. 45 Allie 231
  Andrew S. 143 Anna 224
  Arthur 238 A.J. 127
  Benson 135 Bertha R. 77
  Clancey 125 Delilah 67
  Elvira 262 Enoch 216
  Gertrude 114 G.K. 85
  Hannah 147 250
  Henry A. 130
  Herbert 130 131
  Hiram 224 Infant 114
  131 208 257 Jacob E. 44
  James 148 James P. 239
  John S. 135 John T. 148
  Joseph 264 Julia 141

Brown (continued)
  J.M. 207 208 J.M. (Mrs)
  207 Leon 147 Loueffie
  127 Martha 174
  Martha J. 246 Mary 90
  M.J. 54 M.L. 15
  Nola C. 149 Oscar 257
  Rachel 155 Roina 155
  R.C. 11 R.N. 197 231
  Susan 205 Tom 217 224
  Walter H. 143
  Walter J. 65
Browning, __ W. 222
  Bettie W. 148 J.W. 148
  S. 222 W.A. 222
Broyles, Allie 248
  Aluby H. 104 Arthur 111
  Burney 162 213 215
  B.B. 196 Elizabeth 190
  213 Emme J. 15 Francis
  13 Fred 13 G.W. 2
  Harvy 95 Infant 111 162
  200 213 215 Ira 101
  Jackson 95 101 James
  178 James M. 28 Jane
  196 Jesse 190 Katherine
  174 Lebert 42 Lizzie
  111 Lucy 120 Lula 216
  Mary 113 120 174
  Melda 179 Nola 153
  Rex 174 Rolla 200
  Simeon 3 S.M. 178
  S.M. (Mrs) 253
  William 253 W.M. 14
Brumitt, Minnie L. 50
Brummitt, Hannah E. 183
  Nellie M. 29 W.R. 82
Bryant, Suckey 211
Bryon, Elizabeth 253
Bryson, Owen E. 186
Bubase, Ann 218

Buchanan, Bella 5
  Bessie L. 228
  Betie 247 Dan 14
  Doss 110 George 57
  Henry J. 18 Jane 240
  J.D. 236 Mildred 153
  Stokes 153
Bucher, John 243 Mary 143
  William H. 243
Buck, Jocie B. 153
  Johnathan 141 J.B. 200
  Nathaniel T. 141
  William 67
Buckingham, Alice M. 61
Buhr, Frank 148
Bullis, Mamie 252
Bullman, Lisse 170
Bullock, J.F. 182
Bulwars, __ 194
Bumgardner, F.L. 199
Bunting, Matilda 134
Bunton, F.M. 52
Burchfield, C.E. 79
  Infant 79 Josie 122
Burger, Ambrose D. 151
Burgess, Aden H. 156
  James W. 156 J.S. 156
Burgins, Ann 76
Burgner, Clarence 189
  Conley 189 Olen 130
  131 Sarah F. 72
Burgs, Nannie 253
Burket, Nellie 88
Burkett, Effie 240
Burleson, Alice 232
  Jefferson 230
Burleston, Sarah B. 230
Burnett, Thomas 56
Burns, Porter C. 106
Burnsides, Charles 102
Burton, Hattie 250

Burton (continued)
  Jestan F. 258 June 70
  Marshall T. 234
  Martha C. 189 W.S. 189
Bushage, Infant 32
Butler, C.C. 161 Jim 171
  Julia E. 241 J.A. 241
  L.L. (Miss) 40 Mary 171
  Nora 161 R. Ellis 241
Byerly, J.K. 229
Byley, Sarah 200
Byrd, Nannie 8
  Samuel J.W. 229
Cade, __ 147 Eliza 207
  E.C. 207 Louis 207
  Sallie 123
Caffery, Henry 187
Cagle, Lula 173
Cain, Anderson 185
  John 185
Calloway, Ella 194
  Lee 239 Robert 239
Cambert, Frank 181
Cambridge, Charles H. 249
Cameron, George 147
  Hattie 147
Camp, Charles F. 227
Campbell, Abraham 140
  Archibald 130 Arthur C.
  261 Bertie 65 Cleo 109
  Dave 173 Earle E. 202
  Ellen 233 Estella K.
  261 E.H. 22 George F.
  130 Hassie 33
  Henderson C. 261
  Infant 173 Jack 245
  James 27 James J. 122
  Jane 140 Jessie 43
  John 245 John (Mrs) 245
  Josephine 64 J.F. 202
  Lizzie 101 117

Campbell (continued)
  Louize 52 Mary C. 2
  Mary N. 77 Nora 124
  Rebecca 255 Sallie 175
  Susa 239 S.B. 140 184
  209 246 261
  William 140 261
  W.A. 203 W.A. (Mrs) 203
  W.F. 202
Cane, Raymon 18
Cannon, Elbert M. 95
  Hettie 203
  Maynard 193 195
  Minnie 167 M.S. 167 173
  187 199 203 218
  Patrick 95 Wilmer 203
Canny, Ethel 58
Canter, Eugenie 102
  Mary 226
Carathen, John 127
Carathers, David 35
Carbley, Newton 100
  Richman 100
Carder, Sam 226
  Samuel A. 226
  William 69
Cardwell, Troy E. 198
  T.W. 198
Carethers, Sarah E. 132
Carey, Elijah 68
  Henry 169 Joseph 169
  J.M. 169
Carigar, Lizzie 196
Carlton, Nettie 92
Carmack, Mary M. 90
  Sarah 9
Carmichael, Mary 168
Carmichel, James W. 35
Carmicle, Mary J. 200
Carr, Alford 100
  Elizabeth 127

Carr (continued)
  Fannie B. 201
  Henry H. 100
  James H. 90 John 165
  John H. 148 J.M. 86
  Paul B. 100
  Sallie E. 220
Carrell, Charles 98
  James W. 98
Carrier, R.R. 102
  Sallie 87 Thomas 102
  William H. 102
Carriger, Lizzie 176
  Milton 27
Carroll, Cintha 224
  Earnest 262 Elbert 182
  George 51 182 205
  Infant 21 43 182
  Jesse 197 J.W. 43 182
  Magie 37 Mat 182
  Matilda 245 Vernia 179
  Vina 197 205
Carson, Brookins 233
  Creacy 205 Dick 94
  Ed 215 James 94 Joe 214
  Mary 98 Robert 214
  Clarence 128 Cloyd 120
  Mary 98 Robert 214
Carter, Clarence 128
  Cloyd 128 Cora 69
  Eliga 255 Ella M. 149
  Fannie 179 Frank 246
  F.A. 216 George F. 118
  Lillie M. 118
  Margaret 115 Martha 198
  Martha I. 156 Mary 112
  210 Mary A. 118
  Philip J, 255 Sadie 246
  Venie 59 William 179
Cartwright, Mary 172
Carver, Robert 127

Carwood, Maggie E. 63
Caseday, Glena C. 184
  James 184
Cash, Adie 234 Fry 245
  Ira 204 Jessie 253
  Martha 244 Nancy 183
  Nellie 253
Casper, Maude 198
Cassady, James 170
Caudill, Etta 239
Cauvins, Etta C. 146
Cercy, Blanch 263
  Buran 245 David 245
  Eliza 245 Infant 245
  James 245
Chandess, __ 190
Chandler, Archie R. 24
  Elizabeth 164 Lula 256
  Zachariah 164
Channafin, H.A. 261
  Patrick 261 Andrew 265
  Susan 265
Chapel, Francis C. 149
  J.L. 149
Chappelle, William J. 225
Charlton, E.T. 151
  Sallie 151
Chase, Crinny 222 Edith 2
  John 222 Nancy 102
  Nila M. 11 Ollie 132
  Sarah 260
Chatman, Infant 82
  James 102 106 J.A. 120
  162 Nora B. 106
  Richard 120 Virgie 36
Chesser, John 55
  Elizabeth 8 Richard 149
Childress, J.M. 79
Chinoth, James 26
Chinouth, C.W. 143
  Richard 143 William 143

Christ, John Jr. 165
Christenburg, Alice 60
  Ada 87 Alice 87
Christie, Florence 98
  Kennith 49 Jasper N. 31
Chunewth, Charles 234
  M.E. (Mrs) 234
Church, Bessie 218
  Lee 253 Virgil 253
Clark, __ 257 Bob 243
  Brownie 4 Elbert J. 171
  Elizabeth 175 Ely 175
  George 226 Geo. A. 171
  Henderson 229
  Ira N. 175 Jacob 147
  Joe 38 John 247
  Joseph L. 245 J.F. 238
  J.L. (Dr) 89 Lizzie 18
  Mary 147 M.E. 258
  Nancy 4 Robert 247
  Sarah 174 Will 243
Clarke, Isaac 22
Clauson, Fannie M. 202
  James B. 202 Ben 252
Clawson, James B. 194
  Jim 252 William 194
Clay, Francis 21
  Henry 153
Clayde, Barte 7
Cleek, Jaohnathan 89
Clemons, Dora 190
  Infant 190 Roy 190
Clevinger, Leotis 62
Click, Catherine 95
  Jack 180 Will 68
Clift, William 191
Clineas, Maggie 184
Cloud, T.J. (Mrs) 29
Cloyd, Bessie 110
  Blanch 7 Infant 101
  119 208 James 178

Cloyd (continued)
  Joe 101 J.M. 164
  Maggie 170 Nellie 164
  Roy 119 Will 208
Coaly, Minnie 202
Coff, Sarah E. 108
Coffey, Henry 238
Coffman, David M. 139
  John 218 J.F. (Mrs) 107
  Mary E. 124
Coggins, Nathan 213
Cogins, Nanie 246
Cokelet, Isaac D. 206
Colbertson, Winston 117
Coldwell, __ 26
Cole, Clyde 14 Frank 119
  Gay 194 John 228
  J.H. 119 Mattie 228
  Omer C. 119 Rena 252
  Ross 119 Soloman 211
  Zachary T. 150
Coleman, John 249
Collet, Lizzie 142
  Mariah 263
Collette, Charles 144
  Emily 144 Malcome 21
Colley, Leon H. 112
Collier, Daok 119
  George 230 G.T. 119
  Mahala 6 Martha 119
  Minnie 230
Collins, Bailey 158
  Bordie M. 146 Coy J. 27
  Fannie 119 Fannie B. 27
  Infant 252 Isaac 244
  James 31 244 Jesse 185
  J.M. 146 214 Lena 224
  Malissa 198 Mamie 240
  Nancy J. 244 Sam 252
  Stephen 218 Will J. 240
Combs, Elijah 95 E.J. 95

Combs (continued)
  Marry A. 44
  William E. 95
Conklen, Andrew J. 111
  Hagen 111
Conley, __ 209 J.A. 209
  Lafayette 209 Lydia 209
  Mary 5 M. Ellen 163
Connely, John W. 235
Conner, Hassie 61
Connor, Eva 237 Henry 237
  Henry C. 235 John 245
  J.A. 251 Sarah 245
Constable, Carry 1
  James 110 Lois C. 110
  Nellie L. 47
Cook, Anderson 74
  Cherry M. 74 Eddie 74
  Ethel 73 George H. 117
  Harrison (Mrs) 219
  James D. 137 Jenie 74
  Lillie M. 137
Cooper, __ 210
  Edgan H. 96 Isaac 221
  Jane 251
Copas, Martha 142
Copass, Annie M. 40
  E.C. 183 Ludice 261
Copeland, Mattie 219
Copney, John 33
Copp, Grace 174
  Infant 140 Jacob 120
  John 120 Johnathan 196
  Walt 140
Corathurs, Myrtle 189
Corby, Laura 190
Cornell, Maggie 149
Cornett, Elizabeth D. 221
  Margaret 221
  Montgomery 221
Corson, Infant 35

Corson (continued)
  Lewis 35 Nora E. 232
Couch, Alice 251
Coudler, Sarah 238
Couri, Penelope 153
Courtes, Mary 227
Covington, Martha 189
  Wiley 189
Cox, __ 265 Betsy 163
  Charles W. 177
  Elizabeth 205
  Elvisa 152 Ezeke 255
  E.L. 170 Fred 86
  George B. 55
  Hester M. 187 I.W. 187
  Jane 230 Jessie M. 61
  John D. 284 J. Ada 199
  J. Mat 205 Laura 154
  Lena M. 170 Mahlow 255
  Margaret 107 Mary A 241
  Matthew 141 Mattie 11
  Robert E. 141 Sam F 241
  Virginia B. 204
  Willie 67
Craft, James 229
  Sarah 180
Crane, Mike 259
Crapo, Moses 136
Crawford, __ 237
  Claudie 191 Florida 222
  Georgia 222 Ida 200
  Jake 101 Lola B. 222
  Mary 195 M.G. 192
  Nathan E. 101
  Richard 45 Sarah E. 145
Crayle, Charles 8
Creacy, George W. 229
Creasey, Allen 67
  Bertie 37 Clay 30
Creswich, Walter 145
Crews, Charles R. 242

Crews (continued)
  C.R. 242
Critsinger, Susana 244
Crocker, E.E. 196
Crockett, William 173
Crookshank, Eliza M. 193
  James A. 65
Cropf, Jacob 152
Crosby, O.K. 202 Ward 202
  Ward (Mrs) 202
Cross, Ben H. 12
  Elizabeth 188
  Jackson L. 95 J.H. 95
  J.W. 258 Katherine 258
  Sarah A. 172
Crosswhite, Melvin 204
  Rebecca 204
Crouch, Alfred M. 89
  Cloe M. 176 Decator 30
  George H. 124 James 89
  Jane G. 30 Joseph 124
  Luceil 37 Myra 148
  Nora 257 Paul 251
  Robert 251 R.H. 251
  Sudie 83 William 257
  William B. 124
Crouse, Sussie 113
Crow, Infant 228
  Martha 44 Phoebe 84
  Phoebe M. 81 R.B. 228
  Thomas C. 166
Crowell, J.W. 56
Croyal, Jodie 190
Crumbley, Edd 50
Crumley, B.M. 224
  Daniel 185 D.J. 70
  Infant 224 Jacob G. 237
  James 237 J. 31
  J.C. 219 Mary E. 60
  Mary J. 189 M.L. 185
  T.K. 237 William 190

Crumm, __ 154
Crump, J.P. 212
  Mary D. 212
Crusenberry, John 49
Crutsinger, Nancy 189
Culberson, Haney 25
Culbert, Mary 232
Culverson, Waieta 3
Cummings, Jane R. 127
Cunningham, Barney 70
  Charles H. 181
  Elizabeth 8 Lizzie 166
  Martha 106 Mary J. 259
  Thomas 259
Curtis, A.C. 102 A.M. 157
  169 Delia B. 157 169
  Emeline 208 E.C. 243
  Fannie 102 Henry 243
  James 100 John 117
  Mattie E. 100 M.G. 243
  Nova 28 Rachel 194
Cushing, Frederick H. 238
Dalli--, Florence 38
Dalton, Mose 129
Daniel, Geneva 187
  Greenberry 233
  Riley B. 233 Mattie 153
Darden, Laura M. 144
Dardy, Nancy 103
Daugherty, F.S. (Mrs) 250
  T.S. 250 William 258
Davenport, David 145
  Elice W. 19 Henry L 104
  Isom 145 Judge 93
  Lizzie 93 Lockie 192
  M.N. 126 Richard 104
Davidson, Infant 91
  James 91 J.A. 94
  Lizzie 94 Mildred 21
  Samuel 74
Davis, Alexander R. 165

Davis (continued)
  Bell 213 Charles 154
  Cordia 193 Ida 160
  Infant 76 77 James 77
  John 213 Luna 145
  Mary P. 154 Mollie 174
  Paul 53 Phillip 145
  Sam 76 Susan 130
  Tom 34 William 69
Dawson, Audrey R. 172
  Clema 85 E.S.(Capt) 172
Day, Anderson 206
  James A. 206 Julia 176
  Maggie 206 Mary E. 137
Deadrick, E.L. (Dr) 264
  Jake 196 John F. 264
Deakin, John 197
  Nancy C. 197
  R.E. (Rev) 197
Deakins, __ 131 225
  Acksie 246 Ashia 110
  Cora V. 39 Elizabeth
  109 Henry 62 John 67
  J.J. 206 Vernia S. 139
  Wilham J. 206 W.M. 44
Dearmond, Henry 167
  Infant 103 J.G. 103
Decker, Charles F. 97
  R.H. 97 Thomas C. 131
  Violet V. 131
Deen, James 193
Deglette, Leon 235
Deloach, Matilda 38
Demary, Martha V. 202
DeMichael, Charles 244
  Phebe 244
Dempsey, Edward 187
  John 69
Denney, May B. 188
Denny, Thersa 55
Densmore, Bell 160

Densmore (continued)
    Sarah 172 W.H. 172
Dent, Mary 176
Denton, Arthor 39
    D.B. 206 Henry 206 262
    John F. 262 Julia 265
    Sarah L. 73
    William H. 206
Depew, Carmel L. 183
    Cecil 80 David F. 264
    E.S. 265 John 264
    J.M. 219 William 183
Desantes, Carrie 88
Devault, Jacob 248
    James M. 188
    Matilda 175 Mattie 223
    Nancy 139 Wildon W. 36
    William E. 188
    William V. 248
Dickason, Elizabeth 132
Dickemon, David 126
Dickens, Isaac 3
Dickenson, Garfield 251
    Selma 251
Dickerson, Martha 6
Dickey, M.W. (Mrs) 34
Dickinson, Garfield 206
    Infant 206
Dickison, Bernie 224
    Garfield 224
Dickman, Cora 185
Dickson, Bonnie 58
    Flora E. 223 Glennie 58
    N.H. 223 S.C. 223
Diddle, D.E. 146
Diehl, C.H. 231
    David 231 Samuel T. 231
Diemenlle, Anita D. 167
Dilingham, Mary 51
Dillow, Henry A. 61
    H.N. 157 Ilie 237

Dillworth, James A. 252
    James O. 184
    Mary E. 184
    Oscar F. 178
Dilworth, Charles E. 132
    James A. 132
Dimon, Henry 197
Dipple, George W. 100
Dippre, Christopher 152
Dishner, G.H. 209
    G.K. 180 Katherine 180
Dixon, Delia 161
    Sallie 167
Dobbins, Andy 166
    Hannah 166 Lizzie 173
    Lucretia 154
Dodson, Angie 138
    Lawrence 135 Percy 135
Donnelly, Joseph C. 169
Donohue, Matthew 101
Dooley, William 237
Dope, Margaret 203
Dorney, Nathan H. 217
Dosser, James E. 210
    Mary A. 210
Dotson, Mary A. 257
Dougherty, Alfred 199
Douglas, Elbert 10
    Julia 240 Mollie 143
Dove, C.E. 209 Earl 209
Dowell, Marsh 76
Downer, Margie 132
Doyle, Thomas 182
Drain, Dewy 160 James 160
Drai--, Marcella 50
Droke, Martha 158
Druit, Robert 211
Duarty, __ 219
Dudley, Haywood 254
Duffield, Edgar 234
    Martha 1 Nora 1

Dugan, David 181
  Hugh 247
Dugger, __ 194 Edna 166
  Paul T. 142 Sarah 182
  Thomas 142
Dulaney, Achsah 248
  C.D. 203 E. 210
  E.D. 152 154
  Glennie 203 John W. 152
  154 Milton 152 154
  Nannie 210 Orpha 19
  R.W. 155
Dulany, Millie 133
Dun, Sarah 169
Dunbar, Infant 141
  Isaac N. 13
  M.F. 141 202
Duncan, George R. 180
  Jake 101 John 262
  Joseph 68 Joseph D. 262
  Maggie B. 213 Nelse 213
  Rice 180 Rosa 248
  Rosanna 156
Dunham, Henry 103
  Martin N. 192
Dunn, Amanda 138
  Clinton 240
  Dennis H. 147
  Infant 240 John 119 139
  Margaret 202 Mary 195
  Rhoda E. 6 Robert E 265
  Sabrie 170 Will 265
Durant, Henry P. 225
Durham, Adah 89
  Charles 162 Ellen 151
  Emma S. 162 E.M. 176
  Infant 89 Jessie 257
  Lillie 176 Mary 257
  Roan 162 Thomas 89
  T.N. 151
Durrell, Gardner C. 198

Dwyer, William 150
Dyer, Charlie D. 25
  James P. 143 John A. 88
  John H. 143 Mary 246
  Mary E. 127
Dykes, Abraham 151
  G. 248 Mable 141
  Nellie 248
D--, Ina 22
Eakin, Edgar E. 191
  Harry 191
Eames, Marietta 6
Earnest, Tate L. 59
Earp, Homer F. 241
  J.W. 241 Paul 49
Eastridge, Mary D. 178
Eden, Barbara 183
  Nathaniel 183
Edens, Eugene 155
  Infant 155
Edward, Sam 148
Edwards, Allen 207 208
  B.L. 113 Harrison 207
  Howell 115 Infant 113
  Jerry 64 Lizzie 98
  Martha 208 R.L. 113
  Sam 148 Vista 224
Eickhorn, John 101
Eliott, Martha 100
Elkins, Daniel 199
Eller, Elizabeth 145
Eller, Peter 108
Elliot, George 48
Elliott, Charles H. 171
  Finetta 224 Mike 231
  Mira 223
Ellis, Angia 191
  Frank 160 Gladys 87
  Gustavia 115 H. 115
  H.G. 242 H.H. 25
  Infant 107 175

Ellis (continued)
  James 191 John 115
  Joseph 242 Litia 142
  L.A. 242 Maggie 225
  Maggie M. 160
  Marlin 59 Martha 143
  175 Mary 87 Patsy 108
  S.B. 61 Vollie 107
  Wiley 175
Ellsworth, Catherine 167
Elmendorf, Mary 214
Elrod, David 115
  W.C. 115 117
Elsea, Mary E. 215
Elswick, Infant 234
  Jiles 100 Will 234
Emmert, Andrew J. 127
  Hester 21 23
  Marie E. 127
English, Elizabeth 101
Engomar, Joseph 168
Ensor, Ruth E. 156
  William 70
Epperly, Mary 105
  Nancy 106
Ervin, Dicie 38
  Hattie 147 James 27
  Thomas J. 133
Ervion, David J. 133
Erwin, Eliza 248
  Elizabeth 135 Emery 204
  Georgia 129 Infant 204
  Jacob 217 Mary 129
  Samuel 141 Samuel B 141
  Thomas 129 William 135
Estep, Aletha 227
  Elen 215 Emanuel 16
  John 227 Millie 43
  Moses R. 73 Sallie 244
  Sarah 213
Estepp, Moses R 73

Estes, Jack 239 Lucy 239
  Sarah 225
Evans, A.J. 169
  Charlie 220 David 113
  194 Eliot 244 George 99
  220 Henrietta 240
  Judith 113 Julia 122
  Julina 244 Laura 220
  Louisa 184 Mary E. 169
  Oma P. 263 Perry 99
  Stoward 78 Terry S. 244
  Thomas 22 78 Will 122
Everet, Margaret 188
Everett, Gorden 253
  M.L. 253
Fagans, Salley 46
Fain, Infant 233 Mary 233
Fair, __ 198 Selma M. 111
  William M. 111
Fanning, Cora E. 24
Farmer, Horace L. 150
Faw, Charles 49
Feathers, Carl 48
  Carl E. 228
  Carl L. Jr. 228
  Fronia 168 Infant 20 48
  Lucinda 142 Mary 242
  Mary C. 168 Nannie 100
  Wallie 38
Featherstone, J.M. 168
February, Mariah S. 9
Febuary, A.D. 163
  James A. 163 L.W. 163
Fellers, D.M. 13 Eva 140
  Frank 248 Harrison 120
  Infant 120 248
Felts, Ethel R. 25
  Ralph 50
Felty, Melvina 182
Ferguson, Cora 126
  Courtney 128 Ester 256

Ferguson (continued)
  Ester A. 183 G.W. 126
  185 Harris 156
  Howard T. 128 Jake 95
  Joe 156 J.F. 156
  Lucy 185 Margaret 139
  Polly M. 151 Robert 246
  Sarah M. 195 Thomas 90
  Thomas P. 246
  Virgie 178
Ferrin, Frank 217
Fess, Tempie 58
Fields, Bessie 135
  Charles 214 Charlie 198
  Eliza 214 Kemper 198
  Leonard 208 Minnie 253
  Nancy 99 Samantha 208
  Susie 58
Filips, Elizabeth 110
Filler, Harrison 174
  Infant 174
Filox, Virgie 247
Fine, David V. 115
  D.J. 156 Fhibe 248
  Frank 171 236
  Frank C. 230
  Joseph 200 Orpha 152
  154 Ross 115
  Russell 190 R.A. 115
Fink, Lucy 70
Finley, Florence 178 251
  Francis G. 178
  Hattie 178 186
  John 186
Finnell, James B. 223
Fish, Polly 208
Fisher, Frederick 29
  H.C. 176 Infant 176
  James C. 173
  William 136
Fitzgerald, George 167

Fitzgerald (continued)
  Geroge 173 247
  G.A. 143 208
  Michael 146
Fizer, Maggie 231
Fleck, William 92
Fleenor, Isac L. 205
  Pierce 205 220
  David B. 186 John 209
  Ross R. 186
Fletcher, Dave 208
  John 58 Martha 207
Fleunstein, Alexander 116
Folson, Mary 202
Forbes, Mary E. 228
Ford, Ben 173
  Carie M. 148 Cassie 120
  Curtis 264 Dee M. 197
  Elvira 61 George 227
  George W. 176 Isaac 43
  James 123 236 237
  James M. 250 Jess 250
  John A. 35 John C. 152
  154 John T. 197
  J.C. 236 237 J.H. 83
  J.R. 152 Lauria 183
  Lela M. 61 Lena 189
  Martin 18 Mary 66 176
  Robert 154 Ruth 264
  R.R. 231 Sarah A. 72
  Smith 61 William T. 51
  Willie 50 W.A. 227
  W.D. 135
Forrest, John 258
Fortson, __ 153
Fosdick, Charles H. 224
Foster, Abe 68 Arvel 24
  Elen 24 Elizabeth 233
  Finley 229 John 54
  Lena 56 Marion 119
  Mary M. 119 Watesil 42

Foster (continued)
  W.R. 177
Foust, C.H. 157
  Daniel 157
Fowler, Troy 11
Fox, Adam C. 89 Bessie 3
  Daniel 89 183
  Elizabeth 45 Mary 83
  Mary A. 37 51
  Mary F. 245 O.J. 174
  Rena R. 24 Sallie 183
Foyster, Elen 245
  T.B. 245
France, Chester 250
  D.E. 136 250
  Infant 250
Francis, Andrew 46
  Martha 179
Frank, Charles 99
Franklin, Mary 244
Frasier, Frank 244
Freberg, Marion 149
Freeman, Edith 18
  Margaret 207 Vestie 39
Frieson, Tony 177
Frink, Luman 238
Frisbee, Abram 228
Fry, Julie 201 Mary 192
  Sabery 147
Frys, Tony 177
Fulkerson, Frederick 235
  Infant 20 77 198
  Martin 77 M. 198
  Nettie B. 40 Stella 257
  William H. 11
Fullwood, A.J. 135
  Infant 135
Fulmer, George W. 36
  John W. 183
Fulwiler, Alvin 162
  John 162 Nancy 162

Furches, Daisy 90
  F.W. 201 M.S. 90
Furchess, Charley 213
Furguson, Frank 51
  Franklin 151 Lucy 104
  Susan 63
Gaby, Isaac 115
Gains, Gicy 260
  Nancy 115 Richard 260
Galaspy, Alfred 119
Galloway, G.W. 231
  Noah 172 Robert T. 123
  Robert W. 37 R.M. 231
  Samuel 185 Theodore 123
  Thomas 83 185
Gamblin, Jennie 243
Gammon, Jessie 187
Gann, Mary 101
Garber, __ 156 Isaac 155
  Mae 109 S.H. 65
  William A. 155
Gardner, Charles 73 104
  Hiram G. 242 Infant 91
  145 Isaac 91 James 107
  John 107 Katheline 145
  Lula 57 Sallie 104
Gark, Matilda E. 144
Garland, Lavina 203
  Mary 119 Nancy 89
  Polly 194
Garman, A.L. 185
Garriety, Maggie 107
  Maud 53
Garron, Craig 93
  Curtis 93 Sallie 153
Garst, Infant 109
  John H. 109 Sarah 37
Garvin, J.M. 239 245
  Nellie E. 245
Geagley, Anna 23
Geier, George 123

Geisler, Hugh 130
  Nancy 33 N.H. 130
  William H. 130
Gelaspy, Alferd 222
  Minerva 222 Preston 222
Gentile, Lewis 165
George, Anna L. 208
  J.F. 208 Mary 172
Gerhart, Louis C. 136
Gibbs, Frank 74
Gibson, __ 143 Anna 208
  Arthur A. 105
  Braswell 208
  Cynthia D. 256
  Florence 219 250
  Frank L. 220 George 180
  Hazel V. 169 Henry 208
  H.M. 199 Infant 208
  John E. 169
  J. Pierce 220
  J.E. (Mrs) 169
  J.F. 202 Louise 204
  Mary 129 Mary C. 199
  Mattie 162 Pearl T. 183
  P.P. 143 Starling 148
  Susan 198 Thomas 180
  Thomas J. 105 T.J. 220
  Walter 73
  William 38 180 183
  Zora M. 202
Gifford, L. 111
Giles, J.W. 250 Pearl 250
  Rosie 223
Gilespie, Cora 253
Gillespie, Caroline 132
  Charles A. 174
  Harry 174 Harvy 123
  Landon 123 Lillie 58
  Martha 123 Robert 174
  Robert Jr. 16 Will 253
Gilliam, Infant 265

Gilliam (continued)
  J.M. 265
Gilligan, Edward 96
Gillis, Infant 216
  William 216
Gillspie, George 222
  Marriah A. 216
Gilman, Frank 75
  Nancy 105 Emily 108
  Nancy C. 179
Gipson, David 262
  John 262
Gist, Hannah 163
Gitt, __ 95
Givens, Georgia 23
Glass, Daniel 36 212
  Polly 216
Glean, Jim 34
Glenn, Lizzie 58
Glover, Callie 114
  F.M. 193 John T. 112
  J.C. 180 Nannie 226
  Pollie 104 Susan 188
  195 William J. 180
Goad, Infant 195
  Nate 195 265 Rosa 264
Gobble, Blain 223
  Commadore 250
  Grover 223 John 250
  Maggie 57 Mahala 126
Goble, Henry 215
Godsey, Andrew 94
  Bessie 214 Charles 94
  Daisey 94 John 94 135
  Nauia 55 Robert 135
  Ruth 55 Sarah 114
Goff, Charles H. 105
Goforth, Minnie 184
Goins, Carl 75 Guy 254
  Richard 254
Golden, Laura 189

Goltz, Hugh 181
Gooch, Mollie 198
  Will 129
Good, Agil 244
  Charley 102 D.H. 138
  Infant 102 Jacob M. 199
  Louise 161 Mary 48 212
  Onie L. 19 Raymond 244
  Sam 263 Susan 226
  William D. 80
Goodman, Catherine 110
  Jacob 258 Mary G. 60
Gossett, James 228
Gourley, Adeline 129
  Walter 101
Graham, John 201 Johnie 5
  J.S. 174 Mary E. 195
  Samuel B. 201
  Sara C. 174 Willie 5
Grant, William 161
Gray, Anderson, J. 61
  Burnie F. 11 Dennie 209
  E.D. 53 Fred 240
  Harriett 220 Infant 158
  Infant 158 248
  John L. 158 Josie 44
  Louisa 128 Mary S. 132
  Melvina 67 Robert E. 28
  W. Boyd 132
Graybeal, John C. 71
Graybill, Melvina 146
Grayham, Elia 52
Grear, Will 22
Green, Charlie 201
  Harrison 201 Hobart 62
  Irwin 59 Lula B. 200
  Manson 188 Mary 90
  Paul C. 73 William 188
Greene, ___ 179 Ethel 244
  L.F. 108
Greenfield, Delia 42

Greenfield (continued)
  R.P. 42
Greenlee, Anna P. 8
  Annie 223 Charles H 130
  Clara 64 Fannie 130
  Garfield 195 Jessie 33
  Sam 195 Sherman 195
  S. 89
Greenway, D.S. 1
  Eldridge 127 Eveline 24
  Fannie 136 Hester E 213
  Melvina 5 Sarah 127
Greer, Adam 20 Dora J 239
  Ettie 235 S.C. 239
Gregg, Will 22 259
  Worley 259 P.L. 153
Gregran, Carl 181
Gresham, John F. 245
  Matilda 50
Griffen, Joe 202
Griffith, Amos L. 259
  Henry 194 Jasper B 202
Grills, Iva L. 141
  W.T. 141
Grimes, Guy 149
  Harich 255 Infant 149
  Katie 97
Grindstaff, Burnas 99
Gross, Edith 20
  Minnie 257
Grubbs, Alice G. 127
  A.S. 127
Grump, Caroline 33
Guinn, Bessie 179
  Captolia 234 George 234
  H.G. 179 J.M. 179
  Melda 241 Rosa 241
  Sarah 129
Guire, Elizabeth 209
Gulliver, William H. 128
Gump, Abraham 260

Gump (continued)
　David 260
Gunter, Infant 173
　James 173
Gurvin, Sidney 143
Guthrie, C.W. 43
Guy, Zachariah T. 112
Guyer, Catherine 189
　Katie 229
G__, Elizabeth 77
Hackney, Belle 252
Haga, Mary 196
Hail, __ 234
Haines, Dicea 254
　George 260 Mary T. 111
Hale, Amos 85 Belle 105
　Calidona 110
　Chinouh 102 Cinthie 124
　Cora E. 30 Eliga 260
　Emma 42 Geldra E. 188
　George 98 176 Hany 162
　Henry 247 H.N. 99
　Infant 30 37 67
　Jesse W. 261
　Jessie E. 31
　Jettie 180 John 105
　Julia 176 J.A. 182
　Lizzie 230 Maggie 27
　Mary J. 107 Maud M. 85
　McGagey B. 261
　Mildred 260 Minnie 236
　Robert 151 Robert G 265
　Smith 100 Sue 67
　Susana 256 Thomas 36
　William 230
　William C. 36
Hall, Cora 99 Dolly 118
　E.B. 36 E.D. 83
　Harvey 79 Joseph 148
　loucinda 220 Lucy 239
　Martha 173

Hall (continued)
　Martha E. 148
　Nancy 205 Patsy 79
Halse, Mary 68
Hamby, Allen 231 Wiley 37
Hamilton, Ida M. 142
　J.A. 107 110 175 226
　R.C. 173 Sallie 97
Hamit, Nancy 206
Hamitt, Eddie 85
　Ramon 82
Hamler, Texas 166
Hammer, Bettie 221
　Lou 209 Nola 210
Hammet, __ 102 Fannie 170
　Joseph 119 Reese 190
　William 119
Hammett, Ezekiel 155 178
　John 178 Joseph 238
Hammit, Elizabeth 36
Hammitt, Lena 113
Hammond, Elizabeth 114
Hampton, Acie 135
　H.M. 135 Jessie M. 135
　Mary 262 S.L. 27
Handrop, Henry 102
Haney, G.A. 258
　Infant 258
Hangleter, Henry 259
Hankle, Luke 69
Hanks, Katherine 88
Hannagan, Owen 254
Harden, __ 94
Hardie, Jessie 163
Hardin, Daisey 215
　George U. 147
　George W. 147
　Hooker 215 Lizzie 91
Hardy, John 74
Harell, Waits 247
Harkleroad, Dorothy 185

Harlan, J.E. 83
Harmon, A.L. 116
  A.L. Jr. 116 Hugh 92
  Jim 123 Sallie 207
Harr, Ada M. 32
  Henry 254
Harrell, Abbie 38
  George E. 247
  Vessie 81
Harris, Adoline 143
  Charles 188 Ed 234
  E.B. 232 Grace 69
  Isaac 181 James M. 139
  James Y. 139 Joseph 218
  Lula 146 Mary 139
  Nile 71 Rebecca 94
  Sarah 148 Teddy 232 234
  William H. 168
  William P. 168
Harrison, Daniel 84
  Eliza 255 Herman 104
  Infant 84 John W. 141
  J.M. 148 Lucinda 148
  Mattie 84 Samuel 259
Hartman, Asenth 126
  Elizabeth 231
  Francis E. 85
  J.W.S. 265 Manervia 265
  Nancy E. 151
Hartnett, Timothy 121
Hartsell, Ray 111
Harvey, Isaac 134
  Jennie 105 Maeria 39
  Mary B. 168
  Trephenia 183
Harwood, Dessie 37
  Louisa 12
Hashberger, C.E. 238
  George R. 238
Haskell, Foster M. 197
Hastings, Anna 52

Hatcher, Ira S. 159
  Malinda 102
Hatley, Amanda 242
Hauck, J.E. 138
Hauk, Amanda 217
  C.M. 131 217 Rosie 131
Haun, Ed 122
Hawes, Charlie 263
  Infant 263 Sudie 263
Hawk, Infant 67 Mary 252
  William H. 134
Hawkins, Ella 265
Hawood, J.G. 221
Haws, Anna 79 Charlie 207
  Frank 85 Infant 85
  Julia M. 11 Mable 207
  Mary A. 73 Ollie 85
  William H. 53
Hayes, Bell 175
  Charles A. 191
  Elizabeth 21 G.C. 172
  Infant 172 J.N. 187
  Nellie B. 191
Haynes, Edwin D. 125
  Martha 99 Mary J. 201
Hayse, Charles 165
Head, Carrie 155
  Clarence A. 45
  Infant 155 Jane E. 236
  Walter 155
Headrick, Martha E. 128
Healy, Patrick 239
Heaton, Bettie 259
  Fannie 231 J.S. 231
Hedgepath, Clarence 37
Helbert, S.D. 18
Helsom, Lucy M. 77
Helton, Ida 216
  John H. 226 J.H. 216
  Margaret 69 Robert 163
  William C. 226

Henderson, Cordelia C 120
   Irabela 160 O.P. 11
   Stuart 22
Hendrix, Blain 203
   Nannie E. 203
Henley, Alzenia 178
   Francis 245 Joseph 126
   Joshua 174 Thomas 126
   Wiley 52
Hensley, Deborah 139
   Dicy 40 Eirett 184
   Francis 196 Fred 41
   Lillian 184 Lissa 170
   L. Dora 248 Mary 244
   Mary L. 121 Matthew 170
   Thomas S. 177 Ula 170
   William 177 222
Henson, Clarence 192
   Clyde 260 Frank 92
   Hazel 59 Infant 30 260
   J.J. 192 Lucile 264
   Robert 49
Herman, Charles 146
Herrigton, Kern 259
   Timothy 259
Hess, Mary 180
Hester, Charles W. 153
   John 153 J.M. 153
Hetton, Piny 62
Heubrick, John C. 207
Heues, Sophia 148
Hewet, Nancy J. 107
Hibarger, Martha 115
Hice, Gertrude 144
   Ida 185 Infant 144
Hickman, Nathan 237
   Walter 80 William 145
Hicks, Dennis 78
   Frank 1 Franklin 81
   Henry L. 47 James 121
   Julia 203 Louise 119

Hicks (continued)
   Matilda E. 119
Hilbert, Anna 95 A.T. 70
   Jake 95 John 164
   John B. 255
   Laura M. 160
   Paul B. 255 Rachel 233
   Rettie 45 Robert 62
   Samuel 13
Hill, Carolina 241
   F.D. 226 Mose 214
   Nellie G. 214 Walter 64
Hillard, Mary 171
Hills, Joseph H. 263
Hilton, Joseph 54
   Samuel 28 Toy H. 86
Hinchman, Marcella L. 88
   Walter 88 Walton L. 88
Hines, John 171
Hinley, Maggie 2
Hite, Frank 230
   Howard 207 Hulie 240
Hix, Eli 198 James 198
Hobson, Coleman 228
   Martha 23 Mary 29
   Terry 228
Hodge, Annie 89 Anson 220
   Arch 248 G.W. 51
   Henry 31 James 116 226
   J.S. 89 Lizzie 248
   L.H. (Mrs) 163
   Martin K. 226 Mary 116
   Nathan L. 116
Hodges, Bettie 130
   Denver 12 Gentry 164
   George W. 164
   R.L. 164 209 Wade 209
Holden, Annie 92
Holder, H. 213 Steve 213
Holler, Andy 155
Holly, James 105

Holmes, Charles 211
  Cora L. 221
  George H. 100
  Jane 211 J.E. 221
  Mary 221 Mattie 211
Holt, Flora 240
  Leroy C. 218
Homes, Alexander 63
Honeycutt, Caroline 158
  Julia 192 Julius 192
  Sallie 203
Hook, Paul 128
Hoover, Elizabeth 128
Hope, W.L. 120
Hopper, Chrissie 67
  J.H. 257 Mary 250
  Mary A. 257
  Mattie B. 180
  Richard M. 80
Hopson, Isaac P. 203
  J.P. 203 William 203
Hord, Henry 152
Horne, Alice 71
Horton, Adie E. 172
  Agnes 208
  Arthur 154 208
  Bradis 104 172
  Doss 124 Infant 124 154
  James 91 Selma 91
  Vinie 242
Hoskins, Bell 251
Hoss, Calvin 110
  Glen E. 195
  Henry 110 142
  Howard 27 James 32
  John 55 J.W. 9
  Katheren I. 135
  Learry 122 Nancy J. 17
  Olerry 195 Pauline 122
  Rebecca D. 237 Ruth 88
Hoston, Syman 83

Houck, J.E. 227 Mable 227
Houlder, Mary 130
Hount, Nancy A. 71
Houston, George D. 103
  Grover C. 63
  James M. 170
  John W. 103 J.H. 235
  J.M. 38 Lessie M. 235
  Mary 57 Stephen 176
Howard, Abbie 38 Fred 251
  James 157 John J. 229
  Joseph 251
  Lillian E. 225
  Lula 157 Mary 45
  Robert T. 229
  Samuel B. 157 229
Howell, Alexander 93
  Robert 224
Howern, Charles 251
  David 251 Ella 108
  Lucy L. 190 Onnie 108
Howington, George 138
  W.P. 138
Howuthron, Elizabeth 113
Huack, Cassie 138
Huddle, Laura 206
Hudnall, M.A. 178
Huff, Eliza 112
  Harrison 112
  Preston 64
Huffine, Absolom 248
  Daniel 248 J.A. 115
  J.D. 144 Sarah P. 78
  Walter S. 248
Huffman, B.H. 210
  Henry C. 96 H. 96
  J.D. 96 Luce 211
  Samantha 71
Hughes, Bettie 184
  Fred H. 253
  Josephine 253

Hughes (continued)
  Mary 172 Sallie 189
  Thomas R. 253
Hughs, Rena P. 20
Hulbert, Alice 96
Hull, Lula 225
  Octavia S. 91
Hulse, Angie 105
  David 155 Franklin 180
  Ise 155 John 105 180
  Mary D. 72 Mattie 180
  Sarah E. 248 S.B. 155
Hulsey, Louisa 115
Humphrey, Charles 138
  H.H. 177 Jessie 172
  John S. 172 J.N. 172
  Mabel 51
Humphreys, Clyde D. 140
  C.C. 140 Frec 210
  G.W. 222 Henry 2
  Infant 210 John E. 15
  Leptitia 222
  Matilda 224 N.K. 129
  Sarah E. 68 W.H. 224
Humphries, A.J. 224
Hunphrey, Infant 138
Hunt, Addie 90 Alfred 243
  Anna M. 84
  Delcenia 257
  Elija 139 Jesse 108
  Martain 246 Samuel 142
  Uriah H. 108
  Walter A. 15
Hunter, Alfred 129
  Alice 129 Claude 40
  Frank 51 J.L. 34
  Pkebe 170 Tamer 228
Hurlbut, Alen 187
  Allen J. Jr. 187
Hurley, Effie 198
Hurst, Elizabeth 104

Hurt, Bessie G. 179
  Infant 179 Stuart 179
Hurty, Ben 218
Huskins, Emeline 215
Hustman, Mary 199
Hutchens, Mary A. 243
  O.D. 243
Hutchinson, John 263
Hux, __ 143
Hyatt, Susie 118
Hyder, __ 236 Blanch 241
  F.M. 193 John 99
  Mary A. 193 Mary E. 68
  S.J. 185 Vicie 121
  William H. 99
  William (Mrs) 99
Hylton, Florence 2
  Mollie 126
Hypshire, Silas 4
Hysinger, Martha 126
H--, Charles 76
Ingle, Elmynar E. 108
  Niles B. 142 Sam 212
  S.W. 142
Ingram, Clarence C. 187
  Jane 160
Ireland, William M. 210
Irvin, Jacob 217
  Margaret 151
Irwin, George 89
Isbel, Charles G. 185
Isenberg, Clyde 252
  I.U. 252 Stella 13
Ivans, Dexey 72
Jack, Robert W. 101
Jackson, __ 230 Arbel 102
  A.E. 97 Cardelia 192
  Eliza 241 Ellen 47
  General A.E. 126
  George 164 G.W. 260
  Henry C. 97 Jake 249

Jackson (continued)
　John 34　260 Kissie 250
　Lena 27　L.M. 142
　Mable 94　Marshall 241
　Mary E. 163　Nancy J 255
　Nora 44　Patel E. 102
　R.D. 142　R.M. 34
　Will 56
James, Ida M. 114
Jaynes, Clarence 106
　Infant 106
Jenkins, Bettie 245
　Elizabeth 84　Ellen 6
　Fuson 123　Marie 123
　Mary E. 164　Pearl 88
　Rosco H. 10　Willie 58
Jennings, J.S. 91
Jessie, Bertie 114
Jobe, J.P. 178
　William P. 178
Johnson, Albert 86
　Alfred 169　Anna B. 238
　Aurolia 149　Cecil 12
　Clara 102　Earnest 78
　Elsie 32　E.M. 264
　Hariet 146
　Hattie B. 169
　Henry 238　Hiram 12
　Infant 32　165　169
　James 1　168　178
　James H. 217　Jane 63
　J.J. 32　Loman 26
　Mary A. 179　Munroe 224
　Nancy 180　Nannie 159
　Nelson 149　Rachel 244
　Richard 169　Roy 264
　Steve 168　Viola 165
　Will 159
　William 207　215
　W.B. 249　W.B. Jr. 249
　W.R. 168

Johnston, Bell 87
Joiner, Sarah 122
Jolly, Mary 248
Jones, __ 109　Andy J. 239
　Bert 239　Charles H. 176
　Clara N. 124　Elbert 139
　Eugene 28　Herbert 263
　Herman 240　Homer 263
　Isaac 240　Jake 32
　Joe H. 124　John 265
　John B. 212　John H. 48
　John P. 197
　Julia A. 127
　J.H. 139　155　J.P. 98
　J.W. 220　Margaret 4
　Marthy M. 98　Mary 26　32
　Mary L. 98　M.C. 256
　Nannie M. 108　O.S. 109
　Redgley 50　Rillie 223
　Robert F. 154　Rufus 154
　R.R. 154　Sarah E. 139
　Sue 133　Tebartha 109
　T.S. 184　Virginia 141
　William 53　176
　W.H. 89
Jonnard, William A. 218
　W.A. 218
Jordan, Henry 137　163
　Mary 72　William W. 163
Juste, Herman 218
Justice, Lura 124
Kane, Charles 129
　Thomas E. 106
Kaney, William 210
Keeble, H.K. 140
　Robert H. 140
Keebler, Elizabeth 209
　John 196　Riley H. 11
　Will 196
Keefauver, Deborah 132
　James L. 12　John 97　139

Keefauver (continued)
  Nicholas 97 Shelton 97
  S.U. 257 Terry 257
Keen, __ 265 Amelia 9
  Bartha 224 Clive 221
  Elizabeth 182 Enic 238
  James M. 252
  James W. 221 Joanna 129
  Jonas 252 J.H. 115 116
  Mollie R. 82
  Robert 115 116
  Sallie 82
Keene, Angie 105
  M.V. (Mrs) 190
Keezel, William C. 66
Kegley, C.J. 49
  Ernest 193 Helen 193
Kehoe, Simon 118
Keller, Alexander 177
  John H. 177
  Nathan H. 133 Cordie 31
  Alex 34 Fartha 237
  Infant 138 John 219
  Lena 208 Louisa 219
  Mary 126 Riley H. 75
  Sarah 138 165
  Taylor 138 William 66
Kelly, __ 168 Lannie 154
  Sarrah 243 Stuart 232
  Taylor 243
Kelsey, Lena 141
Kennedy, Wilson 130
Kennell, Hattie 259
Kensey, Lou 229
Kent, Edward 35
Keplinger, Ana L. 164
  Mat 164
Kernick, Albert 103
Ketcham, Fred 79
Ketron, J.K. 50
Keys, Aaron 199

Keys (continued)
  Bessie M. 6 Billie 53
  Bob 184 Clarence C. 184
  Harrem W. 184 Infant 8
  156 James M. 184
  John S. 46 John T. 156
  John W. 199 Julia 106
  Lula V. 85 L.A. 72
  Mary 42 Mary J. 184
  Minnie 219 Niles 85
  Sarah E. 255
  Sarah M. 90
  William W. 255 W.H. 90
Kicker, Ernest 229
  Infant 229
Kilby, J.W. 240 Paul 240
Kilgore, George C. 254
  Infant 98 144
  Thomas 98 144
Killingsworth, Mary 226
Kimerly, Mary A. 14
Kimery, Mary E. 16
Kinchloe, Dicy A. 139
  George E. 195 J.J. 139
  Mary J. 195
Kindle, Emma 93 98
  Lauretta 192
King, Ed 241 Eliza 164
  Elizabeth 100 234
  Emma I. 241 Henry 122
  Jasper 213 Martha F 231
  Samuel G. 183 S.S. 183
  William H. 171 W.R. 135
Kinkade, Martha 56 86
Kinley, Martha 5
  Walter 53
Kinnick, Jacob 232
  John 232
Kiplinger, Anna B. 126
  Ethel 133
Kipplig, W.F. 91

Kirby, James 172
  Monroe F. 152
Kirkpatrick, __ 184
  Amanda F. 142 J.A. 32
  Mary 178 Samuel J. 9
  S. 142
Kirth, Jessie J. 60
Kite, Daniel C. 121
  Eliza 189 Evaline 207
  Hickman A. 189 H.R. 189
  Martha 121 Nimpson 121
  T.E. 207 William A. 189
  Willie B. 121
Kitzmiller, Grace 261
  Polly 226
Kleeper, Mary A. 11
  Jacob 184 John B. 184
  T.B. 184
Knipe, Ina B. 38
Koch, John 196
Koger, William J. 191
Koster, George W. 125
Krause, Susan 147 148
  Jacob 252 Martha J. 252
  Sauana 248
Kyker, Ernest 116
  Infant 68 Jackson 41
  Myrtle 1 Y.N. 149
K--, John 33
Lacey, Mattie C. 146
Lacy, Ester 138
  Everett 57 James A. 100
  John 121 Porter 84
  William J. 100
Lady, Nellie 94
Lafalett, D.F. 2
Laflin, Infant 81
Laingham, Infant 256
Lamkins, James 60
Lamons, Martha J. 172
Lamore, __ 113

Lamous, Mollie 116
  William 116
Landers, Bet 13 Bevie 13
  Viola 14
Landingham, Francis 7 59
Landis, J.F. 21
Lane, Berl 80 James 120
  Mary 95 155
Lang, Jeremiah 144
Langhrein, Julia A. 52
Langhren, Annie 28
Langstaff, John T. 137
Lanpher, Alfred 249
Lapman, Edward 99
Larimer, Chrisley 148
  Donnie 111 Hiram 148
Larkins, Thomas 256
Lausn, Mainard 41
Lawrence, Judy 161
Laws, Alexander 257
  Carrie 69 Infant 257
  Isaac 195 James 109
  John R. 195 Maggie 222
  Martha 135
Lawson, Edgar 21
  F.B. (Mrs) 111
  Grant Jr. 3 Joseph 125
  Susana A. 183
Leab, Bessie S. 106
  Infant 44 Oscar 44 106
Leach, Alice 186
  John 174 Johnie 248
  J.C. 213 J.T. 221
  Landeen S. 174
  Lillie G. 231
  Lucille 39 Mary A. 39
  Mary E. 78 Viner 39
  Will 231 W.H. 138
  W.T. 248
Leadford, Mary E. 44
  Susan 158

Leary, Andrew J. 191
Ledford, G.B. 158
  Sarah 235
  William C. 249
Lee, Benton 97 Carrie 208
  Edith G. 97 Minnie 167
  William 35
  William C. 105
  Zachariah T. 156
Leiber, Anna 163
Leins, Hary 42
Leiter, Rosa 260
Lenen, Elizabeth 29
Leonard, D. 138
  Elizabeth J. 259
  Ethan M. 193 Gladys 78
  Isaac 95 Jacob 166 227
  Louiza 95 Mattie 166
  Minnie 23 Norma 63
  Thomas 193 Vollie 95
Letsinger, William H. 223
Letteral, __ 108
Lewis, Henry J. 59
  Jasper N. 67 John 179
  Milburn 89 S.G. 211
  William 199
Liggett, __ 193
Light, Georgie H. 19
Lilley, Anie 185
Lilly, C.G. 48
  Melvina 176 Sarah A. 39
  Thomas 73
Lincolnfellow, T.S. 25
Lindsey, Albert W. 206
Ling, Frank 54
Link, Sallie 120
Lipps, Charles 174
  Infant 174 Sue 174
Lisenberry, George 260
  James 260
Lisenby, James 148

Lister, Ida 230
Little, __ 169 Amanda 157
  A.P. 85 Hesikiah 103
  Jacob 28 James K. 157
  John 103 157
Littleton, Lena 119
Loal, Alica 240
Lockner, Hannah 162
  Infant 157 James 157
  Joseph 157 Joseph P 206
  J.P. 201 Martin M. 90
  Mary J. 157 Mathas 170
  Mathas D. 170
Lockwood, George W. 168
Loflin, Jude 107
Long, Harvey G. 256
  James W. 152 Jim 260
  John 80 John H. 88
  R.A. 256 Will 260
  William G. 256
Longmire, Ella 122
  Ellen 195 Hannah 134
  Mary 250
Looper, Hazel 80 J.W. 138
Lopez, Antonio 145
Loris, Joseph N. 134
Louderbock, Daisey 94
Loudy, Mary E. 186
  Mollie 136 Nancy 136
  R.L. 136 Thad 186
Louis, Opal M. 186
  Will 186
Love, C.S. 213
  C.S. (Dr) 128 174 179
  216 D. White 132
  Ethel 107 Eva 160
  Henry 160 Jamie 59
  Lois 59 Lulcie 160
  Margaret R. 132
  Marion 211
  Mary E. 80 118 M.D. 107

Love (continued)
  William E. 211
Lovegrove, Albert 107
  Arley R. 190 Callie 107
  Ethel 106 Fannie 205
  J.F. 190 J.R. 190
  Ray 107 Robert 107
Lovel, Elizabeth 177
Lovelace, Infant 91
  Pat 91
Lovell, Marion 4
  Nannie 103
Low, James 23 Jennings 39
  John A. 210
Lowdy, Maggie 144
  Thomas 144 Ella 167
  Gaston P. 210
  Lucinda 222
Lowery, Hassie 201
  Lual 191 Maniard 47
Lowey, E.D. 138
  Robert 138 Nancy B. 156
Loyall, Florence 203
Loyd, Alice F. 149
  Ben 190 George N. 211
  Herald 16 Ida 230
  Lela 190 Mary E. 262
  Ray 81 Robert 211
  Robert C. 262
  Robert R. 47 R.B. 149
  Thomas 190 Vesta 211
  William 189
Lundy, Rosa 73
Lunsford, Andrew 130
  A.J. 228 Infant 130
  Mildred 228 Sarah 227
Lusk, Tennessee 33
Luster, John W. 65
Lustes, Samuel 84
Lutrett, W.M. (Mrs) 105
Luttrell, Bessie 210

Luttrell (continued)
  W.F. 210
Lyemore, James 113
Lyle, Ressa 56 Ruth 57
Lymer, Sam 147
Lynch, Jesse K. 256
  Rosco R. 256
Lyon, Eliza 154
Lyons, Infant 167
  J.R. 167
Lytle, Thomas 140
Lytte, Mary 70
Mabery, Ray M. 41
Mabry, Cora 137
Maden, Mary 62
  Sarah J. 109
Mahoney, Anne E. 122
  Cynthia 81 John 86
  Sarah E. 251
Malier, Mary 214
Mallicot, C.A. 116
  Lillie J. 116
Malone, Alfred 182
  James 182 Kate 214
  William 46
  Willie M. 57
Malonee, Infant 88
  Joe 88 J.M. 227
Maloney, __ 211
  Dililah 169 Will 169
Mangold, Julia A. 211
  J.M. 211
Maples, Johnson 225
Marble, Edward A. 136
Markland, Anderson 52
Markwood, Bertie 139
  D.D. 18 Eleanor 40
  Ester A. 139
Marrion, Mary 209
Marron, Arthur 186
Marshal, Rachel 149

Marshall, __ 151
  Hattie 70 Zell 70
Martin, Amanda 248
  Beulah 255
  Cornelius 105
  Fannie M. 109
  Hattie M. 11 Hazel 5
  Ida 80 Infant 51
  James 88 James G. 125
  James M. 218
  Jesse J. 219 John 139
  J. Mat 4 Louis T. 224
  Lucinda 80 Mary E. 3
  Ollie B. 245
  Sarah A. 72 Sid 51
  Sinde E. 86 Thomas 27
Martinez, Miguel 133
Mason, Angela E. 70
  Charles O. 177
  E. Everton 157
  Francis A. 197
Massengill, Elizabeth 120
  F.T. (Dr) 190
Massey, D.T. 166
Massingill, F.T. 204 215
  F.T. (Dr) 89 173
Masters, Hannah M. 211
  Polly E. 211 Roscoe 85
  T.D. 211 William W. 14
Mathenson, Evie 194
Matherly, Blanch 263
  D. 36 Fred 83
  John 142 263
  Minnie P. 263 Monie 245
  Sarah 142
Mathes, Caroline 71 Ed 1
  Hobart 3 Hubert 3
  John T. 71 Luther 14
  Mary E. 211
Mathews, Mary 35
Mathis, Hillard 222

Mathis (continued)
  Julia C. 127 Lawson 222
  Thomas R. 117 Walter 42
Mattack, John W. 249
Matterson, Francis 117
Matthews, Mahalia 225
Mauk, Alma 135 J.A. 15
  J.M. 232 Samuel M. 113
Maulfair, William L. 150
Maupin, Alie 252 C.C. 218
  Elsie 30 George 233 235
  G.H. 233 James 12
  Jesse 257 John 233
  Rebecca 235
  Robert O. 104 Sam 257
  William C. 235
  Willis 104
Maveric, Pachia 107
Maws, Nancy 208
Maxwell, Sophia 163
May, Lena 14 Mary C. 18
  William 164
  William G. 9
  William H. 164
  W.H. (Mrs) 165
McAdams, David N. 251
  D.N. 251 Flora E. 187
  Samuel D. 211
McAfee, Mary 208
McAlister, Texie 190
McAmis, Sarah 157
McCallister, Annie 27
McCally, Susan 180
McCamey, Marshall 260
McCarey, Harriett 242
McCarty, Emeline 155
McCauley, __ 180
McCavan, Thomas 165
McClain, Fannie 80
  John 263
McClellan, Frank 119

McClellan (continued)
  Rosetta 119
McClelland, __ 134
McClure, E.G. 41
  Francis M. 127
  Horace S. 166 M.S. 127
  Robert R. 127 W.S. 166
McCollum, G.W. (Mrs) 157
  William H. 183
McCorkle, J.J. 105
  Mary J. 105
McCormick, George W. 121
McCourley, Stella 108
McCourry, Ella 258
McCoury, J.O. 12
McCown, G.V. (Mrs) 55
  Lucille 167
McCracken, Alice 66
  Doyle 68 Elizabeth 199
  John 177 J.A. 213
  Louise 213 Mahola 177
  Martha 66 Myrtle B. 11
  Samuel 42 177 213
McCrary, Jennie E. 102
  J.R. 258
McCray, Elizabeth 206
McCrockin, Jeff 171
McCulley, John 107
  Robert F. 107
McCurry, Becky 179
  Rebecca 169 Sarah 240
  S.S. 141
McDonald, Mary S. 219
McDow, Maggie 195
McEvoy, John 96
McFall, Harry 190
  Marilla 251 R.W. 20
  Susan 82 W.K. 190
McFaul, John 167
  Nelson A. 167
McGee, Charley 41

McGee (continued)
  Sallie 199
McGettigan, John 208
  Susan 173
McGhechan, __ 158
McGill, Mary 192
  Patrick 192 Thomas 192
McGrew, Miles 122
McGuire, Dalton 8
McHenry, Daniel F. 158
McIntosh, Leona 230
  W.P. 230
McInturff, Allie 19
  Dave 153 Dora 233
  Israel 201 James 142
  153 195 John 145
  John W. 145 Juliah 195
  Lucy 195 Mary 145
  Unna 141 Will 153
  William A. 201
McIntyre, James H. 20
  Lottie A. 20
McKamey, S.M. 42
McKay, Elizabeth C. 209
McKee, Bertie 213
  Charlie 16 Noah 185
  Willie 140
McKey, Benjamin F. 256
McKinney, Emma 160
McLain, James I. 187
  J.I. 187
McLean, Metchel 46
McLeod, Collin 134
McLin, Susie 9
McLutz, Margaret 195
McMackin, Bell 222
  Howard E. 228 J.D. 228
McMances, Michael 98
McMicaels, Ethel 251
McMillen, Dock 214
  Minervey 251

McMindes, Prescott 103
McNabb, A.L. 215 Ben 215
   George C. 137 G.W. 137
   Margaret 232
McNeal, Doublin 219
   George 219 Thomas C 219
McNear, Hannah L. 220
McNeese, Jacob 116
   J.A. 248
McNeil, Clarence 76
   Henry 63 Johnie M 85
   Sophrona 108
McNeill, Hugh B. 145
McNichols, Albert 230
   Ethel 206 224
   Pansy J. 230
McNutt, Hannah 76
McPeak, Infant 168
   Josephine 253
   Joshua 132 Levi 132
   Sarah 94 Walter 23
   Walter R. 45
McPherson, Alvah 265
   A.A. 265 Charley 8
   Fred 132 178
   James A. 63
McQueen, Ellen 46
   Elva 166 Finley 92
   Jerry 197
McQuerry, Bertha 202
Melear, Hannah 63
Melvin, James R. 204
   Margaret 204
   William 204
Mercer, William 53
Merna, Washington 134
Merrett, Mary 214
Merrick, Charles 136
   Edward J. 136
Merritt, A.E. 194
   Neil A. 194 W.F. 194

Meriweather, Clarence 166
Merwin, Hugh B. 96
Metcalf, C.K. 228
   Harrison 206 R.C. 206
Metz, Frank 150
Mevenick, Peachie 212
Michael, Richard E. 238
Michell, Nora 170
Mikels, John 214
Milburn, Annie 102
   George 102 Infant 102
   John 192 Mary 192
Miles, J.P. 119 Mark 182
   Minnie 228 Nannie E 123
   William 124
   William J. 124
Milhorn, Bessie 26
   Lula P. 59 Martha 44
   Mildred 31 Nannie E 44
Millard, __ 199
   John W 121 Samuel H 121
Miller, __ 198 Addie O 75
   Albert 104 Alex 243
   Alice 17 Axcie 262
   A.R. 138 A.S. 104
   Benjamin 99 Bertha 222
   Bud 109 Clyde 192
   Daniel 114 David 133
   David H. 107
   D.S. 190 221 Eliza 92
   Elizabeth 139 Emma 249
   E.H. 149 E.S. (Dr) 75
   Fannie 62 Fleming 102
   Florence 186 Francis 62
   Frank 116 Frank F. 15
   George 77 86 G.W. 221
   Harrison V. 150
   Henry 93 Herman 174
   H. Stanley 76
   Infant 102 149 154 229
   Isaac 107 114 116 212

Miller (continued)
  Jane 91 Jeniva 76
  Jerry 133 John 116 126
  John R. 108
  Johnathan 115
  Julia A. 138
  Julia H. 221 J.L. 229
  J.M. 194 Kate 88
  Lina 97 Lizzie 116
  Lottie B. 41 Mag N. 106
  Malissa 146 214
  Martha 253 256
  Martha E 179 Marvis 106
  Mary A. 197 Mary E. 113
  Mose 226 Moses 154 156
  222 Monro 179 Nancy 101
  Nora 221 Robert 106
  Ruby L. 109 Sam 192
  Samuel 114 Sarah M. 174
  Susan 109 147 Viola 232
  Virgie B. 31
  Walter H. 108
  William C. 227
  William T. 194
  Woodson T. 145 W.A. 255
  W.H. 104
Millhorn, C.E. 260
  C.S. 130 Elkana 130
  George 130 John 261
  Lula B. 260
Million, __ 145 D.L. 158
  Florence 95 Ida 142
Mills, Arthur 264
  Will 264
Minnick, Mary 208
Mitchel, George 243
  Henry 243 Lodie J. 243
Mitchell, Bertha V. 65
  C.E. 257 Dora 10
  Ettie 163 Haskel L. 44
  Hiram 223 James H. 175

Mitchell (continued)
  Jennie 14 John 13 223
  258 John M. 262
  Lucinda 138 N.W. 71
  Pearl 257 Sallie 197
  257 William 235 262
  W.S. 223
Moathenson, Finley 194
Mohler, John R. 83
  Lavina E. 63
Monroe, Allen W. 144
Montgomery, Amandah 201
  Wilson 201
Moody, Allie 26 Ben 161
  Enoch H. 83 Eva G. 24
  Mary 12 Mary R. 60
  Mattie 258 Maude 260
  Robert 29 Teddy 161
Moon, J.B. 115
  Luscinda E. 115
Moore, Arthur 194
  Benjamin F. 125
  Brazelton 140
  Charlie 176 Cintha A 71
  Daniel 170 David 176
  261 George 161
  George W. 161 Goldie 25
  G.L. 49 H.M. 232
  I.F. 6 Jesse 71 128
  Julia 175 176 261
  J.H. 5 Lucian 25
  Martha M. 170
  Martina J. 229
  Mary 81 262 Nelon 76
  Ralph 43 194
  Richard C. 262 R.A. 14
  Sims 161 Sue 120
  Telete 39 Thomas 262
  William 140 Wilson 101
Moores, Coleman 187
Moran, Thomas M. 254

Morefield, E.D. 219
  Paul 219 Sarah E. 236
Moreland, Lucy 87
  Nancy C. 157 Susie 141
Morelock, A.B. 233
  Caroline 97 215 226
  Georgia E. 126
  Jacob 126 Ollie 126
  Ruth 65
  S.B. 108 109 237 262
Morgan, E.P. 180 Kate 69
  Tom 148
Morrel, John W. 134
  Worley C. 134
Morrell, __ 251 Anna 9
  D.C. 236 D.S. 221
  E.S. 261 Infant 20
  James A. 261 J.S. 146
  Laura 207 Roy E. 236
  Stuart F. 19 Sue 236
  Susan C. 183 S. 91
Morris, __ 91 Anna 87
  Beatrice 119 Ella 90
  Florence B. 163
  James 105 Mose 90
  Verge 105
Morrison, Alonzo 237
  Eloise 237 H.G. 149 194
  Infant 43 149 194
  Katie 81 Lonnie 237
  William E. 218
Morrow, Infant 232
  James F. 232 John 233
  Nora E. 233
Mosely, Nicy 140
  William 140
Moser, Elizabeth 131
Mosier, Arthur 196
  Harold S. 196 T.W. 147
Mosley, Edeline 182
Moss, Caroline P. 74

Mottern, Bettie 110
  Christine 203
  Eugene 110 M.L. 54
Moulton, Amos R. 80
  Barbara 111 Erma 19
  J.W. 177
Moyer, Aaron 165
Moyers, Catherine 200
  Fred 81
Mullen, Harry O. 19
Mullins, Letie G. 213
  Lettie G. 213 N.J. 214
  Thomas 96
Mungen, Theodore 177
Muns, Minnie 166
Murdock, James 205
Murphey, Eliza C. 126
Murphy, James 191
  John 122 Joseph 221
  Thomas 161
Murr, __ 200 Charley 200
  David 51 Elvae 255
  Houston 255 Huston 200
Murray, Annia 107
  Barbry 231 Ella 137
  Ethel 107 Frank 261
  Infant 40 Jessie P. 10
  John 40 137 161
  Joseph 186 Lee 264
  Lucile 264 Matilda 54
  183 Susie 137 Walter 88
Murrell, Eva 176
Murry, John C. 107
Muse, Virgie 98 144
Music, Ollie 138
Myers, Bertha 260
  Kate 262
Nance, Prior 157
  Ruben D. 157
Nash, Joe 220 Will 220
Nave, Christly 115

Nave (continued)
  Ross M. 115 Will 130
  William 115
Naylor, John H. 138
  Nancy 147
Nead, Daniel 185
  Daniel C. 185
Nead, Susan 185
Neal, Ellen 119
Neatherland, Monroe 89
Nelms, Martha E. 63
Nelson, Callie A. 147
  Elizabeth 162 Emily 153
  Harold 208 Jack N. 183
  James 139 John 106 183
  256 John F. 183
  John W. 147 Luther 147
  Mary 139
  T.A.R. (Mrs) 42
Neurath, Elizabeth 181
  Maud 181 William 181
  William J. 181
Neville, John W. 150
Newbrand, George W. 152
Newcomb, Walter A. 201
Newland, Martha 237
Nichols, Ester L. 96
  Ira A. 96
Nichom, Mary 236
Nicodemas, Mary 236
Nieman, Edward J. 175
Norris, Frank 49 H.W. 109
  Infant 49 James 73 109
  Jessie J. 109 Zullie 82
Northington, Lizzie 127
Nuckles, Annie 228
Nuckolds, Lula 111
O'Brien, Dora 113
  George B. 203 John 201
  Margaret 146 Will 203
  William 203

Odell, Anna M. 53 Mag 16
Odom, Infant 247 Will 247
Oellig, Charles (Dr) 247
Oleson, Andrew 113
Oliver, Allen 236
  Arthur 143 221
  Arthur Jr. 143
  Ellen H. 45
  Florence 143 G.W. 62
  Hazel E. 204
  James W. 230 John 125
  204 Joseph 230
  Mildred L. 125
  Virgie 255
Onks, Charley 43 M.D. 194
  Sallie E. 92
Orr, __ 246 Irene 21
  John 180 Laura 171
  Malinda 253 Mary 252
  Mollie 241
Orran, Pauline 84
  Jake 144 Johnie 48
  Paulien 48
Osborne, Dan 7
  Peggie 193
Osgood, Charles H. 118
Ottalou, Rachel 263
Overstreet, __ 104
  Edna 73 Emaline 104
  Infant 23 55
  Robert C. 29 Will 23 55
Owen, Christian 247
  Delia 135 Lucile V 264
  Minnie 228 Wash 136
Owens, A.A. 264
  Minnie 130 William 89
  W.F. 194
Pack, Mina 40
  William 54
Packer, Laura 227
Paine, John F. (Mrs) 216

Painter, Aaron 230
  Anie 25 Annie 101
  Bertice 221 Carl 179
  E.S. 251 Infant 221
  James 102 Jessie 25 128
  John W. 102 114 J.H. 78
  J.W. 102 Lena 162 213
  215 Martin 114
  Otto J. 179 Samuel 230
  Sherman 128 Tempa 111
  Trula M. 5 William 114
Pallet, Sallie 242
Pamter, Glades 13
Parker, F.A. (Mrs) 114
  George W 14 Joseph S 92
  Sarah 174
Parks, Nancy 101
Parnell, Bertha E. 166
Parot, Henry 190
Parsons, Ella 22
Partick, Florence E. 200
Partrum, Janie 94
Patrick, Cary B. 20
  Doris 200 Jina 221
Patterson, Alice 230
  Charles F. 232
  Clara 217 James 200
  John 211 M.S. 230
  Newton A. 35 Polly 211
  P.L. 163 Rufus 217
  S.L. 232 William 217
Patton, Benjamin 226
  Cynthia 128
  Elizabeth Emma 138
  George 157
  J. Montie 157
  Madison 210 Mary 142
  Samuel F. 142
  S.K.N. 140 T.C. 52
  W.D. 50
Paul, Ella M. 142

Paul (continued)
  John 170 Ralph 170
Paxton, Mary 264
Payne, Gabe 42 George 112
  Hester 16 J.R. 16
  Taylor 169
Peak, Levy M. 168
Peaks, Jerry 252
Pearce, Gertrude 33
  John T. 166
  Martha J. 166
Pearson, George R. 254
  Walace W. 235
Pendleton, John 146
Pengh, Easter 260
Penix, Belle 89
Penley, Bettie 120
  Henry 120 128
Peoples, Tabitha 236
  W.R. 236
Peregory, Dimple 114
  D.M. 114
Perkins, Mollie 228
Persell, H.H. 147
  Nancy 147
Peters, John W. 170
  Sam R. 170 Vicie 115
Peterson, Corra L. 230
  D.M. 141 Infant 262
  Marry 141 Sam 230
Philips, Elizabeth 110
  Samuel T. 24
Phillips, Cass 217
  Cumi 20 Donald 4
  Gladis J. 98 John 123
  170 Joseph 220 Lara 7
  Maggie 164 Mary 199
  Nellie 45 Sallie 41
  Sarah 2 217 W.L. 98
Phipp, Sallie 208
Phipps, Eliga 69 J.T. 264

Phipps (continued)
  O.W. 264 William T. 264
Piche, Joseph O. 217
Pickens, Estell 213
  Hattie 207 James 207
  James B. 226
  Marget R. 226 Susie 118
Pickering, Docie H. 187
  Glenie 29 Iris 28
  J.H. 114 Lora 56
  Margie N. 112 Sam 187
  Sam H. 112 Walter B 114
Pickings, Lizzie 196
Pickle, John W. 160
  William 160 W.W. 160
Pickley, Mary F. 163
Pierce, Infant 265
  John E. 265
  Kathlene 265
Pierson, Mae 41
  Sarah 41
Pilb, Fred H. 258
  John 258
Pill, William 70
Pippin, Rebecca E. 135
Pitman, Jane 157
Pleasant, Samuel 142
  Samuel T. 66
  Stella M. 142
Poling, Infant 131
  W.B. 131
Polling, Infant 131
  W.R. 131
Pond, Mary 168
Ponder, William 120
  William T. 120
Pooer, James 162
Poor, Sam 215
  William H. 215
Poore, Annie 101
  Danl 162

Pope, Toney 233
Porter, Anna 89
Postlewait, John M. 136
Poteat, Carl E. 138
  D.S. 138
Potter, Cane 180
Potts, John W. 254
Powell, Martha 143
  Matilda 203
Powers, Winston 216
Presley, Bricen H. 199
Presnell, James 17
  John 253 Margaret 178
Prevett, G.W. 264
Price, Adie 108
  Arthur 259 Eugene 20
  Flora 116 G.W. 108
  Henry 193 Infant 193
  198 Isaac P. 202
  James 149 166
  James R. 1 John 116 118
  Johnie 10 J.H. 198
  Lura J. 137 Mary E. 34
  Mildred F. 166 Nora 192
  Sarah 84 Violet 116
  Wiolet A. 118 Wilber 60
  William 10
Prichard, Eliza 125
  George 125 George W 125
  John 94 Mary 94
  Clandis 133 J.A. 133
Prince, William B. 124
  W.L. 124
Pritchard, Robert 46
  Stella 58
Pritchett, John 252
Privett, Hazel J. 264
Prophet, Mary 189
Propst, James H. 213
  John C. 213 J.C. 142
  J.C. Jr 142

Pugh, Thomas 228
Purcell, Dortha 237
  J.C. 93 Robert A. 93
  Samuel 237
Pursell, Mary V. 8
Pyles, John W. 66
Quade, John F. 118
Quillen, James 167
Radford, William H. 146
  W.H. 146
Raglon, Jacob 134
Raingham, R.L. 256
Rainwater, Joe 29
Ramey, Charles 204
  Lonie 204
Ramsey, Cordie 209
  James 209 James R. 209
Randolph, James 109
  Morgan 240
Range, Albert K. 133
  Barsha A. 237
  Gertrude 22 G.E. 237
  Harry 223 Infant 223
  Jacob 92 Jacob R. 33
  Johnanthan 237
  J.J. (Mrs) 223
  Lydia 227 Maggie 167
  Robert 26 Susan 92
  Thomas 244 William 133
  W.E. 244
Rash, P.C. 180
Ratliff, Henry R. 139
  J.C. 139
Rattigan, John 189
Rawlings, Texie 226
Ray, Ed 188 Edith 99
  Etta 255 Florence 48
  Harriet 104 Infant 99
  Isaac 105 Magnolia 256
  Robert L. 50 Sam 188
  Thomas 104

Raymond, John C. 92
Reaves, Charles 242
  John 242
Redman, Lula 118
Redwine, Infant 146
  James W. 146
  J.W. (Mrs) 113
  Miltie 25
Reed, __ 105
  Benjamin K. 202
  Bird 163 261 Byrd 155
  Cleo 178 Eliza 206
  Etta 187 G.W. 189 229
  James J. 189 July A 126
  J. 229 J.B. 174
  Keith 80 Maggie 159
  P.D. 126 Robert B. 229
  Roy 178 Vergie 185
  W.M. 137
Reedler, William 160
Reedy, Brown 12
  Jennie 46 Jesse 22
Reeser, Joseph E. 211
Reeves, Alice R. 29
  Bulah 242
  Catherine M. 156
  Charles 242 Dan 77
  John D. 175
  John D. (Mrs) 175
  Lois 4 Myra C. 78
  Peter 175 Ula 242
  Walter 166
Regan, Blanch 173
Register, Deborah 224
Reid, David N. 124
  Frank B. 124
  George W. 150
Remington, William 158
Renfro, __ 117
  Florence 47
Rengley, James H. 159

Rengley (continued)
  J.J. 159 J.H. (Mrs) 160
Repass, Delia 61
Rhea, Alice 21 Allen 1
  Bertha 148 Jenie 21
  Jenny 148 John 189
  Norman 189
  Walter 28 76
Rhudy, Mary 6
Rice, Ella 261 Francis 63
  Mary E. 255 Will 255
  William 207
Rich, Lyman A. 133
Richadson, Alsin 234
Richard, Euna 55 John 140
Richards, Sallie 140 261
Richardson, Annie 260
  C.C. 260 Emme E. 28
  John B. 258 Paul 234
  Robert 258 Ruth A. 203
Riddle, Ada P. 178
  A.G. Jr 20 George B. 94
  Gus 201 Infant 201
  James F. 192 John 94
  Margaret 265 Nelson 192
Ridley, Evelyn 196
  R.C. 196
Riffey, Grant 12
Riffy, Elizabeth 83
Riggs, Ethel 79
  Ruby L. 40
Rigsby, Sarah 61
Riley, Hugh 122
  Kathryn 103 Mary 63
  Peter 103
Rinehart, __ 151
  Sarah 244
Riner, Columbus 173
Rines, Alzata 205
  Shadrack 205
Rippey, Clara M. 72

Roadcaff, Elizabeth 143
Roadcap, Barbara 185
Roberts, __ 137 Frank 75
  Henrietta 3 Lucy 149
  Mary 264 S.A. 216
  William H. 216
  Winnie 194
Robertson, Betsy 98
  Nannie J. 134
Robins, Julia 241
  Onida 86
Robinson, Dick 227
  D.V. 49 G. 263
  Infant 49 James 214
  John 134 Lydia 177
  Mary 134 William C. 134
  Willie H. 49
Rodgers, Rosey 258
  William 40
Roe, Margaret 131
  Samuel 131
  Samuel W. 131
  Samuel W., Jr. 131
Rogan, Edward 23
Rogers, Angeline 223
  Calvin R. 114
  Charles B. 166
  David 108 109 G.A. 50
  Henry 109 Mattie P. 178
  Ralph 81 Russell B. 234
  Samuel 178 Viola M. 114
Rogerson, Mary E. 249
Roginson, Sam 263
Rohrbach, Henry C. 240
Rolfe, Carrie C. 243
Rolfs, Walter L. 247
Roller, Lucindy B. 64
Rollin, Nancy 98
Rominger, Sarah L. 143
Rommes, Toy 234
Rose, Bettie 246

Rose (continued)
  Elizabeth 124
  Leslie 129 Roy 213
  William A. 129
Rosenbalm, Hewey 23
Rosenbaum, Abraham 236
  Henry 59 Martha E. 236
Rosenblatt, Lillie 117
Ross, David 4
Rouse, Sarah 24
Rowe, T.D. 22
Rowls, Clyde 66
Royster, Maggie 214
Ruble, David H. 192
  Epram 253 Eva J. 192
  Henry 170 Infant 16
  James A. 253 254
  J.A. (Mrs) 167
  Louise 16
Rudderson, Josiah A. 93
Ruder, W.L. 90
Ruffin, Willie P. 168
  W.N. 168
Rupe, Charles 163
  Elsee 163
Russell, Elizabeth 9
  H. 23 Jacob 136 Jane 17
  Lizzie 107 Pearl 154
  Sam 234
Ruth, Nancy E. 177
Rutledge, Maurine 43
  Tom 110
Ryan, Coy L. 261
  Martha 108 Mollie 46
  Walter 261
Ryans, Horace 75
  Infant 75 Joseph 75
  Ossie 75 William 75
S--, Robert M. 42
Sales, John 216
Salinger, Nona 131

Salinger (continued)
  Nora 131
Sallie, Herbert L. 158
Salts, Elizabeth 90
  Ida 48 126 Isaac 155
  John 155 Margaret 126
  Mariah 221 Sarah 174
  William 14
Sampson, John 128
Sams, Mamie 48 S.E. 255
Sanders, M.J. 255
  Ralph R. 60
Sanderson, William D. 16
Sanford, William 102
Sarron, Nick 175
Saults, Daniel 210
  Guy 2 Ida 210 Jake 180
  Sallie 239 Sarah 9
  Thomas B. 210
Saunders, Flora 118
Saylor, Alice 243 245 247
  Bessie 117 Bonnie A 119
  Dump 123 E.P. 123
  Henry 91 Infant 62
  Isaac 185 James 62 119
  John 156 J.R. 156
  J.W. 149 Ollie 30
  Rachel A. 149 S.G. 167
  Thomas 105 William 156
Scalf, Infant 111
  John 111 Nancy 199
  Nancy J. 252
Scarborough, Micajah 177
Schaver, Lizzie 140
Schowen, Roy 226
Schub, __ 212
Schwab, John P. 160
Scott, Absolom L. 156
  Ada 3 Buna 129 C.E. 134
  Daniel 134 David 156
  Don 214 Elizabeth 239

Scott (continued)
  Harriett 33 Infant 195
  James 203 Julia E. 238
  J.M. 239 Lucinda 92
  Lue 241 Maranda 115
  Marinda 190 Martha 107
  Montgomery 214 M.F. 195
  Richard 214 Sarah 239
  Thomas 64 238 Will 92
  William C. 195
  Wilson 225
Scruggs, Anthony 127
Seaton, A.C. 230
  Bennie A. 108 David 179
  Dora 265 Fred 179
  J.M. 52 Maney 13
  Mark L. 179 Mollie 104
  M.L. 108 Sarah 97
Seaver, George F. 233
  Glen F. 233 Grace 57
See, Gracy 264
Sefford, __ 221
Seicle, Sarah 119
Self, Harry 47
Sellars, Elizabeth 73
  Martha 12
Sellers, Arthur 188
  Jacob 212 Leona 188
  Virginia 212
Sellis, Lula 195
Sells, Henry 261
  Infant 67 Jonathan 261
  Lula 264 Mary 252
  Mary E. 252 Robert B 61
  Rose 83 William 83
Selton, Dabncey B. 203
  G.W. 203
Sercy, Berty 204
  Burran 204 David 25
Sevadley, Edgar 25
Sevier, Anna 142

Seymore, Ida 47 John 47
Sfford, Eliza 236
Shade, Henry 154
  Hyawatha 154
Shaffer, Michael 181
  Westall P. 165
Shamberg, Frederick G 176
Sharp, Thomas H. 158
Sharrett, Laura 264
Shaver, Albert 240
  Gerturde 240 Infant 240
Shaw, Jane 230 Mary E. 7
  Sallie 7
Shearer, Helen 175
  William 175
Sheats, Urban C. 186
  Bertie 256 Lucie 187
  Lucy 112
Shell, Carson 253 256
  Charley 39 Infant 253
  256 Martha 262
Shelton, Arch 230
  Henry 73 John F. 258
  John W. 258 Nora 230
  Sol 230
Shephard, James R. 252
  Bessie M. 184
  Cordia F. 140
  Elizabeth 184
  Howey 252 Robert H. 252
Shepley, Nannie 226
Sherfey, A.J. 82
  Carmel 162
  Catherine 169
  Clifford 39
  Henry W. 147 Hubert 82
  James W. 225 John 162
  Joseph 147 Samuel D 225
  Soloman S. 131
  William E. 44
Sherfy, Jennie 244

Sheridan, Peter 254
Sherrell, Tom 118
Shields, John C 95 Lara 5
  Margaert L. 95
  Mary A. 53 Nancy 95
  Nola 41 Sam 119
  Sam W. 95
Shipley, Adam 10
  Andrew 34 Anna 60 117
  C.f. 151 Elbert A. 64
  Elkana 256 Eugene 256
  George 212 James 132
  Joseph E. 256 J.D. 255
  J.E. 107 Lindsey P. 256
  Lucy 81 Mary 64
  Mary J. 72 Preston 255
  Renah 132 Tollbert 132
  Tom 151 Walter P. 151
  William 160
Shoemaker, J. 151
Short, Bessie 159
  Julia 151
Shoun, J.B. 186
Shoup, Andy J. 124
  Ramey E. 124
Showman, Bertha 75
  George H. 75 John M. 90
  Lulie 90
Shumate, H.M. 253
  Jack 253
Sibley, Corine 187
Sifford, Eliza 237
  George 237 John 10
Silvers, Flora 259
  Infant 103 M.T. 259
  William 103
Simmerman, Infant 133
  J.H. 133 Mary J. 190
Simons, John 165
Simpson, Ely 7
  Sarafine 54

Sims, Sarah 109
  Virginia 46
Singleton, James C. 188
Sisenberry, Ollie 85
Sittin, Edward 235
Sitton, Benjamin J. 246
  Clifton L. 196
Sizemore, Margaret A. 240
Slagle, Andrew J. 45
  Mary E. 115 116
  Sarah 71 William D. 78
Slaughter, Orlena 224
Slemons, John (Mrs) 69
Sliger, Adam 241
  Bertha 149 Charles 257
  Enoch 239 Frank 257
  Infant 239 257
  John 232 241 Mollie 232
  Sarah 116 William 239
Sligerland, Henry T. 259
Slonaker, Elizabeth 142
  J.H. 205 Mary E. 213
Sluder, Idline 91
Smalling, Duke 117
  Louise 60 R.W. 117
  William J. 117
Smallwood, James A. 220
Smith, __ 219
  Alexander 186
  Amelia 227 A.J. 184
  Becky 252 Billy 31
  Calelia 65 Cinthia 128
  Clarence 141 Creed 94
  David H. 223 Dora 232
  Earl 75 Ed 114
  Elias W. 151 Eliza 172
  182 190 Fredrick 225
  George 27 Grace 205
  G.L. 172 264
  Howard P. 158 Infant 41
  Jake 153 Jake W. 19

Smith (continued)
  James 158 James W. 155
  John 21 John T. 227
  John W. 225 Joseph 90
  Julia A. 264
  J. Coson 184
  Lafayette 141
  Levi J. 103 Luke 7 74
  Mamie 3 Martha A. 249
  Mary 121 233 Mary A 113
  Mary E. 154 200
  Nancy 38 Nellie K. 58
  Nora 162 O.A. (Mrs) 161
  Reta 223 Ross 113
  Sam 77 Samuel E. 223
  Sidney 122 Thomas 184
  Troop 56 Virgie 141
  Walter 185
  William 77 159 185
  William P. 229
  William S. 234
  Willie 40 Worley H. 94
  W.H. 41 205
Smithpeters, Delilah 30
  Mike 172 William 172
Snapp, Eleanor 180
  Everitt 68
Sneed, John 114
  Mariah 163 Millie E 114
Snider, Daniel 83
Snoden, Siney 24
Snodgrass, Adron C. 129
  Charles 117 129
  James 110
  Martha C. 159 T.Y. 159
  William 3 Worley M. 129
Snow, Mollie 59
  Nathaniel 57
Snyder, A.E. 182
  Edna 182 Wash 245
Sondy, Infant 58

South, George 167
  Harvy 130 Infant 167
  Jessie 130 John M. 130
  Kate 56 Parley 104
Spain, Ethel L. 48
Sparks, Ida 250
  Mary E. 252 Ruben 134
  William A. 134
Spears, Louise 97
Spencer, Joseph B. 135
  Robert P. 98 Walker 98
Spense, Clara M. 26
Spitzer, Dora 128
  Jessie 128 Sarah 128
Sprance, Amelia 255
Spring, Matthew 206
Sproles, Benage 254
  Sarah 173
Sproul, H.G. 38
Spurgeon, Henry 75
Squibb, I.G. 65
St Clair, Mary 265
St John, Mattie B. 86
Stafford, Charles 126
Stallords, Arthur D. 112
  A.J. 112
Stampton, Dortha 141
Stanfield, Elie 212
  Rebecca 261
Stanley, George W. 181
Stant, ___ 222
  Montgomery 60
Stanton, Birdie 24
  Burson 24 Eli 89
  G.W. 179 Ida G. 162
  Sarah E. 162
Starnes, Bessie M. 226
Staudemayer, Jacob 144
Stebbins, Charles M. 223
Steele, L. 104
Steen, Janie 224

Steffey, Suda 233
Steinlein, Frederick 93
Stephens, John T. 113
   William N. 65
Stephenson, Fanny 244
Stepp, Amantha 15
   John 196
Stevens, Delithia 206
   Hiram 93 Nancy C. 40
Stevenson, Delila M. 123
   Edith 137 J.W. 123
Stewart, Isah 127
   John 263
Stfford, Conie M. 6
Stockton, Peter 111
   W.G. 111
Stonecipher, Jack 43
   Nellie 43
Stonies, Hellen 209
Storie, Arthor J. 204
   James 204
Stornes, Katherine 236
Story, Arthor J. 204
   Brook 110 Clara 41
   Edith 139 Eli 72
   Emeline 154 Frank 110
   George 48 224
   Hubert 200 Ida B. 54
   Infant 200 James 204
   John 47 J.M. 209
   Lavina 204 Margaret 47
   Pearl 210 Rebecca 200
   Rosie 179 Tessie O. 55
   Thomas 204 Thomas A 110
   Thomas N. 224 Tom 179
Stosmer, J. 94
Stout, Allen 120
   Bessie 167 Carrie 155
   Charles E. 193
   Claud M. 6 Clint 117
   Infant 23 117

Stout (continued)
   James M. 188
   Jeamie W. 193
   John 92 J.B. 23 92
   Kate 77 Millard 188 195
   M.E. 193 Rosa 234
   Susan 193 Woodrow 195
Stover, Cehpas 135
Strauss, Annie 103
Street, Josephine 74
Stribling, Albert H. 249
Strickland, Daniel 221
   Lille H. 126
   Margaret 200 Moore 201
   William 200
Strickler, Joseph 231
   Mary 234 Rubin 231
Stuart, Charlotte 204
   Edward 169 174 G.G. 185
   Henry 8 Lee 70
   Lettie 174 Maggie 74
   Maria L. 185
Stull, James A. 112
Stump, J.H. 105 106
   Myrtle S. 105 106
Sturat, Ella 155
Sullanbarger, Rebecca 113
Summers, Estell 265
   Infant 265 Thomas P. 76
Susong, David 251
   Ellie 251
Sutfin, Earnest 38
Sutton, Edward 235
Svoronas, Analtaie 153
   Danepisos 153
   Spero A. 153
Swadley, Elizabeth 85
   George E. 143 Henry 143
   Hunter 143 Ida 60
Swalts, McDowell 49
Swaner, Amos 99 Dilet 99

Swaner (continued)
  William 99
Swatzel, Mary 116
Sweney, Mark E. 92
Swift, Cherry A. 143
  Matilda 234 Ruth 234
  R.F. 203 R.W. 143
Swiney, Eli 251
  Lucy E. 105 Nancy A 251
Swingle, Allie 176
  B.F. 17 Infant 176
Tabor, George W. 250
  Robert C. 250
Tadlock, Arthur 256
  Mary 256 Orland 195
  Samuel H. 195
Taittan, Vestie 109
Talbutt, Susan B. 234
Tapp, W.H. 1
Tarny, John 43
Tate, A.H. 4 Freeman 208
  Sarah 264
Taughy, Elizabeth 199
Taylor, __ 30 242
  Albert 169 Alfred 41
  Alfred D. 23 Alice 118
  Ana E. 255 Andrew 50
  A.P. 206 Bruce B. 117
  Carry 111 Cary 111
  Charles L. 172 C.E. 255
  Ed 43 Elenor S. 225
  Eliza 182 Farrell C. 52
  George W. 200
  Infant 106 113 117
  Jackson 118
  James 69 106 212
  James P. 172 Jane 29
  John 244 John M. 47
  Josephine 172 J.W. 200
  Lyons R. 241 Manuel 123
  Martha 1 Mary 114 124

Taylor (continued)
  Mary A. 255 Mattie 21
  Obelia 118
  Phil S. 97 156
  Robert L. 225 Ruth 240
  Sallie 243 Samuel 186
  Sarafina K. 126
  Sarafine 97 Sarah 244
  Sarah M 241 Skelton 206
  S.J. 113 William 236
  W.E. 255
Teague, Infant 54
Teffetts, Albion W. 175
Telford, Amanda 118
  G.W. 118
Templin, Jacob 162
  John 250 William 250
Tensler, Bettie 53
Tesneer, Addie 66
Thayer, Fritz 152
Thomas, Alice 240
  Carrinth 214
  Charles B. 46
  Goly M. 120 Joe 121
  Luavin A. 144 Mary J 15
  Samuel 120 Sarah 130
  Sauana 141 Viola 53
Thomason, Walker 96
Thompkins, Nathaniel A. 1
Thompson, A.B. 178
  Eliza J. 105 Elvia 247
  James W. 161 John 99
  John R. 161 Josie 192
  Marcure R. 212
  Mary E. 117 Mattie 120
  M.W. 161 Rhea 131
  Tolbert 178
  William A. 186
Thornburg, Margaret 78
Thornton, William A. 186
Throux, Paul 125

Tillard, Samuel T. 121
Tillie, Mary A. 193
Tiner, L.R. 129
  Mollie E. 129
  Richard 198
Tinker, A.H. 108 B.R. 248
  Jake 101 108 James 101
  Maud 248 Mollie 5
  Phillip P. 101
Tipton, Charles J. 108
  Cora L. 104 Edna 199
  Elizabeth 122
  Infant 176 Jane 265
  Joseph 158 Lola 39
  Mose 176 Paul 111
  Tennessee 227
  Walter 111
Tittle, Eliza 190
  Pearl 123
Todd, John 122
Tollie, Elkana 60
Tomkins, Jack 126
Tomlinson, John W. 154
  Sarah C. 154
Tompkins, John 7
Tompson, E. 143
Toney, S.W. 17
Toplins, Marry 175
Topper, Worley 34
Toppin, Caroline 100
Townsend, Martha A. 227
  Rutheuer 155
Trammel, Franklin 111
  Henry 111
Treadway, Alfred S. 160
  G.E. 160 Infant 199
  John 199 J.H. 160
  Mariah 34 Sarah 213
Trent, Hubert 35
  James 189 Wallace 220
  William 248

Trivett, Bertha 241
  Kizzie 262
Trotter, Louis G. 191
Troxell, Bettie 132
  Cassie 111 198
  David 198
Truman, Mary J. 231
  Sam 231
Tucker, Fannie 64
  Fannie W. 97 George 242
  G.W. 164 Isaac N. 232
  Isac 205 James 205
  Jonathan 201 Julia 164
  Laura A. 201 Martha 205
  Mary 162 Nellie G. 232
  Ruth J. 113 S.S. 97
Tunnell, George 87
Turner, __ 173 Alex 32
  T.J. 110
Tuskin, Frank 124
  Infant 124
Tyler, George 249
Tyre, Ruben 30
Tyree, Bessie 197
  Carrie W. 226
  Infant 222 Isaac N. 89
  Nellie 154 222 Nick 89
  Ruben 30 Sam 226
  Thomas 37 51 Virnen 82
  Zacharias 154
Utsman, Martha 138
Valentine, Vincent 96
  William 129
Valley, James 79
Vance, Calvin 154
  Coy E. 113 George 232
  Infant 20 62 James 62
  James A. 113 J.E. 137
  Lizzie 110 Lucy 78
  Margaret T. 137
  Nora 264 Robert F. 154

Vance (continued)
  William 232
Vandenburg, Jacob 159
Vanhoy, Lou E. 161
Vanhuss, Lelia N. 134
Vaughn, David 95 120
  Hubert 95 Lettie 186
  Martha E. 47
Vaught, Charlie 22
  Grace 208 Louise 188
Venabel, Daniel 216
  James F. 216
  J.F. Jr. 216
Vest, John J. 111
  Soloman S. 111
Vile, Alice 159
Vincent, J.H. 111
  Oscar S. 140
Vines, A.S. 170 248
  D.A. 94 Infant 94
  James A. 117
  Joe Anna 117 Mary 170
  Noah 156 N.A. 180
  Retta 110 Walter H. 180
  William 156 248
Vinyard, Mary 157
Voorhes, Mary F. 216
W__, H.M. 4
Waddell, Clyde 155
  F.K. 69 G.W. 106
  Laura H. 155
Wade, J.E. 241
Wagner, __ 222
  Catherine 182 Daniel 15
  Elizabeth 92 James M 17
  J.C. 214 Maud 214
  Nancy 183 Susie 33
Walker, __ 200 Annie 122
  Becky 229 F.M. 246
  Guy 52 Henry 163
  Henry H. 90 Idella 49

Walker (continued)
  Infant 90 109 133 200
  James 133 Joe 154
  John 183 Johnnie 174
  J.B. 246 Lewis 163
  Lute 200 Mary 160
  Ned 53 Nellie 163
  Monroe 183 N.C. 246
  Susanah 198 Walace M 46
  William 90
  William M. 109 Z. 81
Wall, Catherine 140
Wallace, Lockey 54
  Mina E. 33
Waller, Anna L. 149
  Julia 179 Lucinda 211
Walter, Amanda 95
  Franklin 232 Infant 232
  Mary 120
Walters, Cora 195
  C.E. 107 G.W. 3
  May J. 251 William 195
Walton, John 159
Ward, Alva M. 237
  William B. 237
Warlick, H. Howard 8
Warlock, Niles N. 110
Warren, Eli P. 19
  George A. 112
  James D. 144
Wartman, Charlotte 252
Wartmann, Charlotte 132
Washington, Heldie 163
Wassom, Cahrty 2
Wate, Sam 230
Watenburger, Betsy 123
Watkins, Infant 36 50
  Isaac 46 Margie 84
Wats, Ernes 194 James 194
  John 120
Watson, Bird 57

Watson (continued)
  Calud C. 131 Cordia 227
  George 49 Hannah 173
  James W. 131
  Pauline 120. P.E. 120
Watts, Sam 180 Sarah 180
Wealen, Louisa 217
Weaver, Charles E. 124
  Clarence 176 Ethel 196
  Eva 124 E.C. 196
  Gertrude 264 Infant 176
  J.D. 159 227
  Margaret 58 Mary C. 226
  Mary E. 159 Nellie 247
  Rhoda 57 Roy 58
  William R. 243
  Wilson 247
  W.R. 243 245 247
Webb, Martha 240 Ruth 103
  William 240
  William F. 73
Webber, Adam 98
Webster, Elizabeth 87
  G.R. 4
Weisel, Philip 236
Weitz, Sauanna 247
Wells, Dona 168 T.M. 79
  Willie E. 226
West, Amanda E. 118
  George 203 M.J. 15
  W.A. 118 W.E. 179
Wetherby, Albert C. 216
  Mildred 216
Whaley, Bessie 170
  Etter 169 Jacob 236
  Minnie 145
Wheeler, Mary W. 139
Wheelock, Merlin 68
Whetsel, Millie 140
  Suseanna 164
Whetsell, John 250

Whitaker, __ 60
  Alice E. 246 Calvin 189
  Charlie 170 Infant 170
  Jane 231 Maggie 204
White, __ 30 Bettie 34
  Blan 74 B.F. 253
  Carl 70 Carmon 253
  Celia 109 C.C. 246
  Dan 124 246 Dan Jr 246
  D.K. 205 Effie M. 252
  Eliza 204 Elva 36
  Frank 145 George 209
  Hannah L. 220
  Infant 145
  Isaac 220 221 Janie 213
  John 109 John C. 48
  John K. 45 J.B. 29
  J.T. 160 Levis 201
  Louise 205 Maria 49
  N.M. 160 Raymond L 212
  Sarah 127 Sarah L. 221
  Susan 231 Thomas 84 212
  Vernilie 94
  William E. 109
  W.A. (Mrs) 226
  W.E. 212
Whitehorn, Mariah 246
Whiteside, Almira 160
  W.B. 160
Whitker, E.W. 104
  John J. 104
Whitlock, Anna G. 215
  Bettie 237 Carl 91 136
  George 237 262
  George E. 215 J.W. 157
  Mary 136 Nettie F. 44
  Pleasant F. 91
  Robert F. 136
  Virgie 79
Whitlow, Deborah 259
Whittakr, Viola 151

Whittington, Leo 254
Widener, Glenn 250
  Will 250
Widner, Infant 219
  William 219
Wilborn, John 13
Wilborne, John R. 147
Wilbun, Offie 82
Wilburn, Malinda 164
Wilcox, Henrietta C. 127
  Joseph 44 219
Wilder, Ruben 214
Wilds, Agnes 143
Wiley, E.E. 114
Wilhoit, Bonisie 200
  Hannah 170 Philip 162
Wilkerson, Eliza 204
  E.T. 45
Wilkins, Henry I. 235
  Josephine 96
Willard, Jessie 26
Willett, George W. 193
  Joe 222
Williams, Armenta 224
  Bertha 219
  Catherine M. 11
  Earl E. 187 Eli 219
  Elizabeth 77
  Gordon 137 G. 26
  Hampton 191 Henry H 132
  Hop 175 Infant 132 175
  James 122 Leona 77
  Lula 131 Luta 53
  L.W. 170 Patrick 171
  Rebecca 264 Reese J 187
  Rush 103 Thomas 35
  Wash 137
Williamson, Mary A. 64
  Neta 173 T.R. 265
Willin, Margie 173
  Martin 173

Willis, A.J. (Dr) 212 230
  252 John 161 John W 161
  Maud 82 184 Sarah E 146
Willoughby, Mary E. 168
Wilson, Adrout K. 233
  A.H. 168 A.K. 233
  Bruce 164 Cora 113
  E.F. 98 D.G. 121 Ed 155
  Ella 164 E.E. 17
  Foster 94 George 142
  Green F 193 Hildred 168
  Horace C 260
  Infant 24 121 260
  Jake 142 Kennard H 193
  Larkin 193 Lilly B. 155
  Lottie 162 Margaret 173
  Matilda 142 Minnie 150
  Susie 153 Thomas 100
Winbush, Lynn 124
  Rosa L. 124
Wine, Chrisley 248
  Elizabeth 114
Winstead, James M. 249
Winston, Bessie 55 86
  Hattie 56 Robert 56 86
  R.W. 32 Thomas 56 87
Winton, Birnie D. 6
  D.D. 128 Laura 128
Wise, Cecil 4 Isaac 51
Wiseman, Bettie 262
Wishon, David F. 222
  Hunter 222
Wishong, Blanche 50
  D.J. 229 Henry 146
  Leonard 229 Ralph 146
Witt, Jennie E. 124
Wolf, Barbara 177
  Barbie 222
Wolfe, E.S. 103
  Pernesy 78
Wolford, Artie 258

Wood, David 158 Edwin 207
  Eugene 239 M.C. 239
  Nelson A. 165
  Thomas J. 215
Woodby, Mary J. 35
Woodfin, Liddie M. 262
Woodruff, Sarah 170
Woods, John 167
  Mary H. 26
Woodward, Fred 77
Woody, Kathern 176
Woolwine, P.A. 216
  Susie 216
Worley, William P. 198
Worton, Thomas H. 122
Wright, __ 257
  Charlie 138 Clarence 58
  Infant 138 Jonathan 220
  Lane 121 Nancy 36
  Sylvester A. 137
Yancey, Howell 184 223
  Nellie 184 Sophie 184
Yates, Albert 19 Lula 35
  Noah 25
Yeager, Isacher F. 263
  Joseph J. 263
Yeakly, Lydia 127
Yett, __ 190
Yokam, John 128
Yonkey, Martha 209
Younce, Pearl 250
Young, Albert 187
  Anna L. 173 Cora G. 159
  Eva 229 Florence 37
  Ida 135 John W. 187
  Juanita 242 Lizzie J 74
  Ollie 27 Rachel 18
  Sallie 37 Sarah 242
  Tom 159 William 37
  W.R. 173
Zang, Christopher 131

Zang (continued)
  Andrew M. 157
  Bob L. 169 Henry L. 169
  Robert L. 157
  William D.B. 247
Zimmerman, Amanda 234
  Frank 227 Infant 133
  J.C. 227 J.H. 133
  Mary J. 190
  Rachael 209
  Roland G. 97 Samuel 97
  Sarah W. 97

www.ingramcontent.com/pod-product-compliance
Lightning Source LLC
Chambersburg PA
CBHW070936230426
43666CB00011B/2454